Journeying Far and Wide

Journeying Far and Wide

A POLITICAL AND DIPLOMATIC MEMOIR

Philip M. Kaiser

A ROBERT STEWART BOOK

CHARLES SCRIBNER'S SONS
New York

MAXWELL MACMILLAN CANADA
Toronto

MAXWELL MACMILLAN INTERNATIONAL
New York   Oxford   Singapore   Sydney

Charles Scribner's Sons   Maxwell Macmillan Canada, Inc.
Macmillan Publishing Company   1200 Eglinton Avenue East
866 Third Avenue   Suite 200
New York, NY 10022   Don Mills, Ontario M3C 3N1

Macmillan Publishing Company is part of the
Maxwell Communication Group of Companies.

Library of Congress Cataloging-in-Publication Data

Kaiser, Philip M., 1913–
    Journeying far and wide: a political and diplomatic memoir/
Philip M. Kaiser.
        p.   cm.
    "A Robert Stewart Book."
    ISBN 0-684-19350-7 (alk. paper)
    1. Kaiser, Philip M., 1913–   . 2. Ambassadors—United States—
Biography.   3. United States—Foreign relations—1945–1989.
E840.8.K24A3   1992   92-9167   CIP
327.2′092—dc20
[B]

Macmillan Books are available at special discounts for bulk purchases
for sales promotions, premiums, fund-raising, or educational use.
For details, contact:

Special Sales Director
Macmillan Publishing Company
866 Third Avenue
New York, NY 10022

Designed by Nancy Sugihara

10 9 8 7 6 5 4 3 2 1

Printed in the United States of America

For my wife Hannah Elizabeth
and in memory of my mother Temma Giese

Who shall find a woman of valor?
For her price is far above rubies.

Proverbs 31:10

Contents

Acknowledgments

The help of relatives and friends has been indispensable to the writing of this book. My sons, Robert, David, and Charles, urged me to undertake it although they are somewhat disappointed that it is a memoir rather than an autobiography. All three are professional writers who have authored more than one successful book. Not surprisingly, they were uninhibited in their criticisms, usually constructive, of the copy I courageously asked them to read.

My loving thanks are due to my wife, Hannah, who not only kept me going during the difficult periods when the muse evaded me, but also proved to be a most trenchant and constructive critic.

I owe a special debt to my dear friend the late Sir John Wheeler-Bennett. My views as a student about the events that led up to Munich were reinforced by his brilliant books, as well as my conversations with him.

I am also grateful to a host of other friends who have helped me by reading the manuscript, in whole or in part, and giving me the benefit of their criticisms or correcting facts and establishing dates. These include Dorothy Armstrong, William Bader, Michael Beschloss, Tessa Blackstone, Dyke Brown, Gerald Connelly, Susan Crosland, Betty Edwards, Mel Fagen, Catherine Hustead, Sid Korzenik, Paul Laudicina, Ivo Lederer, Jan Marmor, Ron McIntosh, Newton Minow, Mark Perlman, Stephen Schlossberg, Barbara Smith, Elvis Stahr, Ben Stephansky, James Sund-

ix

quist, Ted Tannenwald, Stella Wallinger, Morris Weisz, and Murat Williams.

I profited greatly from Ted Marmor's insightful critique of the manuscript. His own personal journeys made me more sensitive to mine.

Frank Weil's comments and continual prodding were most helpful.

I am particularly indebted to Virginia Newmyer. Her editorial suggestions throughout the manuscript were invaluable.

My assistant, Jean Niesley, patiently deciphered my execrable handwriting, which she then efficiently transcribed on that miraculous modern instrument, the word processor.

Finally, I offer my grateful thanks to Robert Stewart, senior editorial vice president, Charles Scribner's Sons, for his ceaseless encouragement and wise suggestions.

Introduction

This is a memoir of three interrelated journeys. First, a social one—from the ethnic homogeneity of my boyhood to the world of politics and diplomacy. It is the story of an immigrant son's journey from the insular world of Brooklyn to the Midwest, on to Oxford, Washington, and places beyond.

The second is an educational journey—the transition from the Hebrew parochial institution and the New York public high school to a broad, multinational education that provided intellectual ballast throughout my career. The great University of Wisconsin at Madison shaped my unrepentant commitment to political liberalism. Oxford's humanistic traditions and worldwide perspective reinforced that commitment and gave it an international underpinning.

Finally, it is a journey through time: seven decades of political and social upheaval, of economic depression, of three world wars (one bitterly "cold"), of the collapse of empires and the rise and fall of fascism and Communism—seven decades during which I served in political and diplomatic posts for four Democratic Presidents: Truman, Kennedy, Johnson, and Carter, the heirs of Woodrow Wilson and Franklin D. Roosevelt. They have been fascinating years—sometimes frustrating, often enlivening and fulfilling.

The highlights of these journeys are recorded in this memoir: the childhood years in Brooklyn dominated by a deeply religious and ethical mother; the most dramatic event in my early political education, the history-making New York State gubernatorial election in 1928 in which, against the national Republican tide, FDR won with a majority of less than one-half percent; the liberal University of Wisconsin during the years of the Great Depression; Oxford during the tumultuous but politically depressing period just before the war, which changed the course of my life.

Government in Washington is a major part of the memoir, particularly during my four years as President Truman's assistant secretary of labor for international affairs, when I was the U.S. government member on the governing body of the International Labor Organization, and worked closely with America's labor leaders to help Truman's Greek, Turkish, and Marshall aid programs succeed. This was also the time when Senator Joseph McCarthy was viciously corroding government morale by his wild accusations.

Working in Albany, New York, as a special assistant to Governor Averell Harriman, one of America's great public figures, illuminated the contrasts between federal and state governments. It also involved me in social and economic programs that sustained the spirit of the New and Fair Deals.

My memoir then becomes a diplomatic story. After I participated actively in his presidential campaign, President Kennedy appointed me ambassador to Senegal and Mauritania, two West African countries that had just gained their independence from the French empire. Africa intrigued Kennedy, and I found being one of his African ambassadors a heady experience, especially in Senegal, whose president was the remarkable Léopold Senghor, the first African to be elected to the French Academy.

Thanks to Secretary of State Dean Rusk—we were both Rhodes Scholars—I moved from Africa to London where I became the first American minister who was not a Foreign Service career officer. Rusk knew that key members of the Labour and Conservative parties like Denis Healey and Roy Jenkins and Ted Heath had been classmates at Oxford. Almost half of the cabinet members of the newly installed Labour government were old friends. The 1960s were difficult years for Britain as the country was trying to define its international role as a middle-sized power, a fascinating time for an American diplomat, particularly if he were serving as minister to David Bruce, one of our country's preeminent ambassadors.

The next stage in the journey took me inside the Communist world. As a representative of Democrats Abroad in London, I had served as co-chairman of the Foreign Affairs section of the Democratic Party's Platform Committee for the 1976 election. On the recommendation of Secretary of State Cyrus Vance, President Jimmy Carter appointed me ambassador to Hungary. Here I saw Communism at work even though it was a more benign kind than in the rest of the Soviet Empire. The Budapest story focuses on my role in the diplomacy and politics involved in the return to the Hungarian people of the Crown of St. Stephen, the treasured thousand-year-old symbol of their national identity. This courageous act on the part of President Carter initiated a dramatic improvement in American-Hungarian relations. It was a highly successful application of his "differentiation" policy for dealing with the individual countries of Eastern Europe.

My diplomatic journey ended with my appointment as ambassador to Austria, the former imperial partner of Hungary. Austria in the 1980s was special for several reasons: after the terrible prewar years of fascism and a wartime experience as part of Nazi Greater Germany, Austria had become a dynamic, prosperous democracy. In spite of its long history of anti-Semitism, its leading political figure was the chancellor, Bruno Kreisky, who was of Jewish origin and a socialist. Nevertheless, the Austrian people had still failed to confront the realities of their past Nazi relationship. An American ambassador had a lively time because of Kreisky's determination to play a major role on the world scene.

My tour in Vienna came to abrupt end. The Reagan administration instructed all noncareer ambassadors to depart their posts within two weeks. Though previously newly inaugurated Presidents, Democratic and Republican, had treated "political" appointees harshly, none had ever acted so crudely.

Unfortunately, this cavalier attitude toward the country's ambassadors fits the general American tendency to treat the Foreign Service as a stepchild of our government. Although American international commitments have expanded greatly since World War II, State has had the smallest budget of any cabinet department, less than one percent of that of the Defense Department.

Before leaving Vienna, I sent a farewell cable describing in considerable detail Washington's failure to provide the State Department with the resources necessary to perform its role as the country's first line of national defense. The time has come for the American people to appreciate the dedication and competence of the men and women in our Foreign Service, qualities I saw repeatedly during my many years abroad. With the end of the Cold War and the need for the United States to redefine its role in a rapidly changing world, an able, amply supported Foreign Service assumes new importance.

Journeying Far and Wide

1

The Brooklyn Years

Being the ninth of ten children does have some compensations. Whatever political skills I may have I attribute to the fact that I had to develop them early to cope with sibling rivalries and with the demands of a strong authority figure. For it was our mother who ruled the roost. She was a remarkable person. Reared in a Russian *shtetl*, she was deeply religious, and her commitment to Jewish Orthodoxy inspired the highest moral standards. In her, religion and justice, decency and compassion were inextricably intertwined. She brooked little compromise when it came to religious practice or ethical behavior. Though generous beyond measure, especially in dealing with the less fortunate, and deeply committed to the well-being of each of us, she could sometimes be a rather severe matriarch. Her children had to toe the mark. If we met her standards on ninety-nine consecutive occasions—but faltered on the hundredth—her usual response was criticism for a single failure. Praise for good behavior was rare because she thought her high standards were normal and natural.

She had serious doubts about America. It was too materialistic, too secular, too lacking in genuine religious spirit, too threatening to her *shtetl*-shaped world. She feared, too, that her children would succumb to the secular temptations of American life, and fall from religious grace. After spending a year in New York, she returned to Europe, having extracted from her husband a promise that he would follow her twelve months later to live out their lives in the Old Country. Fortunately, my father, warm and always generous, who loved the freedom and challenge of America, found a legitimate excuse for releasing himself from the commitment. He was staying behind to accumulate some capital for the family lumber business in Kolki in which he, his father, and his older brother Jacob were partners. While my father was still in America, Jacob died. Feeling that this absolved him from his promise to return, my father insisted on staying in America.

This was one of the few times he asserted himself against the wishes of a dominating wife. She rejoined him in America only after considerable pressure from her father, who reminded her that a woman for whom moral behavior was imperative must recognize that a wife's place was beside her husband. In addition, her six children deserved the presence of a father. Still, she never fully reconciled herself to life in America. Though quite brilliant, she chose not to master English and rarely spoke it. We never communicated in the same language: she spoke Yiddish to all of us and we spoke English to her. And I felt no guilt about not responding in her language because I was sent to a parochial school where I soon learned Hebrew, which established my credentials as a Jewish boy, and enabled me to feel superior to Yiddish, which I considered the "greenhorn's" jargon.*

My father asserted himself on another occasion that changed the course of my life. At the age of seventeen I was turned down for admission to Harvard because I failed the math College Board exam, even though I'd always received top marks in math. It was a terrible blow, the kind that makes an adolescent feel that the world has come to an end. After recovering from the initial shock, I turned to my second choice: the University of Wisconsin, where I had been admitted. I was attracted by its liberal reputation, which I soon realized was richly deserved.

I knew it would not be easy to get my parents' approval to go to a college so far away from home. Indeed, my mother thought the idea preposterous. She realized, however, how strongly I felt

---

*My mother and father spoke Ukrainian when they didn't want their children to understand what they were saying.

about going and was reluctant to be the parent who said "no" and be solely responsible for my unhappiness. To my great surprise, she said, "Whatever your father decides will be agreeable with me."

He thought it was a splendid idea for me to go to Wisconsin. That was what America was all about, full of challenge and promise. He was in poor financial shape, having been virtually wiped out in the real estate crash of 1928. But he promised to pay my tuition for the first year, $125 a semester, with $100 more to get me started. Thereafter, I would be on my own. My mother was dismayed when I reported this conversation but, completely in character, she stuck to her word.

Leaving my cocoon in Brooklyn for a university about a thousand miles away was the culmination of a weaning process that had been at work for some years. The four older brothers—Max, Abe, Ben, and Oscar—each solicitous in his own way about the younger siblings, pushed Jack, Henry, Jerry, the youngest, and me in that direction. Sisters Ida and Fanny, born between the two groups of brothers, provided much appreciated feminine care and concern about our future development. But it was Oscar, fifteen years my senior, who had the greatest influence on me. Oscar was rather remarkable, intellectually and physically. He was thirteen years old when he arrived in the States, knowing no English. Put into the fourth grade in elementary school, five years later he graduated from high school with an outstanding academic record, having earned varsity letters in baseball and football, games he had never known as a child. New York newspapers chose him as a tackle on the All City Scholastic Team. He had been elected secretary of the school (New Utrecht), where Jewish students were then a small minority.

Six feet three inches tall and ruggedly handsome, Oscar was sensitive, strong-willed, and generous. He was devoted to family and friends, particularly his mother. However, he was not perfect. The tug of football was so strong that he played for his high school team even though he had to do so clandestinely because the games always took place on Saturday. Knowing that his Orthodox mother would forbid him to play on the Sabbath, he had to sneak away after the midday meal. His secret was uncovered when his nose was broken in one of the games and he landed in the hospital. Mother forgave him because the maternal in her overcame the religious disciplinarian. She was undoubtedly relieved that the injury was not more serious.

Oscar always regretted not having attended a university and was determined to see to it that his younger siblings, the last five of whom were born in America, would not make the same mistake. He talked to my brother Henry and me often of his own difficulties adjusting to the new world. He had never managed to break away to take full advantage of the opportunities America offered. He was troubled by his excessive dependence on Mother. Her potential approval or disapproval was a major consideration in anything he planned to do. With one foot in the Old World and one in the New, he became our bridge between the two worlds. He was determined that Henry and I, and Jack and Jerry, should feel at home in the new country. Oscar was our surrogate father.*

A passionate liberal, Oscar had made us more conscious of the acute social problems of the 1920s. Racial discrimination particularly troubled him. In high school he had become a good friend of a black classmate, Chester Washington, an excellent student who played guard beside Oscar's tackle on the football team. After graduation, Oscar had lost contact with Chester until some years later when, getting off a train in Grand Central Station, he ran into Chester, who had become a porter. Sensing that his status upset Oscar, Chester explained that unfortunately this was one of the very few job opportunities open to blacks. He invited Oscar to visit him in his home, so he could see his collection of books and music and appreciate that he was nourishing his cultural interests in spite of his menial job.

Oscar told me of this meeting the day it happened, when he

---

*Mother appreciated what Oscar meant to me. Oscar died of Hodgkin's disease in February 1933, my sophomore year at the University of Wisconsin. Fearing that the shock of this terrible event might result in my not finishing the school year, she contrived a detailed plan which successfully kept word of his death from me until I returned home in June. She did this in spite of the fact that she had originally opposed my going to Wisconsin.

came to pick up his wife, Carrie, who was staying with us while he was out of town. Not long after, Oscar informed me that he had indeed visited Chester in his home and felt much better for what he had seen.

Three decades later, when I was working as a special assistant to Governor Averell Harriman, I looked for Chester Washington. I traveled frequently between Albany and New York, and whenever I was in Grand Central Station I asked for Chester Washington but always missed him. After Harriman's defeat in 1958, I was going upstate for the last time to pick up my family. As I headed toward the appropriate platform, I noted a handsome, rather elderly gentleman carrying bags for two ladies. I walked up to him and inquired if Chester Washington was on duty. "Why do you ask?" he replied. "I've been looking for him for four years," said I, "and have always missed him." "Who are you?" "Phil Kaiser." "Are you kin to Oscar Kaiser?" "He was my elder brother." He dropped the bags and with tears welling up in his eyes, Washington began to tell me what a wonderful man Oscar had been. Unfortunately, Washington was cut short by the two ladies who were baffled by what was taking place and insisted on moving on to their train. I never saw him again.

As an early sports buff, I became an avid reader of the sports pages of the New York and Brooklyn newspapers. Before long, I realized that *The New York Times* had a superior sports section. After reading it, I would turn to the rest of the newspaper and soon found myself intrigued by the political news, particularly the articles from Washington and foreign capitals. Current events began to interest me almost as much as baseball batting averages. Oscar enthusiastically approved of this development and we had frequent political discussions.

Three political incidents during my early life stand out. In the summer of 1923 my parents decided to visit Ukraine to see their fathers and other near relatives. I was one of three children they invited to go along. However, I turned them down, saying that I would prefer to return to the camp where the summer before I had had such a happy time. I never told them the real reason for my decision. Reading the dispatches in *The New York Times* from Central and Eastern Europe, I had become so aware of the postwar upheavals in that part of the world that I decided not to risk that trip. I'm somewhat embarrassed to this day by that precocious display of political anxiety. I was ten years old at the time.

The 1924 convention of the Democratic Party was my initial exposure to presidential politics. My father had just bought the first family radio, the old battery-powered type which, to our great excitement, enabled us to tune to KDKA, the famous Westinghouse station in Pittsburgh. Encouraged by Oscar, I spent hours listening to the broadcasts of the Democratic Convention from Madison Square Garden. The Alabama delegation's proud announcement of "twenty-four votes for Underwood," right up to the 103rd ballot, still rings in my ears. I also remember the one-vote majority against the motion to condemn the Ku Klux Klan.

But the most memorable political event of the 1920s was the election of 1928. After the Democrats nominated Governor Al Smith for the Presidency, the Republican Party of New York threw the Democrats into a funk by nominating for governor Albert Ottinger, the first Jewish candidate for that office in New York history. In order to counteract the impact of Ottinger's candidacy on the Jewish vote, which was largely Democratic, Smith urged Franklin D. Roosevelt, the strongest possible Democrat, to be the party's candidate. FDR had to make a tough decision. Although a future political career was very much a part of his personal agenda, he wasn't sure his recovery from infantile paralysis had progressed sufficiently. He was spending much of his time in Warm Springs, Georgia, where the waters were proving to be especially helpful. It took considerable pressure, with the crucial push coming from his wife, Eleanor, to get FDR to agree to run.

To neutralize further the impact of Ottinger on the Jewish vote, the Democrats chose Herbert H. Lehman as their candidate for lieutenant governor. This turned out to be a brilliant stroke. Lehman was well known in the Jewish community. A generous philanthropist, he was an active member of the prestigious Temple Emanu-El in New York City. Moreover, to many the anomaly of a banker liberal in his politics was intensely appealing. Lehman had been involved in issues relating to industrial relations in New York City and had demonstrated an impartiality that impressed the trade unions. At one time his bank, Lehman Brothers, had actually made a loan to the International Ladies Garment Workers Union when it was in serious financial straits.

Albert Ottinger, the only Republican who held state office, had made an impressive record as attorney general. He was responsible for closing down the notorious "bucket shops" on Wall Street. However, he had not been particularly active in the Jewish world. Twenty-five years later, when I was living in Albany, I learned that he did attend the local temple there regularly. But the Democrats seized upon the fact that Ottinger was a "quiet Jew," comparing him unfavorably with Herbert Lehman. I recall my father receiving letters signed by two of the most highly respected Jewish lawyers of that day, Louis Marshall and Samuel Untermeyer, urging him to vote for the Roosevelt-Lehman ticket. They emphasized Lehman's active role in Jewish affairs in contrast to Ottinger's nonparticipation. They almost went so far as to question Ottinger's Jewishness. These letters were sent to thousands of voters.

The Marshall and Untermeyer letters impressed my father but did not weaken his support for Ottinger. For reasons I never quite understood, he was at the time a registered Republican and remained so until the Depression. Perhaps it was because Teddy Roosevelt was one of his heroes. My father recalled TR's strong condemnation of the terrible Kishinev pogroms of 1905. Actually, the Kishinev massacre was a major reason for my father's emigration to America. So for ethnic as well as political reasons, he became and remained a staunch supporter of Ottinger.

A week before the elections he took me to a rally at the local public school where Ottinger was to speak. Ottinger's performance was fascinating. He devoted a large part of his remarks to proving to his audience that he really was an authentic Jew, sprinkling his speech with references to Jewish subjects and throwing in Yiddish phrases liberally. My father was impressed, not least of all by the fact that a German Jew could speak reasonably good Yiddish.

The gubernatorial contest turned out to be the closest in New York history, until Averell Harriman squeaked through in 1954. Smith, to his great chagrin, lost New York to Hoover by some 250,000 votes. Against the national trend, Roosevelt won by a slim majority of some 25,000 votes, less than one-half percent of the total ballots cast. Brownsville, the district with the largest concentration of Jews in the whole state, produced for the Roosevelt-Lehman ticket its greatest majority ever for a Democrat—against the first Jewish candidate for governor. The Democratic leader of the district was the famed Hymie Shorenstein, the only non-Irish leader of a political district in all of Brooklyn.

The result of the gubernatorial contest was not known until the morning after the election. My father had bought the first electric radio (an Atwater Kent), so we could be certain to hear the returns. We stayed up together all night as the lead seesawed back and forth between Ottinger and Roosevelt. I vividly recall the announcement after midnight by Ed Flynn, the Democratic boss of the Bronx and FDR's campaign manager. He said that because the returns from Republican upstate New York were so slow in coming in, at 6:00 A.M. he would dispatch a large number of especially sworn-in lawyers to determine what was holding them up. That did the trick. Not too long thereafter, FDR's election was announced. More than three decades later I witnessed a similar situation in Illinois, when John F. Kennedy ran against Richard Nixon.

From the time I was seven until I was thirteen, I attended Hebrew Institute of Borough Park, the first parochial school of its kind in America. The mornings, from eight to twelve, were devoted to Hebrew studies and the afternoons, from one to five o'clock, to the regular secular curriculum approved by the state. Eight hours a day of school was rather rigorous but we not only survived, we prospered under this regime. Though little time was left for extracurricular activity, those of us interested in athletics did manage to play ball, particularly in the spring when there was more light at the end of the day. Every now and then, however, the long school hours proved a bit too burdensome and we reacted by playing hooky. Instead of going to school Friday morning—for religious reasons the school week ended on Friday noon—we went directly to the golf course located near our home and served as caddies throughout the day.

At school we were particularly stimulated by the challenge of the Hebrew studies and pleased with ourselves when we realized we were learning the language of the Old Testament. The curriculum was remarkably modern. Emphasis was not on religion, but on learning to understand and speak Hebrew and to appreciate its literature, contemporary as well as traditional. In addition, our teachers emphasized the importance of history. Morning classes were conducted in Hebrew to enhance the students' facility in that language. By the time we graduated from elementary school, most of us were effectively bilingual. I first read *Ivanhoe* in a Hebrew translation.

The Prophets were our favorite subject. We were moved by the passion for social justice they expressed with such poetic eloquence. I remember my favorite Hebrew teacher tearfully talking about Woodrow Wilson the day after the President died. Wilson, he told us, had devoted his life to fulfilling the prophet Isaiah's dream of the time when "nation shall not lift up sword against nation, neither shall they learn war any more."

On the secular side, standards were equally high. All the lay instructors had passed the exams for teachers in public schools. They were enthusiastic about their work and devoted to their students. We were well taught. When I entered public high school, I found no difficulty in adjusting to the new environment. In addition to being a top student in my class, I was active in extracurricular activities. I was a columnist for the school magazine and an editor of the modern language quarterly. I made the school tennis team but dropped out when it became apparent that most of the matches were to be played on Saturday.

I went to New Utrecht, the same high school that my older brothers had attended. Some teachers who had taught Oscar and Ben more than ten years before were still there, and they remembered both brothers warmly. One of them, who was particularly fond of Oscar, never forgave me for not studying her subject, Latin, as he had done. When I ran for president of Arista, the Honor Society, she supported one of her Latin students and I lost.

Although New Utrecht was then the largest high school in the city, students did not feel submerged under a dehumanized mass. The New York public school system was considered one of the best in the country. Academic standards were high. The competition for teaching jobs was so stiff that it showed up in the quality of those who succeeded. To a remarkable degree for so large a school, teachers were student-oriented. Many of them went out of their way to be friendly and helpful. Walter Clayton Leonard, an English instructor, was an outstanding example. A WASP with an elegant background, he was completely at home with a student body that represented a fairly wide range of ethnic backgrounds.

Leonard was married to the daughter of Colonel Tillingham L'Homedieu Huston, one of the owners of the New York Yankees. Under Huston and his partner, the brewer Jacob Ruppert, the Yankees bought Babe Ruth from the Boston Red Sox and then built Yankee Stadium to take full advantage of that shrewd acquisition. Thanks to Walter Leonard's generosity—he always had a batch of Yankee tickets—I saw the Babe play several times. Leonard also invited me to see my first World Series game. Some years after high school, Leonard saw me off when I sailed to England to study at Oxford. I was deeply touched because it was Yom Kippur, the Day of Atonement, and no relatives were present.

I made progress socially, too. Hilda, a classmate in my American History course, had been voted the prettiest girl in the senior class. She had to compete against four hundred other young women. But one look at her and you appreciated why she had been chosen. She was a beautiful brunette: tall, stately, with sparkling eyes that lit up the delicate features of her cameo face. She was also delightfully unpretentious.

I yearned to ask her to be my date at the senior prom, but I was only sixteen and lacked the courage to do so because I couldn't conceive of her accepting. I discussed my predicament with my brother Henry, a year and a half older than I and, in my eyes, a man of the world. He immediately produced the solution: "Our voices are so much alike," he said, "I'll telephone Hilda and pretend that I am you." To my delight his plan worked. She accepted and it wasn't until many months later when we were very much in love and I knew she was fond of Henry that I told her how he had made it all possible.

This was not the first or last time that Husky, who was my closest family ally among the younger siblings, was so helpful. During his lifetime he guided me through many more difficult situations. A model older brother, a sympathetic and reliable confidant, he seemed always to have had the skills that were to make him one of the country's leading labor lawyers.

My brother Oscar was responsible for a crucial turn in our young lives. He encouraged our father, who was prosperous in the early 1920s, to send the younger children to summer camp in Vermont. My mother approved: she liked the idea of healthful outdoor summers for us and was reassured about the religious approach of the camp because one of its owners was a principal of the school we attended.

The camp experience made it easier for me later to attend a university hundreds of miles from home. Camp was an exciting contrast to our life at home and at school. The camp was Jewish, but its ambiance was more secular than that of our year-round lives. Here we were supervised by counselors who were college students on their way to becoming doctors, lawyers, judges, writers, and teachers. Several of them were outstanding college athletes. Exposed to new ideas, attitudes, and interests, we became more comfortable socially and made new friends among our peers. Some of the counselors had a strong influence on our cultural and intellectual development. And, of course, we had an opportunity to develop our athletic abilities. I spent my summers in camp from the time I was nine until I left for Oxford, fourteen years later, the first seven years as a camper, and afterward as a counselor.

Several camp figures made a lasting impression. Moss Hart, one of our great playwrights, was the social director of the adult camp called Crescent Country Club, located next to the boys' camp. It catered to visiting parents. Hart's satirical wit and charm captivated all the guests, as well as the counselors and elder campers whom he invited to the events he organized. He was particularly kind to my brother Husky and me. Saturday nights were usually devoted to a Hart monologue. He would read from a sheet he wrote called "The Laundry—Everything Comes Out in the Wash." The audience rocked with laughter as he cleverly lampooned the guests of the current week. He loved to do imitations of Fanny Brice. He also produced and acted in serious plays; especially memorable was his performance in the leading role in Eugene O'Neill's *Emperor Jones*. The talents displayed at Crescent flowered brilliantly in *Once in a Lifetime, You Can't Take It with You*, and other hit comedies that he wrote until his premature death in the early 1960s.

I last saw Moss and Kitty Hart at Averell Harriman's seventieth birthday party in November 1961 when I was home from Africa on consultation. We talked about his autobiography, *Act One.* Just published, it included a hilarious, highly imaginative chapter on his camp experience. I told him I enjoyed it enormously but any relation between the camp he described and the one I remembered was largely coincidental. Years later when I recalled this incident to Kitty Carlisle Hart, she replied, "George Kaufman and I always disagreed about how much Moss could exaggerate. I said twenty-five percent; he said, 'Oh, at least fifty percent.'"

Herman Wouk was a fellow camper. A year or two younger than I, he was small for his age and a bit pudgy. My brother Henry was one of his idols. Athletics were not Herman's thing, but he became a camp character because he was so strikingly bright and articulate. He wrote clever pieces for the camp newspaper. Herman loved dramatics. He and I acted together in several camp plays and at the end of one summer he won the top dramatics medal, while I was awarded second prize. Years later, Herman wrote *City Boy*, a delightful *roman à clef* about our camp. It should have been read more widely, but was overshadowed by his classic, *The Caine Mutiny*, which followed soon after.

Paul Goodman was another camp figure. His intellect was awesome, but he managed to display his knowledge without making you feel too inadequate because of your comparative ignorance. He came pretty close to being a polymath. He certainly knew more about more subjects than any person I had met before. Philosophy, sociology, poetry, history, literature—they were all his things. But nothing seemed more impressive than his knowledge of medieval Chinese drama.

No one had a greater influence on me than Sid Korzenik, my counselor in my last year as a camper. Sid's background was somewhat similar to mine. He was a first-generation child of Eastern European immigrants. He was four years older. A brilliant student at the then-prestigious Boys' High School, he was offered scholarships to a half dozen top universities in the East. This was a particularly remarkable achievement for a Jewish boy at that time or, for that matter, for any boy at any time.

He chose Harvard, where he graduated magna cum laude and was elected to Phi Beta Kappa. A major in philosophy, he was a student of the great Harvard teachers of that epoch, including Irving Babbitt and Alfred North Whitehead. He was a paradigm of the moderate liberal. Knee-jerk reactions were foreign to him. His extensive knowledge and finely honed intellect were calmly brought to bear on any issue he discussed.

Sid had a great influence on my intellectual development. He encouraged me to expand my interest in history, literature, and politics and introduced me to the study of philosophy. I was grateful to him for recommending books that I had never heard of before, and that I read with great relish. Naturally, he urged me to apply for admission to his alma mater, and no one was more sympathetic when Harvard turned me down.

When I was elected to Phi Beta Kappa at the University of Wisconsin, Sid insisted on putting up the money for the key. We were still in the midst of the Depression, and knowing how broke I was, he said he would fully understand if I used the money to help pay off some of my debts. That's exactly what I did. The key itself, he had observed, was much less important than what it represented. Only recently, he had written me, he had seen a woman in the subway wearing two Phi Beta Kappa keys as earrings. Sid and I have been friends for over fifty years.

Camp also provided an opportunity to develop my athletic ability. I enjoyed baseball, basketball, and handball—but I loved playing tennis. No matter the game, I was intensely competitive, hardly surprising for the ninth of ten children. Happily, among the counselors were star athletes from City College, Columbia, and NYU. Several of them gave me private instruction in baseball, basketball, and tennis.

Archie Hahn was a star baseball and basketball player at City College. In those days, City College, coached by Nat Holman, had one of the outstanding basketball teams in the country. Archie was determined to make me a college athlete no matter which university I attended. He and I were last together in camp in 1927 and we didn't see each other again until we met in Forest Hills a week before I left for Oxford, in September 1936. We had just witnessed the outstanding finals match for the National Tennis Championship between Don Budge and Fred Perry. It was Perry's last performance as an amateur and he won in five torrid sets, saving the win after being down 5–3 in the fifth. Archie greeted me warmly. The first question he asked was, "Did you play any varsity sport in college?" "No," I replied, but added rather proudly, "I did win a Rhodes Scholarship, though, and I'm leaving for Oxford next week." Archie was not impressed. Before departing he made it clear that he thought I had "screwed up" on my priorities.

2

The Wisconsin Years

My stomach turned queasy as I gave my mother a farewell embrace, grabbed my two heavy bags, and dashed down to the train. Twenty-seven hours later, on a September day in 1930, I arrived in Madison, Wisconsin, after stopping at what seemed like every hamlet in Pennsylvania, Ohio, and Indiana. It was the longest scheduled train ride between New York and Madison, and the cheapest. I soon appreciated how ill-equipped I was for dealing with new realities. Having made no previous arrangements for my first night's lodging, I unwittingly landed in the Lorraine, the most expensive hotel in Madison. I felt even more inept when I pulled the shade up the next morning and noticed a sign advertising the Belmont with rooms at half the price only a block away. I made up for the error, however, by finding a nice clean room for the first semester in an agreeable house owned by a pleasant widow. It was two blocks from the main campus and cost only two dollars a week.

Living in the same house a floor below was Rusty, a junior. I became aware of him during that first fall. Prohibition was still the law of the land, but that didn't deter Rusty from working his way through college by selling students, on their way to the football games, his own abominable concoction—raw alcohol with a few drops of brown coloring—for five dollars a pint. As a big-city boy I was shaken by this early encounter with a rugged

15

small-town Wisconsin entrepreneur. I gagged when, at Rusty's insistence, I tasted his terrible brew.

After selecting my courses, finding out whatever I could about different professors, and discovering the cheapest and best places to eat and make friends, I turned to the problem of finding employment, since I could expect very little help from home.

Teaching Hebrew seemed the best bet. I had armed myself with letters testifying to my training in Hebrew studies, which enabled me to meet the Wisconsin state treasurer, Sol Levitan. A La Follette Progressive Republican, he had been reelected several times even when the voters chose conservative Republicans as governor. The people of the state respected Levitan for his technical competence and responded enthusiastically to his charismatic personality. I was delighted by the warmth with which he received me and grateful for his help. An active member of the Madison Jewish community, Sol put me in touch with the local synagogue school, where I was hired as a Hebrew teacher.

Fifty dollars a month, a substantial sum in those Depression days, provided enough economic security for me to confront the challenging university community and the broader Wisconsin world. Wisconsin was radically different from the Brooklyn and camp worlds that I had known during my first seventeen years. They were not quite ghetto worlds, but there was a comforting homogeneity. Most of the people I grew up with came from similar middle-class backgrounds. The sense of identity and feeling of security that they provided were reinforced by a large, affectionate family of older brothers and sisters who often enough had cosseted me.

Now, for the first time, I was completely on my own, not in a hostile setting but in a new and sometimes strange one. People spoke in accents I hadn't heard before about youthful experiences that differed from mine. I discovered, for example, that cemeteries were not only used for interring people; in small, rural towns, they provided the best havens for adolescent romancing. I was taken aback, too, when at the freshman dance during orientation week, for the first time in my life I saw couples dancing cheek-to-cheek.

Navigating through the political and social currents of the campus and the broader Wisconsin world was not easy nor was it relating to a student body made up of young men and women from every section of the country, representing almost every ethnic and racial group. Only later did I realize that during my five years at the university there were only two black students, Hilton Hanna from Panama and Thomas Posey, brought up in the hills of West Virginia.

Before coming to Madison, I was aware of the University of Wisconsin's reputation for liberalism—that was a major reason why I chose it—but it wasn't until I was on the spot that I appreciated the nature and extent of that liberalism.

On my first trip up the campus hill I read the inscription on a plaque under the statue of Abe Lincoln in front of Bascom Hall, the university's main administrative building: "Whatever may be the limitations which trample inquiry elsewhere," it read, "we believe that the great state University of Wisconsin should ever encourage that continual and fearless sifting and winnowing by which alone the truth can be found." This ringing declaration for academic freedom, of which the university was so proud, came from a report by the university's president, Charles K. Adams, in 1894. He was exonerating Professor Richard T. Ely, the distinguished economist who had been charged with economic radicalism for participating in a strike picket line. Ely's action and the university's response set the stage for the remarkable collaboration between the university faculty and the state government known as the "Wisconsin Idea"—Wisconsin's form of liberalism.

This close association began when the elder Bob La Follette, running as a Progressive Republican, was elected governor in 1900. Vigorously pursuing a program of economic and political reform, La Follette turned to the university for expert analysis of the issues involved, and Charles Van Hise, the broad-visioned geologist, president of the university from 1903 to 1918, happily cooperated with the governor. Ideas developed by the faculty, particularly in the economics and political science departments, were translated into legislation at the state level. Often the administrators of the resulting new programs were the very men who had developed those ideas. In 1910–11, for example, there were forty-six faculty members in various state positions.

Leading members of the faculty, in addition to Van Hise, met regularly to discuss projected legislation with state officials at the

Saturday Lunch Club. This collaboration between politician and professor anticipated the FDR "Brain Trust" by several decades. Underlying its activities was the principle that government must be used as an instrument to achieve greater human welfare in a more just society. There was no other way of dealing with the economic and social abuses of powerful special interests in an industrial age. Thanks to the cooperation between state and academia, Wisconsin could boast of some remarkable, ground-breaking legislation during the first fifteen years of the century, including a stringent Corrupt Practices Act; a Railroad Commission; legislation for the protection of health and sanitation and pure food; a law providing shorter hours for railroad employees; a reasonable child labor law; a public utility law to regulate the rates and service of utility companies; a workmen's compensation law, and an Industrial Commission to enforce and carry out its provisions.

It is difficult today to appreciate how bold these reforms were at that time. Wisconsin, more than any other state, was translating the progressive sentiments sweeping the country into practical social and economic legislation. Governor Woodrow Wilson of New Jersey praised the pioneering works of La Follette, while Governor James Cox of Ohio borrowed experts from Wisconsin to help him put into effect new social and economic legislation. Wisconsin also inspired the national movement for reform that reached its apex in the election of 1912, when the combined popular vote of Woodrow Wilson and Theodore Roosevelt, the two progressive candidates, reached seventy percent of the total cast.

Wilson preached a "New Freedom" while Roosevelt, who became the candidate of the newly formed Progressive Party instead of old Bob La Follette, championed a "New Nationalism." Wilson's "New Freedom" program sought to destroy monopolies and restore the free competition that he, like so many Americans, saw as the epitome of the American system. Roosevelt, on the other hand, argued that the government should regulate monopoly, not abolish it, though as President he had gained a reputation as a "trust buster." Both men shared the underlying progressive principle that government must be used as a positive instrument to achieve greater human welfare in the economic system.

Franklin D. Roosevelt, who served as Wilson's assistant secretary of the navy, was greatly influenced by that administration. As President, he revived progressive principles and, in his efforts to achieve economic and social justice within a framework of regulated capitalism, went beyond his old chief. FDR helped to make national government responsible for social security, wages and hours, and unemployment insurance. He was the first President who attempted to use the techniques of macroeconomics to improve the performance of the nation's economy.

Those of us interested in politics who were studying at the University of Wisconsin in the early 1930s, when the country was in the throes of a deep Depression, soon appreciated that the university was still a major center for developing new social and economic legislation. We were impressed that the New Deal was turning to Wisconsin for help in coping with the country's pressing problems. Wisconsin had been the first state to establish an unemployment insurance system, an employment service, and social security. It was natural for FDR to turn to Professor Edwin Witte, the country's leading expert in these fields, to develop national programs. With the help of his undergraduate student, Wilbur Cohen (later secretary of health, education and welfare under President Johnson), Witte devised our Social Security system. William Leiserson, protégé of economist John R. Commons, was a chairman of the National Labor Relations Board, and Arthur Altmeyer, who had directed the Wisconsin Employment Service, became the first chairman of the Federal Social Security Board.

The university was also engaged in a radical educational reform. My first academic decision was whether to enroll in the Wisconsin Experimental College established in 1926. This dramatic expression of the university's academic liberalism reflected the collaboration between Glenn Frank and Alexander Meiklejohn, two quite different individuals. Frank was editor of the liberal magazine *Century*, when, in 1926, he became president of the University of Wisconsin. He was hailed as an excellent choice, although the first individual offered the job was the distinguished Roscoe Pound, dean of the Harvard Law School who, at the last moment, responding to pressure from Harvard colleagues and alumni, reversed his initial decision to accept. Subsequently, when faculty and students justifiably turned sour on Frank, the common wisecrack was, "We thought we were getting a 'pound' but we got a 'frank' instead."* In the course of his twelve-year tenure as president, Frank's bland liberalism deteriorated into cosmetic opportunism.

Meiklejohn, on the other hand, was a passionate academic reformer and a staunch defender of freedom throughout his long life. As president of Amherst between 1912 and 1923, he had tested some of his radical notions about education. For him, substantive knowledge was not the main objective of four years at college. Instead, he emphasized that a liberal education should teach students how to think, and the best way of doing so was to generate genuine dialogue between teachers and students and with individuals in the outside world. He deplored cluttering up college life with vocational training or any other peripheral activities that did not require thinking, and he scorned the notion that "twenty courses made an education."

Practicing what he preached, he established classes at Amherst in cooperation with labor unions, even though at that time most people, particularly his alumni, considered trade unions dangerously subversive. His radical innovations included the establishment of a student council and giving college seniors and young faculty members the responsibility for educational planning. Free speech was a basic ingredient in Meiklejohn's approach. He believed that everyone should have the right to speak freely and frankly and that an individual's feelings should be respected no matter how foolish or dangerous. In later years he even disagreed with Justice Oliver Wendell Holmes's doctrine on "clear and present danger," which forbade free speech in certain perilous situations.

Inevitably Meiklejohn's reforms at Amherst provoked dissent as well as excitement. By 1920 the majority of Amherst alumni, trustees, and faculty were aligned against Meiklejohn. Sloppy administrative practices on his part made it easier for the trustees to force him to resign in 1923. Frank had published some of Meiklejohn's articles on higher education in the *Century Magazine*

*In 1926 a pound was worth $4.87 and a French franc about two cents.

after Meiklejohn left Amherst, and one of Frank's first actions as president of the university was to ask Meiklejohn to organize an entirely new "experimental college" at Wisconsin. It turned out to be Frank's most liberal act during his presidency.

Meiklejohn took full advantage of this unique opportunity to establish a new institution to reflect his educational theories. There were none of the usual obstacles to academic reform, no traditions to worry about, no established curriculum. He organized a new faculty of sixteen members that included colleagues from Amherst who resigned with him, as well as professors from the University of Wisconsin. The student body consisted of 150 men (no women) who lived in separate dorms, newly constructed on the edge of beautiful Lake Mendota. They studied a curriculum never before tried in any American institution.

The entire freshman year was spent in the study of Greek civilization in the age of Pericles. All students studied Greek economics, history, drama, philosophy, and the arts for six weeks at a time through two semesters. The second year was devoted to American culture with similar topics of study. Teaching was carried on in tutorials with small groups, and the whole Experimental College community met regularly once a week for an address by one of the faculty. Each member of the faculty taught in fields other than his own, thus emphasizing that students and teachers were learning together. After two years in the Experimental College, the students completed their studies in the regular university. The existence of the college challenged the established practices of every part of the university system and attracted intellectually and politically motivated students, most of whom were from the East and Chicago rather than Wisconsin.

I was intrigued by the Experimental College, but not sure enough of myself intellectually to apply for admission. The fact that the curriculum was not sufficiently structured scared me off; the contrast with my previous schooling was too great. However, I soon found myself spending much of my time with students from the Experimental College. They were among the most interesting in the university. My Experimental College friends included Sam Berger, who became one of the country's outstanding Foreign Service officers. After serving as Professor Selig Perlman's graduate assistant, Sam became Averell Harriman's labor adviser when Harriman was FDR's Lend-Lease ambassador to Winston Churchill, and subsequently one of our first labor attachés. Later Sam was our ambassador to Korea and deputy ambassador to Vietnam. Our careers intermingled after I joined the international section of the Labor Department. We remained lifelong friends.

When I registered in the College of Arts and Sciences, I was happy to learn that the Experimental College did not have a monopoly on the best faculty. In fact, in the early 1930s the old established university could boast of having one of the country's finest collections of professors still nourished by the great liberal spirit of the preceding two decades. In history there were Frederic L. Paxson, Carl Russell Fish, and John Hicks; in sociology, E. A. Ross, "the father of American sociology," and Kimball Young; in political science, John Gaus, Pitman Potter, and Grayson Kirk (who later became president of Columbia University); in philosophy, Evander Bradley McGilvary and the humanist Max Carl Otto; in English, the poet William Ellery Leonard and the novelist Helen White; in economics, Harold Groves, who taught Walter Heller, President John F. Kennedy's chairman of the Council of Economic Advisers, and Joseph Pechman, the country's leading tax economist; Edwin Witte, the nation's outstanding authority on social security; John R. Commons, the renowned institutional economist and leading exponent and practitioner of the "Wisconsin Idea"; and, last but not least, Commons's disciple, Selig Perlman, the brilliant labor historian and economist.

History, philosophy, and politics were my main interests; in addition, beginning with my second year, I devoted a large share of my time to the study of the classics. There were outstanding professors in each of these fields. Wisconsin's History Department had been among the best in American academia for several decades, certainly since the days of Frederick Jackson Turner, who made his reputation there before moving on to Harvard. Turner's essay "The Significance of the Frontier in American History," delivered before a group of historians at the World's Columbian Exposition in Chicago in 1893, had a major impact on the subsequent interpretation of American history. Turner underlined the importance to our democracy of the characteristics Americans developed in conquering the continental wilderness. This was a sharp break with the emphasis of previous historians on slavery, religion, British tyranny, and nationalism.

I profited greatly from John Hicks's course "Recent American History," which took us from the end of the Civil War to the current scene. Hicks, a disciple of Turner and the author of the definitive *History of Populism*, exposed me to the influence of the West on American history. His lectures—full of substance, beautifully organized, and sprinkled with dry humor—always ended a few seconds before the bell rang. He rarely glanced at his three-by-five note cards, or so it seemed. Once he stumbled, when lecturing on "The Origins of the World War." We realized something was seriously wrong when, uncharacteristically, he rambled on in a disjointed manner and finished the lecture several minutes before the bell. "I owe you an apology," he said. "I'm sure you noticed that I wasn't quite myself this morning. Instead of taking my notes on 'The Origins of the World War,' I took those on 'The Origins of the Civil War.'" He then told the story of the lisping geology professor at the University of Nebraska who, for a quarter of a century, read the same lectures in his course, never changing a single word. The last lecture concluded with the lisping statement: "And every year a hundred thousands of dirt flow into the base of the Mississippi." After twenty-five years, one student had the gumption to ask, "Professor, a hundred thousands of what?" The flustered teacher nervously looked at his notes and then blurted out, "I'm sorry, sir, it doesn't say." We responded with a rousing cheer for Hicks.

A major share of my philosophy studies was under the chairman of the department, Evander Bradley McGilvary, a dapper, soft-spoken professor, highly regarded by his colleagues. Before World War I, he had been a rising star in the American world of philosophy, his articles appearing frequently in the philosophical journals. His essay "The Warfare of Moral Ideals," published in the *Wisconsin War Book* in 1916, was a powerful argument for American entry into the war. At that time the state, with its large German-American population, and the university were racked by conflict over the war issue. A leading member of the university establishment, McGilvary combined a gentle, pleasant style with a vigorous intellectual approach to metaphysical issues. A philosophical determinist, he delighted in sardonically criticizing idealists and pragmatists. Although always available to his students, he covered up his lively interest in them. I never suspected that he would play a major role in shaping my career.

The other teachers who greatly influenced me were Alban Winspear and Walter Agard, both classics professors, and Selig Perlman. Rabbi Max Kadushin, the director of the Hillel Foundation, also enriched my years at the university. A man of great learning, he was deeply respected by the university's faculty. He stimulated my interest in ethics and philosophy. I refreshed my Hebrew by restudying the prophets Jeremiah and Isaiah with him. Sadly, his exceptional intellectual talents were not fully appreciated by many of the Jewish students nor, for that matter, by the national authorities of the Hillel Foundation. They wanted Kadushin to run the foundation as a social club, while the rabbi insisted on developing it as a center for Jewish cultural life.

Alban Winspear was a young Canadian, a Rhodes Scholar, and a product of the Classical Greats course at Oxford. Tall and gangly, with blond hair never quite combed, he spoke rapidly as he puffed away at his ever-present cigarette. He felt that knowledge of the Greek and Roman civilizations provided the answers to every conceivable intellectual problem: philosophical, political, social, or economic. He fancied himself a polymath and was so articulate that he almost convinced his students that he knew practically everything that mattered. Winspear was a stimulating teacher who related the classical world to the issues of contemporary society with great skill. I studied Plato and Aristotle in the original Greek with him, and took several of his special seminars in ancient history and philosophy. Limited to two or three students, they reflected the influence of the Experimental College on the university. On their own initiative, professors could now provide such seminars to honor students. It was Winspear who later suggested that I apply for a Rhodes Scholarship and vigorously supported my candidacy.

Reality did not always temper Winspear's enthusiasm. He thought that the United States should adopt the British system for selecting personnel for the Foreign Service. The British service, many of whose officers had taken the "Greats" in Greek and Roman civilization course at Oxford, was considered the most competent in the world. At one point, Winspear convinced President Frank that this was a viable idea and together they visited Washington in a futile effort to sell it to the appropriate government officials.

No professor did more to shape my intellectual and political outlook than Selig Perlman. His teaching and writings reflected the best in the Wisconsin liberal tradition. His own personal history is remarkable even in the context of the early twentieth century, which is replete with dramatic emigration tales. He came to the United States in 1906 from Bialystok, Russia, under the sponsorship of the American socialist William English Walling, a member of a prominent Midwestern family, and his flamboyant wife, Rose Strunsky, a former "girl friend" of Jack London. Perlman met them by sheer chance. His aunt, living in New York, was a seamstress for Mrs. Walling. When she delivered several dresses to the ship on which the Wallings were sailing for Naples in the late spring of 1905, she told Mrs. Walling that her nephew, Selig Perlman, would also be spending the academic year at the University of Naples. He had been admitted to a Russian university, but when the doctors discovered that he had some chest problems, they recommended that he spend eight to ten months in a southern climate.

After they arrived in Naples, the Wallings looked up Perlman. They liked him and engaged him to tutor them in Russian. A warm friendship resulted, and they urged him to emigrate to America to pursue his studies. The idea appealed to Perlman, but his parents wouldn't think of letting him go. However, two events changed their minds.

The abortive Russian Revolution of 1905 had taken place during Perlman's year in Italy. When he returned to Russia, he was dismayed to learn that a new wave of anti-Semitism had led to the withdrawal of his admission to the university. At about the same time, Walling was arrested by the czarist police due, apparently, to his active support of Milyukov, the Russian social democrat. Walling was released when President Theodore Roosevelt personally interceded on his behalf. The incident received enormous publicity in Russia, and when Perlman pointed out to his parents that Walling was to be his American sponsor, they agreed to let him go. Perlman told me the story when we were together in Wales during the international crisis in September 1938. Immediately after arriving in New York he informed the Wallings of his presence; then, to his dismay, they neglected him for several months. He had reached a state of despair when Mrs. Walling appeared, apologized for their neglect, and, explaining that they had been exceptionally busy, took him in hand. The Wallings decided that the place for him to go was the great liberal University of Wisconsin. They knew John R. Commons and they recommended Perlman to him. Perlman became one of Commons's outstanding disciples and a major collaborator with Commons in writing the classic *History of Labor in the United States*.

Perlman was a young Marxist—a Bundist, not a Communist—when he arrived at the University of Wisconsin in 1907. However, under the influence of Commons, as well as Frederick Jackson Turner and E. A. Ross, and in response to the world that he observed in the United States, Perlman reshaped his *Weltanschauung* and became one of the outstanding exponents of Wisconsin pragmatic idealism. In his brilliant *Theory of the Labor Movement*, published in the mid-1920s, he showed how Communist doctrine on the political role of labor in the modern industrial society had no real relevance to the sociopolitical realities of the United States, the United Kingdom, or Germany—nor, for that matter, Russia. He compared revolutionary movements, institutions, political parties, behavior, and "national character" in all of these countries. The *Theory* was an essential text for his course "Capitalism and Socialism." In this course, unionism, socialism, fascism, and individualist capitalism were each analyzed under the headings of theories and movements. His encyclopedic knowledge of social and political movements of the nineteenth and twentieth centuries provided the base for his shrewd interpretations of current developments. His observations on events of the day were buttressed by an analysis of new books and publications in several languages dealing with political and economic issues. He had command of Italian, French, and German, as well as Russian.

He was an extraordinary figure: short, swarthy, with a high-pitched voice, an intermittent stutter, and a Russian-Yiddish accent that seemed to make his articulate, clear English all the more impressive. A shy man, he never quite looked straight at his students, but instead glanced at the ceiling and moved between aisles while lecturing. At first we found this distracting, but we were soon riveted by the power of his mind and the clarity and originality of his ideas. Remarkably, he never made use of notes. He was particularly impressive when left-wing students tried to heckle him. He demolished their economic, historical, and political assumptions with unmatched knowledge, but softened his blows with his sardonic humor. Perlman deplored the practice of ideologues who tried to force reality to fit their preconceived prejudices.

The structure of the course, limited to fifty students, was quite simple. He would lecture to the class on Mondays and Wednesdays, and on Friday we would be divided up into four small quiz sections where we would discuss the assigned readings for the week. One week was devoted to the writings of Edward Bernstein, the revisionist socialist who had broken away from Marx, and the British Fabians. When Perlman asked us whether the Fabians had any influence on Bernstein, he discovered that none of us had done our homework. One of our fellow students, however, a bright, brash young man, thought he could cover up his ignorance. After the student had thrown out some generalities that avoided an explicit answer to the question, Perlman quietly asked, "Tell me, did they have any influence on Bernstein or not?" The young man, refusing to concede, replied, "Well, Professor, more or less," to which Perlman firmly asked, "Tell me, how much more and how much less?" Since then, I squirm whenever I hear that phrase.

I am deeply indebted to Perlman for at least two important reasons: he shaped my social and political philosophy; and Hannah Greeley, a young woman whom I had met earlier in a protest meeting,* was in his class. In the mid-year exam, the main problem was to explain Marx's concept of dialectical materialism. Hannah received an A and I an A−, a result that was all the more striking because Hannah had asked me to explain dialectical materialism to her a day or two before we took the test.

I was fortunate, too, in seeing Perlman often outside the classroom. After my teaching job lapsed, he asked me to tutor both of his sons in Hebrew and, consequently, I was a regular visitor

---

*More about that later.

to his home. I enjoyed teaching his two bright boys. Mark, who became a distinguished economist, served as chairman of the Economics Department at the University of Pittsburgh. He created the American Economic Association's *Journal of Economic Literature*, and for many years was its editor. The *Journal* has played a major role in restraining the efforts of abstract theorists to dominate the discipline of economics. He has been a valued friend for over half a century. David, the elder brother, became an outstanding scientist. At the time of his early death, he was the dean of the University of Wisconsin's School of Pharmacology. David wrote hundreds of scientific articles and held dozens of pharmaceutical patents.

Above all, I relished the opportunity to converse with Perlman in an informal setting. These talks enabled me to appreciate more fully his exceptional sensitivity to the world around us. His progress at the university had not been easy. We forget that in the years before the Second World War, few Jews became full professors in the country's leading universities. We now know, for example, that it took the personal intercession of Columbia University's powerful president, Nicholas Murray Butler, to secure tenure for the eminent Lionel Trilling in the English Department. Liberal Wisconsin was no exception. Perlman's talents as a teacher and innovative author were unquestioned, but he received his professorship only after two of the university's giants, Commons and Ross, threatened to leave Madison unless he was given tenure.

This experience left its mark on Perlman. He was not bitter about it, but it made him sensitive to any display of prejudice, particularly anti-Semitism. He discouraged bright Jewish students from pursuing academic careers. He was naturally deeply disturbed by the rise of Hitler, a phenomenon that he analyzed with his usual acumen. He was troubled when Governor Phil La Follette, the younger son of the elder Bob, impressed with Hitler's use of mass psychology, tried to apply some of its techniques to the Wisconsin scene. When the governor devised an "X" symbol for his newly organized Progressive Party, Perlman called it "a circumcised swastika."

The simplicity of Perlman's home life was striking. I particularly remember the first time I was invited for Sunday dinner. I was taken aback when I noted that the professor washed the dishes after the meal and stoked the fire before sitting down in the living room to chat with me. I didn't say a word, but he still sensed my reaction to what I felt was behavior beneath his professorial dignity. He remarked, "One of my neighbors, a professor at the university—you know him, so I won't mention his name—when summer comes, he insists that his wife and children leave the house at six in the morning and not return until late in the afternoon so that he can have quiet in order to think. He's been doing that for the last ten years and, between you and me, Phil, he hasn't had a real idea the entire time.

"When I want to work [he didn't say 'think'] I go to my office at Sterling Hall where I can read the latest literature in my fields of interest and have easy access to the John R. Commons Library."

I have always been grateful for the accessibility of the faculty at the University of Wisconsin in the 1930s: not only one's own professors but others as well would happily spend an informal evening with a few students. My roommate Charles Peckarsky and I regularly invited different professors to discuss intellectual subjects and the political issues of the day, and they invariably accepted. They provided an enrichment that is denied to most undergraduates today.

I was troubled, however, when I realized that the liberalism of the faculty and its sensitivity to the crises confronting the country and the world were not matched by the attitudes of some of the students—more troubled than I would have been had I been brought up in a less circumscribed and protected environment.

Students in the early 1930s suffered from the fallout of the great economic depression. I recall the days when the banks closed;* when payments were made by university-issued "script"; when many of us survived by going to the university's experimental farm to drink the milk distributed there without charge, as much as you could drink for a penny paper cup; when during the Christmas holidays, we returned to our homes in the East by hitchhiking across the country in freezing weather. These were the years when, like thousands of their elders, students were desperate for

---

*In fact, I never felt richer than the first day of the bank shut-down because, by sheer chance, I received two ten-dollar money orders that day, one from my father and one from my brother Oscar. I was grandly lending money to my friends.

jobs. Some students were just managing to keep body and soul together. Their courage was daunting. When, for example, I met Ben Stephansky, a student from Milwaukee, he was trying to sustain himself on three dollars a week. He lived miles from campus, literally on the other side of the railroad tracks, to save money on his rent. Bread and cheese—particularly cheap in Wisconsin—were his main sustenance. That didn't prevent him from becoming an outstanding student, an assistant to Selig Perlman, and later in life a professor of economics and an ambassador to Bolivia under President Kennedy.

When we became friends, my brothers Henry and Jerry and I shared our fare with Ben. Jerry, the youngest member of the family, joined Henry and me at the University of Wisconsin after the death of our mother in 1933. Charming, witty, and devoted to family and friends, he was everybody's favorite confidant. I cherished my relationship with Jerry. We brothers were better off than Ben since I had my tutoring job, and Henry and Jerry had found other employment. Together, we earned about $150 a month. After getting established in a very modest apartment—the bathroom was the best room in it—we found we only had about $35 for the next five weeks, hardly enough to live on before our first monthly income. As usual, Henry came up with the solution for our dilemma. We accepted his proposal that we use the $35 to send telegrams to about a dozen friends telling them that we were all set for a good school year, but needed a little financial help, small loans to get us off the ground. We didn't ask for large sums, just $25 to $50. The response was heartening. Only one person failed to answer us; all the others wired us loans. Thereafter we managed to cope financially. We ate breakfast and lunch regularly in our apartment and sometimes dinner as well. We invited Ben Stephansky to share the California sardine sandwiches or cottage cheese and canned pineapple rings, which constituted our daily lunch, and our evening meals, too, when the main course was usually spaghetti, with meat only on special occasions.*

This is not to suggest that we escaped periodic financial crises. During one of them, a crap game on a special train bringing

*We enjoyed restaurant meals when generous, warm-hearted brother Ben visited Madison. Happily, business brought him to the Midwest several times a year.

students back from New York after the Christmas holidays was my salvation. I had returned home against the wishes of my parents, who were distressed about my relationship at the time with a woman four years older than I who lived in Brooklyn. I was warned that if I took advantage of the round-trip ticket bought in September and good for a return at Christmas, Easter, or June, no family member would be able to help me purchase a new round-trip ticket. The family stuck to its word. I had to borrow enough money for another round-trip ticket back to college from friends, and I boarded the train with only four dollars in my pocket and no prospect of any income for at least another month.

The train left New York at midnight and when several students, all of whom I recognized as financially comfortable, invited me to join their crap game in the baggage car, I accepted, feeling that I had very little to lose. My luck was phenomenal. At 6:00 A.M. I had broken up the game with 150 dirty dollars in my hand, a fortune in those days. I felt guilty that one of the losers was the train conductor, who insisted on joining the game.

The social tensions among Wisconsin students reflected the disturbed conditions of the country. There was the usual conflict between the fraternity and sorority members and the "barbarians," students like me who were unaffiliated with the Greek societies. More attuned to the basic liberalism of the university and to the politics of the day, many of us supported Franklin Roosevelt during the presidential campaign of 1932. We cheered the initial measures FDR introduced to revive the nation's economy. We were particularly grateful for the New Deal's National Youth Administration, which helped a large number of hard-pressed students to continue their education. Finding them part-time employment, it provided a margin that made continued study possible. We were proud, too, that Aubrey Williams,* a former Wisconsin state government executive, was the head of the agency. Despite hesitations, doubts, and conflicts, the country began to mobilize for recovery, and we felt that a better future seemed possible.

*Williams, Arthur Altmeyer, chairman of the Social Security Board, and Professor Alexander Meiklejohn were patients of Dr. Hugh P. Greeley, my father-in-law, who shared their liberal social views.

We had witnessed the sad performance of President Herbert Hoover when he appeared at a Republican political rally in the university fieldhouse the weekend before the election. He was en route to his home in Palo Alto, California, in order to vote a few days later. The indoor stadium was almost filled to capacity, with well over ten thousand people present. Walter Kohler, the ex–Republican governor who was running again, introduced Hoover. Instead of the usual, "The President of the United States," he said, "Herbert Hoover, the man who fed the starving Belgians at the end of the World War." Hoover was pathetic, clearly a beaten man. The public address system worked for all the other speakers, but Hoover couldn't make himself heard. Several times the crowd yelled "Louder, louder!"

Members of fraternities and sororities tended to be much more conservative than the "barbarians," often expressing their resentment of the latter's progressive social and political views. They were not very keen about the New Deal. They discriminated against religious and racial groups. Against the background of the rising German Nazism, particularly disturbing was the anti-Semitism on the campus, too apparent to be ignored. In fact, I soon became a member of a club actually called the Anti-Prejudice Society. It was headed by one of the most extraordinary people in the university community, and one of the noblest men I have ever known, "Shorty" Collins, a six-foot-seven Baptist student minister. I was devoted to Shorty, who combined a gentle, friendly personality with a tenacious opposition to any manifestation of religious or racial prejudice.

Several instances when prejudice reared its ugly head remain vivid in my memory. The first was when Marc Connelly's famous play *Green Pastures* came to Madison for a week's performance. Liberals on the campus were appalled to discover that the leading hotels refused to rent rooms to the all-black cast. As always, Collins took the lead in organizing a protest by representatives of concerned political and church groups. There was a special lesson in this incident: although Wisconsin was the only state that had passed antidiscrimination legislation, it had taken no steps to enforce the law. Incidentally, at Shorty's meeting, most of the students wanted to picket the hotels. Hannah Greeley, who turned up for the Congregational students, suggested finding them rooms instead, and thanks to Shorty's efforts they were housed in a decent hotel. This was the first time I met Hannah, and I found it hard to keep my eyes off her and pay attention to the serious business at hand. She was lovely, bright, sensible, and liberal, too, a combination difficult to resist.

Also disturbing was a nasty display of anti-Semitic signs during a Friday night parade that preceded the homecoming football game in 1934. This annual event brought out most of the students in the university. It was shocking to see some signs referring favorably to Hitler, and others sticking closer to the university. One of them, for example, read "Meet you at the Jewnion," suggesting that only Jewish students took advantage of the superb cultural and social facilities at the student Memorial Union. Again, it was Shorty who took the lead in publicly attacking this display of prejudice.

The worst outbreak of prejudice, which occurred in the late spring of 1935, was primarily political. On May 15 of that year, the local chapter of the League for Industrial Democracy, a national social democratic organization, had sponsored a meeting at the university's law school. Monroe Sweetland, a mild-mannered liberal from the West Coast, spoke on "The Beginnings of American Fascism." A group of athletes who had won W's for their athletic achievements, supported by their fraternity brothers, appeared at the meeting and began to heckle Sweetland. He responded by asking them to appoint a representative of their group to present their point of view. One of them then made a speech attacking the "Reds." When Sweetland resumed his remarks, the athletes seized him and forced him out of the building to the shore of Lake Mendota, on the edge of the campus. The audience followed, trying in vain to free him. A riot broke out and the athletes threw Sweetland and three others who had criticized the mob into the lake.

The National Student League, a Marxist group, was holding a meeting in the Memorial Union, also situated on the lake, and its members came out to support the people threatened by the athletes. At that moment some of the letter men announced that they were members of the "Silver Shirts," the notorious anti-Semitic fascist organization. After several fistfights had broken out, the police arrived and escorted members of the National Student

League and the League for Industrial Democracy from the terrace by the lake to protect them from the athletes.

The atmosphere on the campus was tense when the two organizations announced that they would hold a protest meeting the following night. Many feared that it would provoke an even more serious outbreak. Fortunately, the university local of the American Federation of Teachers persuaded the League for Industrial Democracy and the National Student League to call off their meeting, after the college administration had agreed that it would hold an all-university convocation. Representatives of various student organizations, including the LID and the NSL, would be allowed to speak, along with top officials from the university and the church communities. You could feel the tension at the meeting, which took place two days after the riot. The overflow crowd of more than a thousand students filled even the fire escapes outside. The student audience felt badly let down by some of the speakers, particularly President Frank, when he spoke about the philosophy underlying free speech without reference to the events two nights before. We muttered bitterly about his performance. Fortunately, George Sellery, dean of the College of Letters and Science, saved the situation.

Sellery, a medieval historian, was politically conservative but noted for his passionate commitment to the liberal traditions of the university. He was the last speaker, and his first words dramatically changed the atmosphere of the meeting:

> We HAVE belonged to a great university. I have been here at the university for a good many years, and frankly, the event of two nights ago was the most disgraceful thing ever perpetrated at the university.

He suggested that the athletes should throw their sweaters adorned with W's into a public bonfire and as the sweaters went up in flames, everyone should hang their heads in shame.

He excoriated the display of racial prejudice, and concluded by saying, "The principle which lay behind this event will wreck the university unless we wreck the people who support that principle." The audience's response was overwhelming. Sellery was interrupted with thunderous applause after every sentence. The dean had rekindled the true spirit of the university. His speech and the support given the administration by the teachers' union and representatives of liberal church groups helped calm the situation. There were no further ugly outbreaks.

This was the first time I had seen Sellery in action. I had no way of knowing that a year later his unequivocal attitude toward racial and political prejudice would affect me personally.

The university not only experienced internal tensions that had so dramatically exploded; it was also a major target of outsiders with extreme right-wing views. One of them, a precursor of Joseph McCarthy named John Chapple, came from a small town in northern Wisconsin. He set about flagellating the university as a hotbed of red radicalism, where students were corrupted by crypto-Communist professors. Chapple had a following among some students who took classroom notes of remarks by targeted teachers. After distorting their meaning, Chapple used this material as evidence of subversion. One of his targets was Professor Perlman. Chapple himself had taken Perlman's course "Capitalism and Socialism," and attacked him on the basis of deliberate misinterpretation. We were not surprised when Chapple later ran for public office.

Chapple's wild charges, supported by the *Wisconsin News*, the Hearst paper in Milwaukee, led to an investigation of the university's "radicalism" and "atheism" by a special committee of the state senate. A highlight of these bizarre, utterly biased hearings was the committee's embarrassment over the invitation to Professor Perlman to testify on the first day of the Jewish holiday Passover. Perlman calmly declined to appear for religious reasons. This was not the behavior of someone suspected of being a red or an atheist. Perlman was never called again to testify.

The conclusions of the committee were hardly surprising in light of the *a priori* prejudices of its members. After stating that they found abundant "proof" of charges of radicalism, including the labeling of President Glenn Frank as a Communist, they made three major recommendations: first, that "individuals or societies offering or expounding un-American doctrines should be expelled"; second, that "the university cooperate with any organizations whose purpose is the furtherance of Americanism" (this was a call to action by all of the Silver Shirts and similar groups in the state); third, that there be "constant vigilance . . . to secure full and complete information as to anti-American activities." As some observers pointed out, this was a proposal that the Nazis and fascist secret police would easily understand. The committee's report was mere "finding of fact" and had no authority behind it. Wisconsin has been a leader in the country's social reform movements, but unfortunately it also anticipated some of the subsequent national investigations of "un-American activities," including the wild charges of Senator Joseph McCarthy.

The faculty and most of the students rejected the senate committee report. Liberals in the university community had two powerful and articulate supporters, the progressive local newspaper, the *Capital Times*, and the students' *Daily Cardinal*. William Evjue, editor of the *Capital Times*, and Ernie Meyer, its courageous and beloved columnist, were dedicated progressives. In fact, the paper had been founded to support the La Follette movement. Evjue's daily thunderous front-page editorials had considerable influence on people throughout the state. He attacked the conclusions of the senate committee as well as Chapple's wild charges.

The *Daily Cardinal* was equally vigorous in its defense of the university and its faculty. The *Cardinal* had a well-deserved reputation as one of the finest university dailies in the country. Its policies were determined by the student editors without faculty interference. A deliberately provocative journal, it sought to stimulate thought and action, especially through its editorial pages. The paper enhanced the university's reputation as a liberal institution. One of my friends with whom I frequently discussed the paper's activities was Melvin Fagen, chief of the editorial page. Mel was a mild-mannered man with a razor-sharp intellect and the courage of a lion. His editorials attacking the likes of Chapple and the Neanderthal senate committee were rallying cries for the liberal students on campus. Mel has had a distinguished career, serving for many years as the top American official on the Economic Commission for Europe, based in Geneva, and I have maintained contact with him over the last five decades.

The *Daily Cardinal* exemplified for the students the practical significance of a genuinely free press. The *Cardinal* did not always have easy sailing. Sometimes the vigor of its editorials was attacked inside and outside the university world, but it never flinched, and it provided many of us important intellectual ballast during the troubled years of the early 1930s. It defended the right of professors to teach the truth as they saw it, and also the right of students to exercise free speech.

One of its more famous editorial campaigns was leveled against the dean of men at the university, Scott Goodnight. When Goodnight was informed that a student couple was spending the night together in a roominghouse on the campus, he sat in a rocking chair outside the door of the room to capture the pair when they finally emerged in the early hours of the morning. He subsequently suspended them from the university. The *Cardinal* immediately took up the cause of the couple, emphasizing the rights of students to lives of their own making. It proudly printed a letter from William Ellery Leonard, the distinguished poet and star of the English Department, which stated: "Higher than any law made by man is the natural and divine law that when two human beings are engaged in the act of love, they are not to be disturbed."

Clearly, there were no coeducational dormitories in our day. In fact, the parietal rules were strict. All women students, except seniors, had to be in their dormitories or sorority houses by 10:30 P.M. during the week and by midnight on weekends. Seniors were treated more generously with leave to stay out regularly until midnight. I remember how bold I felt when I walked out of Hannah Greeley's home after midnight knowing that her stepmother, the dean of women, was asleep upstairs.*

A young political buff like me found Wisconsin state politics as interesting and as challenging as the university's. My first contact with state politics was the primary election held in late September 1930, just a few weeks after my arrival in Madison. I knew that Phil La Follette, the youngest son of old Bob, was opposing the incumbent, Walter Kohler, a Stalwart Republican, for the nomination for governor. Because the Democratic Party had been moribund for almost half a century, winners of Republican primaries invariably won the general election. I saw posters all over the city asking for support for Kohler but, to my surprise, not a single one for Phil La Follette. When I questioned this, I was told

---

*When I was fifteen, I wrote an essay in my high school English class supporting a Heywood Broun column in which he advocated coeducational dormitories, though he added, "I'm not insisting on coeducational roommates." This was considered a shocking proposal. I never dreamed that I would live to see its fulfillment.

that Kohler was considered a sure winner and consequently there was little financial backing for La Follette.

The experts were wrong, hardly for the first time. Elected at the age of thirty-one, Phil La Follette became the youngest governor in the state's history. Liberals cheered his victory, feeling that the old progressive spirit was reviving to meet the crises confronting the country. Many people believed that he was destined to become President, a not unwarranted view. Bright, charming, and knowledgeable, Phil La Follette was heir to a rich political tradition to which the country was turning during the crushing economic crisis of the early 1930s. Moreover, unlike his more staid brother, Senator Bob, Phil inherited his father's dynamic personality. He was a powerful orator who easily stirred up his audience at a political rally. After hearing him for the first time, I made a point of attending as many of his meetings as I could. Unfortunately, the flaws in Phil's character, particularly his extravagant ambition and the serious mistakes that flowed from them, led to a sad political end for him and his brother Bob.

In 1932 when Phil La Follette ran for reelection as governor, he was defeated in the Republican primary by the former governor Walter Kohler. The FDR landslide swept Alfred Schmedeman into office that year; he became the first Democratic governor in over three decades. Phil La Follette was offered the attorney generalship by FDR but turned it down. Instead, he took the lead in organizing a new independent Progressive Party. Young Phil was riding a wave of progressive enthusiasm that befogged his sense of political realism. At first his tactics worked. He was elected governor on the Independent Progressive Ticket in 1934 and again in 1936, when his brother Bob was reelected as U.S. senator. That year turned out to be the zenith of the new Progressive Party's power.

The Progressives failed in their efforts to organize a national party, once again demonstrating that a two-party structure is an integral part of our system of government. Americans think in terms of majorities. We expect our two parties to be sufficiently flexible to encompass the wide diversity of interests so characteristic of our country. Phil La Follette might have learned from Teddy Roosevelt's experience in 1912 when the Progressive Party disappeared after that election, and from his father's experience of 1924 when old Bob ran for President on the third-party ticket. He managed to win only Wisconsin's thirteen electoral votes and left no institutional legacy. La Follette should also have read Selig Perlman's insightful *History of Trade Unionism in America,* which convincingly argues that no national third party is ever likely to succeed in the United States. Even at the state level, with a long progressive tradition, Phil La Follette had failed to develop locally the kind of organization necessary for the maintenance of a viable political party. Phil was defeated for reelection for governor in 1938 and the party declined quite rapidly thereafter.

In 1944 the Progressive Party was dissolved. By that time Phil had so lost his political mooring that he had become a supporter of General Douglas MacArthur for the Republican nomination for President. (He had served on the general's staff in Japan.) Two years later, Bob was facing a campaign for reelection to the Senate, and with the dissolution of the Progressive Party he had to decide whether to run as a Democrat or return to the Republican Party. He was pressed by a rather remarkable group of young Democrats, including Jim Doyle, Thomas Fairchild, and Horace Wilkie, to join with them. These young men, my contemporaries at the university, were motivated by the idealism of the New Deal. Believing that the future of liberalism in Wisconsin and in America rested with the Democrats, they were determined to revive the Democratic Party in Wisconsin. Subsequently, these three and their colleagues had distinguished careers. Jim, for example, was an active Stevenson supporter and later became an outstanding federal district court judge. He was a generous man who combined fine intelligence with deep commitment to improving the lot of the underprivileged. He showed great courage and wisdom in dealing with some of the cases that came before him during the riotous 1960s. Tom Fairchild served as a federal circuit court judge after a courageous campaign for the Senate against Joe McCarthy in 1952.

The new breed of Democrats felt that Bob La Follette's natural home was their party. They reminded Bob that in his two previous campaigns he had received the blessings of FDR and had no Democratic opposition. In addition, he was a member of the group of progressive senators, men like George Norris of Nebraska and Bunson Cutting of New Mexico, who worked closely with FDR in developing New Deal social and economic programs.

Bob La Follette's decision to rejoin the Republican Party, largely influenced by his brother Phil, angered young Democrats and led some of them to make a decision with unfortunate consequences. I was teaching at the University of Wisconsin Workers' School in August 1946, just before the primary. The school, a pioneer in trade union education, had been founded by John R. Commons. Perlman asked me to join the faculty that summer. I saw several of my young Democratic friends and had lengthy political discussions with them. They thought they could have their cake and eat it, too. La Follette's opponent in the Republican primary was a relatively unknown judge from a small town in northern Wisconsin, Joe McCarthy. On the Democratic side there was only one candidate, Howard MacMurray, an attractive, liberal congressman on leave from the Political Science Department of the University of Wisconsin's Milwaukee branch. They thought that MacMurray would have a good chance of winning the general election if his opponent were McCarthy rather than La Follette. Consequently, some of these Democrats decided to take advantage of the Wisconsin open primary, which enabled them to vote in the Republican contest. They were encouraged by Andrew Biemiller, who at that time was an organizer for the AFL State Federation. He, too, believed that this was the way to revitalize the state Democratic Party. They cast their ballots for Joseph McCarthy. They were impervious to arguments about Bob's outstanding record and about the importance of his seniority, particularly on the Senate Finance Committee. I remember Selig Perlman eloquently making these points to some of the young Democrats.

La Follette faced other defections. In May 1945 he made a speech attacking the Soviet Union for violating agreements to allow elections in Poland and other Eastern European countries, thereby arousing the ire of Communist and fellow-traveler elements in Wisconsin. As a consequence, the Communist-dominated Milwaukee County CIO Council and the United Electrical Workers Local decided to vote against him and for Joe McCarthy in the August 13, 1946, primary. There were other factors at play, but there is no doubt that these votes, as well as those of the Democrats, played a crucial part in the ironic and tragic victory of Joe McCarthy. In a poll of about 700,000 votes in the Republican primary, La Follette lost by less than 4,000. It would be difficult to conceive of a more unhappy denouement for the La Follette dynasty and for the country as a whole. The general election in 1946 was a nationwide disaster for the Democratic Party. In Wisconsin McCarthy easily defeated MacMurray.

Unexpectedly, my candidacy for the Rhodes Scholarship in 1936 became a test of Wisconsin's liberalism. Never before had a Jewish student, or any student who came from the East, been chosen. Consequently, when Professor Alban Winspear suggested that I apply, I appreciated the compliment, but was dubious about my prospects. However, with his vigorous support and the encouragement of my other professors, and because of my faith in the progressive Wisconsin tradition, I followed Winspear's advice.

The selection of Rhodes Scholars involves four basic steps. After filling out a lengthy application that includes the names of five professors who have agreed to submit letters of recommendation, you appear before three committees, assuming you pass muster in the first two: university, state, and regional. Each committee consists of five members—four ex–Rhodes Scholars and a chairman who is usually a distinguished member of the community.

My first hurdle was the university committee chaired by Dean George Sellery, the hero of the university's convocation to protest against the outrageous behavior of the Wisconsin athletes. The committee members, particularly Sellery, questioned me sharply. He raised doubts about my philosophical grounding because I hadn't taken any science courses. At first my replies were respectful. However, when he persisted in heckling me, I abruptly walked out of the room after telling him of an incident that my old friend and mentor Sid Korzenik had described in a recent letter. Korzenik had just returned from a cruise in the Caribbean where he had met Albert Einstein on board ship. When Einstein learned that Korzenik had studied at Harvard under the renowned philosopher Alfred North Whitehead, he asked Korzenik to explain the main thesis of Whitehead's latest book. "I tried reading it," Einstein said, "but I found it incomprehensible."

My brother Henry was waiting for me, and I sadly told him

that this was the end of my quest for the scholarship. The names of the students selected by the committee to compete at the state level would be posted a few hours later. Henry wisely took me for a walk along the lake during which he made a noble fraternal effort to console me, just one example of the invaluable support and advice he provided throughout his life. When we returned to see the results, we were amazed to find that one other student and I had been chosen. In picking only two of us, the committee had broken precedent. Usually, three to five students had been sent on to the Wisconsin state committee, which convened in Milwaukee. I learned the next day from one of the other members of the university committee that Sellery had been impressed by the way in which I stood up to him, and recalling the prejudice that the state committee had demonstrated against Jewish students, proposed that this time only two names be sent to Milwaukee, making it more difficult for the state committee to reject me. His colleagues agreed.

There was good reason to be concerned about the state committee. Its chairman was Judge Ferdinand Geiger, who sat on the federal district court and was notorious for his right-wing views. According to gossip, he boasted that no liberals or Jewish candidates had ever received a Rhodes Scholarship. Sellery had made it clear to the university committee that he was determined to break through that barrier. My source reported one other bit of fascinating information. Professor McGilvary, in his letter of recommendation, stated that he had been on the Wisconsin faculty since 1903, the first year of the Rhodes Scholarships, and, to the best of his recollection, no Jewish student had ever been selected. He could recall three or four who, in his view, certainly deserved to win. Kaiser, he wrote, was at least as good and probably better. His letter made a great impression on the university committee. They couldn't remember McGilvary ever taking such a position before. The letter undoubtedly influenced the state committee as well.

I was now geared to compete before the state committee in Milwaukee. In addition to the two students picked by the University of Wisconsin, there were six or seven candidates who came from other colleges in the state, or were residents of Wisconsin but were applying from universities in other parts of the country.

Under the established procedure, state committees picked two candidates who then competed at the regional level. Each of the eight regional committees covered six states* and chose four Rhodes Scholars, for a final total of thirty-two.

Three or four days before I was scheduled to appear before the state committee, I received a phone call from an old friend, Carol Dempsey. Carol and I had been in the same English class and had become very close friends. Having graduated the year before, she was now living at home in Milwaukee. Carol was an Irish beauty, a brunette with dancing brown eyes and a pertly turned-up nose. Bright, with a dazzling personality, she was one of the most popular coeds on the campus. She had no social prejudices, even though she was a member of one of the more prestigious sororities, which "restricted" its membership.

She reported, "Judge Geiger, who is an old friend of the family, came to dinner last night, and I was shocked when he suddenly said to my father, 'Guess what the university is trying to do? They're trying to force us to pick a Jewish kike from New York as a Rhodes Scholar.'

"Thereupon, I said to Geiger, 'You don't mean my friend, Phil Kaiser?'

"Amazed, he replied, 'How do you know him?' And then I said, 'I've known him for several years. We were in the same English class. He's a great guy and one of the brightest people I know.' I said other things, but I'm not going to spoil you. I think," Carol added with a smile in her voice, "I may have helped you."

When I got to Milwaukee, I discovered that I was lucky for another reason. Under the selection procedure, one member served on several state committees as well as on a regional committee. This was a sensible arrangement because it meant that each member on the regional committee had been able to size up the contestants from more than one state before making a final selection. In my year, T. S. Hume, a liberal minister of the New England Church in Chicago, sat on both the state and regional committees.

I can't say I was treated with kid gloves during my interview

---

*With the admission of Alaska and Hawaii, two committees now include seven states.

before the state committee, but I recall only one pointed question. This was the late fall of 1935, eight months before the 1936 Olympics scheduled to be held in Nazi Germany. I was asked whether I thought the United States should participate in the games in view of the Nazis' racial policies. I sensed the special interest of the committee members in my reply and I unhesitatingly said it would be a mistake for us to participate. Our staying home would send a dramatic signal to the Nazis that we disapproved of their behavior. It would avoid inevitable embarrassment for the black members on our team, or any potential Jewish member. I was happy to see Reverend Hume nodding his approval.

The state committee chose a student from the Naval Academy in Annapolis and me. Inexplicably, Walter Heller, who later became chairman of President Kennedy's Council of Economic Advisers, was passed over. Two weeks later we appeared before the regional committee in Chicago. It was a long, tense day. We drew lots for our order of appearance. I was eleventh on the list. I was called back a second time. It was clear from one member's questions that he doubted that I had any athletic ability. With a little prodding from Hume, I was able to convince the skeptic that I was not just a bookish type, that I had won prizes in summer camp for my athletic prowess and was a member of my high school tennis team.

Elation was the all-consuming reaction to the announcement that I was one of the four chosen. After phoning family members and several professors, I sank into a jubilant state of exhaustion. I had only enough energy to contemplate the fact that the Rhodes award would change the course of my life in ways that I could hardly imagine.

3

Oxford Before
World War II:
An American Perspective

As the *Laconia* docked in Liverpool in September 1936, we American Rhodes Scholars were both excited and anxious at the prospect of studying at Oxford. How would we adjust to a radically different academic ambiance? How would we be received by the British students? Settling in turned out to be an enriching experience. The contrast between the University of Wisconsin and Oxford was striking. Wisconsin was a tension-ridden community reflecting the social diversity of its students and the struggle for individual identity and status. By being both a social and intellectual melting pot, it performed a major function of an American state university. In the early 1930s the University of Wisconsin had about eight thousand students (now it has over forty thousand), while the largest Oxford college contained no more than three hundred. The state university coped with the social and academic problems of large-scale education, while Oxford emphasized individual instruction based on weekly tutorials. No academic institution in the world had a higher ratio of teachers to students.

In my day the Oxford students were relatively homogeneous. A large proportion came from upper-middle-class and upper-class backgrounds, their elite status already established. An increasing number of scholarship students came from poorer backgrounds, but once in Oxford they tended to "aristocratize" rapidly. Admission to an Oxford college made you a member of a special society.

Once you had penetrated British reserve and shyness, you appreciated that the atmosphere was more relaxed and urbane than at Wisconsin.

The center of Oxford life is the autonomous college, and there are differences among the thirty-odd in the university. By a stroke of luck, I had been admitted to Balliol, perhaps the most famous of all. When chosen, scholars were asked to list eight colleges in their order of preference. In my year, 1936, about fifteen of the thirty-two American Rhodes Scholars put Balliol at the top. Out of loyalty to Professor Winspear, who had pushed me to apply for the scholarship, and on his strong recommendation, I had made his college, Corpus Christi, my first choice, and Balliol second.

Fortunately, during my senior year John Fulton, a politics tutor at Balliol, had spent a term in Madison on a Rockefeller Foundation Grant. He was interested in the progressive politics of Wisconsin and in the relationship between the university and the state government. Years later, in fact, when Fulton founded Sussex University in England, the Wisconsin Idea served as something of a model. We became friends, and on several occasions attended political rallies together. When Fulton heard that I was applying for a Rhodes he told me to be sure to pick Balliol as my first choice. When I explained that I would be putting Balliol second, he insisted that I keep him informed. I did so and, thanks to his recommendation, Balliol accepted me after Corpus Christi luckily turned me down. Balliol picked two other Americans that year: Gordon Craig, who became one of the world's leading historians on Germany, and Walt Rostow, the distinguished economic historian who served as LBJ's national security adviser.

In the 1930s Balliol was probably the most cosmopolitan of Oxford colleges and certainly the most politically oriented. It still bore the influence of Benjamin Jowett, the famous nineteenth-century Master of the college. Anxious to relate Balliol to the outside world, Jowett encouraged students to seek glory in politics, the Church, diplomacy, or journalism. He emphasized the importance of teaching without neglecting scholarship and research, and gave success in worldly careers a new impetus. He once admitted, "I have a general prejudice against all persons who do not succeed in the world."

Subsequent masters made their own unique contributions to the college, but Jowett's main thrust was sustained. Balliol men may not be, as the cliché goes, "effortlessly superior," but they have made a marked impact on the world. During this century, with an average student body of less than three hundred, Balliol has produced prime ministers—Asquith, Macmillan, and Heath; foreign ministers—Grey and Curzon; chancellors of the Exchequer—Jenkins and Healey; Archbishops of Canterbury—Lang and Temple; editors of *The Times*—Dawson and Rees-Mogg; and countless cabinet members, MP's, ambassadors, bishops, heads of colleges, vice chancellors of universities, and top civil servants.

A. D. ("Sandie") Lindsay, the master of Balliol when we arrived in 1936, was a natural successor to Benjamin Jowett, although his election as Master in 1924 shocked the university community because he was the first member of the Labour Party to become head of an Oxford college. It seemed fitting that Balliol should take the lead in bringing Oxford up to the times. The early 1920s were a period of great political change. The first Labour government came to power in 1924 and the young Fellows were mainly responsible for Lindsay's election. They knew that Lindsay, who had served as a classics tutor in Balliol for many years before becoming a professor at Glasgow University, was an outstanding teacher and prolific scholar whose extracurricular activities, particularly his deep involvement with the Workers' Education Association, had kept him in close touch with the world beyond academia.

Craig, Rostow, and I first met Lindsay on board the *Laconia*. He was returning from the United States where, as vice chancellor,* he had represented Oxford University at Harvard's tercentenary celebration. He invited the three of us to have tea with him. It was typical of Lindsay to take advantage of an opportunity to meet the Balliol boys in the new crop of Rhodes Scholars.

We were impressed by his physical presence. A tall, handsome man with an open face, his genuine interest in us quickly overcame his shyness. He didn't take long to engage us in serious talk. Knowing that he had recently published a small volume on Karl Marx, we turned the conversation to that subject. To demonstrate

*The vice-chancellorship, the chief executive office of the university, rotated among the heads of colleges.

my knowledge, I asked him whether he had read Croce's *Historical Materialism and the Economics of Karl Marx*. He quietly allowed that he had, without further comment. The week after our arrival in Oxford, I visited the famous Blackwell's book shop and bought Croce's book. I was taken aback when I noticed that Lindsay had written the introduction.

We soon came to admire Lindsay for his intellectual as well as moral power. Though by nature reticent, he had a genuine interest in students, and Americans in particular liked his direct and democratic approach to people and issues. He knew America well and appreciated the contribution Americans made to the cosmopolitan atmosphere in Balliol. He loved to provoke argument, confident in the value of free and frank discussion. I remember his bringing A. C. Coolidge and me together at dinner at the end of my first year, knowing that Coolidge, an old Balliol man and the leading American benefactor of the college, was a passionate Republican, while I was an ardent New Dealer. After we had eaten, Lindsay departed for a meeting, leaving the two of us behind. He was delighted the next morning when Coolidge, his house guest, informed him that for the first time in years, he had been able to have a lengthy, civil discussion about American politics with a New Dealer. We had argued calmly and enjoyably as we walked around the moonlit Balliol quad for several hours.

Americans also found Lindsay's politics congenial. That's not to say that we shared his socialist convictions, but his progressive sentiments suited our views. We agreed, too, on the burning world issues of that period. He was aggressively anti-Nazi and a vigorous supporter of the Spanish Republic. In addition—and this was rather unusual for Oxford people at the time—he was outspoken in his condemnation of Japanese aggression in the Far East. Moreover, Lindsay liked President Roosevelt, and almost all of the American students at Balliol were New Dealers.

The meeting with the Master on board ship was an encouraging beginning. However, having been thoroughly brainwashed about British reserve, we were still anxious about how we would be received. At first blush, the observation of Dan Davin, a New Zealand Rhodes Scholar, that "the English make up in tolerance of the stranger what they lack in warmth" seemed all too true. A few minutes after Gordon Craig entered his rooms for the first time, the former occupant dropped in to solicit his support for some activity. He was so chatty, so apparently out of stereotype, that, in the best American style, Gordon stuck his hand out and said, "My name is Craig." "I know," the British student said, rejecting the proffered hand. "It's written above the door."

The first weeks in college were not made easier by the rules that restricted students' freedom of movement—rules utterly alien to American students. We had to be back in college by midnight, unless we had permission to stay out later, which was rarely given. Moreover, we paid an escalating fine for being out between 9:00 P.M. and midnight. If we hadn't left the college gates by 9:00 P.M., we were stuck inside. The loneliness and frustration these restrictions engendered inspired a series of songs for which Rostow wrote the music and Craig the lyrics. They provided a happy catharsis for British as well as overseas students. "Claustrophobia Blues," "Ninety Mad Englishmen," and "Sherry Party Girl" are a sampling of the song titles.

Once you "escaped" from the college, the main amusements were pub crawling and the cinema. University rules forbade any student from frequenting a pub for a half pint of bitter or lager, and university proctors and their "bulldogs," local citizens, prowled the streets to ensure compliance with this puerile regulation. The proctors were faculty Fellows who served fixed terms, while their "bulldogs," local toughs wearing bowler hats, were permanently employed. If caught in a pub, you were "progged." You paid a ten-shilling fine the first time and were more severely penalized if you continued to sin.

Some of us delighted in outwitting the proctors. One trick worked very well. There were two pubs called Gardener's Arms, one on Plantation Road and the other on North Parade. We soon learned that the proctors regularly invaded the Gardener's Arms located on North Parade. Consequently, we frequented the other Gardener's Arms with impunity.

I was caught one night when we boldly visited The Trout, a well-known suburban inn and pub. Suddenly, hearing the cry "Proctors!" I dashed out before they actually arrived. However, several of my friends were picked up. Unfortunately, one of them—seeing me lurking in the dark—said too loudly, "Did they get you, Phil?" The bulldogs heard him and took me in tow as well.

Some of us became cinema Marxists. One movie house ran all the Marx Brothers' films every year, and Americans were delighted to find that the brothers were as popular among British students as among us. In Balliol we organized an informal Anglo-American Marx Brothers Society whose members happily romped off to each showing of these movie classics. We supplemented Marx with Shakespeare. When we got to know British students who owned cars—a relative few in prewar Oxford—they sometimes invited us to come see a Shakespeare play in Stratford-on-Avon, only thirty-nine miles away. It was just possible to get back to your college before the Oxford bells tolled midnight.

Dates with women students, or "undergraduettes," as they were called, were at a premium. The clichés about "unattractive," "unwashed" undergraduettes were unjustified; but men outnumbered women by about eight to one, and dating an attractive coed was not easy. When you did manage it, tea in your rooms turned out to be one of the more agreeable ways of spending time with her. For some inexplicable reason, there were no restrictions on women calling on you in mid-afternoon. However, if you wanted to host a mixed dinner party, you had to secure prior permission from the dean.

Women's colleges did not make socializing easier. When, for example, I called at Lady Margaret Hall to pick up Nermine Okyar, a beautiful Turkish girl, I was made to feel that I was knocking at the door of a nunnery. Almost all Oxford colleges have now become coed, and reliable reports indicate that students are taking full advantage of their new social opportunities.

Living in college required some physical adjustments. Although each student had his own suite, the only heat available was from a coal fireplace in the sitting room. Warming just the front of the body was not always good enough; and entering an icy bedroom and crawling into bed between cold, damp sheets was a nightly trauma. We felt that we were trying to cope with a concentration of centuries of cold.

Nor were the bath and toilet facilities conveniently located.

There was no running water in the rooms. The Scouts, the indispensable Oxford men servants, brought in hot water for shaving every morning before seven. If I wanted to have a shower, however, I had to walk almost a hundred yards across the open quadrangle. British fellow students thought showering or taking a bath every morning was strange, but they enjoyed seeing me rush out in bathrobe and pajamas, often carrying an umbrella. The fact that Balliol provided showers as well as bathtubs was an unusual gesture highly appreciated by the Americans.

We paid for keeping clean, too—fourpence per bath or shower. This encouraged Cornell, the cheerful one-armed World War veteran who managed the bath facilities, to use the records he kept to run a contest. The student with the largest number of baths or showers at the end of the eight-week term was pronounced "the cleanest man in the college." In the six terms I lived in college, I had the dubious distinction of winning every contest. Cleanliness was not the highest priority of Oxford students. I was suspect in the eyes of many British students because I changed socks, underwear, and shirt every day.

Physical inconveniences soon fell into perspective, as all elements in the Balliol College community—staff, Scouts, Fellows, Master, and students—made us feel welcome. We realized, to our delight, that we had become members of an exceptional society: elitist but democratic, harmonious while catering to diversity. The contrast with a typical American university could not have been more striking.

Our first on-the-ground contact with the college was with the porter, Cyril King, the guardian of the college gate, and the expert on the rules and customs of college life. A wise, kind man, always unflappable, he had the appropriate answer to any practical problem, no matter how difficult or embarrassing, and never made you feel that your questions were gauche or naïve. Students and Fellows respected and loved him.

And then there were the Scouts who, by taking excellent care of the students, made a vital contribution to the quality of college life. They laid our fires, delivered the coal, cleaned our rooms, delivered mail, collected laundry, served meals, and advised us on a variety of practical matters. Since most of them had come to this work at the age of sixteen, their knowledge of college history was exceptional. Although their wages were minimal and their hours far too long, their concern for the welfare of the students under their care never wavered. Oxonians loved to tell stories about their Scouts. A popular one in Balliol was about the venerated Scout who, when entering the bedroom to wake one of his students, noticed a young lady in bed with him. This, of course, was utterly verboten. The Scout didn't bat an eye, but calmly said to his charge, "Shall it be tea for two, sir?"

Arnold Rawlings, my Scout, was a man of inestimable quality. Scouts usually took care of the five or six students on a "staircase." Our staircase was blessed with a very precious facility—a toilet. It was not, however, open to students at all hours. Fellows had first call and controlled the key. Rawlings, who liked the informality of his American charges, always told us where it could be found.

The supervisor of the porter and Scouts was Colonel A. C. H. Duke, the college bursar, a tough boss, but paternal rather than authoritarian and with a strain of kindliness. After my election as president of the Balliol Junior Common Room, Duke and I became friends even though we fought over one or two rather difficult issues. On one occasion, he helped me out of a financial pickle.

Rhodes Scholars received a stipend of four hundred pounds a year, equivalent to almost two thousand dollars, a substantial sum at the time. We were given one hundred pounds every quarter and, thanks to the British practice of generous bank overdrafts, I, like many others, constantly lived beyond that amount. The Oxford academic year consisted of three eight-week terms with six-week vacations for Christmas and Easter and four months off during the summer. When we returned from our holidays we were presented with our bills—"Battels"—for the preceding term. On one such occasion I found that I owed ninety-four pounds, which meant that for the next fourteen weeks I would have six pounds to spend on everything beyond room and board. I decided to turn to Colonel Duke for help. I asked him whether I could pay only seventy-five pounds and take care of the rest out of my next stipend. "That's ridiculous, Kaiser. You couldn't possibly manage if you did that. Why don't you pay me just fifty pounds now and we'll take care of the rest when your position is easier." What a contrast to the practice of American universities where the guillotine fell if you failed to pay your fees on time.

Balliol's tutors made foreigners feel welcome. They were student-oriented and devoted to teaching. They agreed with Lindsay that "Perhaps the greatest characteristic of the Jowett tradition was his insistence that the college existed primarily for the sake of undergraduates . . . 'to train up men to serve God in Church and State.' That included, of course, 'training up' young men to be scholars and teachers but, when the choice had to be made, research was for the sake of teaching, not teaching for the sake of research.' I held to it firmly myself and I hope the college will never abandon it."

The Balliol faculty worked hard to stretch our intellects. They were quick at sizing us up and bringing out the best in us. Humphrey Sumner, the renowned historian—his *Russia and the Balkans* is still a classic—teased me for making too many analogies between New Deal reforms and the British reforms of 1832. His knowledge could be overwhelming. Assigning you an essay on British policy in Eastern Europe, he would recommend for background reading several books in Polish and Russian. When you confessed that you didn't read those languages, he would self-consciously apologize. Sumner, like all his colleagues, was concerned about our general well-being as well as our intellectual development. After I had been laid low with severe flu my first winter term, he told me, "Even though you Americans pride yourselves on being tough, you should seriously consider wearing long woolen underwear to fight the cold damp of Oxford winters." I followed his advice.

We were grateful, too, for the flexibility of A. B. Rodger, the economic historian, who also served as college dean. One evening a mixed tea party in my room was going so well that I decided to telephone him for permission to extend it into dinner, in spite of the rule requiring written permission days in advance. "Dean," I said, "I know I'm out of order, but there's a tea party in my room with some women present that is going so well that I would like to extend it into a dinner party." In his typically pithy manner the dean replied, "If they are women, Kaiser, no go; but if they are ladies, okay."

And who could resist feeling friendly toward Maurice Allen, the very able economics Fellow, when he offered us a gin and vermouth after the subtleties of his tutorials had tied us up in intellectual knots? Years later, Allen became the highly respected economic adviser to the governor of the Bank of England. John Fulton, whose interest in current events meshed nicely with his ideas on higher education, was a stimulating politics tutor. Comparison between the British and American political systems was one of his specialties. He was a fan of the United States and he liked American students. Fulton's easy charm helped make his weekly tutorials especially agreeable. Later he not only was a founder and vice chancellor of the highly successful Sussex University, but also became an active participant in public affairs as chairman of the Commission on Civil Service Reform and as vice chairman of the B.B.C.

In short, Balliol's faculty was admirably suited to challenge a rather remarkable mix of students in the late 1930s. We Americans soon realized that in Balliol there were no foreigners. Students came from a wide variety of backgrounds—every social class in the United Kingdom—and, thanks to Rhodes, from the Commonwealth* and Germany, as well as the United States. Balliol was proud of its cosmopolitan diversity, proud that it was the first Oxford College to admit students from India. Thanks to the social chemistry reflecting the spirit of the college, we all lived together in harmony. Of course, there were groups based on special interests, athletic or intellectual, but the intermingling of students was impressive. Lindsay was proud, too, that even as the composition of the student body was changing, with fewer students from the elitist "public" schools, the college "retained its aristocratic virtues while acquiring democratic ones." His "aristocratic" virtues included "an intense care for distinction and values, a life of the kind of leisure and free conversation among equals which helps to alleviate the things of the spirit, and a wide and generous toleration."

In this setting it was not surprising that, before too long, we Americans found our peers less forbidding than we had feared. Some British students looked up to us because we were three or four years older. They considered us already men of the world. In at least one respect the British students were right: we felt

---

*Since the end of World War II, Rhodes trustees have also established scholarships in former colonies when they achieved independence.

more at ease with the opposite sex. Most of us had studied at coeducational schools and universities, while the British were products of all-male schools. We may have been older, even more socially adept, but not necessarily brighter. We were particularly impressed by the ease with which British students articulated their ideas, a talent developed and nurtured from earliest schooldays.

We soon adjusted to British reserve. Being ignored when you greeted a British student the morning after you had participated in the same drinking party was irritating, but once we realized that shyness had been cultivated as a desirable and respected characteristic,* developing friendships was not too difficult. On the contrary, British students were interested in making us "colonials" feel at home. They liked our openness—even our breeziness—which may explain why they especially appreciated Americans who came from the West.

FDR helped, too. He had caught the imagination of many Englishmen, especially those with a passion for politics. The first Anglo-American party in my rooms took place in November 1936, a month after our arrival in Oxford, when Teddy Heath, Hugh Fraser, and several other British students happily joined Gordon Craig, Walt Rostow, and me to listen to short-wave radio returns of the Roosevelt-Landon election. We stayed up until the early hours of the morning, consuming large amounts of beer and cheering loudly when it became clear that FDR was winning in a landslide.†

---

*See Sir Harold Nicolson's essay "A Defense of Shyness" in *Small Talk* (New York, 1937; reprinted Freeport, N.Y.: Books for Librarians Press, 1971).

†Two years later, a similar group, including Heath, was present in my room to hear the news on the radio of Anthony Eden's resignation as foreign secretary. We were promised an official statement by 10:00 P.M. Instead, after four half-hourly postponements—without any comment or music in between—shortly before midnight we were told that 10 Downing Street had just announced the resignation of Mr. Eden as Secretary of State for Foreign Affairs and that tomorrow he would make a statement in the House of Commons. In the best B.B.C. tradition, there was not the slightest tinge of emotion in the announcer's voice, nor any further comment, only a calm reminder that at midnight there would be the usual weather forecasts for the whole country. Heath thanked me and left without saying another word.

Of course, we also had differences with our British peers. One of them inspired an old but not very respectable American solution. Balliol had its share of dining and drinking clubs, a venerated Oxford institution. The club feasts frequently ended with a group of rowdy, inebriated students breaking up the furniture in the Junior Common Room, the center of student social life. Under college rules, all students, even those who did not participate in the youthful vandalism, had to share in the cost of the damages. After American objections to this unfair rule were rebuffed, whenever we learned a drinking club was meeting, we formed a "vigilante" group that stood guard in the Junior Common Room and prevented any destruction.

In my second year I was elected president of the Junior Common Room, or JCR, further evidence that the Americans were quite acceptable. The JCR was the scene for "local" college politics. Here we gathered to read and discuss articles in newspapers and magazines. Tea was served in the afternoon, and coffee after dinner. Sometimes there were tense encounters when, for example, I ran into one of Balliol's German students, Kurt von Wilmowsky, Krupp's grandson, the evening after the frightful *Kristallnacht* in Germany when rampaging Nazi gangs burned synagogues, sacked Jewish shops, and carried Jews off to concentration camps.

Von Wilmowsky was a serious young man who tried to "explain" rather than defend the Nazi regime in Germany. He was a Hugenberg Nationalist and often suggested that had the United Kingdom and France been more "statesmanlike" in handling the "guilt clause" in the Versailles Treaty, and disarmament and reparation issues, the Nationalists would have prevented Hitler from coming to power. He did not convince many of us at Balliol, particularly since his explanation tended to become a defense of the Hitler regime. That night the headlines in the newspapers were devoted to the pogroms in Germany. On meeting Von Wilmowsky, I quietly said, "You come from a civilized country"; he turned pale and walked out of the Common Room.*

---

*Ironically, the following summer, I found myself helping support a German Nationalist. I had just arrived in Paris and looked up two Oxford friends, Guy Nunn and Dan Davin, both vigorous anti-Nazis, who were spending their summer

The business of the JCR was handled by an executive committee and a president chosen annually by the students. The presidency entailed amusing, challenging, and time-consuming responsibilities. First of all, the president chaired several JCR meetings each term, all well attended and lively. I realized how articulate, boisterous, and witty Oxford students could be. The agenda consisted of one or two fixed items, but "other business" produced most of the fireworks. One item was always lively, adding newspaper or magazine subscriptions. We boasted that Balliol had the best collection of periodicals in Oxford. Under our rules the Common Room had to subscribe to any journal approved by only thirty students, and less well-known, more quixotic magazines had a special appeal. This was characteristically Balliol: a willingness to cater to minorities, even though it sometimes led to an increase in the annual dues for the members. When the British students in Balliol discovered that in their copies of the American magazine *Time*, distributed through London, references to the affair between Edward VIII and Mrs. Wallis Simpson had been deleted, they sought uncensored copies which came directly from the States. A motion to order three subscriptions directly from New York carried unanimously!

Replying to the complaints, observations, and anything else any student cared to write about in the JCR Suggestion Book was another presidential responsibility. We were expected to be knowledgeable about every conceivable subject: plumbing, politics,

---

vacation in the French capital. They urged me to join them in helping keep Fritz Oberender alive. Fritz was a successful German architect who had joined the Hugenberg Party. Participating actively in the last free election in Germany, he found himself debating Goebbels on several occasions. The fiendish propaganda minister neither forgot nor forgave. About a fortnight before my arrival in Paris, a Nazi friend of Oberender secretly informed him that Goebbels was now planning to have him arrested. Oberender, a handsome, blond, blue-eyed German—almost a caricature of the Nazi male model—wangled permission to leave Berlin for a five-day "business" trip to Paris. He departed with just enough baggage to keep him going for that short visit, never intending to return. I don't recall where Guy or Dan met him, but when they learned he was not a socialist, a Communist, or Jewish, they assumed the responsibility of keeping him alive. They asked me to share the burden. The three of us used money from our Rhodes Scholar stipend to keep him going until just before the war, when he managed to emigrate to South America.

poetry, science, literature, sports, sex, and especially college food, about which the complaints were legion. If the president's answers were not timely or clever enough, he was subjected to a barrage of written criticism. One student, a zoologist, would indite the Latin names of the bugs he claimed he saw on the lettuce and other vegetables, and raise written hell if corrective action was not taken immediately. When biographers of Heath, Healey, and Jenkins called on me in the early 1970s to ask what these three were like as students, I recommended that they read the JCR Suggestion Books for the years each was president of the Common Room.

During my presidency, the executive committee pushed for some significant changes in the college's labor policies. Scouts' salaries were shamefully low even though during term they worked seven long days a week. Discovering that we controlled the salary of the JCR Scout, we voted him a substantial increase, hoping to set a precedent for all the other Scouts. Colonel Duke, their supervisor, didn't particularly like our action, adjusting to it reluctantly and slowly.

We had more trouble, however, when the JCR passed a resolution demanding one night off a week for the Scouts. This time Duke resisted vigorously. The colonel and I were on our way to an embarrassing impasse when the Master stepped into the picture.

Under a written constitutional agreement between the faculty's Senior Common Room and the students' Junior Common Room, the Master's formal point of contact with the student body was the president of the JCR. Consequently, I saw Lindsay quite often. Whenever there was business to transact between the Master and the Junior Common Room, he would invite me to breakfast in the Master's lodging. He did so when Duke and I were having our hassle over the Scouts. As usual, the Master got down to the subject very quickly. He said that as a member of the Labour Party, he was embarrassed that it took an American to focus attention on the college's exploitation of its Scouts. Soon thereafter, they got one night off a week.

Sometimes the president of the JCR had an unusual assignment. During my term the college dedicated new pews in the chapel. The guest of honor for the occasion was one of Balliol's illustrious old boys, Cosmo Gordon Lang, Archbishop of Canterbury. As president of the JCR, I acted as the official student host throughout the day, personally amused at having this unique ecumenical responsibility. The Archbishop was so charming and so friendly that I almost forgot his strong support for Chamberlain's appeasement policy.

Even Balliol men recognized that Oxford life wasn't limited to your own college.* You made contact with the wider university world in several ways. At the beginning of every term the university published a schedule of lecture courses offered by faculty in the various colleges. Attendance was voluntary and open to all students. We were a tough audience: if what we heard didn't satisfy us, we drifted away. Occasionally, the lecturer found himself facing the proverbial Greek audience of "four walls and three benches" weeks before the conclusion of his course. The system enabled us to listen to a full series of lectures by the more famous Oxford faculty. Thus, among others, I heard Roy Harrod on Keynes;† Oliver Franks on philosophy; G. D. H. Cole on British labor; Richard Crossman on politics; Denis Brogan on America and France; and Isaiah Berlin on political philosophy and the history of ideas.

These lectures provided a rich intellectual addition to the weekly tutorials with Fellows in your own college. Three of the faculty members, Richard Crossman, Isaiah Berlin, and Denis Brogan, became my lifelong friends.

Crossman, a big bear of a man with horned-rimmed glasses, had great personal appeal. His lectures sparkled with provocative ideas. He loved to shock students with iconoclastic comments that he cleverly managed to make, at least temporarily, plausible. Mocking accepted wisdom was one of his specialties and he was never inhibited by the need to be consistent. As Leonard Woolf observed in his autobiography, Crossman could passionately defend a position on a particular issue one week and the opposite view with equal emphasis a fortnight later—and not bat an eye-

---

*As Harold Macmillan put it at the eightieth-anniversary Rhodes Scholar Reunion in 1983: "What is Oxford? There is Balliol, [pause] and then Wadham, Worcester, and the other colleges."

†Many years later, in the late 1960s, I asked Roy Harrod why, in his massive biography of Keynes, he never mentioned the latter's homosexuality. "I was afraid," he replied, "it would damage his reputation in America."

lash. He could be an intellectual bully, but he respected you if you stood your ground. Politics were his passion. His *Cabinet Diaries*, published after his early death, provide a uniquely intimate picture of how British government actually works.

I saw quite a bit of Crossman during the post-Munich Oxford by-election campaign in which he was a key participant. We kept in touch after I left Oxford. We again met in Washington in early 1946 during the hearing of the Anglo-American Commission on Palestine, an assignment that was a turning point in his career. Prime Minister Clement Attlee, a friend of Crossman's father, never forgave Dick for supporting the recommendation that 100,000 Jews be allowed to enter Palestine. Crossman had to wait until Harold Wilson became prime minister to be appointed to the cabinet.

During that stay in Washington, I introduced Crossman to the ebullient Meyer Weisgal, the president of the Israeli Weizmann Institute of Science. They hit it off immediately and their friendship flourished as Crossman became the leading pro-Israeli politician in England. Characteristically, Crossman never hesitated to castigate the Israelis when he thought they were off base, without, however, provoking a hostile reaction. I saw him do this when we were in Israel together in 1970. In fact, Crossman enjoyed chiding his friends. As one of his close friends once jokingly said to me, "If you're around when I die, please see to it that Dick, whom I love, doesn't deliver the eulogy at my funeral. He will almost certainly concentrate on my warts."

Isaiah Berlin was and still is the most remarkable of all Oxonians. Prodigiously wise and witty, he is a perpetual source of knowledge. Trained as a philosopher, he is equally at home in literature, music, and politics. He illumines every subject he addresses, whether it be Marx or Disraeli, Chekhov or Mozart, Weizmann or Roosevelt, or Russian or American politics.

Berlin is an extraordinary conversationalist. His mind, always teeming with brilliant ideas, works at supersonic speed. Since his tongue never lags behind, it is difficult to keep up with him, but the effort to do so is more than worth it. You're always captivated by what he has to say. He loves to gossip. He can be critical when the facts demand it, but he is always fair and gracious in his comments, never mean or petty. Unlike most exceptionally articulate individuals, Berlin is also a good listener. When in his company, you feel wiser than you really are. It's rather like playing tennis with someone much better than yourself; you sometimes rise to the occasion and your game improves—at least temporarily. Berlin has a special gift for making friends. They invariably turn to him for advice and help and he never disappoints them. He could easily have inspired Verdi's aria on friendship in *Don Carlos*.

I met Berlin my first year at Oxford when he spoke at a meeting of the Oxford Jewish Society. His subject was "Disraeli and the Conservative Party," in which he outlined some of the ideas brilliantly elaborated in his later essay "Benjamin Disraeli, Karl Marx and the Search for Identity." Berlin noted that unlike Marx, Disraeli, far from rejecting his Jewish background, glamorized it, substituting his romantic imagination for the real facts when talking about his Sephardi, Spanish-Jewish ancestors. Disraeli claimed to be an authentic aristocrat because of the antiquity of his race, its regard for tradition and authority, and the contribution it had made to the Christian religion. Having established his identity, Disraeli was still sufficiently detached from it to articulate for the traditional British Tories the historical significance of their party and its mission for the future. Through his remarkable alchemy of romanticism and political pragmatism, Disraeli became the father of Tory democracy, and a Conservative prime minister who successfully combined deep concern for the exploited masses with contempt for those who belittled tradition and true merit.

Berlin's own background made him more apt to appreciate what others had missed in their study of Disraeli. Berlin's Jewishness has always been an integral part of his character and personality, without diminishing in any way his Englishness. The two have been mutually sustaining and enriching. Thanks to the liberal, civilized character of British society, his deep Jewish commitment has not prevented him from becoming one of Oxford's outstanding figures (today he is generally recognized as the "guru" of Oxford) and one of the most respected and popular individuals in British intellectual and cultural circles. He helped found and was the first president of Oxford's Wolfson College and served as president of the British Academy from 1974 to 1978.

Seeing Berlin regularly over the last fifty years in Washington, in Oxford and London, even in Budapest and Vienna, has always been a special treat. We met quite regularly during the war when he was an officer at the British embassy in Washington and writing a wise weekly letter that was a lively mixture of Washington politics and gossip. Churchill valued it so highly that he asked his staff to invite "I. Berlin" to 10 Downing Street when he visited England. Shortly thereafter, when Irving Berlin came to London with the cast of his wartime show, *This Is the Army*, Churchill's secretary dutifully invited the songwriter to a lunch given by the PM. It didn't take Churchill long to realize that he had the wrong I. Berlin in tow. According to one of his secretaries, John Peck, who later was my British ambassadorial colleague in Senegal, the prime minister was so angry at his staff that he threatened to fire them all and didn't talk to any of them for several days.

Another remarkable Oxonian was D. W. Brogan. Americans particularly appreciated him. As his writings and lectures demonstrated, his knowledge of our history and politics was extraordinary. Like de Tocqueville and Bryce, he used his outsider's perspective on our country to great advantage, observing and understanding events and issues that Americans often took for granted or overlooked.

Most impressive were the thoroughness with which Brogan kept up with the current U.S. political scene and his wide range of American friends. He liked American students and we, in turn, loved to hear his stories about American politics and politicians. He knew everybody in the United States, or so it seemed. It was not enough to tell Brogan the state you came from; he also wanted to know the county, and then would reveal the names of the local Democratic and Republican Party leaders who, of course, were his friends. His encyclopedic knowledge was matched by the brilliance of his historical and social analysis.

He was a nonstop talker (often a nonstop drinker, too), but most of his hours-long monologues were informative, witty, and replete with anecdotes. After a George Washington's birthday party which Brogan gave for American students, he kept Guy Nunn and me up all night. A bottle of Scotch was polished off, mostly by Brogan, while he enlightened us about American politics. His books on the United States and France—he knew as much about France as he did about the United States—reveal the skill with which he used his vast store of anecdotes to illuminate a personality or an event. You missed a great deal if you failed to read Brogan's footnotes. In his book *The Development of Modern France* Brogan refers to the concern of some Germans about the improvement of relations between France and Italy at the turn of the century. Would Italy remain loyal to her alliance with Germany? "It was all very well," Brogan writes, "for the German government to minimize the secession of Italy, to talk of wives waltzing with men other than their husbands and yet remain faithful. No one knew better," Brogan emphasizes, "than Chancellor von Bülow, that Italian flirtations were liable to have quite serious consequences." And then in a footnote he writes, "The chancellor's wife was an Italian lady of very high rank who had eloped with von Bülow when she was still the wife of the German ambassador in Rome. And von Bülow was on her husband's staff."

You couldn't have a more loyal friend than Denis Brogan. He would happily overlook your faults, exaggerate your good qualities, and vigorously defend you against any criticism. We remained friends for almost four decades, from the time we met at Oxford until his death, and saw each other regularly on both sides of the Atlantic. He gave a pre-wedding dinner for Hannah and me and stood up for us at our nuptial ceremony in Oxford the following morning. Two hours later, he weaved into our wedding reception, having received a telegram shortly before, informing him that he had been named professor of political science at Cambridge University.

Hannah and I celebrated our thirtieth wedding anniversary when I was minister in our London embassy. We invited the people who were present at our wedding ceremony and other close British friends to dine at our residence. Altogether there were about eighty of us that night and it was a happy "family" occasion. Brogan was one of the two or three postprandial speakers. He was in excellent form, reminiscing about prewar Oxford, and reminding us of friends who sadly were no longer with us. He concluded by indulging the Brogan habit of exaggerating the accomplishments of his friends. "I have a secret to tell you about

Phil," he said. "When he was a student at Oxford he studied under
Harold Wilson, and I can tell you that Harold Wilson learned
more about politics from Phil than Phil did from him."

A nice compliment, but there was no truth to it. I had met
Wilson at Oxford when he was a tutor in economics, hardly knew
him, and never had any tutorials with him. You could confidently
believe anything Brogan wrote; his pen was completely reliable.
When he talked about his friends, however, his imagination took
hold and they often emerged bigger than life.

Denis Brogan was our natural choice for faculty adviser to the
United States Society, where Rhodes Scholars and other American
students met regularly to listen to distinguished speakers. One of
the latter was Joseph Kennedy, the American ambassador to Great
Britain, who came in the fall of 1938. Foolishly, he had no prepared speech. Instead, he boldly announced that he would make
no preliminary remarks and was ready to devote all his time to
answering questions. We couldn't resist this opportunity to
bloody him. It was no secret that Kennedy strongly supported
Chamberlain's appeasement policy and favored Franco in Spain,
which most of us deplored. Kennedy arrogantly emphasized his
position in his replies to the first few questions, and we reacted
by prodding him with one sharp query after another, adding
provocative supplementaries whenever we felt his responses were
unsatisfactory. For about twenty minutes there was a rising cre-
scendo of hostility between students and speaker. Fortunately,
Brogan, who had no love for Kennedy, intervened and called a
halt before the meeting could spin out of control.

Rhodes Scholars helped provide entrée to each other's Oxford
college. Our natural camaraderie was reinforced by the eight days
we had spent together on our sea voyage to Europe. In the early
uncertain days at Oxford, we turned to each other for moral
support, sharing our worries and our dilemmas. We took advantage of Oxford's intensive social activity. Breakfast (including
champagne on special occasions), lunch, tea, and dinner parties
were held frequently in students' rooms. Sometimes we just plea-
sured ourselves with too much drink and trivial talk, but often
there were serious political, literary, and cultural discussions. At
first, Americans invited only each other, but before too long we

broadened our social net. At these parties we encountered students and faculty from other colleges. It was in Murat Williams's rooms at Christ Church that I first met Alastair Buchan, who later founded the International Institute of Strategic Studies, and Frank Pakenham (later Lord Longford) and Patrick Gordon-Walker, both Fellows in politics at Christ Church. When the latter two became members of Harold Wilson's government in the 1960s, I saw them often officially, as well as informally.

The American friendships made at Oxford were a special Rhodes dividend. Rhodes Scholars were top students in their universities, chosen after a tough selection process. They had a wide range of interests—law, politics, literature, economics, journalism, science—and came from every region in the country. Among the seventy-five or eighty American scholars in residence, there was as good a geographical distribution as you would find in a full student body of American universities. From my class of '36, for example, I enjoyed the friendships of Dyke Brown from California; Carlton Chapman from Alabama; Gordon Craig from New Jersey; Bob Ebert from Illinois; Walt Rostow from Connecticut; Elvis Stahr from Kentucky; and Murat Williams from Virginia, with whom I roomed my third year in lodgings outside our respective colleges.

All are individuals who have had outstanding careers. Brown, after helping write the Gaither Report, which launched the Ford Foundation, became one of its first vice presidents. Later he founded the Athenian School, a liberal prep school on the West Coast. When Carlton Chapman was dean of the Dartmouth Medical School, he turned it into a full four-year medical college. Subsequently, he served as president of the prestigious Commonwealth Foundation. Gordon Craig, a leading diplomatic historian, has served as the president of the American Historical Association. During his years at Princeton and Stanford, students considered him the outstanding teacher on the campus. Bob Ebert, an eminent physician, served as dean of Harvard Medical School for many years. Walt Rostow was President Johnson's national security adviser. Elvis Stahr was president of West Virginia University when President Kennedy appointed him secretary of the army; subsequently he became president of Indiana University. Murat

Williams, the model of a Virginia gentleman and a dedicated liberal, has had a distinguished diplomatic career, ending up as ambassador to El Salvador.

This is a fair sampling of the careers of hundreds of Rhodes Scholars since the first class of 1903. In founding the scholarships, Rhodes stated, "I also desire to encourage appreciation of the advantages which I explicitly believe would result from the union of the English-speaking peoples throughout the world." The scholarships have not united Great Britain and the United States, but if there has been a "special relationship" between our two countries, the Scholars have certainly contributed to it. And they have fulfilled their benefactor's hope that a Rhodes Scholar would "esteem the performance of public duties as his highest aim."

Rhodes Scholars have held almost every important position in American life, except the Presidency. Inevitably they have been influenced by their Oxonian experience. Many American colleges have followed the lead of Swarthmore in adopting the Oxford tutorial system, and Yale's "colleges" and Harvard "houses," though pale imitations, have been modeled after the autonomous Oxford colleges. Rhodes Scholars have been presidents of our universities, and many faculty members across the country were Rhodes beneficiaries.

Law has also been a favorite of Rhodes Scholars, not surprisingly, in view of the common Anglo-American legal heritage. Oxford-trained lawyers are partners in major U.S. law firms and sit on our judicial benches; John Marshall Harlan was a Justice of the Supreme Court, and Byron White and David Souter are currently members.

Journalism seized the interests of a large number of scholars—Hedley Donovan became editor-in-chief of *Time*, and Jason McManus is today. John Fischer was editor of *Harper's Magazine*, while John Oakes was for many years chief editorial writer of *The New York Times*. Michael Kinsley is editor of the *New Republic* and Charles Maynes is editor of *Foreign Policy*.

In recent years, politics and government, too, have provided an outlet for Rhodes Scholars' talent. When Dean Rusk was secretary of state, William Fulbright was chairman of the Senate Foreign Relations Committee. Senators David Boren, Bill Bradley, Richard Lugar, Larry Pressler, and Paul Sarbanes, as well as several congressmen, including Speaker Carl Albert, were also Rhodes Scholars. Dick Celeste has been governor of Ohio; Bill Clinton is governor of Arkansas and campaigning as the Democratic Party's candidate for President in 1992. Oxonians have served as ambassadors and as top civil servants. Apparently, thanks to Rhodes, Oxford has not only been a training ground of the British elite; it has also helped form a fair share of the American establishment.

Sometimes, unwise attempts were made to apply British political practice to the American scene. When Republicans won control of the Congress in the elections of 1946, Fulbright suggested that Truman appoint Senator Arthur Vandenberg secretary of state and then resign so that Republicans could take over the Presidency.*

Small wonder Truman never felt kindly toward the Arkansas senator, calling him "an overeducated Oxford son-of-a-bitch." In spite of this mistake, Fulbright became one of our outstanding senators. Oxford must have inspired what may have been his greatest achievement. Undoubtedly, he had the success of the Rhodes Scholarships in mind when he pushed for the establishment of the Fulbright Scholarships, a worldwide exchange program that has become a major factor in strengthening America's international ties.

Unlike the 1920s, when sybaritic behavior dominated Oxford life, national and world politics were major interests in the Oxford of the 1930s. This was particularly true in Balliol, whose students represented every shade of political opinion from Conservative to Communist. One of the most articulate, Peter Geach, now a distinguished philosopher, was a Jacobite who believed that the last legitimate king of England was James II, and that every occupant of the throne since his removal in 1688 was a usurper.

Edward (Teddy) Heath, Denis Healey, Roy Jenkins, Hugh Fraser, and Julian Amery were some of my Balliol contemporaries politically active during their student days who later became members of Parliament and government ministers. These five students made an interesting contrast. Heath came from a lower-middle-class background. A grammar school boy, he won Balliol's Organ

---

*At that time, the secretary of state succeeded as President if the Vice Presidency was vacant.

Scholarship. Politics, music, and sailing became his lifelong interests. As a student he was serious, agreeably ambitious, friendly and rather outgoing, good company at a social occasion. Later, when he became leader of the Conservatives, Oxford contemporaries puzzled that reaching "the top of the greasy pole" turned him inward, rather than making him more expansive. A man of great courage, Heath championed causes that might have damaged his political career. In the famous Oxford by-election, held a month after the Munich Agreement in the fall of 1938, Heath supported Lindsay against the Tory candidate, Quintin Hogg, because he had no confidence in Chamberlain's appeasement policies.

Hugh Fraser and Julian Amery were true-blue Tories with radically different backgrounds from Heath. Both exuded the social confidence that reflected their upper-class background. Hugh, the youngest son of the fourteenth Lord Lovat, belonged to a Scottish Catholic family. Julian's father, L. S. Amery* (another Balliol man), was a leading Tory member of Parliament and a strong supporter of Winston Churchill. Hugh and Julian enlivened the Balliol scene with the vigor of their political views and with their capacity for friendship and fun. Hugh gave me my first tip on the Derby. (The horse lost.) They both invited me to a dinner at the conservative Raleigh Club to hear Chaim Weizmann talk off the record. The future president of Israel skillfully combined intellect and charm to win over his audience of aristocratic young Tories.† Julian and Hugh disagreed over Munich. Julian actively supported Lindsay, the antiappeasement candidate in the post-Munich by-election, while Hugh, then president of the Oxford University Conservative Society, unenthusiastically supported Quintin Hogg, the Tory candidate. In later years, both served in

---

*L. S. Amery was probably the only man who proposed a toast to FDR and Hitler together. As chairman of the Rhodes trustees, Mr. Amery hosted the annual trustee dinners to honor the new Rhodes Scholars. In 1936 he raised his glass "to the President of the United States and the Chancellor of the Third Reich" in order to avoid the embarrassment of the previous year when he toasted Roosevelt and Hitler separately and only German Rhodes Scholars stood up for the latter.

†Fraser and Amery continued to be friends of Israel throughout their political careers.

Tory governments as members of the right wing of the party and did not always support Heath. In fact, Hugh ran against Ted for the leadership of the party in the election that culminated in Margaret Thatcher's victory.

Denis Healey, like Heath a grammar school product, represented the other end of the political spectrum. In his student days, he was a member of the Communist Party, because only Moscow seemed to be standing up to the Nazi threat. Other moderate students had joined the party for essentially the same reason. Denys Hoyland, the son of a distinguished Quaker family, was one of that group. Ruggedly handsome, physically tough with craggy, Norse-like features, he was one of the kindest, most idealistic Balliol contemporaries. He joined the army in December 1939 and was killed in action on the Italian front five years later. Neither he nor Healey fit the stereotype of the tough hard-boiled Communist. Instead, they were moved by deep idealism. Distressed over the country's mass unemployment as well as Chamberlain's policy of appeasement, they deplored the fact that England and France were complying with the policy of "nonintervention" in the Spanish Civil War while Nazi Germany and Fascist Italy were flagrantly supporting Franco. They were seduced by the notion that Communism was the "wave of the future," so eloquently articulated in John Strachey's *The Coming Struggle for Power*. The Nazi-Soviet Pact shattered these illusions.

Healey's charm and exceptional intelligence* made him popular with his Oxford contemporaries despite his political radicalism. He was frank and articulate, and there were few signs of the intellectual arrogance that years later turned off some of his Labour MP colleagues, and may well have cost him the leadership of his party.

I appreciated the wide sweep of Healey's appeal when I asked a very attractive young Oxford undergraduate, Edna Edmunds, for a Sunday noon date. She was busy, she replied, because she was going to London to participate in a political rally with Denis Healey. After the war they became husband and wife.

Roy Jenkins was a child of the new Labour establishment. His

---

*In later years John Fulton, who taught most of us, told me he thought Healey was the brightest.

father, the son of a Welsh miner, became a Labour MP and served as Attlee's parliamentary private secretary. Roy's impressive intellect, quiet self-assurance, and moderate socialist views appealed to his fellow students. They were among the qualities that later accounted for the formation of a "Jenkins Group" among Labour MP's. In later years Jenkins, like Heath,* strongly supported the United Kingdom's entry into the Common Market, with costly consequences to his leadership ambitions. He resigned as deputy leader of the Labour Party when the Labour shadow cabinet voted to support a national referendum on whether the United Kingdom should remain in the European Community, even though it was the previous Labour government that had applied for membership. When James Callaghan became prime minister in 1976, three years after Labour returned to power, he denied Jenkins the Foreign Office. Jenkins accepted the presidency of the European Community and, when his term expired, became a founder of the new Social Democratic Party.

Although the late 1930s were a difficult period for students interested in public life, these young men still believed they would be making their careers in a world in which the United Kingdom would be playing a leading role. This fact shaped their attitudes on major political and economic issues when they became ministers in a postwar world that saw so dramatic a change in the position of Great Britain. It has not been easy for that generation to adjust to the status of a middle-sized country.

Inevitably, personal as well as political strains have marked this transition. I remember a conversation with Ted Heath in the early 1950s when I was passing through London on the way home from an ILO governing body meeting in Geneva. Heath, then the Conservative Party chief whip, had invited me to lunch in the House of Commons. When discussing America's new leadership of the Free World, he emphasized how new we were at the game and how much we had to learn. We could find no better teacher than the British. There was bite, and a slight tone of condescension in his remarks.

Heath used the standard Harold Macmillan line when the latter

---

*After the death of Macmillan, both Heath and Jenkins stood for the chancellorship of Oxford. Jenkins won.

served as the British liaison with Eisenhower in North Africa. Macmillan always told newly arriving British officers that they must recognize the changing roles of the United Kingdom and the United States on the world stage. The Americans were the new "Romans" and the British were the old "Greeks." The sophisticated British had much to teach the rough-hewn, unworldly Americans. Heath's subsequent commitment to the Common Market—the UK's entry in the early 1970s was due primarily to his political and personal tenacity—reflected a desire to reestablish Britain as an important player in international politics and no longer too dependent on special ties with the United States.

Later, in the 1960s, when I was minister in the American embassy, I couldn't help but observe the anguish with which a Labour government dealt with the question of maintaining a military presence east of Suez. Not surprisingly, Denis Healey, then minister of defense, resisted withdrawal and the consequent diminution of Britain's international role until Britain's stagnant economy compelled him to cut defense expenditures.

Political activity in Oxford was organized mainly around the Oxford Union and the university party societies—Conservative, Labour, and Liberal. The Conservatives had their more exclusive Raleigh Club, and there were nonpartisan groups such as the Bryce Society,* which was devoted to the discussion of international affairs at regular white-tie dinners.

The Communists' October Club was dissolved in 1935 when apparently a large number of its members joined the Labour Society. In addition, the fascists had a branch in Oxford with offices across the street from Balliol. Their ideas and tactics had little appeal to Oxford students, who held frequent anti-fascist meetings. When Oswald Mosley, the leader of the British Union of Fascists, spoke at a party rally in Oxford in the spring of 1936, fighting broke out between the stewards of the meeting and left-wing anti-fascists in the audience, drawing blood and doing con-

---

*The fifty members of Bryce were shocked when we learned that the family of one of our speakers, Leonard Einstein, a former American minister in Czechoslovakia who lived in London, had been threatened after he had criticized Hitler and Mussolini in off-the-record remarks at one of our functions. This was a painful example of the ugliness in the years leading up to the war.

siderable damage. The violent behavior of the stewards made a bad impression on most students and townspeople. We were told that Frank Pakenham, later Lord Longford, who had been a respectable Tory, reacted to the events that evening by joining the Labour Party.

At the Oxford Union, the historic university debating society, students formally argued about the political and social issues of the day, often with distinguished guests participating. The world outside became aware of the Union in February 1933 as a result of its debate on the motion "That this House will in no circumstance fight for King and Country." When the motion carried, it created a public furor. Its significance was exaggerated, or misunderstood.

Several factors accounted for the Union vote. It reflected, first of all, a hangover from the antiwar sentiment so strong in the 1920s. More significantly, it symbolized a drastic change in attitude between the pleasure-loving Oxford of the 1920s, so imaginatively evoked by Evelyn Waugh in *Brideshead Revisited*, and the more politically conscious Oxford of the 1930s, which was reacting to the worldwide economic collapse after 1929 and the breakdown of international political order. An overwhelming majority in England still supported the League of Nations, even though it had failed to stop the Sino-Japanese conflict in 1931. In particular, the young were not inclined to be pushed into fighting for what they felt was mindless jingoism. For the moment, "my country, right or wrong" was not a popular sentiment.

The Union, modeled on the House of Commons, was a major training ground for future parliamentarians. New officers were elected every term and the presidency of the Union was considered a rich prize. It marked you as a potential cabinet member, if not a prime minister. Balliol men were president in each of the eight years between 1932 and 1939, including Ted Heath and Hugh Fraser.

The Labour, Conservative, and Liberal societies provided rostrums for leading national figures. A week after our arrival in Oxford I heard Winston Churchill speak. His message was as clear as it was eloquent. Hitler's Germany was determined to overrun Europe and destroy democracy. To resist this threat to freedom, England and France had to collaborate with the Soviet Union. He recalled how vigorously he had always fought Communism; but Nazism was now a much greater danger and was growing so powerful that the free nations had to cooperate with Moscow against a spreading fascism. Churchill's party leaders continued to ignore him.

In the course of the next three years every other political leader except Chamberlain spoke at Oxford. Clement Attlee, the leader of the Labour Party, was the speaker at the meeting of the University Labour Society a few days after Anthony Eden resigned as foreign secretary in February 1938, to protest Chamberlain's policy of appeasement. A hyped-up standing-room-only crowd was yearning for a speech full of red meat, but the bland, cool Attlee only offered pabulum. Let down, but still enthusiastic, the students then carried Attlee on their shoulders to the train station. I've never seen a political leader look more unhappy or more self-conscious. Charisma was not Attlee's outstanding characteristic.

We were living during the "nightmare years" in world affairs. By the fall of 1936, Hitler had dismantled the postwar treaties, alliances, and guarantees of the League of Nations, which were to ensure Europe against international violence. The process started soon after Hitler assumed power in January 1933, a development that few professional observers thought possible in the preceding months, or even weeks. When it happened, Walter Lippmann could approvingly suggest that perhaps the Nazi phenomenon represented the "wave of the future." Hitler moved rapidly, cunningly, and with impunity to implement the program laid down in *Mein Kampf.* On October 14, 1933, he announced the formal withdrawal of Germany from the Disarmament Conference and the League of Nations. This was Hitler's angry response to a proposal by the United Kingdom, United States, France, and Italy that after a probationary period of five years, Germany be granted equality of status in armaments. Unfortunately, no such offer had ever been made to Hitler's predecessors.

In March 1935, Hitler reestablished compulsory military service in Germany and announced the creation of the Luftwaffe. The final blow against the Treaty of Versailles came in March 1936, when, using France's ratification of the Franco-Soviet Pact as his excuse, Hitler convened the Reichstag to denounce the Locarno

Pact, the treaty that had been the foundation of postwar stability in Europe, and to announce that even as he spoke, German troops were occupying the Rhineland's demilitarized zones.

British and French acceptance of German remilitarization was depressing. Britain made some of the right noises, but when it became clear that the French would not march against the Germans, there was no chance of Britain acting on her own. We learned after the war, when the relevant documents became available, that the German generals had opposed Hitler's plan on the grounds that it would certainly lead to war at a time when German armaments were not yet able to cope with the Western powers. Hitler contemptuously accepted the generals' condition that German troops be immediately withdrawn in the event of French opposition. The failure of both France and Great Britain to act reinforced Hitler's contempt for them.

Students were not only aware of Hitler's international behavior; we were familiar, too, with developments inside Germany: the destruction of democratic institutions, the book burnings, the murderous purge of Hitler's own Brown Shirts in June of 1934, the establishment of concentration camps, and the incredibly cruel treatment of the German Jews. How could any free people have had doubts about the true nature of this fascist society? How could any government put its trust in a policy of appeasement when Hitler continuously broke his "promises"?

Oxford went out of its way to welcome German Jewish scholars whom the Nazis had expelled. One of them was Edward Frankel, whose appointment as Oxford's Regius Professor of Latin was an unusual example of Oxbridge cooperation. Several British academicians competed with Frankel for this prestigious chair. The Oxford committee making the choice solicited the advice of A. E. Housman, the distinguished poet and Regius Professor of Latin at Cambridge. He is reputed to have replied, "I hope you don't appoint Frankel because we would like to have him take over my chair when I retire." Naturally, that tipped the scales to Frankel.

Another incident indicated Oxonian feelings about the Nazis. A. D. Lindsay told me of a visit to Oxford by a group of German classicists and philosophers. As vice chancellor, Lindsay entertained them at dinner. One of his British guests was W. D. Ross, the famous Oxford Aristotelian and author of *The Right and the*

Good. Ross, a serious, competent, and rather dry lecturer, rarely indicated any interest in current politics. That night, however, whenever the Germans digressed from philosophical discourse and tried to suggest that the Nazis were much better than some people thought, Ross stopped them in their tracks by asking, "What about their treatment of the Jews?" Ross made no other comments in the course of the evening.*

I had a taste of Fascist Italy and Nazi Germany during my Oxford vacations. Though repelled by both, I was struck by the difference between the two. The Italians would rally by the thousands in front of the Palazzo Venezia to shout "Duce, Duce"; but I soon observed that in smaller groups, or individually, their hearts were not passionately behind Mussolini. Italian soldiers marching down the streets of Rome or Florence did not inspire fear. Their casualness suggested they were not taking their soldiering too seriously. Individually, Italians told you of their concern about Hitler's increasing influence over Mussolini. I was in Rome a few days before Hitler's visit in the spring of 1938 and met several Italians who expressed dismay and anger over the fact that Italian Jews had been moved out of the city in preparation for the Führer's stay. Anti-Semitism was not endemic in Italy, and many Italians resented Mussolini's increasing susceptibility to the Nazi infection.

An incident in Florence also indicated Italian attitudes. I was spending a fortnight in that lovely city and had my mail forwarded to the American Express office. One day I walked in with a copy of Salvemini's devastating *Under the Axe of Fascism* in my hand. There were other people around when the Italian clerk with whom I had become quite friendly said loudly, "Why are you wasting your time with that propaganda?" I ignored his comment. When I turned to leave, after picking up my mail, all the other clients had departed. The clerk's attitude had changed dramatically. "Why don't you give me that book," he then asked, "so that I can read it and pass it around to my friends? You can easily get another copy." I happily gave it to him.

*Also noteworthy was the vote by Oxford's Congregation, the faculty legislative body, against the university's participation in the celebration of the University of Heidelberg's five-hundred-and-fiftieth anniversary.

I had another unusual book experience in Italy. Among my baggage was a valise full of books that I was hoping to read during my six-week vacation, almost all of which were forbidden in Italy. The valise mysteriously disappeared on the train between Rome and Florence. I reported the loss to the police, gave them my Oxford address, and all the other information about parents, grandparents, and so forth that was always requested by fascist and Nazi officers, never expecting to see the valise, the books, and my notes again. Five weeks later, to my delight and surprise, it turned up at Balliol College with everything in it intact.

Nazi Germany, which I visited in the summer of 1937, was grimmer than Fascist Italy. Dyke Brown, a tall, talented, and handsome Rhodes Scholar from California, and I had spent late July and August of that year at the Salzburg Festival. Dyke wanted to buy a Leica camera in Munich illegally by using verboten "Reisemarks." Tourists were given a special exchange rate, which was much more favorable than the official rate, for a limited amount of foreign currency. Reisemarks—tourist marks—could be used legally only for room and board and entertainment. We soon discovered, however, that tourist and regular marks were identical, so that the restrictions about the use of the Reisemarks could be violated with impunity. Dyke pointed out that together we could accumulate enough marks in Munich to buy his Leica camera in one week, whereas he alone would require a fortnight. Moreover, he added, we should experience the evil of Nazism on the spot so that in later years we would be able to tell our children and grandchildren about it. He convinced me to join him in striking a blow against the Nazi economy.

Munich, the capital of Nazism, was scary, quite different from Rome or Florence. Being greeted in Munich with outstretched arms and *"Heil Hitler!"* was a shocking experience. It set the disturbing tone of the city's ambiance, an eeriness reinforced by the anti-Semitic hysteria of the press as well as by the plethora of men in black SS uniforms. The difference between Italians in uniform and Germans was striking. There was nothing relaxed or casual about an SS soldier strutting alone down a deserted Munich side street as if he were on full parade in the presence of his Führer. He reflected the new mood of Munich, which, in more normal times, had been famous for its *Gemütlichkeit*. So did our visit to a plaque on the sidewall of the Feldherren Halle on the Residenz-strasse commemorating those killed when Hitler launched his aborted putsch in 1923. It was guarded around the clock by black-shirted troops, and everyone who passed it, whether on foot or in a bus, was forced to give the Nazi salute.

The museum of *"entartete Kunst"*—degenerate art—was also a grisly expression of the Nazi mentality. An exhibition of some of the finest avant-garde art, which the Nazis considered "degener-ate," was mounted in an old army barracks with low ceilings and narrow claustrophobic walls. There were outstanding paintings by Marc Chagall, Ernst Ludwig Kirchner, Paul Klee, and George Grosz. I remember George Grosz's *Armistice Day*, a powerful picture of soldiers with their guts hanging out marching before a stand of well-groomed army officers. On the wall next to this canvas the Nazis had inscribed in bold red letters "For this degen-erate painting Kurt Eisner, the Jewish prime minister of the Social-ist Bavarian Republic, paid thousands of marks of the German people's money." Similar statements in either red or garish green were written beside other paintings. One legend read "Revelation of the Jewish Racial Soul," though only six of the 112 artists represented were Jewish. The impact was sickening, precisely the objective of the Nazi authorities.

We also visited the Nazis' antidote to "degenerate art," the New House of German Art. Here paintings were beautifully hung in a high-ceilinged, superbly lit museum. A large share of the canvases pictured insipidly happy peasant and sea scenes that made you feel as if you had eaten too many chocolates. Almost a dozen were portraits of Hitler, all of which focused on his blue eyes. Un-wisely, I burst into laughter when I saw the last one, Adolf Hitler dressed in medieval armor, staff in hand, and sitting on a white horse. Dyke, a man much taller than I, grabbed me by the scruff of the neck and moved me down to the exit as quickly as possible.

The attitude of the young Germans we met in the student hostel where we were staying provided little comfort. They parroted the Nazi litany of hate. It was unlikely that any of them would have asked to borrow an anti-Nazi book if they saw one.

The happiest moment of my stay in Munich occurred when I boarded the overnight express train to Paris. Munich had become so oppressive that I left a day earlier than planned. Discovering that I had thirty or forty marks more than I was allowed to take out of the country, I used the surplus to buy the best wine the dining car could provide to share with a congenial French orchestra leader from Strasbourg who had sat down at my table. Upon discovering that our views on Hitler's Germany coincided, we discussed a wide spectrum of political, social, and cultural subjects. We also drank a boisterous toast to freedom when the train crossed the Franco-German frontier, only parting when the car was closed at midnight.

From 1936 to 1939, the crucial years leading up to the war, students at Oxford followed intently the political events that were so close and so threatening. Concern about the Spanish Civil War never subsided; concern about Nazi Germany continually increased. Although we were obviously not privy to government meetings or to confidential exchanges between ambassadors and foreign ministers, what we saw, heard, read, and experienced during our vacation travels enabled many of us to realize what was happening and to anticipate what was likely to occur. We were smart enough to appreciate that Churchill was right and the others were wrong.

The Spanish Civil War broke out in July 1936, two months before our arrival in Oxford, and by the end of the year students from Oxford and other British universities were fighting on the side of the Loyalists. Many of us were skeptical about the "nonintervention" policy. We were especially distressed when it became apparent that, while Britain and "Popular Front" France, responding to British pressure, were complying with it, Nazi Germany and Fascist Italy were intervening with a vengeance, trying out new weapons and testing new military strategies. Nazi bombers made Guernica the first city ever to be destroyed by aerial bombardment, an event that inspired Picasso's great painting.

Unfortunately, because the Soviet Union became the major supporter of the Spanish Loyalists, Germany and Italy could stir up anti-Communist sentiment in France and Great Britain. This also created serious problems for the Loyalists as George Orwell learned when he witnessed the bloody encounters in Barcelona between the Communists and the other elements supporting the Madrid government. Kingsley Martin, the editor of the left-wing *New Statesman*, refused to publish George Orwell's account of Soviet-led purges, claiming that it would damage the Loyalist cause. When, thirty years later, our son, David, who was writing his Harvard senior thesis on Orwell's politics, questioned Martin about this editorial decision, he still insisted he had done the right thing.

Watching Britain's reactions to the rising Nazi threat was increasingly distressing. The government's behavior reflected the fact that British public opinion was bedeviled by contradictions. The minority, led by Churchill, saw in Hitler's Germany a challenge to Western civilization, and were prepared to act against the Nazis as they violated one pact after another. They urged an increase in British military expenditures and an alliance with the Soviet Union in order to match German rearmament. Against this group were the majority, who felt guilty about the terms of the Treaty of Versailles and believed that German desires for its revision should be met.

In addition, both ideology and a widely felt pacifism affected British public opinion. There were those who, finding Hitler's anti-Communism appealing, were willing to forgive or overlook his aggressive behavior, a sentiment the Nazis were skillful in exploiting. Some, like followers of Oswald Mosley, the founder of the British Union of Fascists, not only approved Nazism but were ready to imitate it.

Pacifism also served Hitler's interests. There were two strains in Britain: the absolute, often religiously motivated conscientious objectors, such as George Lansbury, the leader of the Labour Party until 1935; and the "practical," a much larger group, many of them older men and women who remembered the terrible losses suffered during the First World War, which they thought left more problems in its wake than it solved. Anxious to prevent a repetition at almost any cost, they were easy targets for Hitler's propaganda, particularly when the Nazis stirred up fears of the terrible and inevitable aerial destruction of another war. It was widely believed that London and other British cities would be leveled. *Schrecklichkeit*, or "frightfulness," became an important Nazi psychological weapon. It was reinforced by Charles Lindbergh's report on the overwhelming power of the Luftwaffe written after he visited Germany in 1938, a report used by Joseph Kennedy, our ambassador in London, to push the case for appeasement.

Chamberlain's policy of appeasement reflected the views of the groups in England opposed to war. Chamberlain believed that only revision of the Treaty of Versailles could preserve European peace. An arrogant man and an amateur in foreign affairs, he refused to recognize the accumulating evidence of Hitler's duplicity. In spite of warnings from his Foreign Office, Chamberlain thought he could deal with the Nazi chancellor on the basis of mutual trust and understanding. Turning Hitler toward Eastern Europe also had its appeal. Moreover, as a former chancellor of the Exchequer, Chamberlain was obsessive about restraining expenditure for armaments. He continually resisted Churchill's call for a greater increase in armaments, arguing that the Exchequer couldn't afford it. We students were quick to notice that even after Munich, Chamberlain was reluctant to strengthen British defenses and resisted cabinet changes that would guarantee high-level attention to preparations for a possible conflict.

Lord Noel-Buxton, father of Rufus, a Balliol classmate and close friend, exemplified the Englishmen who, against another war at almost any cost, supported Chamberlain's policy. I met Lord Noel-Buxton in 1937, when Rufus invited me to spend the Christmas holidays at their country house in Epping Forest. At the time, Noel-Buxton was seventy years old, a tall, handsome man, quietly charming, and delightfully at ease with young people. The grandchild of Sir Thomas Buxton, a distinguished Quaker who was largely responsible for the freeing of the slaves in the British colonies in 1833, Noel-Buxton had had an impressive political career. Before the First World War, as a Liberal member of the House of Commons and expert on the Balkans, he was one of the few members of Parliament who supported the Young Turks during the revolution of 1908. He belonged to the group of radical Liberals who opposed the foreign policies of Asquith and Grey, arguing that they would lead to war.

After the outbreak of hostilities in 1914, Noel-Buxton's Liberal colleagues David Lloyd George and Winston Churchill asked him to visit Romania and Bulgaria in order to persuade his personal friends, the kings of both countries, to join the Allied cause. Ironically, the Young Turks tried to assassinate him when he was in Bucharest. One bullet luckily ricocheted off the silver cigarette case pocketed close to his heart, and the other pierced his chin, where subsequently he raised a Vandyke to cover his scar.

At the end of the war, like several other radical Liberals, Buxton joined the Labor Party. Ramsay MacDonald chose him as minister of agriculture in both his cabinets, and when Buxton resigned in 1930 because of ill health, he was made the first Labour peer in British history. His wife, Lucy, a lively, intelligent lady, twenty-five years younger, was elected to his seat in Parliament. The family's two beautiful tawny shepherd hounds were named Ramsay and Arthur after the prime minister and the foreign secretary, Arthur Henderson.

Noel-Buxton's political background made his active support of appeasement particularly valuable to Chamberlain. Noel-Buxton enjoyed political discussions with young people, so I had no difficulty in talking to him about his attitude toward Hitler's Germany. His position was clear: World War I had been a terrible mistake that must not be repeated. I could understand his attitude toward the war, but pointed out that the Kaiser's Germany was radically different from Hitler's. It included lively free institutions: a multi-party system, one of the world's leading trade union movements, and a free press. Moreover, it would be dangerous to allow Hitler to dominate Europe. Noel-Buxton appreciated all of this, but still felt that another war with Germany must be avoided. The resulting destruction would be disastrous, with incalculable social and political consequences.

This was his position despite the fact that he had few illusions about Hitler. When I saw him shortly after he had been received by Hitler in Berlin, he told me that Hitler seemed a "normal" person until Noel-Buxton criticized his cruel treatment of the Jews. Then, according to Noel-Buxton, "he raved and ranted like a wild man."

We watched the excruciating developments in the spring and summer of 1938 with heightening emotions. We were dismayed by Hitler's brutal occupation of Austria in March, which occurred just before our spring vacation. In spite of British, French, and Italian commitments to preserve Austrian independence, Hitler pulled off the Anschluss with no more international reaction than diplomatic slaps on the wrist. Forgotten was Hitler's statement of 1935: "Germany neither intends nor wishes to interfere in the internal affairs of Austria, to annex Austria, or to conclude an Anschluss."

A few days after the Nazis marched into Austria, I met a Viennese couple on a train heading for Florence where I was planning to spend the spring break. Their boast that they were hoarse from shouting *"Heil Hitler!"* when the German leader entered Vienna hardly improved my morale. This encounter recalled my previous summer at the Salzburg Music Festival when I was shocked by the extent of Nazi sentiment. Kurt von Schuschnigg, the last pre-Nazi chancellor, was present at one of the concerts I attended and the reaction to him was cool. There were no cheers, no applause, only indifference or hostile glances.

On our return to Oxford for the summer term we faced the fact that Czechoslovakia was next on Hitler's list. In May, when the Czechs mobilized their military in response to the German threat, and the British, French, and Soviets indicated their support of Prague, we thought that at long last Hitler would face resistance. However, instead of consolidating anti-Nazi cooperation, Chamberlain resumed his policy of appeasement with even greater determination.

Chamberlain's objective seemed clear: to preserve European peace he would accept a peaceful transfer of the Sudetenland to Germany. Ironically, Hitler believed such a transfer was an essential step in his preparations for war. Effecting it would not be easy. The Czechs were determined to defend their sovereignty, their democracy, and their territorial integrity. The Sudetenland was particularly important because of the modern fortifications built into its mountainous terrain. Presumably the Czech position was supported by a mutual defense pact with France, the Russian commitment to come to Prague's aid if France stood by its commitment, and the general belief that Britain would back up her French ally even though she had no formal obligation to do so.

It took Chamberlain and Hitler six months to overcome these obstacles, an effort that culminated in the Munich Agreement in September 1938. It was frustrating and frightening to witness the way Hitler kept Czechoslovakia in continuous turmoil to achieve his objective. It was sad to observe how Chamberlain cooperated by helping destroy Czechoslovakia's will to resist Nazi intervention.

The Nazis applied salami tactics. The Sudeten Germans started off with a modest request in regard to their minority rights, but as the Czech government moved to meet them, they continually escalated their demands, justifying them by organizing demonstrations and riots to prove popular support.

Hitler's man, his Trojan Horse inside Czechoslovakia, was Konrad Henlein, the leader of the Sudeten German Party. In the beginning, Henlein, who had secretly joined the Nazis in 1935, played the role of a loyal Czech citizen seeking to find reasonable relief for the legitimate grievances of the German minority. After the Austrian Anschluss, he shed that disguise, suddenly becoming the leader of an "oppressed minority," clearly under the orders of his masters in Berlin. Seven weeks after the Nazis marched into Vienna, and after rejecting several Czech concessions, Henlein, on instructions from his Nazi superiors, presented the "Karlsbad Program" to the Czech authorities. It made eight demands that no sovereign government could accept. They called for full autonomy for the German minority, in effect demanding the right to set up a Nazi state within Czechoslovakia. Moreover, the program implied that Czechoslovakia would have to give up its treaties with France and Russia. The main objective was perfectly clear: when Prague rejected the Karlsbad Program, Hitler would step forward and openly assume the role of "Protector of All Germans."

To allay public anxieties aroused in the West by the Karlsbad Program, Berlin had Henlein visit London in the spring of 1938. He saw several of the outstanding opponents of appeasement, including Churchill, Anthony Eden, and Harold Nicolson. Not surprisingly, he assured them that the Karlsbad Program was not an ultimatum, but rather a basis for negotiations. They were not taken in.

I heard a firsthand report about the visit from Harold Nicolson. His son, Nigel, another Balliol friend, invited me and three others to a breakfast party for his father, who was staying at Oxford's Randolph Hotel the weekend after he had seen Henlein. Harold Nicolson gave us a vivid account of the meeting.*

---

*My request for grapefruit that morning provoked a caustic comment from Nicolson about the barbarity of eating that fruit, particularly at breakfast. I thought he was joking, but after I reaffirmed my order, Nicolson ignored me for the rest of the meal. Years later, when Harold Nicolson's dairies were published, Nigel, in one

Aware of Henlein's shifty character, and of his recent behavior in Czechoslovakia, Nicolson was not impressed by Henlein's attempt to prove he was a moderate acting on his own.* He had tried to convince Nicolson that he wanted to negotiate an agreement with the Czech government that would provide local autonomy to the Sudeten Germans without affecting the federal government's responsibilities in finance, foreign affairs, and defense. He claimed he did not wish to join Germany, like many of his followers, but if there were no agreement with Prague, nor a settlement by an international commission, German occupation would inevitably follow, and that would mean war. Nicolson replied that British opinion would support a reasonable approach on local autonomy, but would turn against the Sudeten Germans if their demands were likely to provoke hostilities.

The Henlein performance was a typical example of Nazi deception. He got little comfort from Nicolson, Churchill, or Eden, but he did much better with two leading supporters of Chamberlain policies—Geoffrey Dawson, the editor of *The Times*, and J. L. Garvin, the editor of *The Observer*—who assured Henlein that Britain was indifferent to the fate of Czechoslovakia. Apparently he brought that message back to Hitler.

Dawson was a member of the coterie of appeasers familiar to Oxonians. It included Sir John Simon, chancellor of the Exchequer; Lord Halifax, foreign minister; and Cosmo Gordon Lang, Archbishop of Canterbury, all Fellows of All Souls. These men often spent weekends at this prestigious college,† and Oxford was full of gossip about what they were "plotting" to advance Chamberlain's policies. In his book *All Souls and Appeasement*, A. L. Rowse, who was a young All Souls Fellow, recounts some

---

of his editorial notes, stated that among his father's aversions were people who ate grapefruit.

*It was only after the war that we learned that the day before he arrived in London, Henlein had made a secret visit to Berlin, where Ribbentrop instructed him on how to deceive the British.

†All Souls was a unique Oxford College, a highly respected "think tank." It had no students attached to it. Its Fellows in residence were outstanding academics, while its visiting Fellows included leading political, church, and legal figures.

of the conversations among his distinguished elders. He confirms the suspicions we had about the depth of their support for appeasement and their cynical attitude toward Czechoslovakia.

Tensions mounted in Europe in the summer of 1938, as the Nazis prepared for their annual Nuremberg rally the first week of September. When we sat down on September 12 to hear Hitler speak in Nuremberg, we feared his words might lead to war. It was a vicious speech with vulgar attacks on President Beneš and the Czechs. Hitler's hysterical outpourings, interlaced with the audience's staccato shouts of *"Sieg heil!"* were alarming. Hitler did not declare war, but he promised the Sudeten Germans that if they did not obtain justice on their own behalf, he would secure it for them. He demanded a rapid settlement of the Sudeten problem through self-determination, but he made no mention of a plebiscite. Hearing Hitler on the radio viciously attacking his enemies, in this case Edvard Beneš, the Czech president, was a frightening experience. We listened to Radio Luxembourg, which provided the best reception in England. The contrast between Hitler's fiery oratory and the suave, soft-spoken French announcer summarizing Hitler's remarks after each paragraph increased the eerie impact of Hitler's hysteria.

Hitler's speech left Europe in a state of desperate anxiety about his next move and caused a crisis in the French government. French sociopolitical schizophrenia was striking. Beginning with my Christmas vacation in 1936, I had visited France regularly over the next two years. The sharp ideological conflicts in France and the absence of an underlying social consensus so characteristic of Great Britain made a deep impression. The Roosevelt haters at home paled in comparison with the right-wing haters of Léon Blum, the Socialist Popular Front prime minister of France. The fact that he was Jewish intensified their hostility. Blum was the most cultivated political leader in Western Europe, a brilliant student of French literature, but that made no difference to the French right. Charles Maurras, the editor of *Action Française*, the Royalist paper, openly invited his readers to assassinate Blum. "Any kitchen knife would do," he wrote. Anti-Semitism, deeply rooted in French society, was stimulated by the rise of Hitler in Germany and the election of Blum as prime minister.

My very first contact with a Frenchman had given me a sense

of the mood of some of the people in the country. On the boat train from Dieppe to Paris, I asked a mild-looking, middle-aged, middle-class French passenger how the country was doing since Blum came to power. (Léon Blum had been in office for six months, the most fruitful period of his premiership.) His response was unequivocal and uncivil. "Why would a young man, and a foreigner at that, be interested in that terrible man, that vile social-ist who is doing so much damage to the country?"

I soon learned that this was not an isolated opinion. "Rather Hitler than Blum" was the cry of too many groups in French society—fascists, reactionaries of the right, the clericals, upper classes, and petite bourgeoisie. Passionate supporters of appease-ment, these people believed that a French defeat of Hitler would be a disaster because it would destroy the main power resisting the spread of Communism in Europe. Unfortunately, the democratic elements in France, including the trade unions and the Socialist and Radical Socialist parties, were riddled with pacifism. As the danger of war increased, they became less keen about fulfilling France's commitment to defend Czechoslovakia.*

Given the divided opinions in France, it was not surprising that the government found itself incapable of deciding what action to take after Hitler's speech. Edouard Daladier, the Radical Socialist prime minister† who replaced Blum, reflected the country's uncer-tainty, confusion, and reluctance to take any action that might lead to war. His cabinet divided between appeasers and those ready to stand by Czechoslovakia, he was unwilling to come down on either side. Instead, he abdicated to Chamberlain responsibility for dealing with the Czech crisis.

The stage was now set for the dramatic announcement that amazed the world: Neville Chamberlain was to fly to Berchtesga-den, Hitler's lair, to prevent the outbreak of hostilities. The British

---

*Although the Popular Front was in power during the height of the Spanish Civil War, the French government failed to come to the support of a neighboring democracy for two reasons: the country was deeply divided on the issue on ideologi-cal grounds, and the British government would not support Paris had it decided to come to Madrid's aid.

†The Radical Socialist Party was neither radical nor socialist.

public cheered the news. It broke the terrible tension generated by the fear of war and the widely held belief that London would be destroyed. Some Englishmen hoped that Chamberlain would warn Hitler that a German attack on Czechoslovakia would be opposed by France, Russia, and Britain, but the prime minister had no such plan in mind.

Those of us who were convinced that Chamberlain was wedded to his policy of appeasement feared that he was flying to Berchtesgaden to arrange to give Hitler what he wanted. We didn't like the Canossa-like overtones. There was courage in what Chamberlain did, but it was pathetic, too; taking the first airplane flight in his life to visit a man twenty years his junior to see whether he could satisfy the latter's unreasonable and threatening demands. We were also bothered by the fact that he took with him his favorite civil servant, Sir Horace Wilson, chief industrial adviser, rather than any top Foreign Office official. We all knew that Wilson, the amateur in diplomacy, was a strong supporter of appeasement. Chamberlain didn't even have his own interpreter in his meetings with Hitler, but depended entirely on the latter's Dr. Paul Schmidt, a fact that shocked the professionals in the British Foreign Office.

The summit at Berchtesgaden set in motion the dismemberment of Czechoslovakia. During a tough three-hour conference, Hitler made his position perfectly clear. The. Sudeten Germans must have the right of self-determination and the right to return to Germany if they so desired. What's more, if they couldn't achieve this by themselves, he would help them do so without further delay, even if it might mean war. Chamberlain, who had hoped for a compromise, was taken aback. He felt he deserved better treatment from Hitler, but he was also convinced that Hitler was actively preparing to invade Czechoslovakia. Hitler proposed that if Chamberlain could assure him that the British government would accept the principle of self-determination, he was ready to discuss the means for peacefully implementing that policy. In response, the prime minister pointed out he couldn't make that commitment on the spot, but he was prepared to present this proposal to his cabinet as quickly as possible, provided that Hitler held back military action in the meantime. Arrangements were made for another meeting after Chamberlain's consultations.

Tense drama dominated the next two weeks with war or peace in the balance. Upon his return from Berchtesgaden, Chamberlain immediately went to work to meet Hitler's demands. He secured French agreement to jointly urge Prague to transfer to Germany all territory with a population of over fifty percent Sudeten German inhabitants. The British and French would then guarantee the new Czech borders, a commitment of dubious value once Czech fortifications had been handed over to the Germans. London and Paris then pressured Prague to accept their new Anglo-French proposal. Britain and France had become Hitler's accomplices.

Chamberlain was stunned when, during his second trip to Germany a week later, he found that Hitler was no longer satisfied with the peaceful transfer of Sudeten territory in an orderly manner, as he had agreed at Berchtesgaden. At Godesberg, the venue of this second meeting, Hitler demanded that all Czech troops and officials be evacuated from Sudeten areas where the German population exceeded fifty percent, to be replaced by German troops. A plebiscite would follow in November to determine the new frontier to be drawn by a German–Czech or an international commission. Areas in which the German minority was substantial, but less than fifty percent, would also be subject to a plebiscite.

Chamberlain tried to dissuade Hitler from this unnecessary and provocative use of force, particularly when there was agreement in principle to give him what he wanted. Hitler responded by insisting that the Czechs would have to begin the evacuation of the predominantly German areas on September 26 and complete the operation by September 28. In response to further efforts by Chamberlain, Hitler made a minor "concession": he would extend the time limit to October 1. Hitler's demand and his new timetable were incorporated in the "Godesberg Memorandum," which Chamberlain agreed to transmit to Czechoslovakia while emphasizing that he couldn't accept it personally, nor recommend it to Prague.

As a result of Hitler's behavior at Godesberg, the mood of the British changed from relief and hope to deep anxiety, and then a determination to resist Hitler. To avoid war, Chamberlain was willing to satisfy Hitler's demands, yet he had to go along with a majority of his cabinet, which insisted that the British government reject the Godesberg Memorandum. London assured France that if she became engaged in hostilities, the United Kingdom would feel compelled to support her. It was heartening to see how the country rallied behind this decision. Even leading appeasers like Garvin of *The Observer* now attacked Hitler. In an editorial on September 25, he wrote: "The Nazi power last week threw off the mask before the British prime minister and demanded, in effect, his total capitulation on their own soil. They considered that their armed advantage had made them already masters of the earth. Not yet!"

Once again, Europe focused on a Hitler speech in Berlin on September 26, when he viciously attacked President Beneš and stated that if Prague had not given up all of the Sudetenland by October 1, Germany would occupy it by that date. "If war breaks out," Hitler shouted, "it will be Beneš's responsibility."

In his speech Hitler shrewdly played up to Chamberlain. He praised the prime minister's effort for peace and stated that after all minority claims, Hungarian and Polish, as well as German, were satisfied, he would guarantee the integrity of the Czech state. He also added his usual promises. Once the Sudeten-German question was settled, he would make no further territorial claims on Europe. Yet again, he guaranteed the inviolability of all Germany's neighbors.

It would be difficult to exaggerate the tension in Great Britain, as well as the rest of Europe, following Hitler's speech. It was generally believed that war would break out on September 28 and that London and Paris would be leveled. The British navy had been mobilized, London children evacuated to the country, and hospitals cleared to take care of expected casualties. Londoners dug trenches, but kept that traditional British cool that was to serve them so well during the *Blitzkrieg*. No such sangfroid was displayed across the Channel. Parisians caused traffic jams on roads leading out of the city as large numbers fled to the country.

During this critical period, I was the guest in Cardiff, Wales, of my old professor Selig Perlman, who was spending a year at the University of Wales. I couldn't have asked for better companionship while following the international crisis. Perlman's pragmatic idealism had helped shape my basic political outlook. We shared, too, of course, a deep revulsion to Nazism. His personal history and his knowledge of the European scene enhanced his sensitivity to the evolving drama. Most of the day our ears were glued to the radio. Perlman's language skills came in handy when we heard a broadcast in an Eastern European language. Perlman listened intently, and when the announcer signed off, he said, "It's unfair, I've never heard that language before, but I understand every word that was said. It's the Czech government's mobilization order." Russian, his native tongue, had enabled him to comprehend the related Slavic language.

We were certain now that war would break out within hours. I had told Perlman that I had become engaged to Hannah Greeley, who had also been a student in his class at Madison and who was staying in London. He knew her well. "You must wire her to come to Cardiff immediately," he now insisted. "It would be irresponsible to leave her in London, which will almost certainly be leveled by German bombers." I sent the telegram and then, to relieve our tensions, we took a long walk in the hills outside the city during which Perlman told me the remarkable story of how he emigrated to America and settled in Madison, at the University of Wisconsin.

All of England awaited Chamberlain's radio speech on the evening of September 27, unaware of his behind-the-scenes machinations. We expected, or at least hoped for, a measured appeal to resist Hitler's unreasonable demands. Instead we heard the speech of a tired man beset by the apparent failure of his policies. He revealed again his determination to do everything possible to prevent the outbreak of war. "I would not hesitate to pay even a third visit to Germany," he said, "if I thought it would do any good." We were struck by the fact that he showed greater sympathy for the German case than for the Czech. He revealed, too, his bewilderment that the German and Czech behavior threatened to cause a war over issues that had already been settled in principle. Surprisingly, he continued to express belief in Hitler's promises. We were taken aback when he described the crisis as "a quarrel in a faraway country between people of whom we know nothing," adding that, "however much we may sympathize with a small nation confronted by a big and powerful neighbor, we cannot in all circumstances undertake to involve the whole British Empire in a war simply on her account."

I heard Chamberlain's speech with Professor Perlman at the

home of a Welsh businessman who had invited us and several local people to dine with him that evening. We were all puzzled and let down by Chamberlain's remarks. We still expected the worst the next day. The local people thought that Cardiff as well as London would be destroyed.

The following day we were stunned by the news of Chamberlain's last-minute announcement in the House of Commons that he was accepting Hitler's invitation to meet in Munich with him, Daladier, and Mussolini. At first, like almost all of Britain, we were greatly relieved. But after catching our intellectual breath, we feared that we were about to witness the final step in the sellout of Czechoslovakia.

I tried to sort out this ambivalence as I rode to the railway station to meet Hannah. She had left London before the news of Chamberlain's flight to Munich had been announced. Stepping off the train, her first words were, "Has the war started?"

When Chamberlain unexpectedly told the House of Commons that he would fly to Munich for a four-power meeting, members cheered. Some wept with joy as they threw their papers in the air. Only a handful of MP's, including Churchill, Eden, and Nicolson, refused to join the mob. The behavior in the House was reflected in the wave of relief that swept through the whole country, which felt as if there had been a last-minute reprieve from a death sentence. To a large degree Hitler's policy of "frightfulness" had succeeded.

The meeting in Munich inevitably resulted in a victory for Hitler. The four-power accord gave him practically all he demanded at Godesberg, while providing a fig leaf, however transparent, for Chamberlain and Daladier.

Under the Munich Agreement, the Sudeten territory was ceded to Germany. An international commission was set up consisting of German, British, French, Italian, and Czechoslovakian representatives to provide for the evacuation of the territory beginning on October 1 and ending on October 7. Britain, France, Germany, and Italy agreed to join in a guarantee of Czechoslovakia's new frontiers once Hungarian and Polish territorial demands had been resolved.

Hitler had achieved his main objective of having his troops enter the Sudetenland by October 1, and completing the occupation in ten days without opposition. Churchill's comment was typically acerbic: "at Berchtesgaden . . . one pound was demanded. When it was given at Godesberg, two pounds were demanded at pistol point. Finally, at Munich, the dictator consented to take one pound, seventeen and six, and the rest in promises 'of good will for the future.' "

The agreement on the Sudetenland was not the only result of the Munich conference. On Chamberlain's initiative, he and Hitler signed a joint declaration that stated: "We are resolved that the method of consultation shall be the method adopted to deal with any other questions that may concern our two countries, and we are determined to continue our efforts to remove possible sources of difference and thus to contribute to assure the peace of Europe." They also expressed their determination "never to go to war again." When the prime minister arrived at Heston, the London airport, he flourished the document containing the joint declaration before his fellow cabinet members and the press correspondents, and made it clear to his countrymen that he was particularly proud of it. Cheered when he returned to 10 Downing Street, and succumbing to the euphoria of the hour, the prime minister said to the crowd: "My good friends, for the second time in our history a British prime minister has returned from Germany bringing peace with honor.* I believe it is peace for our time." In the event, "our time" would last less than a year.

The elation in Britain over Munich quickly subsided as relief gave way to reality, and people recognized the price that had been paid for a dubious peace. There was shame and guilt over selling out democratic Czechoslovakia and concern over the implication for France and Great Britain of yet another bloodless Hitler victory. The Munich Agreement divided the country, with bitter disagreements in political parties, family, and class.

Back in Oxford the first week in October to begin the new school year, I heard stories about sharp family disagreements over Munich. Christopher Cadogan, a student at Magdalen College and one of my closest friends, told me of his anger when his father, a retired naval commander, ordered up a case of vintage

---

*He was referring to Disraeli's remark after the signing of the Treaty of Berlin in 1878.

champagne to celebrate the Hitler-Chamberlain agreement. Christopher had stalked out of the house.

Christopher was not a hotheaded young man. On the contrary, he was the quintessential balanced, bright, and idealistic young Englishman, one of the most attractive students I met during my time at Oxford. He was tall, lean, with a loping walk, which made him seem in a hurry, though never at the expense of his easy self-assurance. He combined his deep commitment to his Liberal Party politics with a tremendous sense of fun, playing endless practical jokes and giving wickedly accurate imitations of almost everyone. He loved music, skiing, good food and good wine, car racing, and attractive women. His intelligence and wit delighted his friends. We were sure that one day he would be a leading figure in British politics.

Christopher and his future wife, the bright, beautiful Stella Zilliacus, stood up for Hannah and me at our wedding in June 1939. Stella was also deeply involved in politics. At Oxford, she studied politics, philosophy, and economics. The daughter of Koni Zilliacus, she had been brought up as a League of Nations child in Geneva. Her father, who later became a left-wing MP and a close friend of Tito, was a top official in the political section of the League. During the 1930s, his books on European politics, particularly *The Road to War*, written under the pseudonym "Vigilantes," alerted many of us at Oxford to the true nature of Hitler's Germany.

Early in the war, Christopher, an army officer, was killed in a naval incident in the eastern Mediterranean. After surviving the Dunkirk evacuation, he had been assigned to British Middle East headquarters in Cairo. He was a member of a small group that flew to Istanbul on a special mission. They completed their work in short order, and the day they were scheduled to return to Egypt, Christopher took ill and was unable to fly back. He stayed behind to recover and, several days later, boarded a Turkish ship sailing to Cairo. The Italians torpedoed the vessel and Christopher was not among the survivors. The race is not to the swift but to the lucky.

In the autumn of 1938, no one at Oxford was more bitter about Munich than Denis Brogan. I ran into him a few days after the Munich Agreement. He was furious over Chamberlain's performance. "When I saw Arthur Goodhart* in Blackwell's yesterday," Brogan said to me, "I told him how fed up I was with the spineless sellout of the government and how annoyed I was with myself for being so stupid as to think only a few days before Chamberlain capitulated at Munich that at long last the prime minister was going to stand up to Hitler. I should have known better. I should have accepted Harvard's offer of a chair, or Minnesota's, and quit this cowardly country.

"Goodhart," Brogan added, "was shocked. 'You're not the kind of person, Denis, who would leave a sinking ship,' he said. 'You're right,' I replied, 'but there's a difference between leaving a sinking ship and scurrying from a scuttled one!'"

All of Oxford soon had a chance to express its views on the policy of appeasement. The first parliamentary by-election held after Munich was fixed for the city of Oxford on October 27. Students, faculty, and town residents participated in what turned out to be a passionate contest. The Tories picked Quintin Hogg† as their candidate, a young Fellow of All Souls and the son of Viscount Hailsham, a member of Chamberlain's cabinet. Labour chose Patrick Gordon-Walker, a Fellow of Christ Church. The Liberals put up Ivor Davies.

Because a divided Labour-Liberal opposition would ensure the election of Quintin Hogg, who fully supported Chamberlain's policies, three of Oxford's leading academics took the lead in pressuring A. D. Lindsay to run as an "Independent" or "Popular Front" candidate against Hogg: Roy Harrod, who became the biographer of Keynes; and Frank Pakenham and Richard Crossman, both of whom later served as ministers in Harold Wilson's government. A Lindsay candidacy would involve a radical departure in British politics for two reasons: no head of an Oxford college, let alone a retiring vice chancellor, had ever stood for

*Goodhart was the very respectable American-Anglophile barrister and professor of jurisprudence who was master of University College, Oxford.

†Thirty-two years later, Quintin Hogg, as Lord Hailsham, became Lord Chancellor in Prime Minister Edward Heath's 1970–74 government. When the Tories returned to power in 1979 under Margaret Thatcher, Lord Hailsham became her Lord Chancellor.

Parliament, nor had there ever been a "Popular Front" candidate in a British election.

Lindsay felt so strongly about the issues involved that he cast tradition aside and agreed to run if Liberals and Labour would support him. He thought that "something most frightful" was happening. "The thing that makes me angry," he told a meeting, "is the calm, smug, complacent way in which people talk about it, especially the high-class papers. . . . I can't stand the smug hypocrisy with which they say how very nice it is for the people of Czechoslovakia now." He was appalled that the Germans were forcing the Czechs to hand back some 400,000 Sudeten Germans who had opposed the Nazis so that they could be put in concentration camps. Many of the students shared Lindsay's sentiments.

It took considerable effort, diplomatic skill, and precious time to organize the Popular Front candidacy. The Liberal candidate stepped down voluntarily, but Gordon-Walker was reluctant to yield. After the necessary negotiations were completed, only eleven days were left for campaigning. Lindsay's first meeting sticks in my mind, particularly the nominating speech by the chairman of the Oxford Labour Party. The latter was the Chief Scout at Christ Church, and it seemed appropriate on this historic occasion that a college Scout should be nominating a Master of a college and a recent vice chancellor. The overflow crowd responded with enthusiasm to Lindsay's powerful protest against the government's policy and his appeal for support across party lines.

Most of all I remember the impact of Lindsay's candidacy on Balliol. It was the most memorable event in my three years at Oxford. No issue aroused the students more than the Munich Agreement, and it was a source of particular excitement that the first referendum on it should occur in Oxford, and that the man carrying the anti-appeasement banner should be the Master of Balliol. It would be difficult to forget the drama of the evening when the Master spoke to the students in a Junior Common Room meeting about his decision to stand for Parliament.

Most of the students at Balliol were anti-Munich, but by no means all of us. In his shy but dignified and direct manner, the Master explained why he felt obliged to stand for Parliament. He emphasized, however, that no student should feel that this action on his part should influence their own views. He recalled that he had said the same about his line of action during the General Strike of 1926. The Americans in Balliol were particularly moved that night in the Common Room. We were anti-appeasement and stirred by the fact that a person of Lindsay's stature and position should be willing to undertake a tough political campaign with the odds so heavily against him. We demonstrated our support in the most practical way by canvassing vigorously for the Master during the campaign. The fact that this was hardly legal added zest to our activity. I recall with gratitude how friendly Oxford citizens were when we rang their doorbells, even though we were Americans.

I remember the Master standing outside Elliston's, a local emporium, one day at noon in order to shake hands with the shopgirls as they emerged to go to lunch. It was the kind of campaigning that shy Lindsay found particularly difficult. When he turned to leave, he noticed that three or four of us Americans were watching his performance. Still self-conscious after his harrowing experience, he was pleased to see some friendly faces and blurted out, "If you damn Americans could vote in this election I might have a chance of winning it!"

This campaign was my baptism in practical politics. The ability to overcome party parochialism and the short duration of the campaign, as well as the relative unimportance of financing it, left a permanent mark. Any American who has lived through a British election must bemoan the length and cost of our political contests. Most impressive was the extent to which candidates and their supporters concentrated on the issues confronting the electorate: peace, national unity, political morality, and defense of democracy. Ted Heath and Harold Macmillan were among the people who felt strongly enough about these issues to desert the Tory party and support Lindsay. In the Oxford Union, Heath proposed a motion that "this House deplores the government's policy without honor." It carried handsomely.

Both sides in the election appealed to emotion as well as intellect. Some of Lindsay's supporters used the slogan, which Lindsay deplored, "A vote for Hogg is a vote for Hitler." It was amusing that Dick Crossman, the left-of-center Labourite, and Julian

Amery, the right-of-center Tory, both claimed to have been the authors of this slogan. Either was capable of it. Some of Hogg's people falsely charged that Lindsay had received telegrams of support from Stalin. Isaiah Berlin who, like Hogg, was a young Fellow of All Souls, recalled how one night during the campaign, at dinner in the college, Hogg, responding to a comment made by Berlin, said, "You disapprove of Hitler's Germany only because you're Jewish."

Rarely have students and faculty been so involved in a parliamentary election. Crowded meetings, numerous speeches, self-conscious handshaking, letters to newspaper editors, and intensive canvassing of voters marked the eleven hectic days of campaigning. I remember the crowd nervously waiting outside Town Hall to hear the mayor announce the results. Lindsay lost. His supporters were deeply disappointed, but we took some comfort from the fact that the Tory majority had been cut in half.

Lindsay bore his defeat with great dignity. Thanking his supporters for the good fight, he predicted that the movement begun by the Oxford by-election would continue. He was right. The country had been awakened to the dangers of Chamberlain's policies. In the three by-elections held soon after Oxford's, the Labour opposition won two Tory seats and sharply reduced the Conservative majority in the third.

During my remaining eight months at Oxford, many of us watched with dismay the fulfillment of our fears about the policy of appeasement. It was an eerie period, with reality competing with political fantasy. Chamberlain persisted in defending the Munich Agreement in spite of ominous developments that belied his confidence. When, in a public speech a week after Munich, Hitler warned the Germans that if Duff Cooper,* Eden, or Churchill came to power they would aim immediately to start a war, Chamberlain not only failed to defend his former colleagues; he indicated sympathy for Hitler's point of view.

Noel-Buxton told me of the letter that he had received from the prime minister bemoaning Churchill's and Eden's criticism of Hitler. Publicly in the House of Commons, Chamberlain stated

---

*Duff Cooper had resigned as secretary of state for war to protest against the Munich agreement.

that criticizing Munich was like a bird fouling its own nest and expressed his confidence in Hitler's commitment to both the Munich Agreement and the Anglo-German declaration. This encouraged Hitler to repeat his attacks on the "British warmongers."

Most baffling and troubling during the five months between Munich and the invasion of Czechoslovakia on March 15, 1939, was Chamberlain's continuing confidence in his appeasement policy. Newspapers and magazines, books and radio were full of accounts of the Nazis tightening their economic and political grip on Eastern Europe in probable preparation for the next aggressive act, but that didn't bother the prime minister. He seemed to think that this development was the logical result of his policy, and that Germany had a right to a dominant position in Central and Eastern Europe. Not a few of us suspected that Chamberlain shared the view held by some of his compatriots that encouraging the Nazis to turn eastward would result in a conflict with the Soviet Union that, by weakening both dictatorships, would serve the interests of the West. It still seems incredible that on March 10, 1939, five days before the Nazis marched into Prague and annexed Czechoslovakia, Chamberlain could state that "Europe was settling down to a period of tranquillity, and that the government was therefore contemplating the possibility of a general limitation of armament."

No one who lived in England at that time can ever forget the impact on the country of Hitler's takeover of Czechoslovakia. The wave of guilt after Munich had been somewhat assuaged by the promise of a four-power guarantee of Czechoslovakia's new borders and Hitler's statement that the Sudetenland represented his last territorial demand in Europe. There could no longer be any doubt about the worthlessness of Hitler's promises and his determination to dominate Europe. The former appeasers now agreed with those who never had any illusions about Hitler that the Nazi leader had to be stopped. You could feel the relief that permeated the country, the exhilaration over the realization that Great Britain could once again play its authentic role in world affairs.

But it took time for Chamberlain to respond to the public clamor. On March 15, when the German troops were marching into Czechoslovakia and Hitler himself was entering Prague, Chamberlain still refused to associate himself with "charges of breach of faith . . . which did not seem to me to be founded on sufficient premises." His main concern was to demonstrate that the disintegration of the Czech state, which Hitler had blatantly organized, absolved Britain from implementing her Munich commitment to guarantee the new Czech borders. Forgotten was the prime minister's statement shortly after Munich that "The new Czechoslovakia will find greater security than she ever enjoyed in the past."

I was in the House of Commons gallery the next day—Lord Noel-Buxton had secured a pass for me—and I recall the quiver in Chamberlain's voice when he bemoaned the fact that Hitler had broken the promises he had made to him personally. Chamberlain sounded like a man who was distressed to learn that Hitler was not really a British gentleman. You could almost feel the members' dissatisfaction with Chamberlain's performance, his failure to articulate the country's sense of outrage over Hitler's new act of aggression. In reply to a question, the prime minister stated that he had not yet protested to the German government and gave no assurances that he was prepared to do so. He would only say that he was considering recalling for consultation Sir Nevile Henderson, the British ambassador to Germany, who had been a fervent supporter of appeasement.

But a stubborn old man had to realize that the British people and their representatives in the House of Commons, including people from his own party, demanded unequivocal condemnation of German aggression and commitment by the government to resist any future Nazi attempts to dominate the world by force. Realizing that his position as prime minister was now in question, less than twenty-four hours later Chamberlain announced a basic change in his government's policy. In a speech in Birmingham, his hometown, after again lamenting Hitler's failure to consult with him as provided in the Munich Agreement, Chamberlain abandoned appeasement and stated that Britain, with the support of the Commonwealth and in alliance with France, would resist any attempt to dominate the world by force.

Three days later I sat in the gallery of the House of Lords with what an attendant told me was the largest crowd of visitors since the outbreak of World War I. We had come to hear Lord Halifax, the foreign secretary, speak. He reinforced the diplomatic volte-face announced by the prime minister in Birmingham, but his speech was less tortured and more emphatic than Chamberlain's. Halifax, who had long since lost his faith in Munich, influenced Chamberlain's decision to change course.

Shortly after Hitler took over Czechoslovakia, I became involved in an enterprise that reminded me of what Nazism meant and what personal heroism could do about it. My fiancée, Hannah, who was living in London at the time, was asked by Peggy Guggenheim whether she knew anyone who would be willing to undertake a dangerous mission. Guggenheim had secured British visas for thirty-six artists and writers hiding in Prague since the Nazis marched into Czechoslovakia a week or two before. These thirty-six refugees from Germany and Austria were on the Nazi most-wanted list. Guggenheim needed an individual who was willing to try to get into Prague, find them, hand over some money, and tell them if they escaped from Czechoslovakia and reached a British consulate they could pick up the visas and be on their way to London.

Hannah immediately thought of Guy Nunn, who was planning to spend his spring vacation quietly in Oxford studying for his exams. Guy, a contemporary Rhodes Scholar and close friend, was just the right person. He was tough, poised, spoke excellent German, and was more than smart enough to extract a visa from the Nazi authorities in Berlin to visit Prague, although the Czech border had been closed to foreigners.

Guy leaped at the suggestion. Hannah and Peggy decided that his posing as an art dealer would be the best cover. He would ask for a visa to spend five days in Prague in order to buy some paintings. The expenditure of foreign exchange would be the bait to hook the Nazis. Before reaching Berlin, Guy memorized the names of the refugees and hid the money in his shoe. Fortunately, he had been reading Hegel the preceding months. When he saw the appropriate official at the infamous Nazi headquarters in Alexander Platz, he convinced him that he was a bona fide art dealer by displaying his knowledge of Hegel's aesthetics. Guy was granted a five-day visa.

In Prague it took him three days to contact enough of the refugees to spread the word and distribute the funds. On the fourth day, through traps he had set, he realized that he was being followed and that his hotel room had been entered. A day earlier than scheduled, he slipped out of Prague. Thirty-five of the thirty-six escaped and made it safely to England.

I shared the relief of many Oxonians over the dramatic change in government policy, though we regretted that Chamberlain had not made his stand over Czechoslovakia. Before Munich, he had stubbornly refused to accept any proposal in regard to Czechoslovakia that could result in Britain's going to war as the result of a decision of another country. Then, on March 31, 1939, he officially reversed that position, stating in the House of Commons, "In the event of any action which threatened Polish independence, and which the Polish government accordingly considered vital to resist with national forces, His Majesty's government would feel themselves bound at once to lend the Polish government all support in its power."

This was an ironic turn. It would have made much more sense to stand up for democratic Czechoslovakia, powerfully armed with fortifications that contained Maginot Line secrets, than to rally behind Poland, a country governed by a military oligarchy that collaborated with Germany in the dismemberment of Czechoslovakia. The British declaration in support of Poland represented a remarkable change in policy but it also underlined how dismally appeasement had failed in the months before.

Chamberlain didn't stop with Poland. With the passion of converts, within a few weeks the British and French extended guarantees to Greece, Romania, Denmark, Holland, and Switzerland. In addition, over vigorous Labour and Liberal opposition, Chamberlain pushed through a bill calling for conscription, and finally decided to set up the Ministry of Supply to accelerate rearmament.

These were important steps, but one more seemed essential. An effective front against Nazi aggression required Soviet participation, and Chamberlain moved gingerly in seeking Moscow's collaboration. From mid-April 1939 until the Hitler-Stalin Pact at the end of August, political attention focused on the tortuous negotiations between Britain and France and the Soviet Union, while the world was unaware of the conversation going on between Moscow and Berlin.

It was difficult to follow all the twists and turns in the negotiations between the Western democracies and the Soviet Union.

Mistrust and prejudice were serious obstacles to a successful conclusion. As Sir John Wheeler-Bennett, the distinguished diplomatic historian, wrote, "Few negotiations in history have been conducted in a such a spirit of mutual mistrust among all parties."

Vyacheslav Molotov's replacing Maxim Litvinov as foreign minister seemed ominous. We knew that Litvinov, a highly trained diplomat, supported an alliance with the West. His behavior during the Czech crisis had been responsibly supportive. Molotov, on the other hand, lacked Litvinov's international outlook and experience, was tougher and more cynical. Except for this change, the public was aware only that negotiations between the West and the Soviets were not going smoothly. I must have sensed something radically wrong, because in June I wrote to my brother Henry that I would not be surprised if Stalin made a deal with Hitler.

A personal event, the imminence of my marriage, proved to be even more distracting, and much more agreeably so, than the prospect of an international conflict. Rhodes Scholar rules prohibited my marriage until I had completed my studies. Hannah Greeley and I were married on June 16, a week after my last exam.

We had been students in Selig Perlman's class, "Capitalism and Socialism," in 1934. I found her enormously appealing: she was pretty, bright, wonderfully sensitive and sensible. She combined a strong will with a remarkable generosity. In her concern for the less fortunate, her sense of fairness and her determination always to be helpful, she was a match for my mother. When it came to assisting others, there was no limit to Hannah's or Temma's energy. I continue to marvel at the similarities between my *shtetl* mother and my Yankee wife.

An inheritance from Hannah's grandfather had enabled her to visit Europe in the summer of 1938. We toured England and Scotland together in a car borrowed from a Japanese classmate at Balliol. After she accepted my proposal during the intermission at a symphony orchestra concert in Glasgow, we agreed she should spend a year in England. She succeeded in getting a job in London with the Spanish Youth Food Ship Committee. She lived off her salary, two pounds a week, later raised to two pounds ten shillings. We saw each other almost every weekend and, of course, during my vacations.

Friends at Oxford helped with wedding arrangements and acted as surrogate relatives at the ceremony and the reception that followed. The British are particularly warm and generous on these occasions. J. C. H. Whitehead, a nephew of the famous philosopher, was the mathematics tutor at Balliol. I had never exchanged a word with him until a week before the wedding, when we crossed in the quad. To my surprise, he stopped and said, "Kaiser, I understand you're getting married next week. Well, I was married a year ago and I can tell you the economics of married life is very simple. A penny bun costs tuppence." And he walked away.

At a dinner given by the Master and Fellows to the graduating students, Dean Rodger rose and said, "Usually only one toast is offered: to the health and prosperity of the students; but tonight," he added, "we are breaking tradition. I also propose a toast to Kaiser who, on Friday, will be losing his amateur status."

We spent a week in Stratford seeing Shakespeare plays. Then we continued our honeymoon in the beautiful Cotswolds, staying at the magnificent Hatherop Castle of Sir Thomas Bazley, the half-brother of Christopher Cadogan. We completed our stay in Europe with a week in Paris where, thanks to a letter of introduction from Lord Noel-Buxton, we visited William Bullitt, the American ambassador. I was surprised when he asked whether I thought war would break out that summer. I appreciated the compliment, but I expected him to know the answer.

The concern about the possibility of war never left us. I had hoped to remain in Europe at least until the crisis was resolved one way or another. Ed Murrow had asked Denis Brogan to recommend a few young Americans who might join him at CBS. Brogan had suggested Guy Nunn and me. But Murrow then told him that CBS was not yet ready to go ahead with its projected expansion. With no prospect of employment in Europe, Hannah and I boarded the *Nieuw Amsterdam* on August 4, 1939, and docked in New York six days later.

4

The Truman Years:
Labor and
International Affairs

Remember," President Truman said, "in this new assignment, you must be sure that you treat all Americans equally and fairly, and I mean *all* Americans"; and then, with that warm Truman grin, he added, "Whether we like it or not, Republicans are citizens of this country, too." We were finishing a half-hour meeting in the Oval Office in July 1949, during which the President informed me that he was appointing me assistant secretary of labor for international affairs.

This meeting with the President was the high point of the ten years I had spent in Washington after my return home from Oxford. Two years as an economist in the Research Division of the Board of Governors of the Federal Reserve System was followed by four years as chief of the project operations staff on the Board of Economic Warfare and as chief of the planning staff in its successor agency, the Foreign Economic Administration. I had joined the Labor Department in 1946 after a brief tour in the State Department's office dealing with international organization affairs.

I was naturally touched by the President's warm reception. The appointment had been in the works for months. Several times I had heard that it was on the verge of being announced. However, the opposition, particularly from India Edwards, vice chairman of the Democratic National Committee and one of Truman's favorites, had succeeded in holding it up. India had nothing against me personally (we subsequently became good friends), but she was pushing hard for more women in top government jobs and she had particularly targeted this one.

There was another important hurdle. After my appointment had unanimously cleared the Senate Labor Committee, an anonymous woman, an employee of the Federal Security Agency (the predecessor of the Department of Health and Human Services), had phoned Forrest Donnell, the conservative Republican senator from Missouri, to tell him that I had security problems. The senator asked that my confirmation be delayed until he was satisfied about my loyalty. Senator Elbert Thomas of Utah, the chairman of the Labor Committee, responded by appointing a subcommittee of two, Donnell and Hubert Humphrey, to look into the matter.

Like so many other loyal civil servants I was a victim of the hysteria generated by Senator Joseph McCarthy. Succumbing to the hyped-up anti-Communist crusade, Truman established a Loyalty Board in every government department to check the security of all employees. At a time when he was rallying the American people to support the Greek-Turkish aid programs and the Marshall Plan in order to resist Moscow's aggressions abroad, the President was particularly sensitive to charges that members of his own administration were "soft" on Communism. Unfortunately, the move did not satisfy the right wing. Instead, it exacerbated the hysteria.

Loyalty boards were administrative bodies; there was no provision for due process or for judicial review. Subjecting an individual to a hearing suggested that there was derogatory information about him serious enough to require an appearance before the board. In other words, he was being accused without the protective presumption of innocence so basic to our legal system. He was not guaranteed the right to face his accusers or cross-examine witnesses. People were considered untrustworthy because of their ideas or imputed motives, and, worst of all, adjudged "guilty by association." Furthermore, as John Lord O'Brien, assistant attorney general in Hoover's administration and a leading lawyer, observed, loyalty boards stimulated the growth of anti-intellectual movements, and of anxiety and insecurity in our society. In later years Truman expressed regret over the abuses of the loyalty program. He was particularly unhappy that once an individual was cleared by one board, he was subject to a new investigation if he were transferred to another government job. In his memoirs, Truman wrote, "This is not in the tradition of fair play and justice."

During a meeting in the mid-1950s when he was in New York visiting his daughter, Margaret, President Truman and I talked about McCarthyism and the loyalty boards. He told me of a monograph, *A Study of "Witch Hunting" and Hysteria in the United States*, which he "had gotten up" while he was in the White House. He later sent a copy to me, saying he intended "to elaborate on it at a later date and possibly give a series of lectures on it. It will be some time, however," he added, "before I get to that point."*

The monograph does not discuss McCarthyism but in his "Concluding Observations" the President makes an impassioned plea for the protection of the freedoms guaranteed in the Bill of Rights that "serve to counteract the effects of hysteria." While recognizing the dangers of Communism in the late 1940s, Truman points out that "democracies have discovered that the most powerful antidote to Communism is a virile government which can fulfill the needs of all classes of people." In the United States, he adds, "Communism has had few internal successes, and has always polled an infinitesimal percentage of the popular vote in elections." Moreover, Communist efforts to capture private organizations, particularly trade unions, through infiltration have been frustrated. By using democratic processes, President Truman points out, trade union leaders have defeated the underhand tactics of the Communists or driven them into isolated organizations where they were easily identified.

In my own case the Labor Department Loyalty Board presented me with an "interrogatory." My loyalty was not questioned and I was not asked to appear at a hearing. I was required to clarify my relationship with certain people I had known. One in particular appeared troublesome—a fellow Rhodes Scholar, member of a

---

*His monograph on hysteria includes chapters on witchcraft in Salem, Massachusetts, 1692; the Alien and Sedition Acts, 1798–1800; anti-Masonry, 1826–40; the Know-Nothing movement, 1840–56; Reconstruction and the Ku Klux Klan, 1865–77; and post–World War I hysteria, 1919–29.

famous Virginia family, and a law partner of General "Wild Bill" Donovan, who brought him to Washington when the general became head of OSS. This was hardly a suspicious background. I had no trouble satisfying the Labor Department board that my relationship with that individual did not reflect on my loyalty or security since fellow Rhodes Scholars inevitably got to know each other. Moreover, I had no reason to believe there was any question about his loyalty. I was given a clean bill of political health. The fact that some outsider had learned about the interrogatory and could distort its significance in order to prevent my confirmation was typical of what was occurring during this sad period in our history. Subsequently, I was called upon to vouch for the loyalty of several of our labor attachés, some of whom were subjected to hearings simply because they operated in the sensitive trade union world. There were other shameful cases and, perhaps the worst of all, one involving a decent, liberal U.S. senator.*

Senator Donnell finally approved my nomination after a Missourian, Stanley Rector, who had taught my wife and me at Wisconsin, and who was a friend of Donnell, assured him that I was a completely loyal American. Other civil servants were not so fortunate in their connections.

During my first meeting with President Truman, his charm, warmth, and ability to relate to people became apparent. He immediately set you at ease; he had that talent, too often lacking in top officials, of making you feel that while in his presence you had his full interest and attention. As I was about to leave, the President said, "I understand, Phil, you were a Rhodes Scholar." Mental telepathy led me immediately to associate this question with Senator Fulbright because I knew how strongly the President felt about him. I didn't quite hang my head in shame, but quietly admitted that I had been a Rhodes Scholar. The President's face then lit up with the famous Truman smile, and he said, "But Maurice here assures me that you're a different kind than Senator Halfbright." Maurice Tobin, the secretary of labor, was a favorite of Truman's, having been one of the very few individuals who vigorously campaigned for the President in the fall of 1948 when

*See pages 144–45.

almost everybody thought that Truman's chances for election were practically nil.

The Friday before that election, as Tobin was preparing to leave for Boston, he said to me, "Phil, take all the money you have plus all that you can borrow and bet it on Truman. He's going to win and the odds couldn't be more favorable." I didn't follow his advice because I didn't have much money and was in no position to borrow any. At the inaugural ball three months later, as I observed Tobin helping his wife put on a beautiful new mink coat, he smilingly remarked, "Truman won it for Helen."

I had come to the Labor Department as an executive assistant to David Morse, the first man appointed assistant secretary of labor for international affairs, a position established by Congress in 1946 in response to a new appreciation of the increasing importance of labor's international role, particularly during the Cold War.

My brother Henry, at that time an associate general counsel for the American Federation of Labor, had supported the nomination of David Morse and had helped him in the Senate confirmation proceedings. Morse needed help, too, because some officials of the AFL thought he was too liberal, and in their view not sufficiently anti-Communist. Morse had asked Henry to join him in the new Labor Department enterprise, but Henry was committed to his legal career. He suggested that Morse have a look at me. International affairs were my principal interest, Henry emphasized, pointing out that I had done academic work in the labor field at both Wisconsin and Oxford. At the time, I was in the State Department dealing with U.S. participation in international organizations. The idea of being involved in the launching of a new international enterprise appealed to me. I was delighted when, after several interviews with Morse, he asked me to become his executive assistant.

It was a happy association. Morse, who before the war had been a regional attorney for the National Labor Relations Board, had served in a high labor post in the military governments in Italy and Germany. He had done an outstanding job in laying the foundations for the revival of free labor movements in those two countries. He was full of enthusiasm for his new assignment, to which his new staff happily responded. We were impressed by his competence, and by the way in which he used his exceptional administrative skills to implement public policy. We appreciated, too, his warmth, his generosity of spirit, and his genuine concern for the welfare of those who worked for him. We also relished being involved in a new and challenging government effort in the front line of the Cold War.

Tobin, the former mayor of Boston and governor of Massachusetts, had become secretary of labor shortly before Morse left the department to take up the position of director general of the International Labor Organization in Geneva. By then I was director of the newly established Office of International Labor Affairs, and in frequent contact with the new secretary. We became warm friends. After Truman's victory in 1948, Tobin recommended my appointment as assistant secretary for international affairs to succeed Morse. His proposal to the President was supported by leaders of the AFL and the CIO, who wrote strong letters to President Truman urging my appointment.

Handsome enough to be a matinee idol, Tobin was a paradigm of the liberal, pragmatic Boston Irish politician. His political success—he was able to defeat the legendary James Curley—depended largely on his ability to relate personally to every ethnic group, in addition to his fellow Irishmen, and on his marvelous skill as an orator. He was a poor administrator, but an intelligent and exceptionally decent individual. He loved people. His day was made when he helped someone, and the less important the person involved, the more pleasure it gave him. On several occasions he invited me to a "business breakfast" in his apartment in the Winthrop House on Massachusetts Avenue. When I arrived I always found other people—at times up to ten—waiting to see him, all obviously seeking help.

His generosity of spirit was matched by political courage that has been too little noted. During the height of the McCarthy period, when so many politicians were running for cover, he attacked McCarthy at a convention of the Veterans of Foreign Wars, an audience that was predominantly sympathetic to the Wisconsin senator. It was a magnificent speech, eloquently emphasizing the violation of basic American civil liberties by McCarthy and his followers, and delivered at a time when Congressman John Kennedy avoided taking any stand on McCarthy. The speech made such an impact that McCarthy asked for and received equal time to respond.

On more than one occasion, Tobin publicly supported his colleague, Secretary of State Dean Acheson, a leading target of McCarthyites. Tobin admired Acheson, a fact that undoubtedly contributed to the friendship I developed with the secretary of state after my responsibilities brought me into contact with the top level of the State Department.

Unfortunately, Tobin died in 1953 at the early age of fifty-three. President Truman and all of Tobin's cabinet colleagues except Dean Acheson attended the funeral in Boston. I was so disappointed by Acheson's absence that when I returned to Washington I called on him to inquire why he had failed to attend. He explained that because he was in the midst of a complicated legal situation, he couldn't leave. There followed a discussion about loyalty during which Acheson told me a remarkable story about the repercussions of his public statement "I will not turn my back on Alger Hiss." The very next day, Acheson called on President Truman, and, as he handed him a letter of resignation, Acheson said, "Mr. President, you must accept this to avoid unnecessary political damage." According to Acheson, the President responded that he was amazed that Acheson would even think of resigning. It indicated that Acheson didn't appreciate what loyalty meant to him. "He got out of his chair," Acheson said, "came around the desk, put his arm around me, and said, 'Don't forget, Dean, that out of loyalty I followed a criminal to the grave.* As long as I am President, you're going to be my secretary of state.'" And, concluded Acheson, the President never mentioned Alger Hiss to him again.

By the time I joined the Labor Department in September 1946, it had become clear that the world's democratic labor movements would play an increasingly important role in shaping international developments. After the breakdown of the wartime alliance between East and West and the advent of the Cold War, the Soviet Union interpreted the resulting atmosphere of social ferment, po-

---

*Truman was referring to Tom Pendergast, the Missouri political boss who had helped launch his political career. Years later Pendergast was jailed for criminal activity. While President, Truman attended Pendergast's funeral.

litical instability, and faltering economic systems as the profound "crisis of capitalism," which Marx had predicted would provide the opportunity to launch the political warfare whose main target was the working classes. According to Moscow, Marxism-Leninism represented a conception of society in which labor for the first time was truly emancipated, and the world was in the grip of historical forces that would inevitably validate its theory. Communism had thrust the issue of labor's role in society into the very heart of the international crisis created by the Soviets.

In addition to an effective military alliance, the Western democracies' defense against the spread of Communism required economic and social policies that would guarantee political stability. This stability could not be achieved without the development of free and responsible trade unions together with sound and constructive labor-management relations and progressive management practices in a free-market economy. Such a combination would provide a solid bulwark against political and social unrest and become a positive force in the strengthening of democracy. The emergence of the Solidarity movement in Poland is the most dramatic contemporary example of the significance of free trade unions. Fortunately, the American trade union movement, collaborating with other free trade unions, was prepared to resist the Communist drive to subvert free labor, and to assist the development of authentic trade unions in former enemy countries and later in the new nations of the Third World.

Today, when American trade unions have been declining in numerical strength, it is easy to forget their amazing growth in the period just before the war and in the two decades thereafter. In the United States trade union membership in 1947 was five times what it had been in 1935. American labor was then at the height of its political power. Its support of Truman in 1948 proved indispensable to his dramatic victory. Due to Truman's veto of the Taft-Hartley bill, labor had never worked harder for a presidential candidate or devoted more resources to a presidential campaign.

The Truman administration, with the support of American labor, was prepared to play its part in coping with Moscow's challenge. The task was not easy. We had to face the fact that the Communists had scored some important successes. In Europe, Communist control of the main trade union organizations made

PMK, center, with (left to right) brother Jerry, eldest son Bob, sister Fanny, and brother Jack.

PMK on table with brother Henry at his right, Jack at his left and, left to right, cousin Eva, sisters Fanny and Ida.

PMK's family plus two sisters-in-law when he (second child from left) was nine or ten years old.

PMK, on far left, with (left to right) brothers Henry, Ben, Jack, and Abe.

Wisconsin students picketing Madison's leading hotel, the Loraine, for refusing to rent rooms to the cast of *Green Pastures*. PMK stands third from left. *(University of Wisconsin-Madison Archives, #x251446)*

Professor Evander Bradley McGilvary, PMK's philosophy teacher and key supporter of his Rhodes Scholarship application. *(University of Wisconsin-Madison Archives, #x25781)*

Professor Selig Perlman, a model of pragmatic idealism and a great influence on PMK. Behind him is a portrait of Professor John R. Commons, Perlman's mentor and a major architect of Wisconsin's historic progressivism. *(University of Wisconsin-Madison Archives, #x251951)*

PMK after a squash game on the Balliol College team.

PMK, left, with American Oxford classmates Dyke Brown and Murat Williams.

The Balliol trio of the 1936 class of Rhodes Scholars: Walt Rostow, PMK, and Gordon Craig.

President Truman receiving J. Oldenbroek, general secretary of the International Confederation of Trade Unions. Behind, left to right, are Averell Harriman; Secretary of Labor Maurice Tobin; PMK; Sir Vincent Tewson, general secretary of the British Trade Union Congress; William Green, president of the AFL; and Jack Potofsky, vice president of the CIO. *(UPI/The Bettmann Archives)*

PMK with Giulio Pastore, secretary general of the ItalianConfederation of Labor, Rome, March 1951. *(AP/Wide World Photos)*

To the Philip M. Kaiser, with kindest
regards, best wishes.
Harry Truman

Harry Truman.

PMK with George Meany, center, and Arnold Zempel, PMK's top
assistant, on board ship before departure for an ILO conference.

Averell Harriman speaking to a meeting of Marshall Plan labor officials and Foreign Service labor attachés in Paris, 1950. George Meany on his right, PMK on his left.

PMK being sworn in as assistant secretary of labor by Supreme Court Justice Hugo Black.

Chatting with Paul Ramadier, the former French prime minister, at an ILO Governing Body meeting. Ramadier was the French delegate.

John Fitzgerald Kennedy.

PMK's father with Secretary of Labor Maurice Tobin at PMK's swearing-in as assistant secretary of labor.

France and Italy precarious participants in the democratic camp. As the new global leader, the United States had to learn hurriedly how to deal with issues that other leading nations never had to face. We had to develop new diplomatic concepts and make psychological and economic readjustments to our new position as a superpower. We had to learn the art of public diplomacy. We had to win not only the support of governments, but the support of their working people, whose "natural" leader the Soviet Union claimed to be.

The United States had to overcome the historic distrust of foreign labor organizations that, although not Communist-dominated, contained motley strains of Marxism, anarchosyndicalism, and Christian socialism that prevented them from seeing the difference between American competitive capitalism and their own national monopoly capitalism built on old feudal structures. American offers of assistance were often viewed with suspicion in underdeveloped areas where technological progress in the past had been associated with imperialism and economic exploitation. Latin Americans either criticized the United States for giving them insufficient aid, or suspected that the aim of such aid was to revive "dollar diplomacy" and "Yankee capitalist exploitation" of cheap labor. Many Europeans regarded American aid as a device to prevent or export a depression or to convert their countries into economic vassals. All watched for any move that they thought encroached on their independence. In 1949, after the launching of the Marshall Plan, I discussed these problems with William Rappard, the highly respected professor of international relations at the University of Geneva, and my colleague on the governing body of the International Labor Organization. He told me that Europeans, "steeped in cynicism," suspected American motives. They could not conceive of any generosity underlying the action of any great power.

To allay these misgivings, the U.S. government launched a variety of programs to win foreign worker support, and to relate these programs to the international activities of the AFL and CIO. The Labor Attaché Program was established toward the end of the war as a new arm of American diplomacy. We encouraged the rebirth or development of free trade unions in Germany, Italy, Austria, and Japan. In addition, the United States set in motion labor information and exchange-of-persons programs to counter-act the false ideas about America sown by Communist opponents. We strengthened our participation in the International Labor Organization, created under the Treaty of Versailles as a result primarily of the efforts of Samuel Gompers, then president of the AFL. Most important, the U.S. government sought to alleviate postwar economic distress, taking steps to ensure that the working man abroad participated in as well as profited from our aid and technical assistance programs.

As assistant secretary of labor for international affairs, I was deeply involved in these activities. I had the never-flagging support of Secretary Tobin, who made the resources of the entire department available for foreign programs, and the help of the superb staff of the newly organized Office of International Labor Affairs: Arnold Zempel, Leo Werts, Ned Persons, James Taylor, Olen Warnock, and George Ewing. One of our major objectives was to expand the Labor Attaché Program and ensure that key embassies were staffed with labor experts. This required the grafting of a whole new program on the Foreign Service, not an easy task. The Service was still dominated by a hidebound bureaucracy that depended on an out-of-date elitism.* The newly recruited labor attachés did not fit the traditional Foreign Service stereotypes. The established bureaucracy did not like the idea of the labor movement getting involved in their operations, nor were they always happy about the Labor Department's active role.

Fortunately, the Foreign Service Act passed in 1946 provided for Labor Department membership on the board of the Foreign Service and we used the leverage this gave us to press for more labor attaché positions. The board consisted of seven members, three assistant secretaries of state and one each from the Departments of Agriculture, Commerce, and Labor, with the undersecretary of state for administration. The board had considerable power, particularly in regard to personnel matters. Its "Appointments and Assignments" sub-board approved all professional ap-

---

*The Service has opened up dramatically during the last two decades, though the public is not generally aware of that fact. Too many Americans still respond to clichés about "cookie-pushing" diplomats, most of whom they erroneously believe are graduates of Ivy League colleges.

pointments in the Foreign Service. I took full advantage of our membership, never hesitating to do some logrolling to add to the corps of labor attachés. On several occasions when the director of the Office of Foreign Service asked for my support on other Service issues, the price I exacted was the allocation of an additional labor attaché position.

Membership on the board also enabled me to develop highly valued friendships with high-ranking officials of the State Department. After almost five years on the board, I became its senior member as there was considerable turnover of assistant secretaries of state. Among my colleagues were "Doc" Matthews, Jimmy Riddleberger, George Allen, Dean Rusk, William Benton, Norman Armour, Howland Sargeant, and Jack Peurifoy, who, as deputy undersecretary for administration, was ex-officio chairman of the board.* All of them came to appreciate the importance of labor in the postwar world. I never hesitated to seek their help, and quite often they turned to me for advice and assistance, not always on matters affecting labor.

A good example of my cooperation involved Foy Kohler, an outstanding Foreign Service officer. While stationed in Washington, Kohler and his wife had provoked Virginia police, who they claimed had treated them roughly in the aftermath of an automobile accident. The police, on their part, stated that the Kohlers had hardly been respectful, comparing the law officers unfavorably with those in Moscow. The Virginia police claimed that the Kohlers were not entirely sober. The story appeared the following day on the front page of the *Times Herald*, which, with its anti-administration bias, gave it a particularly nasty twist. Early that morning I received a call from Jack Peurifoy asking whether I would take the lead in coming to Kohler's defense. Peurifoy feared that in the McCarthy atmosphere prevalent at the time, Kohler might be unjustly driven from the Service. Jack thought that it would be better if a non–State Department member of the board were the first to defend Kohler. As I respected Kohler and deplored the influence of McCarthy, I was happy to comply with Jack's request. Together we devised a punishment that controlled the

*Peurifoy had pushed hard for my appointment as assistant secretary of labor.

damage: Kohler would have to go on leave without pay for thirty days. The board agreed. Later Kohler became ambassador to the Soviet Union.

My participation on the board provided an opportunity to observe closely the functioning of the Foreign Service as it began to come of age and adjusted to the demands of the postwar world. The changes did not come easily. Under the act of 1946 the board was responsible for recommending to the secretary the removal of members of the Foreign Service for reasons other than security. We pressed for the removal of dead wood from the Service. In 1949 or 1950 the State Department's Division of Foreign Service Personnel presented its first recommendation for removal. After reading several hundred pages of hearings on the case, the board met to make its decision. The first member to comment was the elegant, distinguished Foreign Service veteran Norman Armour. "I'm glad," he said, "to see that the Service is acting on my recommendation. In 1921 when I was counselor of the embassy in Lisbon and this man was serving in his first post, I wrote in my efficiency report that he was definitely not Foreign Service caliber and steps should be taken to move him out as early as possible." A minority of the board voted against the officer's removal because he was scheduled to retire six months later. Acting Secretary Lovett agreed with that position.

Collaboration between Commerce and Labor Department members on the board made possible a radical change in the promotion procedure in the Foreign Service. We insisted that the promotion boards include public members, distinguished individuals from academia, the corporate world, and trade unions who had no connection with the government. Old-time Foreign Service officers resisted this change but, after years of experience, they acknowledged that opening up the Service to public scrutiny has proven to be invaluable. Without exception, the outsiders who have participated in the promotion process have become strong supporters of the Foreign Service.

Another institution, although informal, enabled under- and assistant secretaries in the Truman administration to get to know each other as well as the cabinet secretaries. Every month a different cabinet member hosted a "little cabinet dinner" in his department at which the President turned up regularly. After dinner the host would speak about the problems of his department and then field questions. I remember Dean Acheson speaking for an hour and a half without a note during which he brilliantly analyzed the problems we faced around the world. A warm spirit of comradeship permeated these dinners from the first drink before we sat down until the end of the evening. The President was always at his best: informal, friendly, and interested in each of us. There were far fewer under- and assistant secretaries than there are today, and the dinners enhanced their collaboration. They provided an opportunity for me to discuss the new role of labor in the international arena. Years later, in his speech at the dinner celebrating President Truman's seventy-fifth birthday, Dean Acheson observed that there were, of course, bureaucratic fights during the Truman administration, "but the resulting wounds were always in the front of the body, never in the back."

This comradeship was evident when I served on President Truman's Committee on Executive Personnel, established to deal with the problem of excessive turnover of top-level officials. The other members were Jack Peurifoy, deputy undersecretary of state; Archie Alexander, undersecretary of the army; Eugene Zuckert, undersecretary of the air force; Graham Morrison, assistant attorney general; and Donald Dawson, the President's executive assistant for personnel.

I remember our first meeting with the President. After outlining the problem and asking us to develop a plan to create a national register from which he could choose qualified men and women for top government positions, Truman concluded, "I am told people leave the government for two reasons, financial and health. Now I can appreciate why individuals leave to earn more money, particularly if they have children going to college. But"—his face lit up with the famous Truman smile—"I can't understand why anybody would get an ulcer while working in Washington." My colleagues and I later agreed that the last person who would get an ulcer was our very normal and sensible President.

The first American labor attaché, Dan Horowitz, was appointed in 1943 to Chile where the liberal Claude Bowers, the biographer of Jefferson and Hamilton, was FDR's ambassador. He was the

only chief of mission at that time who would accept a labor attaché. Horowitz had government and academic credentials in the
field of industrial relations. The United States had been influenced
by Great Britain, which had launched its labor attaché program
a few years earlier by sending Archibald McDonald Gordon to
Washington. McDonald's performance served as a model for future U.S. and British labor attachés. During his long tour, he
developed warm personal relations with all the American labor
leaders in Washington, and with those at the local level around
the country. I saw him regularly. He used his contacts to advance
the best interests of his country. On several occasions he influenced
directly the international policy statements of the CIO and AFL.
Years later, in the 1960s, when I was American minister in London, I gave a reception for the visiting George Meany, president
of the AFL-CIO. I invited all of Britain's labor leaders, whom
Meany naturally knew, and Archie Gordon. I couldn't help but
observe that Meany paid much more attention to Gordon, by then
retired, than to any British trade union colleague.

After a modest beginning, the U.S. labor attaché program became an accepted part of our Foreign Service. By 1953, a total
of thirty-three full-time labor attachés, twenty labor reporting
officers, and seven labor information officers were assigned to
more than fifty embassies. These labor attachés were the lifeblood
of our activities in the international labor field. They provided the
Departments of State and Labor with regular reports on developments in foreign labor movements, including estimates of the
effectiveness of Communist and non-Communist forces; on the
trend of wages, employment, and unemployment; and on the
causes and outcomes of major labor disputes. They also evaluated
the interaction between the labor movement and the various political movements of the country. They added new breadth and depth
to political and economic reporting.

Yet reporting is only part of the attaché's job. He has to explain
to unions, governments, and employers abroad the unique philosophy underlying American labor-management relations. The labor attaché is expected to develop contacts with key leaders in
the trade union movement, and to influence their thinking and
decisions in directions compatible with American goals.

Compared to the traditional diplomat, the labor attaché spent little time with the Foreign Office. His contacts were with union members, employers, labor political parties, ministries of labor and social affairs, and academics in the labor field. He roamed around the country to contact local trade union leaders and ordinary workers. In countries where labor parties were in power, he often provided the main personal liaison between top government officials and our ambassador. He had, in short, an unusual opportunity to enhance American influence among individuals and institutions that historically have had no contact with U.S. diplomatic missions. At the same time he could bring to his own government an authentic account of grass-roots developments in the country to which he was accredited. By focusing attention on the labor movement, he represented a new kind of diplomat.

Choosing the labor attachés was a major challenge. They came from within the Foreign Service and other government agencies and from academia and the labor movement. The State and Labor Departments cooperated in the selection process. Before nominating an attaché we tried to ensure that he met with the approval of both the AFL and CIO. The special cachet that this provided made it easier for him to develop a strong personal relationship with the trade unions in the host country, and in some situations to act as liaison between them and their American trade union colleagues.

Getting trade union "approval" of the labor attaché selected, while maintaining the government's authority to make the final choice, was not always easy, particularly during the years when the AFL and the CIO were separate organizations. They did not necessarily agree on international policies, and intense, sometimes bitter, competition arose between the international officials of both organizations. This inevitably spilled over into their attitudes about particular individuals. In addition, both organizations had a natural bias toward candidates from the trade union movement. We were anxious to hire people with a working-class background, but these nominees did not always have the requisite qualifications. The AFL and CIO resented our rejection of any of their recommendations. Dealing effectively with this situation required considerable diplomatic and negotiating skills.

Once appointed, labor attachés faced another problem—maintaining a working relationship with AFL and CIO international officials. This was particularly true in Europe where Irving Brown represented the AFL and Vic Reuther the CIO. These two able, aggressive men didn't always agree on strategy and tactics. While cooperating with both Brown and Reuther, the labor attaché had to maintain his integrity as a government official, and avoid being caught in the crossfire between them without being perceived as the "agent" of either one.

On the whole the labor attaché program was reasonably successful. Labor attachés were often key members of their respective embassies. Twelve subsequently became ambassadors. Two outstanding examples were Sam Berger in London and Ben Stephansky in Mexico City. Sam had spent a year in England just before the war (1937–38) on a Social Science Research Fellowship to study the British labor movement. Sam developed personal friendships with the leaders of the Labour Party and the trade unions at a time when the American embassy was paying little attention to them. These friendships proved invaluable during the war, when Sam served as Averell Harriman's labor adviser, and after 1945 when Sam became a labor attaché in London. With the Labour Party now in power, Sam had extraordinary access to many members of the cabinet, including the prime minister. It was universally recognized that he was the key member of our embassy. Later Sam served as our ambassador to Korea and, during the critical Vietnam years, was deputy ambassador in Saigon.

Stephansky's experience was equally interesting. Ben was teaching at the University of Chicago when he took a year off to work in the International Bureau of the Labor Department. He did such a fine job that after a year we convinced him to take up the position of labor attaché to Mexico. He quickly learned Spanish and assiduously cultivated trade union leaders and top officials in the Ministries of Labor and Social Affairs. He became a close personal friend of Adolfo Lopez Mateos, the minister of labor, who subsequently was elected president of Mexico.

Before Lopez Mateos was inaugurated, he was visited by the then–majority leader of the U.S. Senate, Lyndon Johnson. The Mexican president-elect had already received the names of the

American delegation to his inauguration. It was to be headed by Secretary of State John Foster Dulles. Lopez Mateos complained bitterly to Johnson that it did not include the one American who really understood Mexico, his dear friend Ben Stephansky, whom he had personally invited but who had not been named because it was a "high-level" delegation. At Johnson's insistence, President Eisenhower added Ben to the American delegation. Dulles, not very happy about this development, never made Ben feel quite welcome. In 1961, President Kennedy appointed Ben as ambassador to Bolivia, where he did an outstanding job.

Parallel to the developing governmental activities and essential to their effectiveness was the autonomous international activity of the American labor movement. Our government had to recognize the stake of American workers in foreign affairs and to accept labor's international political activity outside the traditional channels of diplomacy.

The AFL had a long history of international activity, dating from its first convention in 1881. It inspired the designation of May 1 as an international labor day to advocate the eight-hour work day, an event, ironically, later taken over by the Communists. Since 1894, the AFL had been exchanging delegates with the British Trades Union Congress to their respective annual conferences. Under the leadership of its first president, the dynamic cigar maker Samuel Gompers, leaders of the AFL joined with trade unionists in Europe to organize the International Federation of Trade Unions (IFTU). In the 1920s, however, responding to widespread isolationism and reacting against the insistence of socialist affiliates that a majority decision should be binding on all IFTU affiliates, the AFL withdrew from the organization.

By the late 1940s, as Communist pressure on labor mounted throughout the world, the American labor movement had broadened the scope of its international activities. It continued to take an active part in pressing for and supporting such government policies as military and economic aid, technical assistance, and a strong labor attaché program. It also had begun to develop its own machinery for directly assisting labor in other areas of the world, actively cooperating with foreign free trade union movements in their common struggle against totalitarianism. American trade unions had also shown a greater willingness to support practical economic concessions necessary for mutual assistance in the free world, such as reduction of tariff barriers.

In addition, American labor began to resolve its own internal differences. The formation in the mid-1930s of the CIO led to intense competition with the older AFL. The AFL had little sympathy with ideological movements that had an unbroken record of failure in the United States and that had sometimes caused the American trade unions serious difficulties with European trade union movements. The CIO, on the other hand, from its beginnings in 1936 became interested in international affairs, and in the mood of the times demonstrated greater tolerance and willingness to live with those who mix political ideology and trade unionism. Moreover, in its zeal to organize mass-production workers, the CIO was willing to utilize cadres from different radical groups. As a result, several of the CIO unions were led by left-wing ideologues who followed the Communist position on international issues.

The differences between the AFL and the CIO on international affairs were submerged after the Nazi invasion of the Soviet Union. They reemerged, however, in 1944 when, in the glow of the wartime alliance, the CIO and the British Trades Union Congress (TUC) joined with the Soviet Labor Organization (AUCCTU) to form a new international labor organization, the World Federation of Trade Unions (WFTU). The CIO and the British TUC hoped that the wartime alliance would continue. The AFL, however, not only refused to join the WFTU but attacked the CIO and British TUC for participating. The AFL, finding no common ground between legitimate trade unions and labor organizations formed and operated by the Soviet government, declared that mixing them in a single international trade union would have disastrous consequences for democratic trade unionism and for the Free World. Consequently, the AFL established independent international machinery and formulated its own policies, a chief objective of which was to neutralize the activities of the WFTU.

In 1947, Philip Murray, president of the CIO, responding to the confrontation between Moscow and the West, took steps to isolate the Communist-dominated CIO unions. His choice of Arthur Goldberg as his general counsel to replace the left-wing Lee Pressman* signaled his new course. Assistant Secretary Morse took advantage of this turn of events to form a high-level Trade Union Advisory Committee on International Affairs, with members from all sections of the American labor movement. This brilliant bureaucratic move was a historic breakthrough, highlighting the fact that the American trade unions indeed had a special role to play both in advising our government and in explaining America to labor abroad. Our unions were perhaps the most experienced sector in the American community to deal with Communism and to sort out the various idealogical strains running through Europe's non-Communist labor movements.

The Trade Union Advisory Committee made it possible for the first time for leaders of the CIO and the AFL to work regularly together, and to overcome the differences that had formerly kept them from even talking to each other, thereby weakening their impact on international affairs. The committee consisted of ten members, four each from the AFL and the CIO and two representing the railway brotherhoods, all key figures in their organizations. The AFL members were George Meany, who was then the secretary-treasurer; Matthew Woll, who was in charge of the International Affairs Committee of the AFL Executive Council; David Dubinsky, president of the International Ladies Garment Workers Union, and deeply interested in foreign affairs; and Philip Delaney, a full-time international representative of the AFL. The CIO contingent included James Carey, secretary-treasurer; Jack Potofsky, president of the Amalgamated Clothing Workers Union; Clinton Golden, a highly respected official of the United Steel Workers, and an intimate of Philip Murray; and Michael Ross, the CIO's international representative. The railway union representatives were Arthur Lyon, executive director of the Railway Labor Executives Association, and Thomas Harkin, an official of the Brotherhood of Railway Trainmen.

Two dynamic members of the committee were George Meany and David Dubinsky. Though their backgrounds were radically

---

*Long after, Pressman admitted that he had been a Communist and a member of a Communist caucus which determined political policies for Communist-controlled unions.

different, they were good friends and close allies, particularly on international issues. Meany, broad-shouldered and powerfully built, was a New York Irishman from the Bronx who, in his early twenties, had served the usual apprenticeship before becoming a full-fledged member of the Plumbers Union. His intelligence, vigor, and toughness, and his commitment to the broader objectives of American labor, enabled him to rise above the parochialism of his craft union background. He soon assumed leadership positions in the AFL—first as head of the New York State AFL and then, by the late 1940s, as secretary-treasurer of the national AFL and heir-apparent to the presidency.

Meany became president of the AFL in 1953 when William Green died, and for the next three decades dominated the American labor scene. He loved power and knew how to use it. He fought corruption, effected a merger with the CIO in 1955, pushed civil rights and health care programs, and greatly increased the AFL-CIO's political muscle. Although a supporter of the Democratic Party, his advice was sought by Republican as well as Democratic Presidents. Meany bore his power with easy self-assurance. In 1972, when I was attending the Democratic Party convention in Miami as a delegate of Democrats Abroad, I ran into Meany as he was sitting down in the Hotel Americana to have lunch with Lane Kirkland, his secretary-treasurer. While we were talking a bellboy came along and told Meany the White House was calling. Somewhat irritated, Meany got up and went to the lobby to pick up the phone. He returned about ten minutes later and said, quite ingenuously, "Who does Nixon think he is, calling me while I'm having lunch."

In the late 1940s when he was still secretary-treasurer, Meany became restless because President Green, in spite of his age, gave no sign that he had any intention of stepping down. There were members of Green's staff, particularly Thea Glenn, his executive secretary, and Florence Thorne, his elderly research director who had been an intimate of Samuel Gompers, who seemed determined to sustain Green in the presidency indefinitely and to frustrate Meany.

Meany overcame some of his frustration by asserting himself on international issues. As a dedicated disciple of Samuel Gompers, he vigorously opposed Communism and was an active participant in any program aimed at containing it. Nor did he like the European socialists. For decades he was one of the leading hard-liners in the country, refusing to countenance any contact with the Communist state-controlled "unions" in Eastern Europe. He rejected the argument of some Western European labor movements that they could influence the Communists rather than the other way around.* This attitude led to Meany's support of the temporary withdrawal of the United States from the International Labor Organization in the late 1970s because the organization's secretariat was suspected of catering to the Soviet and Eastern European members.

Meany was tough, frank, but reasonable, if your argument had merit. He was a guardian of AFL interests. I remember his refusal to agree to the appointment of a man from the CIO Newspaper Guild to head our labor information program. He recognized that the candidate was qualified, but Meany felt strongly that this was a job that "belonged" to the AFL. I enjoyed working with Meany. I appreciated his support for my appointment as assistant secretary of labor. I saw him regularly at our Advisory Committee meetings and at ILO conferences, and consulted with him often on matters of common interest.

Several times we crossed the Atlantic together on our way to ILO conferences. On one occasion I disembarked at Cherbourg with Mr. and Mrs. Meany because we were being driven to Paris to be on time for a meeting he and I were having with Averell Harriman. When we stopped briefly for lunch, Mrs. Meany asked me whether my French was good enough to order fruit salad without brandy. I assured her that it was, and told the waiter in my best French that Madame would like some fruit salad *sans*

---

*Years later, Anton Benya, the powerful leader of the Austrian trade union movement, and a devoted friend of the AFL-CIO, told me several times that he couldn't understand why Meany and Kirkland disapproved of his willingness to receive delegations from Eastern Europe. When the latter came to Vienna, Benya said, he always found them envious of what the free Austrian trade unions had been able to achieve.

Ironically, when I met Gaspar, the Hungarian labor leader who was also president of the Communist World Federation of Trade Unions, he praised Meany as one of the world's great trade union leaders, unmatched for what he had achieved for his country's workers.

alcool. Back came a large bowl of salad that Mrs. Meany realized, after one taste, was full of brandy. When I called over the waiter and chastised him for disregarding my request, he replied, "Whoever heard of eating fruit salad without brandy!" I'm afraid Mrs. Meany suspected that my French had been inadequate.

David Dubinsky differed from Meany in size and style as well as background. DD was short, stocky, dynamic, and domineering. He was a leading figure in New York politics, using the then lively Liberal Party as his instrument, and he relished his personal relationships with FDR, Truman, Kennedy, and Johnson. He was born and brought up in Poland, where he became a member of the Jewish Socialist Bund, which opposed the Communists. Soon after his arrival in America he joined the International Ladies Garment Workers Union and fought his way up to the presidency, after first serving as secretary-treasurer, the typical number-two post in many American trade unions.* In the course of his rise to power he had to defeat a Communist effort in the late 1920s to gain control of his union. This experience reinforced his hostility to Moscow's minions.

An active participant in the meetings of the Trade Union Advisory Committee, Dubinsky expressed his opinions bluntly and colorfully. He was skeptical at first about the government's willingness to participate in international labor programs. When, for example, I informed the Trade Union Advisory Committee that we were planning to bring over labor leaders from Germany and Austria to see how American trade unions operated, Dubinsky expressed doubt that the government would ever spend money for that purpose. Later his union cooperated handsomely with the program, acting as host to the visitors in different parts of the country.

We became close friends. I sometimes dined in New York with him and his wife, Emma, before taking off for Europe. On one occasion when my brother Jerry and his wife joined us, I made a genuine attempt to pick up the check. DD grabbed it the same moment. There ensued a struggle between Dubinsky and me. I

---

*Dubinsky told me that he retained his position as treasurer after becoming president because of the trouble he had caused his predecessor when he, Dubinsky, was secretary-treasurer.

yielded when he scoffingly said to me, "On your six dollars a day, you're gonna pay for this?" At that time six dollars was the figure for federal employees' per diem expenses.

Dubinsky's support for my work was invaluable, particularly when I had problems with Jay Lovestone, his adviser on international affairs. Lovestone was brilliant, but highly contentious. As a young man he had been chairman of the American Communist Party. When Stalin ordered him out of the Comintern, Lovestone formed his own splinter group called the Communist Party (Opposition) but generally referred to as "Lovestoneites." By the time he joined Dubinsky's staff he had become one of the most rabid anti-Communists in America. As is often the case with apostates, he was suspicious of those who, in his view, did not fully share his hostility toward Moscow. Liberals were frequently his *bêtes rouges*.

The Trade Union Advisory Committee became a major instrument for coordinating the activities of labor and government in the international field. It met regularly, first under the chairmanship of David Morse and then, after I was appointed assistant secretary, with me in the chair. The agendas for the meetings covered the full range of international issues, and discussions were vigorous and uninhibited. You would expect no less from a George Meany, a David Dubinsky, a Clint Golden, and a Jake Potofsky.

We solicited the committee's advice on what our position should be on issues before the ILO and what our policies should be on international trade; on how we should encourage the development of free trade union movements in Germany, Austria, and Japan; and how we should strengthen those movements around the world, particularly in Western Europe, which was struggling against the onslaught of the Communists. In the late 1940s and early 1950s the Communists dominated the national unions in France and Italy. The Communist-led organizations included a majority of the workers even after the free trade unions in both countries, with the help of American labor, broke away and established their own organizations. The Trade Union Advisory Committee's cooperation was essential for the success of our exchange program for foreign labor leaders and our labor information activities.

As assistant secretary of labor for international affairs I served as the department's representative on a large number of interdepartmental committees dealing with the full range of international issues. These included labor policies in the occupied countries; the administration of aid to Greece and Turkey under the Truman Plan, and later under the much larger Marshall Plan; and Point IV technical assistance. The backing of American labor added strength to the position of the Labor Department in these forums.

One special case where labor's backing was helpful involved reversing a decision by General MacArthur when he was ruling Japan. MacArthur had appointed trade union experts to his staff and had supported instituting a National Labor Relations Board for Occupied Japan. Later, in order to break a strike of workers in a government-controlled industry, he violated a contract that he had made with the government workers' union. The Labor Department, which was deeply involved in the development of free labor unions in Austria, Germany, and Japan, feared that MacArthur's action would stifle the normal legitimate growth of Japanese trade unions. When our demand for a reversal of MacArthur's decision was rejected by Undersecretary of the Army William Draper, we requested a hearing before Secretary Kenneth Royall. I vividly recall the meeting in Royall's vast office in the Pentagon. Draper brought along a retinue of about ten generals and top civilian officials. I was accompanied by one assistant, Arnold Steinbach, a refugee from Nazi Austria, who had become an expert on labor affairs in military government. Before the meeting I had learned that Secretary Royall, though a conservative Democrat, knew and respected both Philip Murray and Arthur Goldberg. I briefed the latter on the issue and he volunteered to speak to Royall about it.

Draper and his people made a powerful presentation, which emphasized that it was unwise for Washington to overrule a decision of the man in charge on the spot. I responded by stressing that compliance with contractual agreements was essential to the growth of free labor unions. When we were finished, Royall, a tall, impressive figure, stood up, looked out the window, turned about and, to the consternation of Draper and his people, said, "Order MacArthur to reverse his decision. There is nothing more disruptive to orderly development of a democratic society than the breaking of a contract."

The Trade Union Advisory Committee was particularly helpful in securing labor's support for Truman's Greek and Turkish aid program and for the Marshall Plan. The committee was informed of Truman's historic initiative in Greece and Turkey before it was made public. In a secret meeting arranged by David Morse, Dean Acheson, then undersecretary of state, explained the reasons for the President's historic decision and asked for labor's support in implementing it. The trade union leaders appreciated this recognition of their importance. They realized how essential the policy was to stop Moscow's threat to the Mediterranean and were eager to support it. Subsequently, when we asked the committee to choose a trade unionist to head the labor section of the mission established in Athens to run the program, they picked Clint Golden, a superb selection. Golden was knowledgeable, able, charismatic, and highly respected by his colleagues in the labor movement. Moreover, he had fought against Communist influence in the CIO. It was the first time that the AFL and the CIO had made a joint personnel recommendation for a position of this importance. It was particularly impressive that the AFL had proposed Golden. The way was cleared for subsequent collaboration although the path was not always smooth.

This new cooperation was put to the test when Golden chose as his deputy Alan Strachan, who had been an official of the United Auto Workers, another CIO union. The AFL initially felt that Golden should have chosen one of their people. When I pointed out that if we didn't allow a man of Golden's stature to pick his own deputy it would look like a vote of no confidence, they quickly withdrew their objection.

Most important was the Trade Union Advisory Committee's backing of the Marshall Plan. The American effort to rehabilitate Europe's economy represented one of the most remarkable initiatives in modern diplomatic history. At stake was the survival of free institutions in the nations of Western Europe at a time when postwar poverty and dislocation made them more vulnerable to Communist subversion. Essential to the success of the program was the support of the trade unions. Not surprisingly, Moscow's efforts to sabotage European recovery concentrated on France and Italy. The collaboration of American labor and the democratic sectors of the French and Italian trade union movements helped frustrate Communist attempts to prevent the unloading of Marshall aid equipment and supplies.

Thanks to the Marshall Plan, Richard Nixon also came to realize the importance of free trade unions. In 1949, when he was still a congressman, he visited Europe with a delegation of colleagues to see how the Marshall Plan was working. After returning to Washington, he asked me to come up to the Hill to talk about the role of labor in Europe. He had discovered that the survival of democracy depended on strong, free trade unions. In implementing the European Recovery Plan, the United States had to encourage their growth. In subsequent years Nixon and I discussed the subject several times, once in 1951 during a lengthy lunch at the Hôtel Crillon in Paris. He was on his way home from Geneva after serving as a delegate to the annual conference of the World Health Organization and I was en route to the annual conference of the International Labor Organization. As we were finishing the meal, Vic Reuther, the CIO representative in Europe, who had been eating alone, came by. I introduced him to Nixon and Nixon asked Reuther to join us for coffee. Nixon was keenly interested in Vic's comments on the European labor scene. Nineteen years later, when Nixon came to London as President and I was still minister in the embassy, he recalled the lunch and the meeting with Reuther.

Happily, Paul Hoffman, the director of the Mutual Security Agency that ran the European Recovery Program, and Averell Harriman, who directed its activities in Europe, needed no new experience or education to appreciate the role of labor in achieving the objectives of the program. At the very beginning they came to us in the Labor Department and to our Trade Union Advisory Committee for help in providing trade union personnel to staff their labor divisions at the Washington headquarters as well as at Harriman's operating headquarters in Paris and in the aid missions in each of the European countries receiving Marshall assistance. This was no small or easy task. However, able people were found, and the AFL and CIO were satisfied that both had been fairly treated in staffing the labor side of the Mutual Security Agency.

My trips to Europe—three times a year for ILO meetings between 1948 and 1953—enabled me to keep in touch with Marshall Plan developments on the Continent. I always stopped off in Paris en route to or from Geneva, invariably visiting with Harriman. After we exchanged notes on labor's international efforts, he was anxious to hear the latest news and gossip about labor's activities at home. He was clearly interested in trade union support should he decide to run for political office. On one occasion I saw Harriman in Geneva at six-thirty in the morning. He was attending a meeting of the Economic Commission for Europe and invited me to the first of three breakfasts he had scheduled for the one day he was in town.

The Marshall Plan was a major factor in resolving a festering conflict between the AFL and CIO on how to deal with the international organization of trade unions. As related earlier, when the CIO had joined the new World Federation of Trade Unions, the AFL had refused to do so because the government-controlled Soviet labor organizations were members. When Moscow attacked the Marshall Plan, not only refusing to participate itself, but forcing Czechoslovakia and Poland to do the same, the WFTU also came out against it. As a result, the CIO, which was then in the throes of expelling its Communist-controlled unions, withdrew from the WFTU. The British TUC followed suit. The scene was set for a new free trade union international, the International Confederation of Free Trade Unions (ICFTU), which, for the first time, included the AFL and the CIO as members.

While the Marshall Plan provided the context, it was the history of their cooperation in the Labor Department's Trade Union Advisory Committee that had helped clear the way for this historic collaboration between the leaders of the AFL and the CIO.

When the organizational meeting of the ICFTU took place in London in June 1948, AFL and CIO members of the American delegation asked me to attend as an observer. The invitation reflected the fact that, thanks to frequent contacts with labor leaders over several years, I had developed warm personal relationships with them. It was unusual for a government official to be included in purely trade union meetings, but the Americans requested that I be allowed to be present, and the British hosts raised no objections. I had, in fact, become acquainted with high-level British trade unionists during a visit to Europe in 1947.

Several incidents outside the regular meetings illustrated the relationship between American and foreign labor leaders. I was having tea in the Hyde Park Hotel with David Dubinsky, when he received a message from his old friend Ernie Bevin, the former head of the British Transport Workers Union who had become Britain's foreign secretary. Dubinsky had asked to see him, to ease the tension resulting from Bevin's surly remarks about the influence of New York Jews on the American attitude toward Palestine. Dubinsky's union, the ILGW, had sent Bevin's transport workers a gift of $50,000 during the war to finance a special mess for bombed-out members. In his message, Bevin stated that he would be happy to receive his old friend Dubinsky on condition that Dubinsky not talk about the Middle East. When Dubinsky asked me how he might respond, I told him he had no choice but to proceed with the meeting. He was unhappy about the restriction, but told me later he nevertheless enjoyed reminiscing with his old trade union friend.

Earlier Dubinsky had told me of an experience in Germany the week before his arrival in London. He and four or five other American labor leaders had met with a group of old German trade unionists. He knew they were not Nazis but he was unable to say a word during the session of several hours. When Dubinsky's American colleagues, accustomed to his indefatigable ebullience, asked him why he didn't speak, he replied that he felt too hostile toward the Germans and didn't want to cause any embarrassment. He couldn't forget that over thirty of his relatives had lost their lives in the Holocaust. He was stunned, however, when he was told that together the ten German trade unionists in the meeting had spent over one hundred years in concentration camps. He felt guilty, he told me, about his behavior. This was a dramatic reminder to him that not all Germans were Nazis, especially the trade unionists. He did penance by talking about this incident in public several times after his return to New York.

The meetings in London proceeded smoothly, and resulted in the foundation of a new labor international, which was to become a rallying point for free labor around the world.

Forming the ICFTU was not the first attempt at organizing free world labor. However, it differed from its predecessors in several respects. For the first time in a century-long history, the free trade unions were able to overcome ideological differences that had previously limited the scope of their activities. Neither the constitution of the ICFTU nor its manifesto mentioned "socialist," "nationalization," or, in fact, "free enterprise objectives." Free trade unionism rather than political ideology became the cohesive force in the organization and the program of the ICFTU. The new organization also shunned the pacifism that so conspicuously weakened previous labor internationals. From its inception the ICFTU actively supported resistance to the totalitarian threat against free labor. It became a strong partisan of the Marshall Plan and NATO.

These provisions reflected the practical needs of the European unions as well as the new power and influence of the American trade unions. Antagonistic to Communism, American trade unions provided a successful example of economic unionism that had made large gains for its workers within a capitalistic society. American unions emphasized the importance of experimentation and flexibility in letting workers determine the type of organization that best met their needs. The American experience was in practical contradiction to the concept of class struggle, which taught that, with the insoluble barrier between employer and employee, labor-management cooperation was little more than a truce in the unremitting struggle between classes. American labor's record of militancy, industrial struggle, and fighting for the rights of the common man enabled it to communicate, with fraternal feeling, with other workers of the world.

The third new factor in the ICFTU was its universality. Earlier internationals were predominantly European in membership as well as in outlook. Europe's unions play a major role in the ICFTU, but the new international's affiliates and activities were to cover the world to an extent unknown before, including Latin America, Australia, the Middle East, Southeast Asia, and Africa. In the developing areas of the world the ICFTU has encouraged the creation of new democratic unions capable of satisfying the legitimate needs of their members, a difficult objective because in the newly independent countries political parties with a labor base are often tempted to control workers' organizations.

The U.S. government, particularly the Labor Department, cooperated with the new international, but we were always conscious of its genuine independence. When the first secretary-general of the ICFTU, J. Oldenbroek, a Dutch trade unionist who, during the war, had been active in the underground movement, visited the United States, I arranged for President Truman to receive him. We were not surprised when the President demonstrated that he was familiar with the main international labor issues, but he bowled us over, particularly Oldenbroek, when he displayed a rather remarkable knowledge of Dutch seventeenth-century naval history.

The ICFTU complemented and strengthened the activities of the International Labor Organization. Established in 1919, the ILO is the oldest functioning international institution. When the Communist revolution that had engulfed Russia by 1918 threatened the stability of other European countries, the Allied powers were faced with the urgency of creating some democratic machinery through which they could raise workers' living standards. Otherwise there was a danger that labor would lose faith in democracy and, in frustration, succumb to the promises of the Russian revolution.

As a consequence, the Peace Conference in 1919 created the International Labor Organization as the instrument through which labor could participate in solving economic and social problems and help in the development of international labor standards. The ILO was unique in one other respect. Its tripartite structure gave labor and management, as well as government, direct representation with full participating and voting rights.

In spite of the role Samuel Gompers played in the creation of the ILO, the United States did not join it after the Senate rejected the Treaty of Versailles. Ironically, before that rejection the first session of the ILO governing body was held in Washington. I learned from Léon Jouhaux, the French labor leader who attended the meeting, that Samuel Gompers, acting as host, took special care of the foreign members. The Volstead Act, which provided for the enforcement of the Prohibition Amendment, the eighteenth, had gone into effect just before the meeting convened. Familiar with the tastes and habits of his foreign colleagues, Gompers apparently arranged to have a bottle of whiskey placed under the table in front of the chair of each participant.

Thanks to the initiative of Secretary of Labor Frances Perkins and the support of President Roosevelt, the United States did join the ILO in 1934, in spite of nonmembership in the League of

Nations. This action reflected some movement away from the isolationism that had dominated the 1920s. Madame Perkins took an active interest in the work of the organization. She led the American delegation to the annual conferences and later was largely instrumental in maintaining the ILO during the war years when its headquarters were temporarily moved from Geneva to Montreal.

After becoming assistant secretary I called on Madame Perkins because I had heard of her continuing interest in the ILO. She was then a member of the Civil Service Commission and from time to time I lunched in her office, invariably with the same menu: a rather tepid bean soup, a tuna fish sandwich with slightly stale white bread and, the *pièce de résistance*, apple pie à la mode. Except gastronomically, these were always special occasions for me. Madame Perkins was a remarkable person—warm, wise, knowledgeable, and a dedicated New Dealer. One of her favorite subjects was the "overrated male species." A superb raconteuse, she told me about the top executives of American industry who came to Washington after FDR's inauguration and begged the government to take over their companies.

During one lunch she recalled her first visit to Independence, Missouri, when campaigning for Al Smith, the Democratic candidate for President in 1928, and the first Catholic nominee for that office. She was told to ask the county judge, Harry Truman, for help in arranging a public meeting. Truman was very supportive. He was impressed with her courage, but concerned about her security because of the prevalence of anti-Smith sentiment in that predominantly Protestant area. He insisted that a Protestant clergyman open her meeting, but could find only a lay minister who was willing to do so.

In the spring of 1952 Madame Perkins asked me to arrange for her to be an adviser to the U.S. delegation to the annual ILO conference. Before retiring in December, she wanted to participate in the world of the ILO once more and see her old friends. I thought it was a splendid idea and Secretary Tobin felt the same way. Her presence made it the most respected delegation in the four years I served as delegation chairman. I recall vividly the tears that welled up in the eyes of some delegates when they greeted her, and the ovation she received when, in my speech before a plenary session, I expressed the pride of the American delegation in having Madame Perkins as one of our colleagues.

One of the main responsibilities of the new assistant secretary of labor for international affairs, David Morse, was the direction of our government's participation in the International Labor Organization. He naturally became the U.S. government's member on the governing body and chairman of the delegation to the annual conference. His commitment to the work of the organization, his competence in handling its problems, and the skill with which he managed the U.S. tripartite delegation of government, worker, and employee representatives made a deep impression not only in Washington but also among the representatives of the other countries. In June 1948 the governing body elected him director of the organization. He served for twenty-two years and made the ILO a major force in world affairs, particularly on social issues. In 1969 the ILO received the Nobel Peace Prize for its contribution to social progress and stability.

As the successor to Morse in the Department of Labor, I served as the U.S. government member on the governing body from November 1948 to June 1953 and chaired our delegation to the annual conference each of those years except 1953. That year, with the Republicans in power and my term approaching its end, I suggested that my fellow delegate, Senator Irving Ives of New York, be chairman. Martin Durkin, President Eisenhower's Secretary of Labor, agreed that this would increase the Republican Party's interest in the work of the ILO.*

I also chaired our delegation to the regional meeting of the American state members held in Brazil in 1952. At that meeting we coped successfully with the Argentine Peronista delegation, which was aggressively opposed to the United States. Peronism was a radical populist movement. Though nominally anti-Communist, it had some features of Italian and Spanish fascism, particularly its support of state control of trade unions and its emphasis on strong-arm government. It often voted with the left, and its influence in Latin America was rising. In a speech before the conference I emphasized our commitment to strengthening

---

*We later arranged for Ives to be elected president of the conference.

free labor unions and our determination to improve the conditions of Latin American workers.

I have a special reason for being greatly indebted to my Brazilian hosts. The conference was originally scheduled to end on a Monday afternoon and I had planned to fly back to Washington that night. The Brazilians decided to ask the delegates to take a day off to visit their new modern steel plant, Volta Redonda. As a consequence the conference ended on Tuesday. The Pan Am plane which left Rio Monday night crashed in the Amazon jungle with no survivors.

Like Morse, I found my responsibilities relating to the ILO challenging as the organization coped with postwar demands. Until 1948 the ILO had concentrated on the development of international labor standards. These standards, developed at the annual labor conferences, were in the form of either conventions or recommendations. Conventions are similar to international treaties and subject to ratification. When a member state ratifies a convention, it is obligated to bring national legislation in line. Recommendations, on the other hand, do not require ratification and do not have the force of law. They are important, however, as norms and goals. Together the ILO conventions and recommendations constitute the international labor code that provides a model for national legislation and practice in member countries.

In the late 1940s the United States successfully pushed for the approval of two conventions that have had a major impact on social and political developments around the world. The first, approved in the annual conference of 1948, dealt with freedom of association. It stipulated that "workers and employers, without distinction whatsoever, shall have the right to establish and, subject only to rules of the organization concerned, to join organizations of their own choosing without previous authorization." The convention goes on to guarantee the right of organizations to operate free from government interference.

These fundamental rights were strengthened by a convention passed the following year on the right to organize and bargain collectively. I chaired our delegation that year when we government delegates and the American labor delegates actively supported this convention while the American employers opposed it. A governing body committee on freedom of association was set up to handle complaints in this field. It has examined over one thousand cases since its creation, including the Polish government's early oppression of Solidarity.

While continuing its traditional work on the development of labor standards, in the late 1940s the ILO initiated an extensive operations program focusing on technical aid to developing countries. Assistance was provided in many fields—vocational training, cooperatives, social security, employment services, industrial training, industrial safety, and labor legislation—all of great importance to newly independent countries. Regional offices were set up in Asia, Africa, and Latin America to direct these programs on the spot. The ILO is now devoting a large share of its resources to technical assistance.

The ILO program was initiated before President Truman launched his Point Four program in his 1949 inaugural address. The ILO proposal for technical assistance was on the agenda of the first governing body meeting I attended, in November 1948, and, ironically, my instructions were to vote against it because we had doubts about the ILO's ability to run such a program, and because it involved additional expenditures. When it became apparent that the proposal was enthusiastically supported by every member of the governing body except me, I decided that it would be a mistake to oppose it. There was not enough time to ask Washington to change its instructions before the vote was scheduled. I turned for advice to David Zellerbach, president of the Crown Zellerbach Corporation and for several years the U.S. employer member on the governing body. He was a highly intelligent man, sensible, and dedicated to the work of the ILO, who five years later became Eisenhower's ambassador to Italy. He had earned the respect of all his governing body colleagues, government and workers as well as employers. He strongly supported the proposed technical assistance program and thought it would be a mistake for me to vote against it. He suggested that when the vote came up I could manage to be engaged in the men's room. I followed his advice.

The ILO was the beginning of my education in diplomacy. There could be no better training than being a member of the governing body and chairman of the U.S. delegation to the annual conference. The governing body met three times a year, and each session involved a fortnight of intensive meetings when compromises had to be worked out, not only among government representatives but also with workers and employers.

After participating in several governing body meetings, I became aware of the national and professional predilections of each member. It was not always easy to reconcile the differences between a British employer delegate who was head of the Federation of British Industries and a French trade union leader, or, for that matter, between the American worker and employer delegates. Happily, personal relationships often proved useful in calming troubled waters.

Among my cherished friends were two Frenchmen: Paul Ramadier, who, as the socialist prime minister of France, had driven the Communists out of the cabinet in 1947; and Léon Jouhaux, the French trade unionist who had been a member of the governing body from its inception in 1919, and won the Nobel Peace Prize some thirty-nine years later. Ramadier, the most prestigious member of the governing body, sat next to me, the youngest and newest member (we were seated alphabetically—France followed États-Unis). I was grateful for his wisdom and kindness. Never condescending, he always treated me as a colleague and taught me a great deal about parliamentary procedure and the importance of being firm but tactful with representatives of other nations. He had a delightful Gallic sense of humor. He would make amusing comments about our colleagues, sometimes in the form of written couplets that he would pass on to me.

Ramadier and I often exchanged friendly barbs. I remember trying to tease him when we walked out of a committee meeting together and were informed that North Korea had invaded South Korea. At that very moment the French were lacking a government after one of those political crises that were so frequent under the Fourth Republic. "We have an international crisis," I said to Ramadier, "and once again there is no French government." Smiling wisely, he replied, "You're right, my dear colleague, but when you have nothing to say and there is nothing you can do, it is pretty smart not to have a government."

I had my differences with Ramadier when he was chairman of the governing body, usually about procedural matters, but we found ways to resolve them. During a coffee break after a heated exchange between us, he walked over to me and asked whether I liked Roquefort cheese. When I told him I certainly did, he said he would send me "the real Roquefort produced only in my native southern France." A month later I received a ten-pound box of Roquefort, enough to keep the family awash in this excellent cheese for many months.

My ILO friendships with Italians proved helpful in a rather special situation. Before I left Washington for a governing body meeting in 1951, Tom Lane, our labor attaché in Italy, urged me to spend the weekend in Rome between the fortnight sessions. When I got to Geneva I found that there were no commercial flights to Rome that Friday evening. I phoned Lane to tell him that I would have to cancel my trip. "Oh, no," he replied, "we must get you here." He called back in a few minutes to inform me that Ambassador James Dunn was sending his air attaché to Geneva to pick me up. Lane came along to describe his "plot." He had organized a reception in my honor and invited Rodolfo Rubinacci, the minister of labor, and Giulio Pastore, the head of the non-Communist trade union movement. Lane was sure they would come because they were friends of mine. And that was the reason for the reception. Rubinacci and Pastore had been quarreling and were so angry with each other that for weeks they had refused even to meet. This was hurting our efforts to strengthen the democratic elements in the Italian trade union movement. Lane's plan worked. They came, they shook hands, and thereafter resumed their personal relationship.

Not surprisingly, I found the bureaucracy of international organizations even more frustrating than that of national governments. Developing consensus on important issues among several dozen governments, their employers, and workers took special effort and skill, and administering a secretariat made up of representatives from the different member nations was not an easy task.

Two things soon became clear: First, the members of the ILO staff were adept at playing off labor members of the governing body against government and employer members to serve their own ends. The secretariat staff could always count on the support of the workers' group when it made unreasonable demands about salaries, holidays, and pensions. And, second, most members of the governing body loved to come to Geneva, not only for governing body meetings, but for the large number of other meetings, technical and regional, to which a tripartite group was always sent as "observers." For most employer and worker representatives and some of the government membership on the governing body, this was their full-time job, and the more sessions in Switzerland and other parts of the world the better.

When I realized that the ILO was the only specialized agency of the United Nations whose governing body met three times rather than twice a year, I proposed that the ILO hold only two meetings. This would save a good deal of money—employers, particularly, were always complaining about "unnecessary" expenditures—and a good deal of time for those of us who had other responsibilities. We lobbied the members of the governing body and got a strong negative reaction from both workers and employers. They just loved to attend the meetings for which they received a handsome per diem from the ILO. Nevertheless, I managed to line up enough votes among the government members to carry my proposal, including the Cuban, in this pre-Castro era, whose enthusiastic support I clinched with a bottle of bourbon.

I was always in close touch with our consul general in Geneva, Ed Ward, whom I knew well from Washington. The Cuban member on the governing body was also their consul general in Geneva. When Ward told me that he and the Cuban were good friends, I asked for his help in securing the Cuban's vote for my proposal. "That's as easy as a bottle of bourbon," said Ward. "This guy loves bourbon. I'll arrange a lunch for you and him. You give him your pitch and when he leaves you hand him a bottle of bourbon. And he'll vote for you on any issue you name." I agreed to Ward's plan and it worked like a charm. In fact, it worked too well. In an impassioned speech in the governing body the Cuban talked about reducing the meetings from three to two as if it would be one of the greatest achievements since the invention of the wheel.

Our proposal carried by a majority of two. However, as soon as the vote was announced, the leader of the workers' group, Alf Roberts, a British trade unionist, rose and said, "I hereby serve notice that every year we will automatically take advantage of the provision in the standing orders of the governing body which stipulates that any time eight members of the governing body ask for a meeting, the director must comply with that request. We eight worker members will always make that request." I had no alternative but to withdraw my proposal.

Paul Finet, the Belgian labor member and the able head of the Belgian Federation of Labor, later chairman of the Iron and Steel Community, came to see me before the governing body met. He was a member of the workers' group. "Phil," he said, "I want you to know how delighted I am with your proposal. I have a full-time job: I'm trying to run the Belgian labor movement. These meetings take too much of my time." Nevertheless, Roberts got Finet to vote with the workers' group against my proposal—an example of international bureaucracy at its worst.

I had difficulties with the American employer delegate and some of his advisers. The U.S. Chamber of Commerce selected Charles McCormick, president of the McCormick Spice Company, to replace David Zellerbach. This choice represented a fall from grace. Apparently the original idea was to select Fowler McCormick, the chairman of International Harvester, an enlightened employer like Zellerbach, whose employees were represented by the United Automobile Workers. Fowler couldn't accept and instead they chose Charles, no relative, blood or otherwise. The latter, a hard conservative, had a company union, a grievous mistake for a U.S. employer delegate to an international organization where all of the worker delegates, except those from Eastern Europe, represented authentic trade unions. The United States spent millions of dollars on its information program to help develop a favorable attitude toward our country among workers around the world. In the ILO we had a unique forum for doing precisely that. A liberal employer delegate like David Zellerbach helped us achieve our objective; a Charles McCormick did just the opposite.

McCormick antagonized not only the workers; the employer delegates from other countries also found him difficult to digest. He was bombastic, showy, ignorant about the international scene, and, perhaps worst of all, obviously not sympathetic to the objectives of the ILO. Moreover, McCormick was dominated by his chief adviser, Will McGrath from Ohio, an authentic reactionary: anti-FDR, anti-Truman, and, above all, anti-labor. I tried again and again to educate McCormick about the realities of the ILO world, but once he came under the influence of McGrath it was impossible to get him to see the light.

McGrath, who was also an isolationist, stirred up the American employers' concern about ILO conventions which, if ratified, superseded domestic law. McGrath—and McCormick—were sure that the Truman administration, with the help of labor, was planning to "socialize" the United States by having the Senate ratify conventions on social issues approved at ILO conferences. This was pure fantasy. They refused to recognize that there was adequate protection against any such development, particularly the requirement for a two-thirds Senate approval of any proposal. McGrath encouraged his senator from Ohio, John Bricker, to introduce the Bricker Amendment, which would have radically changed our treaty-making process by requiring House as well as Senate approval, and in some instances involve action by individual states as well.

The Bricker Amendment never carried, but it did generate sufficient political paranoia to inhibit sensible government action. In the early 1950s, thanks to the efforts of the American government and labor delegates, the ILO conference approved a proposed convention on slave labor, which was aimed at the vicious practices in the Soviet Union. Because of the atmosphere generated by Bricker, Secretary of State John Foster Dulles refused to submit the convention to the Senate for ratification, and until today we have taken no action on it. This in spite of the fact that the provisions of the Thirteenth Amendment to our Constitution put us automatically in compliance with the convention's provisions.

The McCormick-McGrath concern about the danger of conventions was utterly unrealistic for another reason. Because of our federal structure, ratification of conventions meant that every one of our states had to pass legislation meeting the convention standards in order for us to be in compliance. As a result, we ratified few conventions. In fact, we took the initiative in having the constitution of the ILO revised with new provisions stipulating that if a federal government could show that the laws and practices of each of their states met the standards of the convention, the country would then be in compliance without the need for formal ratification at the federal level.

There was an additional aspect of the new ILO constitution,

which had unfortunate consequences. When, in 1948, the U.S. Senate ratified it—technically it was a treaty—the Senate stipulated that henceforth every individual attending an ILO meeting, either as a delegate or an adviser, had to be investigated by the FBI and cleared by the secretary of labor.

When this proposal about FBI investigations was first made, Senator Elbert Thomas, chairman of the Labor Committee, asked me to check whether the White House was willing to go along with it. Thomas himself was against it. Morse was away attending an ILO conference. I urged the White House to oppose it but they decided that, due to the atmosphere at that time and our desire to secure ratification of the new ILO constitution, we had to go along with the amendment.

Tobin was never happy about this provision. If there were any question about the loyalty of a proposed delegate to an ILO conference or one of the advisers, the secretary had to make the final clearance decision. The issue came up dramatically on two occasions. The first involved the popular Jack Potofsky, president of the Amalgamated Clothing Workers, scheduled one year to be a member of the workers' delegation to the ILO conference. Jack was one of our best-known and highly respected labor leaders. The official in the Labor Department who read the file in the first instance was the director of personnel, a serious young man who was neither liberal nor conservative but rather a political cipher. Potofsky had made some harmless public statements about the Soviet Union that were included in this FBI report, and that McCarthyites could easily misinterpret. The director of personnel used them to raise questions about Potofsky's loyalty and insisted that he and I take the matter up with Secretary Tobin.

When we walked into the secretary's office—I had told him why we were coming to see him—Tobin said to me, "I will waste no time reading the FBI report on Jack Potofsky. I'm amazed that you suggested that I do so. I have known Jack for many years, as you have, and he is a better American citizen than you and I. Of course he's cleared to go to the ILO conference."

The second case did not have such a happy ending. It involved the liberal senator from Utah, Elbert Thomas. After the election in 1948, when the Democrats retained control of the Senate, he again became chairman of the Senate Labor Committee. The ILO

delegation to the annual conference was made up of two government delegates, one employer and one worker, with advisers for
each group. The first government delegate and chairman of the
entire delegation was the assistant secretary of labor for international affairs, and we had developed the practice of picking the
chairman of the Senate Labor Committee as the second government delegate. Early in 1949 we asked Senator Thomas to attend
the conference in June and he happily agreed. This automatically
triggered an FBI investigation of him.

However, President Truman had other ideas. The first item on
his agenda after his victory in 1948 was repeal of the Taft-Hartley
Act (which he never succeeded in accomplishing). The President
stated that we couldn't take Thomas to Geneva because, as chairman of the Labor Committee, he was needed by the President to
handle the repeal legislation. About a year and a half later, in 1950,
Thomas was running for reelection to the Senate. He and other
liberals, like Joseph O'Mahoney of Wyoming and Scott Lucas of
Illinois, were special targets of the right-wing Republicans led by
McCarthy. The latter ran a filthy campaign uninhibited by decency or fairness. Early in October I received a desperate call from
Senator Thomas. "Phil," he said, "can you get the secretary to
come out and help me? I'm in real trouble here. They're murdering
me with that FBI investigation that was launched when you first
invited me to be an ILO delegate. My opponents are going around
the state saying, 'We told you what a dangerous radical the senator
was. He's so dangerous that the FBI has had to investigate him.'"

I immediately reported this conversation to Secretary Tobin.
He was sick about it. He went out to Utah and campaigned for
Thomas who, like several of his liberal colleagues, was defeated.
Subsequently, on more than one occasion, Tobin expressed his
distress over this development.

Unexpectedly I stayed on as assistant secretary of labor until
July 1953. I had declined the chairmanship of the ILO governing
body in June 1952 because I thought it unfair to take on this
responsibility when it was uncertain that I would be available for
a one-year term. A Republican victory in the fall would mean that
I would leave office shortly after the new President's inauguration
in January. My refusal was not a vote of no confidence in Adlai
Stevenson. On the contrary, I thought a candidate so exceptionally

talented would appeal to a majority of American voters. I cheer-fully made campaign speeches for Stevenson during a two-week swing along the West Coast. Stevenson, however, understood the American electorate much better than I. When someone told him not to worry about the outcome because all the intelligent people in the country would vote for him, he replied, "If that's the only vote I receive, I'll surely lose."

After Martin Durkin, whom I knew well, was appointed secre-tary of labor in Eisenhower's cabinet (a plumber surrounded by eight millionaires), he asked me to stay on long enough to attend the ILO conference in June as a delegate with Senator Irving Ives of New York to help educate Republicans about the importance of the ILO. I agreed to go. There was an additional personal reason for doing so—a celebration in Oxford of the fiftieth anniversary of the Rhodes Scholarship was to take place two days after the conclusion of the ILO conference. I resigned soon after my return to Washington in mid-July.

The Communist world has been dismantled, and it is altogether fitting that Poland played a crucial role in that development. There is social justice, too, in the fact that Solidarity, a free labor union movement, has been the major instrument in the unraveling of Poland's dictatorship and its move toward democracy. The road for Solidarity was long and difficult. No one, no expert on Com-munism, believed that a free labor union movement could survive in a Communist-controlled country. But the idea of Solidarity refused to die, and its leaders, followed by millions of loyal mem-bers, refused to give up, in spite of Solidarity's being outlawed after its initial recognition. Throughout its struggle, and particu-larly during the years of its underground existence, Solidarity was helped by the free trade unions of the world, particularly the AFL-CIO, which maintained regular contact with the Polish labor movement, and by the ILO.

Poland, like all Eastern European countries, had ratified Con-vention 87, Freedom of Association and Protection of the Right to Organize, passed in 1948, and Convention 98, The Right to Organize and Bargain Collectively, passed in 1949, without any intention of complying with its provisions. But these ratifications opened the door for subsequent ILO action. In 1978, responding to complaints from the International Confederation of Free Trade Unions, the ILO found that the Polish Labor Code, which required that all Polish unions had to register with the government-controlled Central Council of Trade Unions, violated Convention 87. The ILO repeatedly requested that Poland change its labor legislation.

In 1981, the year after Poland initially recognized Solidarity, Lech Walesa attended the sixty-seventh session of the International Labor Organization conference as Poland's worker delegate. This provided a unique opportunity for Walesa to make contact with the mainstream of Free World labor, to tell the Polish story to an international audience, and to develop a wide range of new, invaluable friendships. After Solidarity was outlawed, the ILO kept up its institutional pressure on the Polish government to cease violating Conventions 87 and 98.

Walesa did not forget the support he received from both the ICFTU and the ILO. In May 1989, on the eve of Solidarity's great victory in Poland's free election, he told the director general of the ILO that "the International Labor Organization played an important part in the process leading to the restoration of trade union freedom in Poland." He expressed the wish that cooperation between the ILO and the Polish trade union movement would continue in the future. Walesa made his statements the day after his historic first appearance at the executive board meeting of the ICFTU. In his speech before the world's free trade union leaders Walesa praised the ICFTU for its support of Solidarity in the ILO, as well as its material aid. At that time, he also singled out the AFL-CIO for years of steadfast moral and material assistance. At a critical moment in Solidarity's early years, Monsignor George Higgins, the beloved American labor priest, was able to secure an entry visa to Poland and carry a message of support from the AFL-CIO's president, Lane Kirkland, whom the Poles would not allow to visit their country.

With the collapse of the Communist world, it is too easy to forget the intensity of the Cold War in the late 1940s and early 1950s. The threat from Moscow was painfully real and the United States had to take the lead in institutionalizing our containment of Communism's challenge. I was fortunate to be involved in the role that labor played in that effort, a role not widely known by the American public, for it meant participating in the crucial socioeconomic sector of that struggle. I remain grateful to those who made this participation possible, particularly my brother Henry, David Morse, Maurice Tobin, the leaders of the American labor movement, and, of course, President Truman.

5

Albany After Washington: Averell Harriman, Governor of New York

On a September evening in 1954, Averell Harriman, George Ball, and I were driving around the Sixty-ninth Street Armory in New York City while the delegates to the Democratic State Convention were nominating Harriman for governor. (The old, sensible rule that candidates must not appear on the floor until one was actually chosen was still in effect.) Harriman's victory was the culmination of an intense battle with Franklin D. Roosevelt, Jr. The long-standing personal relationships between the Roosevelts and the Harrimans added an extra dramatic dimension to the contest. Harriman's sister Mary and Eleanor Roosevelt had worked together in the 1920s in support of New York State's liberal social legislation that had marked the administration of Governor Al Smith. Their allies in this effort were their old friend Frances Perkins,* whom Governor Al Smith had appointed to the State Industrial Commission, and Belle Moscowitz, who was the governor's able executive assistant. Mary Rumsey encouraged her brother Averell to join the Democratic Party in 1928 and to sup-

---

*Many years later, during a visit to Albany when Harriman was governor, Miss Perkins talked to me about some of the boyhood obstacles Harriman had to overcome. People knew about his dynamic and domineering father, but his mother, Perkins emphasized, was also a powerful personality. When a student at Yale, Harriman had been an extreme stutterer and, remarkably, he had completely overcome that severe handicap.

port Al Smith in the presidential contest that year. And later Harriman emerged as a key figure in the Roosevelt administration, serving as FDR's special Lend-Lease ambassador and subsequently as his ambassador to the Soviet Union.

In the late spring of 1954, FDR Jr. seemed to be the popular Democratic choice for governor. Cashing in on the still potent attraction of the Roosevelt name, reinforced by his own ebullient personality so reminiscent of his father, he had garnered the support of most of the upstate and suburban Democratic leaders. FDR Jr. had also recruited a talented group of advisers, including Jack Bingham, who served as his research director; Lou Harris, the well-known pollster; Daniel Patrick Moynihan, a young political activist; and Justin Feldman, Roosevelt's administrative assistant. Roosevelt had hoped that the combination of his personal popularity and the competence of his staff would make his candidacy irresistible to the New York Democratic bosses, particularly Carmine DeSapio, who, as the Democratic National Committeeman from New York and the party leader in Manhattan, dominated the bosses of the other four boroughs. Because the city's delegates to the state nominating convention surpassed in number the total of the rest of the state, DeSapio would, in fact, pick the nominee. Inevitably, his support became the main target of both Roosevelt and Harriman.

FDR Jr. might have bypassed DeSapio and won the nomination had he decided to put up his own slate of delegates in Brooklyn to oppose the machine's candidates. It was generally recognized that anyone running under the Roosevelt banner was unbeatable in Brooklyn, the largest borough in New York City. But FDR Jr.'s advisers urged him not to challenge the machine, arguing that by the time of the nominating convention, DeSapio would support their candidate, and it might harm FDR Jr. in the general election if he had antagonized the Manhattan leader by upstaging him in Brooklyn.

Though lacking the charismatic personality of FDR Jr., Averell Harriman had important assets as a candidate. He was a world-renowned figure who had played a major role in the victorious struggle against the Nazis. As a close associate of Presidents Roosevelt and Truman, he carried the mantle of both the New Deal and the Fair Deal. He had made a respectable run for the presiden-

tial nomination in 1952 as the candidate of the New York delegation. A tall, handsome man, his patrician background and
aristocratic mien made his liberal politics all the more attractive
to many Democratic voters. Labor liked Harriman, not only because of his relationship with Roosevelt and Truman, but also
because of his collaboration with the trade unions when he administered Marshall aid. George Meany, president of the AFL and
former head of the New York State Federation of Labor, particularly approved of his tough position on how to deal with the
Soviet Union. Happily for Harriman, labor preferred him over the
Republican candidate, Senator Irving Ives, in spite of the latter's
favorable record on labor legislation when he had served as speaker
of the Assembly in Albany.

Most important, Harriman had the support of New York's
followers of Adlai Stevenson, led by the venerated Senator Herbert Lehman, and Alex Rose and David Dubinsky, the leaders of
the Liberal Party, whose voters could prove crucial in a close
election. Tom Finletter, Truman's secretary of the Air Force, and
George Ball were important members of the Stevenson camp,
which was looking forward to his presidential candidacy in 1956.

Two motives dominated the attitude of these men. First, they
thought Harriman would make a strong candidate for governor.
FDR Jr., in their view, was too erratic, still too immature to be
governor of the Empire State. Second, if elected, FDR Jr. would
undoubtedly seek the nomination for the Presidency two years
hence. Another Governor Roosevelt would be a real threat to
Stevenson while Governor Harriman, they thought, would be too
old to still have presidential ambitions. Little did they know their
man. Two individuals in particular, Alex Rose and Julius
Edelstein, Lehman's able administrative assistant, both skillful political operators, were largely responsible for finally convincing
DeSapio that Harriman would be the better candidate. DeSapio
might have also calculated that he would have an easier time
dealing with Harriman as governor than with a young, seemingly
ambitious Roosevelt.

I became involved in the fight for the nomination early in 1954
as a Harriman supporter. At that time I was an adviser to the Free
Europe Committee spending Mondays to Fridays in New York.
I had soon reestablished contact with Harriman. We had become

friends during my frequent trips to Europe in the late 1940s and early 1950s. We had worked together then on issues involving labor's role in strengthening European democracies and continued our collaboration after he returned to Washington to become Truman's mutual security administrator. When Harriman asked me to help with his campaign for governor, I was happy to do so. I had enormous respect for his public record, and was impressed, too, by his imposing persona. I thought him a better candidate than Roosevelt, whom, incidentally, I had not yet met.

Vigorous trade union support was essential for Harriman's victory, and he used me mainly as his contact with the labor movement. He found my close friendships with David Dubinsky, Alex Rose, George Harrison (president of the Brotherhood of Railway Clerks), and Jack Potofsky particularly helpful. Louis Hollander, head of the State CIO Political Action Committee and a strong FDR Jr. supporter, was an officer in Potofsky's union, the Amalgamated Clothing Workers. Consequently, by securing Potofsky's backing for Harriman, we helped reduce the impact of Hollander's intensive efforts on behalf of FDR Jr.

After Harriman's nomination, I raised money from the unions for the campaign. Harriman also asked me to help draft his speeches to labor and liberal party groups and to accompany him to those rallies. In addition, I spoke at several meetings where I used my personal experience with both candidates (Ives and I had been fellow delegates to the ILO annual conference the year before) as the basis for preferring Harriman.

The polls taken shortly after the nominating conventions of both parties gave Harriman an impressive lead. He was profiting from the widely felt sentiment that the Republicans had been in power in Albany long enough, from voters' concerns over increasing unemployment in the country, particularly in New York State, and from the decision of Governor Thomas E. Dewey not to run again.

By October, however, the Republicans had cut into Harriman's lead. Harriman was a tense, plodding candidate who rarely turned on his audiences at political rallies. A chain-smoker for many years, he gave it all up when, at the outset of the campaign, he developed laryngitis and his doctors told him he would have no voice for the duration of the contest unless he stopped smoking. This was a remarkable demonstration of will power, but it did not make for a more relaxed and effective campaigner.

A major reason for the decline of the support for Harriman was Governor Dewey's aggressively negative campaign on behalf of Senator Ives. Dewey produced a copy of a newspaper showing that Harriman had been indicted many years before for trying to influence a Brooklyn judge's decision on a river dock lease in which a Harriman company was interested. Of course, Dewey did not mention the fact that the indictment was soon dropped. Another Dewey "revelation" was an old report that representatives of the Teamsters Union had been handled roughly when they tried to organize the dairy workers on Harriman's Arden farm. George Meany defused this one by quickly coming to Harriman's defense and emphasizing labor's enthusiastic support for him.

The last "charge" was that Harriman had been sympathetic to Nazi Germany. According to Dewey, Harriman's bank, Brown Brothers Harriman, had maintained some of its interests in Germany after Hitler came to power. I remember that this charge appeared in the press the day Harriman was scheduled to speak at the principal election rally of the Liberal Party. Harriman was troubled when I picked him up at his home on East Eighty-first Street, but he cheered up when I pointed out that, given his wartime record, this attack was so ridiculous it vitiated all the previous charges. We agreed that making fun of the accusation that he was pro-Nazi before this predominantly Jewish and politically sophisticated audience was the best way to handle it. Harriman was superb—much better than his usual pastel performance on the political rostrum. The large crowd laughed and cheered when he concluded his lively, off-the-cuff remarks with "and now they're accusing me, who was President Roosevelt's wartime ambassador to Winston Churchill, of being pro-Nazi."

The Dewey attacks hurt but they were not as damaging as a public comment made by a member of Mayor Robert Wagner's staff about ten days before the election. He stated that New York City was not getting its fair share of school aid from the state. Because Republicans controlled both branches of the state government, the formula for such aid was skewed in favor of the upstate communities, almost all of which were Republican, in contrast to Democratic New York City.

Although Harriman disassociated himself from that position, emphasizing that the individual involved had no connection with him, that did not stop the Republicans from unleashing a massive scare campaign upstate. They insisted that, if elected, Harriman would change the school-aid formula, and produced phony statistics to show how that would greatly increase local taxes.

The election was too close for comfort. I listened to the returns with Harriman and his wife, Marie, in their suite in the Biltmore Hotel. It wasn't until 2:00 or 3:00 A.M. that Harriman could claim victory with a meager majority of just over eleven thousand. It was the closest election in New York history, closer than FDR's victory in 1928. The damage done by the school issue was apparent. Harriman carried New York City by a whopping 690,000 majority. On the basis of previous gubernatorial electoral patterns, that should have provided a statewide majority of 300,000 to 400,000. However, upstate Republicans produced a much larger vote than usual for their candidate.

Harriman's camp was deeply relieved, but sad, too. While he had squeaked through, FDR Jr., who had agreed to stand as a candidate for attorney general after losing the nomination for governor, was defeated by Jacob Javits, whom the Republican bosses put on their ticket to cut into the Jewish vote, which usually favored a Roosevelt. As soon as it became clear that FDR Jr. had lost, Harriman excused himself, saying, "I must go down and talk to Franklin."

Fortunately, even a close win is a win. Within forty-eight hours after the election a new Harriman had emerged. He was more sure of himself, eager to assume the role of chief executive of the Empire State. He was also very aware of the fact that the two Roosevelts, Charles Evans Hughes, Al Smith, and Tom Dewey, all former governors of New York, had been presidential candidates. On the Monday after the election Harriman talked to me about running for President in 1956.

His old friends and colleagues Robert Lovett, John McCloy, Dean Acheson, and Paul Nitze deplored Harriman's demeaning himself by running for political office. Their condescension may have blinded them to an essential element in Harriman's character. Although aware of his lifelong ambition, they did not recognize the significance of his persistent desire to reach the pinnacle of political power. Being a top aide to both Roosevelt and Truman seemed a natural prelude to becoming the top man himself. His friends overlooked another factor. Harriman understood and relished politics, even though he lacked the personality, the easy charm of most successful politicians. His old friends felt that he was compromising his principles by entering the electoral arena. They failed to appreciate, however, that Harriman realized compromise was the lubricant of effective government action at the highest levels. To operate effectively even the McCloys and Lovetts needed the support of a skillful and compatible top political authority.

Harriman was determined to make an outstanding record as governor, to be a worthy successor of his famous liberal Democratic predecessors, Smith, Roosevelt, and Lehman. He lost no time in keeping the first promise made during the campaign: his first act, before his inauguration, would be to inspect conditions in Schenectady, Gloversville, and Jamestown, areas with the highest rates of unemployment in New York, to see what could be done to revive these communities. I was a member of the small advance team that Harriman dispatched three days after his election, and we accompanied him the following week. He received a warm and hopeful reception from the people in these cities. Their predicament, neglected for so long, spurred Harriman to make unemployment and poverty major concerns of his administration.

The government team Harriman put together included several Washington figures who stood out among the state commissioners, most of whom owed their appointments to the patronage of political bosses. Paul Appleby, who had been FDR's undersecretary of agriculture and Truman's assistant budget director, now became the state's director of budget; Isador Lubin, FDR's commissioner of labor statistics and a close Harriman associate in the early war years, was named industrial commissioner; Ed Dickinson, who had been an official in the U.S. Department of Commerce, became New York's commissioner of commerce; and

Mark McCloskey, the witty, redheaded Irishman who had been in charge of the federal recreation program for military personnel, served as Harriman's youth commissioner.

Another former Washingtonian was Jonathan Bingham, whom Harriman appointed to the key administrative position of secretary to the governor. Bingham, after heading up Truman's Point Four program, had been a top member of our UN mission in New York. He was an exceptional public servant: knowledgeable, able, a superb draftsman, loyal to his chief, a tireless worker, and blessed with an even, unflappable temperament—all the qualities that Harriman needed. Bingham was blessed, too, with a lovely, talented wife, June, the author of a biography of Reinhold Niebuhr, the Protestant theologian. Later, Bingham became one of our most effective liberal congressmen, a star on the House of Representatives Foreign Affairs Committee.

Bingham chose young Daniel Patrick Moynihan, also a former member of FDR Jr.'s campaign staff, as his deputy, and Elizabeth Brennan, Pat's future wife, as his secretary. Today Pat is the liberal, articulate senior senator from New York and Liz his political manager. Although Jack and Pat had supported FDR Jr. for the gubernatorial nomination, Harriman hired them, as well as others from that camp like Roger Tubby, a Truman staff alumnus.

Harriman knew that I wanted to be industrial commissioner. Before picking Lubin, an excellent choice,* he invited me to lunch to tell me of his decision and to assure me that he wanted me to join his administration in another position. I suggested chairman of the State Mediation Board or the Labor Relations Board, either of which would have meant residing in New York City. Harriman made no commitment but said he would prefer my being part of the Albany team, an idea that appealed to me.

At lunch in the Executive Mansion the day after his inauguration, Harriman asked me to serve as a special assistant with the primary responsibility for developing and directing a new state program to deal with the problems of an increasingly older population. During his campaign, Harriman had promised to break

---

*The Republican-controlled Senate threatened to reject Lubin because he was too liberal. I participated actively in the successful behind-the-scenes struggle that led to his confirmation.

new ground in this field and in consumer protection, both crying for effective statewide action, by appointing two officials directly responsible to the governor to initiate new programs and coordinate the relevant activities of all state agencies. He chose Professor Persia Campbell of Queens College, an expert in consumer affairs and an extremely effective individual, to be his consumer counsel.

I had hardly expected this kind of offer. However, I liked the idea of coming to grips with a subject that encompassed the whole range of the state government's activities, including employment, pensions, social welfare, housing, physical and mental health, insurance, recreation, and adult education. Harriman made the offer even more attractive by asking me to be a political adviser and to continue as his personal liaison with the trade union leaders and with the officials of the Liberal Party, particularly Rose and Dubinsky.

After finding a large, rambling, old, almost-winterized summer home on thirteen acres of uncultivated land, bisected by two active streams, I moved Hannah and our three young sons, Bob, David, and Charles, up to the Albany area. We were able to enjoy country life all year round, with my office in the state capital only fifteen minutes away. The next four years provided an education in state government, and hard-core politics at the state and local level. Most interesting of all, I had a chance to work with and observe a complicated, driven, able, difficult, sometimes charming, intensely ambitious, and fascinating man direct the affairs of the state while trying to ride the governorship of New York to the Presidency of the United States.

Being governor was a watershed in Harriman's life. Never a man who won popularity contests before, he had been chosen by the people of New York as their top political figure. You couldn't help but sense his feeling of fulfillment and his exhilaration; and his delightful no-nonsense wife, Marie, who earlier had made it clear she had little interest in being the wife of the governor, soon shared Harriman's enthusiasm for his new status. Harriman loved being governor and she came to relish her role as the chief executive's wife. His four years in Albany were among the happiest in Harriman's life. No title gave him more pleasure than "Governor."

Harriman adjusted impressively to the political life in Albany, which differed markedly from that in Washington. Lobbying was more blatant, legislators were more easily controlled by their leadership, and politicians more brazen in asserting their influence. In addition, the Democratic governor had to deal with a legislature always controlled by the Republicans.

During its annual session of four months, the state legislature met for three days at the beginning of every week in a clublike atmosphere. Except for members who lived in the Albany area, senators and assemblymen stayed at the two large downtown hotels, the DeWitt Clinton and the Ten Eyck. Members of both parties dined and wined together as they cooked up their deals. They were often joined by the horde of Albany lobbyists who, representing every conceivable interest, had no trouble in developing cozy relationships with the legislators and powerful pols. The convivial atmosphere was reinforced by the fact that, like the British House of Commons, legislative sessions were held in the evening after frequent cocktail parties and ample dinners in Albany's best restaurants. But that was the main, if not the only, similarity with the Mother of Parliaments.

The fact that almost all legislators had jobs in the private sector—service in Albany was part-time—made them easier prey for the lobbyists. The latter could promise rewards that profited the legislators' private interests. Lobbyists also targeted local political leaders. They knew that state senators and assemblymen were particularly responsive to pressures from their district and county party chairmen. The latter had selected the legislators in the first instance, and their reelection—their terms were only two years—depended on the continuing goodwill of their political patrons. On their frequent visits to Albany, the pols did not hide their presence under a bushel. The governor's office had a special staff of four telephone operators, two of whom dated back to the days when FDR was governor. They were remarkably efficient. If, for example, you wanted to know whether Carmine DeSapio was in Albany, they could tell you on which train he arrived and whom he was seeing at that very moment.

Among the most powerful lobbies were the banking industry, insurance, railways, teachers, church groups (particularly Catholic), trade unions, and medical services. The banking and insurance representatives were especially active because New York City is the country's center of both industries, and legislation passed in Albany had nationwide ramifications.

One of the most effective lobbyists was George Baehr, an outstanding physician and organizer of New York City's HIP, the nation's first prepaid medical care program. He cleverly managed to become the personal consultant physician of the legislative leaders of both parties. Not typical of other lobbyists, Dr. Baehr pushed legislation that invariably served the best interests of the general public.

In June 1958 I attended a dinner in New York City in honor of Dr. Baehr's seventieth birthday, a gala event attended by the state's and city's leading political figures. I sat at a table with Oswald Heck, the genial, able Republican speaker of the Assembly. At the end of the evening I happily accepted Heck's invitation to drive back to Albany with him in his official limousine next morning. It was a bright, sunny day, the kind that made you aware, once again, of the beauty of the ride upstate. As good friends Heck and I enjoyed a long, uninhibited conversation. During a discussion about the current state of lobbying, I remarked to Heck that I had the impression that lobbyists had become somewhat more subtle—that instead of direct bribes they would, for example, indicate to the targeted legislator that by his voting in their interest they could generate new business for his law firm, since a large number of assemblymen and senators were lawyers. "There's a good deal of that," Heck smilingly replied, "but if you think money isn't still being passed under and over the table, then you're not up to date on present-day practice." In the best bipartisan spirit, Heck dropped me off at the state capitol so that I could be in time for a Harriman cabinet meeting.

Bipartisanship necessarily predominated in Albany when a Democrat was elected governor. The Republicans had what many years before Al Smith had called "a constitutional majority" in both houses of the legislature. He was referring to the fact that prior to the U.S. Supreme Court's "one man, one vote" decision in 1963, the excessive representation from the less-populated rural areas guaranteed a Republican majority in the Senate and the Assembly. In the 1950s New York State was still operating under a system of legislative apportionment incorporated in the state constitution drafted in 1894. Thanks to clever Republican manipulation, the constitution stipulated that each of New York's sixty-two counties was guaranteed representation by at least one member in the Assembly, no matter how small its population. This provision assured Republican control of the lower house because most of the counties were rural, and they invariably elected the GOP candidate.

To maintain Republican control of the Senate the constitution simply provided that no two counties divided by a river could ever have half of the Senate seats. The targets here were Manhattan and Brooklyn, the two largest New York City counties—both overwhelmingly Democratic—which, except for this provision, could have provided a Democratic majority in the Senate.* Consequently, to achieve a fair part of his agenda, a Democratic governor had to be skilled in the art of political maneuvering, while at the same time generating popular support for his liberal policies.

Harriman was ready for the challenge. He was aware of the skill with which Smith, Roosevelt, and Lehman had handled Republican-controlled legislatures. They cleverly manipulated the legislative leaders into supporting policies that they knew were so popular with the electorate that the Republicans could not afford to oppose or block them. Moreover, Harriman himself was familiar with the problems of a Democratic executive dealing with a Republican-controlled legislature. As Truman's secretary of commerce, he was a major architect of the Marshall Plan, a key player in getting it approved, and later the program's European administrator, all of this during the Republican-controlled Eightieth Congress.

The governor's success in dealing with the legislature was helped by the leadership's tight control of members. Even Sam Rayburn, the last of Washington's imperial speakers of the U.S. House of Representatives, would have envied the powers of Albany's speaker of the Assembly and majority leader of the Senate. The speaker's authority rested on the fact that he appointed the chairmen as well as the members of all committees, particularly

*On one unique occasion Democrats gained control of the legislature. In 1934, when Lehman was reelected governor by a majority of over 800,000, the Democrats won the Assembly by a margin of one vote. They had already won the Senate as a result of the FDR presidential landslide two years earlier.

the Rules Committee, his chief instrument for running the business of the Assembly. The majority leader of the Senate had similar control. Back-bench mavericks were rare in either House: no Albany equivalents of Washington's Hubert Humphrey, Wayne Morse, or Jesse Helms bedeviled the legislative leadership. And if any such voices were raised in Albany, the leadership could call upon a member's county political chairman to bring an errant legislator in line.

Harriman, like his Democratic predecessors, exploited the close relationship between the leadership and the county political chairmen in dealing with the legislature. Whenever Republican leaders realized that the governor's proposal was seen to be in the public interest, or, if opposed, was exploitable politically by the Democrats, the Republicans usually saw to it that the back-benchers went along with it.

Another Albany practice helped the governor. Although the state, like the federal constitution, gave the legislature the power to override the executive's veto, it was never used in Albany. The threat of a veto by the governor therefore had a telling effect on the legislature's leadership. On more than one occasion the leaders changed the text of a bill to satisfy the governor's demands in order to avoid his veto. Harriman used this weapon with considerable skill.

Harriman was justly proud of his accomplishments during his four years as governor. He pushed through programs for protection of the consumer, for better care of mental health patients in the state hospitals, for more middle-class housing, and for improving the lot of the elderly. As a result of his prodding and his effective handling of the Republican-controlled legislature, new laws were passed for expanding senior-citizen housing, for health insurance, for providing federal Social Security for state employees and pensions for retired teachers who were too old to have been included in any insurance program. For the first time anywhere in the country discrimination in employment because of age was outlawed. Such legislation reflected Harriman's commitment to the liberal objectives of the New and Fair Deals. His program on poverty, also the first of its kind, anticipated the Great Society.

Harriman not only worked overtime on social legislation; he

was determined to be a governor widely known and liked by the average voter throughout the state. He tried to prove, too, that he was at home in the rough-and-tumble of practical politics. He made bread-and-butter speeches at formal political functions while, ironically, Carmine DeSapio's speech writers had the political boss talk about broad domestic and international issues. As Mark McCloskey put it, "Harriman, who was brought up on the sidewalk, tried to prove he was at home in the gutter, while DeSapio, who was brought up in the gutter, tried to prove he was at home on the sidewalk." This made for an odd couple with the efforts of neither quite convincing. Harriman evoked respect and admiration but hardly ever enthusiasm as a political leader.

Harriman was the first governor since Al Smith to actually live in the Executive Mansion in Albany rather than using it as a three-day hotel during the legislative sessions, and then departing "home" for the weekends. He was anxious to show that he was a full-time governor, as interested in Republican-dominated upstate as in Democratic New York City. He traveled frequently to all parts of the state, and encouraged projects in rural areas. He supported, for example, the use of state funds to build a ski center near Saranac Lake, and promoted the construction of the toll-free North Way, a long-overdue, modern, four-lane highway between Albany and Montreal. Harriman also reestablished the long-dormant custom of holding open house at the Executive Mansion on New Year's Day for any citizens who cared to visit. Hundreds came, many from rural areas, thrilled to see the home of their governor.

Harriman revived another Smith practice by sometimes dining in one of Albany's restaurants. On one occasion, after a cocktail party my wife and I gave in honor of Governor and Mrs. Harriman, we moved on to dinner at the Twenty-one Club, a restaurant located in the center of the city. We also invited Mr. and Mrs. Jim Reynolds, old friends of both the Harrimans and ourselves. We had a delightful time, with Harriman obviously enjoying the friendly attention of the other diners in the restaurant. When the check arrived, for the first and only time in the many years I knew Harriman he made a move to pick it up. He and I both seized it. I insisted it was my party. I yielded, however, when, behind Harriman's back, Reynolds raised five fingers on one hand and a

single finger on the second hand to remind me that a week before
Union Pacific stock had split five for one. Harriman then produced
an old, crumpled envelope from which he extracted two hundred-
dollar bills. He paid the check with one of them.

There are many stories about Harriman's parsimony, and none
are apocryphal. During the 1954 election, his campaign finance
director called on the venerable Senator Lehman for a contribution. The director responded enthusiastically to the senator's proposal that he give the same amount to Harriman that the latter
had contributed to the senator's campaign two years earlier. Lehman then produced a check for one hundred dollars.

Harriman hardly ever carried any cash; nor did he sign checks,
having provided the power of attorney for that purpose to an
officer of his bank. Usually, when you dined or lunched in a
restaurant with him, he turned to one of his guests and asked if
he had any cash to cover the bill. On one occasion when my son
Bob and I were dining with Governor and Mrs. Harriman at the
Jockey Club in Washington's Jefferson Hotel, Harriman offered
to sign the check. "Are you a guest here at the hotel?" the waiter
asked. "No," came the reply, "but I'm Averell Harriman." The
waiter, unimpressed, responded with the ultimate insult, "Do you
have a credit card?" The situation was saved by Mrs. Harriman,
who, fortunately for me, was carrying enough money to pay for
the dinner.

Clearly, Harriman had psychological difficulties with dispens-
ing money, but he could be generous. David Bruce told me that
Harriman paid him five times more than the salary he was earning
when he hired Bruce in the 1920s to work at Brown Brothers
Harriman. And, according to former House Speaker Tip O'Neill,
his aunt, a Maryknoll nun, regularly received a generous contribution for the order from Governor Harriman, although she had to
promise that she would never make the gift public.

I witnessed another generous contribution by Harriman, one
that was the result of careful maneuvering. In the late 1960s, when
I was minister at our embassy in London, Hugh Fraser, my old
Balliol classmate and then a Conservative MP, took up the cause
of raising an endowment for a Felix Frankfurter fellowship in law
at Balliol. It was to commemorate the year that Frankfurter was
the American Eastman Professor at Oxford and a Fellow at Balliol.

Fraser decided to ask Harriman for a contribution. Soliciting the aid of old Balliol boys, Hugh asked me to broach the matter to Harriman during one of my trips to Washington. The governor's response was less than enthusiastic. "I never had any connection with Balliol," he said, "and what's more, I never really liked Felix Frankfurter."

But Hugh knew that Harriman was close to the Kennedy family, and he got them to soften Harriman up. Shortly thereafter, Harriman came to London for an official visit, and stayed with us because Ambassador David K. E. Bruce was out of town. Hugh rang me the evening before Harriman and I were due to have breakfast with Ted Heath, the leader of the opposition and future prime minister. Hugh said, "Don't forget to remind Ted to thank Harriman for planning to make a generous contribution to the Frankfurter fund. If Ted does that, it'll be the clincher." Harriman winced when Ted thanked him; he knew he had been taken. Subsequently he made a generous contribution. He kept silent about the matter until he returned to the States, when he wrote, "By the way, Phil, when I reported on my visit to Dean Rusk, I told him that one thing in England really worried me: the all-pervasive power of the Balliol mafia!"

To underline the fact that the governor had made Albany his home, the Harriman Executive Mansion became the center of an active social life. During the week the staff and legislators were usually the guests; and on weekends the Harrimans transplanted to the Executive Mansion the elegance and gaiety of their East Side brownstone in New York City. They filled the mansion with old friends from the political, theatrical, and artistic worlds. We loved the evenings when Richard Rodgers sat down at the piano and played a medley of his own songs, and when Hervé Alphand, the French ambassador to Washington and a superb mime, after his perfect portrayal of de Gaulle, Churchill, and Roosevelt, gave us his *pièce de résistance*—an imitation of a Chinese diplomat at an international conference who didn't really know English but tried to give the impression that he did.

I particularly remember Dean Acheson's first visit to Albany. He and Harriman had been friends for almost half a century— from their school days at Groton and Yale through their service together in the Roosevelt and Truman administrations. They were different in style and temperament: Acheson brilliant, witty, cool, and articulate, the son of an Episcopal bishop; Harriman intense, aristocratically aloof, but highly ambitious and competitive, son of one of the richest men in America. They sometimes disagreed, but their collaboration contributed to the institutionalization of America's new international role in the postwar world. Acheson, however, had been the more important player, particularly after Truman chose him as secretary of state, a job that Harriman had sought. Later, when Harriman was appointed Truman's assistant for national security, he loyally supported Acheson in his conflicts with Secretary of Defense Louis Johnson.

In the spring of 1955, when Acheson arrived in Albany as the governor's guest, it was the first time since the days when Harriman was Yale's crew coach, and had picked Acheson to coach the freshmen eight, that Harriman was clearly the more important figure. He was the newly elected governor of the Empire State while Acheson was an ex-secretary of state affected by the cloud of unpopularity still hanging over the recent Truman administration. Harriman relished the situation but handled it with consummate grace. First of all he insisted that the Democratic leaders in the legislature introduce Acheson to the Republican-controlled senate and assembly. The latter had no choice but to respond hospitably.

Later Harriman hosted a stag dinner for his old friend and colleague, to which he invited only the five of us in his administration who had known Acheson from Washington. Always an elegant host, Harriman was more relaxed and charming than I had ever seen him before. Sitting down at the table we found three champagne glasses at each place. When the first course was served, the butler filled the first glass with Taylor's New York champagne. "Dean," Harriman said, "I have a confession to make. For years you and I worked hard to reduce tariff barriers to international trade. Since January 1, however, I have realized that it was a mistake, particularly for alcoholic beverages. How do you like this wonderful New York champagne?" After a sip Acheson made no comment, but his mustache bristled and the look on his face made it clear that the Taylor concoction had not caught his palate's fancy.

When the second course came, and New York's Widener champagne was poured into the second glass, the governor smilingly remarked, "We produce not one but two outstanding champagnes. How do you like this one, Dean?" "Well," Acheson replied, "it fizzes." A vintage French champagne accompanied the main course. As Acheson savored the taste he grinningly said, "I don't know what corrupted you on January 1, Averell, but I am still in favor of lowering tariff barriers, particularly on alcoholic beverages." Amusing nostalgia, which Acheson and Harriman enjoyed thoroughly, enlivened the rest of the evening.

Harriman entertaining socially in the Executive Mansion contrasted sharply with Harriman working in the governor's office in the state capitol. There was no charm during business hours, no small talk, and business could begin at 6:00 A.M. when the governor would phone and ask whether you had read the lead editorial in that day's New York Times. "It was all wrong. Why don't you call your friend John Oakes [the chief editorial writer] and tell him so?" The governor was disappointed, or rather surprised, when you told him that you hadn't yet read the editorial. After a while we compared stories about these calls. The best one involved Gene Bannigan, the Democratic leader in the State Assembly. Early one morning when Harriman phoned Bannigan he solicitously asked whether he had woken him. "Heavens, no," replied Bannigan. "I've been waiting up all night for your call."

There was little letup in the intensity that the governor generated during "office hours." He was like a fox terrier when he zeroed in on any issue of immediate interest, and considered raising another subject before its time an inexcusable diversion. On one occasion in his office I was surprised to hear him fussing over some seemingly trivial details in a phone conversation. "You're the governor," I said to him when he hung up, "and you have staff to deal with details of that nature." "Let me teach you an important lesson," he replied. "Whenever a particular issue is of special importance to you, be sure you yourself handle all of the details relating to it." I dubbed this "the Harriman principle," in recognition of his relentlessness in almost everything he did.

I had a phone call one day from George Harrison, the president of the Brotherhood of Railway Clerks. Intelligent, moderate, and responsible, he was one of our finest trade unionists, a favorite labor leader of both Roosevelt and Truman, and a loyal supporter of Harriman. Harrison and I had become friends during my years as assistant secretary of labor. Harrison told me that the Railway Clerks had a problem with the Union Pacific that could be easily cleared up if the governor would phone the railway's president and point out that since the union request involved a relatively unimportant administrative matter, granting it would prevent serious industrial trouble. Would I urgently bring the matter to the governor's attention?

I asked to see the governor immediately. Heavily engaged in the issues of the day, he was annoyed by my interruption. "Doesn't George know that I no longer have any connection with the Union Pacific and can do nothing about it?" he asked. As I got up to leave, I said, "Well, I'll just tell him that you have no influence with Union Pacific. I know he'll be disappointed." When I reached the door the governor blurted out, "Just a minute," picked up the phone, and asked his secretary to call the president of Union Pacific. In a few moments the president agreed to take care of the matter Harrison had raised.

Such behavior was not untypical. His first reaction to any request or suggestion not on the day's agenda was invariably negative. The intensity of his reaction increased by several decibels if you criticized something he had done; and he was even more provoked when, in response to one of his proposals, you had the courage to say, "Governor, you can't do that." But if you stuck with your point of view, not always an easy thing to do, he would give it reasonable consideration. He was particularly responsive if you demonstrated that your recommendation was in the best Roosevelt and Truman tradition.

Being involved in the preparation of a Harriman speech was a trying experience. Jim Sundquist, his talented speech writer, got hardened to the fact that Harriman almost always scoffed at the first draft. One sometimes felt that even if a draft had combined the Ten Commandments and the Sermon on the Mount, it would have been called unsatisfactory.* In any case, the governor usually

---

*Among the many stories about preparing speeches for Harriman, perhaps the most popular one involved Charles Collingwood, the CBS political correspondent, who took leave to be Harriman's speech writer during his bid for the presidential nomination in 1952. One evening, after making extensive suggestions for revisions of a Collingwood speech draft, Harriman said that he was going off to dinner with

asked one or two people to join him and the original drafter as they reviewed the text sentence by sentence, a long and tedious exercise. During these sessions you didn't mind Harriman rejecting your suggestion, which he frequently did, but you were annoyed when he ignored your proposal, exploiting the fact that his hearing was a bit deficient.

On one occasion he was compelled to respond to any suggestion I made. In the spring of 1956 he was gearing up to run for President later that year. I had just had a polyp on my vocal cord removed, and the doctors had ordered me not to talk for three weeks to prevent a recurrence of the growth. For twenty-one days I behaved like a Trappist monk—up to a point—never opening my mouth, almost driving my family mad with voluminous notes. In the middle of my enforced silence Harriman's secretary, Bernice McCrae, phoned and told Hannah that that evening the governor was reviewing a draft of a speech he was scheduled to make at the Wisconsin Democratic convention. He would appreciate my joining the editorial group. Hannah replied that I would be happy to accept but because I couldn't talk I would have to make my suggestions in writing. After checking with the governor, Bernice reported that in view of my knowledge of the Wisconsin scene, he would still like me to come.

I couldn't resist taking advantage of a unique situation. As soon as I realized that the governor was compelled to read whatever I wrote, I made more suggestions than ever. I don't think my host enjoyed my presence that evening.

In two settings it was particularly agreeable to deal with Harriman—in the Executive Mansion after a swim in the heated pool and in the governor's limousine between Albany and New York City. Early in my stay in Albany I developed serious back trouble and Harriman insisted that I hasten my recuperation by swimming regularly in the heated pool that had been built for FDR in one of the Executive Mansion's greenhouses shortly after he had become governor. I took full advantage of Harriman's generous offer and

General Omar Bradley and would like to see a new draft when he returned about ten o'clock. "I'm sorry," Collingwood responded. "I can't do it because I've got a special date tonight." "Why not see her after I get back?" Harriman asked. "Because," Collingwood replied, "her husband will have returned home by then."

quite often met him there, because he loved to swim himself. On these occasions he would invariably invite me for a drink, providing an opportunity for easy, relaxed conversation about substantive issues. He was the host *par excellence*.

Similarly, during the motor trips between New York City and Albany, I had his full attention. I recall, too, the picnic lunches we had in the car without any interruption in our conversations. They were modest repasts: soup, sandwich, pie, and hot coffee, which had been prepared in the Executive Mansion. It avoided the need to stop and spend money for a restaurant meal. If we were remaining overnight, the governor usually invited me to stay at his brownstone on East Eighty-first Street. Harriman and his wife were always generous in making their several houses available to their friends.

During those rides Harriman sometimes reminisced about his experience in the Roosevelt and Truman administrations. On one occasion he bemoaned the fact that Truman had not appointed him secretary of the treasury when Acheson was secretary of state and Robert Lovett secretary of defense. "What an unusually effective trio we three old friends and colleagues would have made," he observed. Until then I had naïvely thought that Harriman, having fulfilled a fair amount of his ambition by being elected governor of New York, had been able to forget previous political disappointments.

In both places, the mansion after a swim and during a ride in the governor's car, Harriman often talked about international affairs. He found it frustrating not to be directly involved in shaping our foreign policies. I recall particularly his deep concern about developments during those critical days in October 1956 when Moscow crushed the Hungarian revolt and the British, French, and Israelis moved against Nasser's Egypt. He was distressed about our government's impotent reaction to the Hungarian situation, particularly after what many Hungarians had interpreted as promises of aid by Secretary of State Dulles, and upset over the way in which Eisenhower and Dulles handled the Middle Eastern developments. While he disapproved of the British-French-Israeli action, he felt it was a serious mistake to be so determined and so hasty in repudiating our British and French allies in the face of Soviet threats. He particularly deplored Dulles's calling a midnight session of the UN Security Council to expedite the condemnation of Britain and France. That was no way to treat allies.

Harriman was appalled when Eisenhower induced a sterling crisis in order to compel a British capitulation. In Harriman's view the proximity of the presidential election influenced Eisenhower's reaction. Having campaigned as the "peace candidate," Eisenhower mistakenly feared that the outbreak of hostilities in the Middle East would hurt him at the polls. He failed to realize that his military background was a special asset during an international crisis. In fact, the events abroad in late October undoubtedly contributed to his landslide victory.

Driven by deep ambition, Harriman could not resist running for the presidential nomination in 1956. He was convinced that Stevenson could not possibly win. Moreover, he believed that his successful experience as chief executive of New York, combined with his rich background in foreign affairs, made him the better candidate. He spent a large amount of his own money to finance his campaign, as he had when he sought the nomination in 1952. (Unwisely, as we shall see, he refused to contribute to his campaign for reelection as governor two years later.)

Once again I served as his liaison with the American labor movement. The campaign made some progress with old trade union friends like George Harrison. For the most part, however, the labor leadership stuck with Stevenson. The most satisfying development for Harriman was Truman's vigorous support of his candidacy at the Chicago convention, which for several hours shook the Stevenson supporters. I recall Theodore White, who was covering his first convention, coming in to see me at Harriman headquarters to inquire whether Truman's unqualified backing of Harriman would make any difference. I told him that it was too early to answer his question and recommended that he see what effect Truman had had on two key delegations, Pennsylvania and Michigan. When White came back and informed me that there had been no change in either state, it was clear that the Truman endorsement would have little effect. Stevenson was nominated by an overwhelming majority of the delegates.

Harriman's determination to run for the Presidency was costly politically as well as financially. Governors who run unsuccessfully for the Presidency almost invariably suffer some decline in prestige. In this case Harriman's determination to take on both Stevenson and Eisenhower reflected considerable ambition and courage but raised doubts about his political judgment.

By the spring of 1958 Harriman had sufficiently recovered from the setback in Chicago to begin focusing on his campaign for reelection as governor in November. There was ample reason to be optimistic. The polls reinforced the generally held view that a fair majority of the state's electorate supported the governor. The voters liked what he had done substantively in the previous four years and apparently approved of the tone and style of his administration even though he lacked charisma. Nor did the Republicans seem particularly threatening. Leonard Hall, former chairman of the Republican National Committee, was competing with Nelson Rockefeller for the gubernatorial nomination, and Harriman and the Democratic Party leaders took neither the professional politician nor the well-intentioned rich young man very seriously. In fact, because of his misguided assessment of Rockefeller, Harriman chose him as the chairman of the state constitutional convention. In session in 1957 and 1958, the convention provided Rockefeller with the kind of experience that enabled him to demonstrate later his familiarity with state government.

Harriman was confident and relaxed, unusually so, that spring and early summer. Unwisely, however, he decided not to spend his own funds on the forthcoming election. In light of his performance as governor, he felt that the Democrats in the state should finance the campaign. This saved him some money, but it proved to be a costly political mistake in a contest against a Rockefeller.

Unfortunately, Harriman delayed dealing with the one issue that should have been settled before the party convention in September: the Democratic nominee for the vacant seat in the U.S. Senate. The Liberal Party, a crucial ally, was pushing hard for Tom Finletter. On several occasions Alex Rose, the party's leader, phoned me to underline the depth of the Liberal Party's commitment to Finletter. By that time I was the only person in the Harriman administration through whom the Liberals were communicating with the governor. When I passed Rose's messages on to Harriman, it became all too clear that he did not share the

172 · PHILIP M. KAISER

Liberal Party's view. He had no intention of accepting Finletter as his running mate. He argued that it would be a mistake to have two Protestants, particularly two with rather similar backgrounds, heading the ticket.

Historically there was some merit to this point, and in Harriman's case it was reinforced by the fact that he had never quite forgiven Finletter for supporting Stevenson for the presidential nomination in 1956. Harriman felt that as a New Yorker Finletter should have supported the nomination of New York's governor. At a private dinner in the Executive Mansion a week before the convention—the only guests were former governor Charles Poletti, my wife, and I—Hannah, in her characteristically nononsense manner, suggested to the governor that he support Finletter for the Senate because he was clearly the most qualified candidate. Harriman emphatically rejected the idea.

Instead, belatedly, only a few days before the nominating convention in September, Harriman indicated that his candidate was Thomas Murray, a respectable Catholic (in fact a papal knight), who had served as chairman of the Atomic Energy Commission. Unfortunately, he had little political experience and less rank-and-file support.

While Harriman was floundering on this issue, Carmine DeSapio moved in to fill the vacuum in a way that would suit his personal interests. He picked as his own candidate Frank Hogan, who had served with distinction as district attorney for New York County (Manhattan) for many years. In the preceding two elections for that post, Hogan had had bipartisan support, and no opposition, because of his outstanding record. He might have been an excellent choice except for the fact that he was DeSapio's candidate. It was assumed that DeSapio wanted to promote Hogan to the U.S. Senate so that he could pick the next district attorney in Manhattan, a position of more than academic interest to the Democratic leader.

When we arrived in Buffalo for the Democratic Party convention, the disagreement among Harriman, the Liberals, and DeSapio was all too apparent. The fact that Harriman's choice was being ignored led to disarray on the eve of the convention, with an adverse effect on the morale of the delegates. Inevitably, too, the lack of consensus on the senatorial nominee became the media's leading story, with the failure of Harriman's leadership high-lighted.

The first order of business of the convention was the nomination by acclaim of Harriman for reelection as governor. The convention then recessed before proceeding the next day to nominate the candidates for the U.S. Senate, comptroller, and state attorney general. It had become painfully evident that the governor's prestige had been damaged and that, if possible, the nomination of Hogan for the Senate should be stopped.

Apparently, DeSapio had made a deal with Peter Crotty, the Democratic leader in Erie County—whose capital, Buffalo, was a major center of Democratic strength. Crotty would support Hogan for senator, and in return DeSapio would support Crotty for attorney general, in spite of the fact that the Liberal Party had made it clear that under no circumstances would they back Crotty for that position. My major responsibility during the convention was to act as the governor's liaison with Alex Rose,* the leader of the Liberal Party. At Rose's request, I had informed Harriman of the Liberal Party's attitude toward Crotty. Irrationally, De-Sapio and Mike Prendergast, the state party chairman, were annoyed with me for bringing this news to the governor.

Late in the afternoon of the day before the candidate for the Senate was to be chosen, Harriman called in Milton Stewart, one of his political aides, and me to discuss his embarrassing predicament. Aware of the fact that Murray could not be nominated and that he was about to suffer a serious rebuff, Harriman asked us whether it was too late for him to adopt Hogan as his candidate. We pointed out that that was not feasible. Because everyone knew that DeSapio had picked Hogan, if Harriman now embraced him it would be interpreted as a complete victory for the political boss.

Late that evening a last, desperate strategy emerged. If Bob Wagner, mayor of New York City, would agree to run for the Senate, Hogan was willing to withdraw. Wagner had run for the Senate against Jacob Javits two years before, and, although

---

*Theoretically, Rose was incognito while attending the convention. He holed up in a suite in the same hotel that housed Harriman and his aides, and every reporter knew he was there.

defeated, had made a respectable showing at a time when Eisenhower had carried New York against Stevenson by a staggering majority.

Wagner, reluctant to run again, asked for time to consider the offer, promising to give his final decision the following morning before the convention reconvened. I was in Alex Rose's suite that evening discussing the latest developments with him, Julius Edelstein, and Aaron Jacoby, a Brooklyn politician, when, at about 11:30 P.M., I received a phone call from Harriman's secretary, Bernice McCrae, asking me to send Rose up immediately to see the governor. As he left, Rose exacted a promise from the three of us to remain until he returned.

When he came back an hour and a half later, he bemoaned the irony of politics. "During the last six months," he told us, "at least once a week I had breakfast, lunch, a drink, or dinner with Bob Wagner, in order to convince him that it would be a mistake for him to run again for the Senate. I did that because we Liberals knew that if Bob decided to run, we would have to support him instead of Finletter." He went on to explain that, moreover, the Liberals didn't want Wagner to give up the mayoralty, particularly since they were primarily responsible for his election the previous year against the opposition of the Democratic political bosses. "Do you know what I've been doing this past hour and a half?" Rose asked us, his face wreathed with a sardonic smile. "I've been practically down on bended knee begging Bob to run for the Senate." Rose, a shrewd politician, realized that now only a Wagner candidacy could prevent what might be irreparable damage to Harriman's reelection campaign.

We hardly slept that night, waiting restlessly for Wagner's decision. When morning came, Wagner announced that for personal reasons he could not run for the Senate. He did not reveal that his wife was suffering from cancer.

Harriman maintained his support for Murray, but the convention proceeded to implement the DeSapio plan by nominating Hogan for the U.S. Senate, and Crotty for state attorney general. These acts of political bravado, and stupidity, boomeranged on their perpetrators and were largely responsible for the subsequent defeat of Harriman for reelection. I remember the remark of Marie Harriman, the governor's colorful wife, about what had happened at the convention. "In Buffalo," she said, "they gave Ave what in Philadelphia they call a rat fucking."

Harriman tried to rally the Democrats immediately after the convention, but the Republicans lost no time in taking advantage of the fissures that had been opened. In his first speech after being nominated, Rockefeller recalled the most dramatic incident of the 1922 Democratic state convention, also held in Buffalo, which had long since been forgotten. The Democrats were ready to nominate their hero, Al Smith, for governor by acclamation. Smith had been first elected the state's chief executive in 1918 but was defeated two years later, a victim of Harding's presidential landslide.* It was generally believed that Smith, who was very popular with the mass of voters, would easily defeat Nathan Miller, the Republican incumbent, in 1922.

When Smith arrived in Buffalo, he was appalled to discover that William Randolph Hearst, the father of yellow journalism, had lined up the support of the political bosses for his senatorial candidacy. Smith, who despised Hearst, refused to go along. Before the convention nominated him for governor, Smith called in the political nabobs and bluntly said to them, "You can have me as your gubernatorial candidate or Hearst for the Senate, but you can't have us both. Make up your minds whom you prefer." The convention proceeded to nominate Smith for governor and Royal Copland for the U.S. Senate.

Rockefeller's speech, highlighting the difference between the wobbling Harriman and the courageously forthright Smith, had a powerful impact. It enabled the Republicans to portray Harriman as a man incapable of controlling his party's political bosses. The speech, repeated regularly for the next several weeks, provided the springboard for an aggressive Republican campaign that spared no money in portraying Rockefeller as a young, dynamic candidate who would bring new vitality to the governance of New York.

Rockefeller made full use of his vast fortune. Rockefeller forces flooded the state with mailings to every conceivable group, placed advertisements in every ethnic journal, and filled the airwaves with paid messages. Rockefeller's personal charm, energetically

---

*Until 1938 the gubernatorial term was two years.

displayed, became a valuable asset. The young wealthy WASP seemed completely at home among Italian, Jewish, Hispanic, and black groups. Moreover, the family charities, widely dispensed over many years, also helped the Rockefeller candidacy. Hospitals, universities, Latin American countries, blacks, and Jews were all among the recipients. The Rockefeller name was associated with the Rockefeller Institute (now Rockefeller University), the philanthropic Rockefeller Foundation, the site of the United Nations. Every day tens of thousands of people passed Rockefeller Center in mid-Manhattan. The Rockefeller candidate had no problems about name identity.

We had evidence of the potential impact of Rockefeller's charm in the spring before the election. One day in late May, Harriman had called me in to tell me that he had heard that Jack Potofsky, loyal Democrat and active supporter of Harriman four years earlier, was being effectively wooed by Rockefeller. I found this hard to believe, and agreed to take lunch with Jack in New York City to ascertain whether he was seriously considering supporting the Republican candidate. We met at Luchow's, Jack's favorite restaurant, located near his headquarters on Union Square. To my dismay I found Jack full of praise for Rockefeller and surprisingly cool to his old friend Averell. When I pressed him for his reasons he shamelessly told me, "Nelson always accepts my invitations for dinner while in recent months Averell kept saying he was too busy to come to the city and spend an evening with me." I couldn't resist commenting that Rockefeller's sociability hardly demonstrated that he was a better friend of labor than Harriman. I reminded Potofsky of how supportive of trade unions the governor had been down through the years, and that running the state kept him from spending as much time with old friends as he would have liked. Potofsky blushingly acknowledged that perhaps he was allowing personal sociability to affect his political judgment unduly. He told me to go back to Albany and tell the governor that, of course, he and his union would actively support him for reelection. They would remain loyal Democrats.

Early in October, when the Harriman entourage was beginning to realize that the election was slipping away, I dined at the home of the Israeli consul general in New York. Most of the evening was devoted to a general discussion of the forthcoming election.

As the guests were leaving our Israeli host asked me to stay behind for a few minutes. When we were alone he said, "You know your man is going to lose." "Why do you say that?" I asked. He replied that in recent days he had met many Jews who normally voted Democratic, had supported Harriman in 1954, but were now planning to vote for Rockefeller. They gave as their main reason the fact that, although both families were very wealthy, the Rockefellers were generously philanthropic, while there was no public record of charitable contributions by the Harrimans. This reaction to the different behavior of the two families undoubtedly influenced a large number of New York City's voters. In 1954 Harriman carried the city by a majority of 690,000; four years later Rockefeller reduced Harriman's majority in the city to 310,000.

While the Rockefeller campaign flourished, Harriman's floundered. From its inception defeat seemed to be its ubiquitous companion. The governor campaigned vigorously throughout the state, but his substantive achievements of the previous four years were overshadowed by the conflicts between him and the politicians, so dramatically apparent during the Democratic Party convention. Liberal support was relatively apathetic because of the nomination of Crotty for attorney general. The campaign also suffered from a lack of adequate financial support.*

There was no limit to Harriman's bad luck. Even Dorothy Schiff, the owner and publisher of the *New York Post*, defected the day before the election. Schiff was a friend of both Harriman and Rockefeller, their families having moved in the same financial worlds for many years. As expected, her newspaper, which was known for its liberal editorial policy, had come out for Harriman. However, during the last weekend of the campaign, when Harriman criticized Rockefeller's position on the Middle East, Schiff announced on the front page of her paper on the Monday before the election that she thought Harriman's charges grossly unfair.

---

*Ted Tannenwald, who had been Harriman's counsel when the governor was Truman's mutual security administrator, now acted as the campaign's financial director. While Harriman remained adamant about no personal contribution, Ted told me members of the Harriman family were willing to make the maximum contribution allowed. Tannenwald was a very able lawyer who later became chief judge of the U.S. Tax Courts.

The *New York Post* was therefore withdrawing its support for the governor and was now backing Rockefeller. The Rockefeller campaign took full advantage of this shift. When voters appeared at the polls the next morning they found Rockefeller supporters distributing leaflets highlighting the *Post*'s decision to support their candidate rather than Harriman.

On election night, hours after Harriman had conceded to Rockefeller, I was with the governor and his wife at their home on East Eighty-first Street listening to the last returns. He could not quite hear the final figures. At his insistence, I had the sad task of telling him that he had lost by a majority of 573,034.

It was a stunning blow to Harriman. For several weeks thereafter he was a sad, discouraged figure. Many thought this was the end of his political career. They underestimated him. By January 1 when he left Albany, he had regained his poise, and was looking forward to moving to Washington and participating actively in national and international affairs.

Before long, Harriman was adding weight to the Democratic Party's efforts to regain the White House. A major adviser on international affairs in the 1960 election, he campaigned actively on Kennedy's behalf. Subsequently, neither age nor hearing difficulties prevented Harriman from making significant contributions on international issues in both the Kennedy and Johnson administrations; and Carter sought his counsel on American policy toward the Soviet Union. Perhaps his outstanding achievement during these years was his negotiation of the Nuclear Testing Agreement with Moscow in 1963.

A major Harriman frustration was the U.S. failure to reach an agreement with North Vietnam to end the war before the 1968 presidential elections. In the spring of that year President Johnson had appointed Harriman and Cyrus Vance to talk with Hanoi's representatives in Paris about negotiating a peace agreement. The two Americans persevered through several unproductive months. In October, however, a few weeks before the presidential election, Johnson finally met Hanoi's condition for beginning formal negotiations by stopping all bombing. Harriman, who for several years had pushed for peace, tried desperately to reach an agreement. He and Vance were making progress, but their efforts were sabotaged when Nguyen Van Thieu, the Vietnamese president, secretly encouraged by Nixon to hold out for a more favorable deal from a Republican administration, refused to sit down at the table with the NLF (the Communist National Liberation Front). Harriman believed that if Nixon were elected President, the war would drag on in spite of Nixon's statement that he had a secret plan for ending hostilities. Harriman derived no satisfaction from the fact that his doubts about Nixon were justified.

After Nixon was elected President, Harriman and Vance were forced to withdraw from the negotiations. Subsequently, on several occasions Harriman told me that the agreement he and Cy Vance were in the process of negotiating with Hanoi's representatives was more favorable than the one signed by Nixon and Kissinger four years later, after the loss of thousands of additional lives. The United States, he stressed, was in a much stronger bargaining position in 1968, when it still had 500,000 troops in Vietnam, than in 1972, when almost all of the Americans had been withdrawn.

Until the end of his life (he died in 1986), Harriman maintained a vital interest in public affairs, particularly encouraging the development of positive but realistic U.S.-Soviet relations. He would have been delighted with the end of the Cold War, the liberation of the Eastern European countries, the collapse of the Berlin Wall after Gorbachev came to power, and the disbanding of the Communist Party in the Soviet Union after the aborted reactionary coup in August 1991.

6

The Kennedy Years: Ambassador in Africa

What's it really like to be an African ambassador?" asked President Kennedy after I had given him an oral report on a recent crisis in Senegal. Kennedy always found time for his African ambassadors when they were home on consultation. The fact that a crisis had involved an aborted attempt by the prime minister to oust the more moderate president naturally interested Kennedy. He wanted to hear the full story, the juicy political details. He was curious about the two personalities involved: what and whom they represented, and what brought their differences to so dramatic a head. He was relieved that bloodshed had been avoided. He mused that, unfortunately, too much of his time was devoted to dealing with "crises," and not enough "to helping keep noncritical areas from becoming critical."

As Arthur Schlesinger, Jr., observed in *A Thousand Days,* his authoritative account of Kennedy's presidency, Africa was a continent that had intrigued Kennedy for some years. In 1957, when the only independent countries on the African continent were Egypt, Ethiopia, Liberia, and South Africa, he had created a furor with his Senate speech supporting independence for Algeria. "No amount of mutual politeness, wishful thinking, nostalgia, or regret," he said, "should blind either France or the U.S. to the fact that, if France and the West at large are to have a continuing influence in North Africa . . . the essential first step is the independence of Algeria." He emphasized that the United States must use its influence to help achieve that objective.

The speech provoked a storm of protest not only from the French government but also from the American administration and the foreign policy establishment in the United States. *The New York Times* and the Council on Foreign Relations criticized Kennedy for jeopardizing the unity of NATO by attacking our French ally.

But Kennedy persisted. In the 1960 presidential campaign, Kennedy made Africa an important issue, charging that "we have lost ground in Africa because we have neglected and ignored the needs and aspirations of African people," and on assuming office he made Africa a high priority. He selected his own ambassadors for the new African nations, changed U.S. policy, and moved to develop personal relationships with most of the new African leaders. He wanted ambassadors who were knowledgeable, experienced, and sympathetic to his African policies. The ambassadors he appointed couldn't help but feel the President's own excitement about Africa. There, Kennedy pointed out, a chief of mission was on his own, in contrast to Bonn, Paris, and London, where the main business was done by telephone from Washington and through regular visits from the secretary of state and other top officials.

Thanks to Byron White, I was an active participant in the 1960 presidential campaign. Byron and I first became friends when we were students at Oxford. I had returned to Washington, having become a professor at American University, when Kennedy appointed Byron chairman of Citizens for Kennedy. Byron asked me to serve as one of his deputies. This gave me an opportunity to get to know Bobby Kennedy. Although I had met Jack Kennedy on several occasions when he was a congressman and senator, I had never known Bobby before. The Citizens group was one of Bobby's favorite operations and we saw him quite frequently.

Bobby was an impressive campaign director. Campaign organizations are notorious for hyped-up inefficiency—the stakes are high, time is short, and staff is constantly jockeying for position while trying to cope with the candidate's pressing demands. Fatigue sets in early and persists throughout the contest. As the candidate's brother, Bobby's authority was unquestioned and he made good use of his unique position. By his wise delegation of responsibilities, he minimized turf battles among staff, who appreciated that Bobby was the campaign's "universal joint." He knew how to use volunteers and recognized the importance of making people who couldn't be used feel that they were, nevertheless, welcome supporters of the candidate, a skill glaringly lacking in many campaign managers.

Bobby's energies were unflagging. Although extraordinarily busy, he was always there when you had something important to discuss. Early in the campaign he quizzed me about the complicated political situation in New York, a scene I knew as a result of my work with Governor Harriman. The regular party, the Liberals, and several key trade union leaders were all supporting Kennedy but refusing to cooperate with one another. I told Bobby it would be a waste of time and energy to try to bring them together. He would have to deal with each group separately to secure all-out support during the campaign.

At Byron White's suggestion I also discussed with Bobby the problem his father's reputed anti-Semitism was creating among Jewish voters. Bobby, aware of the situation, was realistic about it. We discussed what action might be taken to offset the unfavorable attitude of Jews toward his father, which was adversely affecting his brother's candidacy. He told me about the contributions his father had made to several Jewish hospitals but didn't know when he had made them.

Protestant bigots helped solve this problem when they tried to stir up anti-Catholic support for Nixon. The reaction of many Jews, particularly Democrats who were concerned about Kennedy *père*, was not surprising. They found it easier to rally behind Jack because the bigots were supporting his opponent.

When the campaign was over I was told I would be welcome in the new administration. I suggested a diplomatic post, which would follow naturally from my education and experience, and indicated I would prefer serving in Western Europe.

My experience in foreign affairs included working at the Board of Economic Warfare and Foreign Economic Administration during the war and briefly later in the State Department. As assistant secretary of labor for international affairs, I had been that department's statutory member on the Board of the Foreign Service. Under the Foreign Service Act of 1946, the board at that time had considerable power over operations of the Service. The Labor Department was also responsible for developing the Labor Attaché Program and integrating it into the Foreign Service. This involved almost daily contact with the State Department. On my triannual trips to the ILO meetings in Geneva, I usually arranged to stop at one or another embassy in Europe to check on the activities of our labor attachés.

I was more than a little surprised when Chester Bowles, who was handling ambassadorial appointments, informed me that President Kennedy would like to send me to Senegal. I had a general interest in African developments but Europe was certainly the part of the world I knew best. "Why me to Senegal?" I asked Bowles. "Well," he replied, "the president of Senegal, Léopold Senghor, is a brilliant intellectual who was trained in France and has a social democratic background. Among his heroes are Jean Jaurès and Léon Blum. That's a world with which you are familiar and I believe you speak French."

As I discussed the proposal with Bowles and thought about it later, the prospect of serving as ambassador to Senegal seemed challenging. There was a certain cachet about being one of Kennedy's African ambassadors, and the more I learned about Senghor the more intrigued I became about being accredited to his government.

The offer became even more attractive when I was told that I would also be named ambassador to the Islamic Republic of Mauritania that bordered on Senegal. Mauritania was strikingly different from its southern neighbor. Bigger than Texas, but mostly desert, it had a much smaller population than Senegal, a different ethnic makeup, and different social and economic problems. Mokhtar Ould Daddah, Mauritania's president, trained in France as a lawyer, was an intelligent and interesting political leader, but lacked the stature of Senghor. Senegal was a much more important country, with an attractive westernized capital, Dakar, where I would live. The prospect of covering two contrasting African countries added spice to the assignment.

After being confirmed by the Senate, I went through the usual briefing process for new ambassadors, involving several weeks of meetings in the State Department, and at Commerce, Agriculture, Labor, Defense, and the CIA, all of which had African interests. Some briefings were useful, some trivial, and some actually misleading. The CIA expert on West Africa informed me that, in the agency's opinion, "President Senghor would probably not last more than six months." This was a bit of a shocker because one of the main reasons for my accepting the post was the attraction of being accredited to Senghor, but other information indicated that perhaps the agency was wrong. In fact, Senghor was the first African president to retire from office voluntarily, some twenty years later. In Senegal, I was to learn that French intelligence could also be mistaken.

About a week before I was scheduled to leave for Africa, I received a call from the Israeli ambassador to Washington, Abe Harmon, whom I had known for several years. He thought it would be useful for me to meet Ehud Avriel, the Israeli government's leading African expert, who had served in several posts on the Continent and who happened to be in Washington. Indeed, it was useful. Avriel alerted me to the complicated nature of the relations between the Senegalese establishment and the large French community in Dakar. As is often the case with outsiders, he had a keen appreciation of the role an American ambassador should play in that setting. "It is important," he said, "to maintain good relations with the French in Dakar," but not to allow them to overwhelm you. "The Senegalese," he added, "have a very special love-hate relationship with the French. They want the American ambassador to have good relations with the French, but not at their expense. A sensitive balancing act between the two would make for greater effectiveness on the part of the American representatives."

Avriel underlined a major built-in advantage enjoyed by American ambassadors. Representing the most powerful nation in the world, they have no identity problems. There is no need for them to be unduly aggressive, to puff themselves up in order to perform effectively. A touch of modesty is always an attractive quality, but particularly so in an American ambassador, a fact U.S. representatives have not always appreciated.

When I was received by President Kennedy before leaving for

Africa, he opened the conversation by saying, "Now, in regard to Mongolia—" "You mean Mauritania," I interjected, but he knew what he was talking about, while I turned out to be embarrassingly quick-on-the-draw. At that moment there was actually an important policy issue involving Mauritania, Mongolia, and the United Nations. Earlier that year Mauritania had applied for admission to the UN, which would have meant international recognition of Mauritania's independence. Claiming that Mauritania was a Moroccan province, the year before, in 1960, Morocco had gotten the Soviet Union to veto Mauritania's application. But in 1961 the Soviets were reluctant to repeat their veto, and for good reason. Moscow did not want to antagonize a large group of African countries, the twelve Francophone African nations. The Soviets indicated that they would not veto Mauritania if the United States or any other country on the Security Council did not veto Outer Mongolia's application.

This gave the black African states a chance to do some hard bargaining. They told us that unless we abstained and got Nationalist China to do the same on the Outer Mongolian vote in exchange for Soviet abstention on Mauritania, they, the African States, would vote as a block to admit Communist China to the UN. Their votes would tip the balance in favor of Peking. At that time Kennedy could not afford to allow the Chinese Communists to be admitted to the UN because American public opinion was still strongly against it. Subsequently, Kennedy not only agreed to abstain on Outer Mongolia but, after putting considerable pressure on Chiang Kai-shek, got him to abstain, too. Mauritania and Outer Mongolia were admitted and the African states kept their part of the bargain. Once again the Chinese Communists' application for admission was rejected.

My wife and I, with our two youngest sons, David, then fourteen, and Charles, almost eleven, arrived in Dakar in July 1961 at the height of the hot, humid season. The warmth of our reception by both the Senegalese and the French helped ease our adjustment to this new world. We were particularly concerned about how our sons would cope. To make it easier for them to bridge the language gap, we had asked Marianne Wurlitzer, a Vassar graduate in French, to join us for a year. She was a great help. The boys entered the Dakar lycée, one of the finest outside of France. By the end of the first year they were at home in French and had proved themselves fine young diplomats. They still treasure their experience with their Senegalese classmates.*

Senghor was the most appealing aspect of my new assignment. A poet as well as a statesman—he had been nominated for the Nobel Prize in Literature in 1962—Senghor was probably the world's most cultivated chief of state. Later, he was the first black to be elected to the French Academy. The French in Africa tried to make Frenchmen out of the Africans and Senghor was a model product of that effort. The closest British parallel was India's Nehru, who had been educated at Harrow, the elitist public school, and Cambridge University. After attending the lycée in Dakar, Senghor received a scholarship to study in Paris at the renowned Lycée Louis-le-Grand and at the Sorbonne, where one of his classmates was Georges Pompidou, the future French prime minister and president. They became lifelong friends (Senghor often talked to me about Pompidou). In the mid-1930s Senghor became the first African Agrégé in French language and literature, a degree the French consider superior to our Ph.D. He taught French at the Lycée Henri-IV, one of Paris's most prestigious schools.

A soldier in the French army, Senghor was captured in 1940 and spent two years in a Nazi concentration camp, where he managed to write some of his best poetry. On his release he joined the French Resistance, and soon after the war launched his political career. He was the chairman of the French Constituent Assembly's subcommittee, which vetted the draft of the Fourth Republic's new constitution for grammatical correctness, a remarkable tribute to his knowledge of the French language. In 1946 he was one of the two Senegalese elected to the National Assembly in Paris on the French Socialist ticket. Thereafter, he founded his own African Socialist Party. He served in the French National Assembly until the French territories became independent in 1960, and was a leader of its Overseas Block (some twenty-three members),

---

*As professional writers they have found being bilingual invaluable. David, who is a professor of modern European history, is the author of *Politics and War: European Conflicts from Philip II to Hitler*, a History Book Club selection; Charles, who has taught journalism at Columbia and Princeton, is the author of *1968 in America*.

which helped make and unmake French governments. He was a secretary of state in several French cabinets.

When independence came to the former French colonies, Senghor failed in his efforts to create a federal African government to replace the French West African empire. He always deplored "micronationalisme," the emergence of too many small, less viable states. He was elected president of Senegal in 1960 after the breakup of the Mali Federation.

Senghor advocated an "African socialism," which he described as being "open, democratic, and humanistic." "We stand," he said in 1959, "for a democratic socialism which goes far to integrate spiritual values, a socialism which ties in with the ethical current of French Socialists." Referring to Léon Blum's *À l'Échelle Humaine*, written while Blum was a prisoner of war, Senghor added, "Historically and culturally we belong to this current." He sought to remove the old colonial barriers between Anglophone and Francophone Africa—while continuing to cooperate closely with France.

Though a product of French culture, he never lost his pride in being an African. Writing extensively about African culture, he was one of three originators of the concept of "negritude," which stressed the uniqueness of the African heritage and the contribution it could make to international culture. Senghor was also familiar with the works of American black writers, some of whose poetry he had translated into French.

Given the similarities between Senghor and Kennedy, it seemed inevitable that a special bond would develop between these two men. They were both intellectuals, both highly cultivated, both Catholic in countries predominantly Protestant or Moslem, and, not least of all, both creative, pragmatic politicians.

I soon realized the extent to which President Kennedy had prepared the way for his ambassadors. When I presented my credentials to President Senghor, he recalled Kennedy's 1957 speech on Algeria and the enthusiasm it had aroused throughout Africa. He liked the way Kennedy had dealt with Africa since becoming President. He particularly appreciated the change in U.S. policy toward Africa. Eisenhower and Dulles had pressed the new African countries to ally themselves with Washington. It was not good enough if they were neutral or "nonaligned." Kennedy took a different position. He understood why they didn't want to be enmeshed in the Cold War. If these new nations were genuinely neutral, this would serve U.S. interests. The new Kennedy policy made moderate "nonaligned" states like Senegal more favorably disposed toward the United States, and helped change the attitude of more radical states like Guinea toward Washington.

Nor did it take long to appreciate why those who predicted Senghor's early fall proved to be wrong. Few chiefs of state could match his political skill or his personal charisma. A Catholic and a member of the minority Serer tribe, he became head of a Moslem country where the Wolof tribe predominated. He maintained a close personal relationship with Moslem religious leaders. Although a brilliant intellectual, he drew his main support from the Senegalese peasants. Reflecting the historic association between France and Senegal, he envisaged a future that was a blend of African and French cultures. (He practiced what he preached by marrying a Frenchwoman.) He was an outstanding orator, too, who communicated easily with all sections of his society. In short, he created a consensus from a diversity of groups and interests in a new country struggling to create a viable democracy, though poorly endowed with natural resources. And, except for one serious crisis which he successfully overcame, he deftly sustained that consensus over two decades.

Three months after my arrival in Dakar, I accompanied Senghor on a visit to Washington. The trip provided me with an extraordinary opportunity to see President Kennedy's legendary charm in action. Senghor was excited about the prospect of meeting Kennedy and, at his request, I provided him with a copy of the just published *Strategy for Peace*, a collection of Kennedy's speeches that had been translated into French.

With Arthur Schlesinger's help, we arranged for Senghor to lecture at Harvard before he arrived in Washington. It was the first subject Kennedy raised when the three of us flew in a helicopter from Andrews Air Force Base, where the President had greeted Senghor, to the White House lawn. I acted as interpreter. "I understand you visited my old university," Kennedy began. "Yes," replied Senghor, "I enjoyed it very much. I read some of my poetry and discussed it with them, and there were a lot of young men and women there who could obviously handle French." For Senghor, an essential requirement for being a cultivated individual was the ability to understand and speak French.

This opened things up nicely. Then Senghor said, "Mr. President, before coming over I read your *Stratégie pour la Paix* and I was impressed with what you wrote. I'm sorry I didn't read it in English, but I wanted to read it quickly. I agree with practically everything you wrote." "Well, thank you," Kennedy replied, "but I've been in office now for eight months and I've learned that it's much easier to write about these things than to act on the basis of what you've written."

When Senghor expressed awe at the Lincoln Memorial as we approached it, the President immediately called the pilot on the intercom and ordered: "Fly slowly around the Lincoln Memorial and let President Senghor have a good look at it." As we did, Kennedy gave a brief history of the structure including some interesting details on its architecture. Senghor was charmed.

After landing on the White House lawn we went directly into the Oval Office. The two presidents were now completely at ease, and serious substantive talks began immediately. "I've a very important decision to make in regard to an African country," Kennedy said, "and I need your advice. We have this Volta dam project in Ghana, which involves a large amount of aid for Nkrumah. And," he added, "you know, I'm sure, what the problem is with this man. I must be frank with you. If I give Nkrumah this much aid, other African countries won't receive as much aid as they otherwise might have."

Senghor rose to the compliment. He obviously appreciated Kennedy's asking for advice on one of the White House's toughest African problems. The key to Kennedy's new African approach was his willingness to live with policies of genuine neutrality or nonalignment of the new countries. In October 1961, however, he couldn't be certain about Ghana. Nkrumah's frequent tilts toward the Communist countries raised legitimate doubts about his "nonalignment," and his repressive domestic policies added to the concern about his regime. The issue had come to a head over the Volta project originally conceived by the British colonial administration. A dam in the Volta River would make Ghana much more viable economically by creating a large lake to help irrigation and transport, and by generating hydroelectric power, which would facilitate the construction of a smelter to convert Ghana's large bauxite deposits into aluminum.

When the British and Canadian aluminum industries were unable to finance the project, it drew the attention of Kaiser Industries, an American aluminum producer. (No relation, alas.) After a study on the spot, Kaiser decided that the dam was economically feasible, and in 1961 they were the main partner in a group that pressed the new administration for financial support for the project.

After receiving Nkrumah in March 1961, Kennedy, who was impressed with him, was inclined to support the Volta project. But soon thereafter Nkrumah toured the Communist countries, from Eastern Europe to Peking. His statements in each capital were so favorable to his hosts that he raised new doubts about his commitment to nonalignment.

Kennedy then became subject to considerable pressure against providing the large loan to Ghana. Among those who were opposed to it were his brother Bobby, and Senator Albert Gore of Tennessee, the President's old colleague who was chairman of the Senate Sub-Committee on African Affairs. Before making a final decision the President sought the views of the heads of African governments, particularly those who were unfriendly to Nkrumah.

Senghor's reply to Kennedy was characteristically charming, and frank. "Mr. President," he said, "I appreciate your asking me for advice. Let me start by saying what Nkrumah needs more than anything else is a psychiatrist—and a very good psychiatrist. I know the character. I visited him last year on a state visit. I could tell you about the stunt he pulled to prevent me from speaking to the students at the University of Ghana, most of whom were not friendly to him. Earlier in the day he had seen the text of my speech. It had ideas and views that he didn't find congenial. And he managed to sabotage my appearance by touring me around until it was too late for me to see any students.

"But," concluded Senghor, "in spite of this man's instability, in spite of his radical politics with most of which I disagree, Mr.

President, you have no alternative but to go along with the project, particularly if it's economically feasible. Otherwise the Africans will accuse you of violating your own policies in regard to neutrality and nonalignment." And Senghor concluded by underlining that Kennedy should approve the Volta project even if it meant that other African countries would get less aid. A few months later Kennedy did approve it.

Ghana was the most pressing item in a two-hour *tour d'horizon* that covered the other major African issues, such as the Congo, as well as the broader international problems. Senghor couldn't help but be impressed by Kennedy's detailed knowledge of African affairs, and his genuine regard for Senghor's own views on the subjects Kennedy raised. Senghor was delighted, too, when Kennedy asked him about "negritude" and "African socialism," two of Senghor's favorite subjects.

The personal rapport established in the Oval Office was delightfully reinforced at the lunch Kennedy gave in Senghor's honor. In his toast, Kennedy said that he knew some chiefs of state who wrote poetry, but luckily didn't have the courage to publish it. Happily however, Senghor was one who did publish and in doing so enriched the world culturally. Kennedy's toast was translated into French by a professional interpreter.

Senghor's response was elegant, clear, and simple, a little simpler than usual because I had told him that Kennedy's French was rather elementary. (In the three years I heard Senghor speak it in a wide variety of circumstances, he always performed superbly.) Kennedy was so delighted that he could understand Senghor's response that when the interpreter rose to translate, the President jumped up and said, "I'm terribly sorry, but we're not going to have President Senghor insulted by having his remarks translated. If there was anybody who didn't understand this elegant, wonderfully clear French, it's their misfortune." Senghor beamed, and like Kennedy didn't seem to mind that there were people at the lunch who knew no French at all and couldn't possibly understand, even if Senghor's French was easily comprehensible.

As we got up from the table, Kennedy asked me to bring over Walter Lippmann. When he introduced Senghor to Lippmann, following the usual "What a great honor it is to meet you,"

Senghor added, "Ah! Mr. Lippmann, needless to say, I have read you regularly down through the years and thanks to you I have been enlightened on many complicated issues. . . . I've been able to understand things that otherwise would have been beyond my comprehension." Kennedy poured it on: "Well, President Senghor, I know exactly what you mean. The trouble is, however, that Mr. Lippmann writes his column only three times a week. On Tuesday, Thursday, and Friday, when his columns appear, life is simple for me. I know what to do, what decisions to take. But the other days," Kennedy concluded, "when there is no column, I'm lost. I flounder. I don't know the answers." Lippmann lapped it up. He beamed like a child who had been given the largest ice cream cone imaginable.

Senghor purred over the visit as shortly before midnight we flew back to New York in a government plane. About twenty minutes before we were due to land at La Guardia, he said to me, "It's been an exhilarating and long day. I'm tired, so if you'll excuse me I'm going to the back of the plane to catch a quick nap. We blacks have one advantage over you whites: we have no trouble sleeping whenever we so desire."

Senghor's visit paid off handsomely. It established a warm personal relationship between the two dynamic, highly literate presidents, and it solidified my position as the on-the-spot interlocuteur. Senghor couldn't help but notice how Kennedy went out of his way to make it clear that I was his man in Senegal.

Historically, the prime responsibility of an ambassador is to interpret the views of his own government to the government to which he is accredited and to report with equal accuracy the views of that government to the leaders of his own country. To do this effectively, access to top officials is essential. A president or a prime minister will happily receive an ambassador when he knows the latter has the confidence of his president and will look forward to developing the kind of rapport that makes for full and fair discussions, even on difficult and embarrassing issues. Kennedy knew that by associating his ambassadors with himself personally he would stimulate that kind of relationship.

Not all Presidents have been so wise. When President Nixon made his first trip abroad in 1969, he decided to meet with groups of influential private citizens in Western Europe. He insisted his ambassadors not be present because he believed that private citizens would then speak more frankly to him. This absurd request belittled his ambassadors.*

My first meetings with Senghor had been friendly enough, but after his visit to Washington he became even more accessible, and our discussions were more wide-ranging, relaxed, and frank, whether we were talking about agreeable items or contentious issues. It was a pleasure "to do business" with Senghor. He was the epitome of the cultivated gentleman. Of medium height, his tailoring was impeccable, his bearing dignified and easy. There was a wise, friendly twinkle in his eye and his pride in being an African seemed to enhance his stature. He spoke deliberately, making sure that every word was heard and easily understood.

He was always on schedule. I was never kept waiting for a moment, and he usually covered the agenda briskly, thoroughly, and invariably with a touch of humor, with a single exception. During one of our meetings I had barely begun to cover my agenda when Senghor said that unfortunately he had to break away to attend the funeral of the son of the president of the National Assembly. I was surprised by this unusual behavior since I, too, was planning to be present at the funeral and knew it was scheduled to take place three hours later.

Five minutes after my return to the embassy, a special presidential messenger appeared to convey the president's apologies and to ask me to return to the palace to resume our discussion. The president had made a mistake, the messenger reported, about the time of the funeral, and would appreciate my returning. I was glad to do so.

Senghor liked general discussions, too—about socialism, capitalism, and Communism; about the failure of Soviet agriculture and the remarkable productivity of America's farmers; about colonialism and neocolonialism; about de Gaulle's role on the world stage; and, not least of all, about race relations. We were engaged in a continual dialogue (one of Senghor's favorite words), aimed at discovering common ground between our two countries in

*See pages 258–59.

spite of differences in institutions, economic development, and social forms, in a world beset by the ideological struggle between East and West.

Senghor was particularly interested in developments on civil rights in America, and when we talked about racism he showed his understanding of our problems. Though not uncritical, he approved of the efforts made by the Kennedy administration to fight segregation. "Racism is as old as mankind," he would say, "and it's essential that governments fight against it." On one occasion he was smilingly reassuring: "You Americans are not so bad when it comes to prejudice against blacks. The Arabs were worse, followed by Asian Indians and the Lebanese.* Americans are fourth on the list."

No African chief of state was so sensitive as Senghor to the political winds blowing across his continent, nor so aware that cultural and educational relations between countries now supplemented traditional diplomacy. He appreciated the several millions in American aid: Food for Peace, funds for four secondary schools, and road-building equipment. He seemed even more grateful, however, for the $35,000 the Ford Foundation granted, on my recommendation, to help finance Senghor's conference, African Roads to Socialism,† and the $50,000 from the Rockfeller Foundation for Nigerian student scholarships to study French at the University of Dakar.

Senghor was enthusiastic, too, about the Peace Corps. He was impressed that young Americans were prepared to devote several years of their lives to helping the Senegalese. When I first discussed the work planned for the Peace Corps—digging wells, building one-room schools, and teaching English in the *brousse*, or countryside, where scattered trees and sparse underbrush provided the only relief from the hot sun—Senghor asked, "Do you intend to leave the young people here even during the Hivernage?" The

---

*For decades the Lebanese had been the small shopkeepers in French West Africa.

†It was at this conference that I first met James Callaghan, the future British prime minister who represented the British Labour Party. We spent the weekend together in Gambia, the neighboring British colony. This was the beginning of a friendship that flourished during my years as minister in London.

Hivernage covered the six months of exceptionally hot, muggy climate. "Of course, we expect the Peace Corps to carry on throughout the year," I replied. *"Excellence,"* said the shocked Senghor, "that is cruelty itself! My own family sent me to France during the hot season. It is almost unbearable to stay here."

Senghor liked to receive American visitors, too, private as well as official. It gave him a chance to learn about our society. He related to all of them and invariably charmed them, too, regardless of background. He could discuss dancing with Gene Kelly or Martha Graham; education with Father Theodore Hesburgh or Grayson Kirk; literature with James Baldwin; civil liberties with Justice William O. Douglas; and women's athletics with the Olympic champion Wilma Rudolph.

He was impressive in his meetings with official visitors. G. Mennen ("Soapy") Williams, the assistant secretary of state for African affairs, was so charmed that he stopped in Dakar three times during my three-year tour. Senghor was masterful in dealing with Senator Alan Ellender of Louisiana, who came to Africa looking for material that would enable him to cut back appropriations for U.S. aid and information programs. He insisted, too, on meeting the chiefs of state in the countries he visited. When I told Senghor of the purpose of Ellender's visit, I added that he was a conservative and a racist, but chairman of the powerful Senate Appropriations Committee. With a twinkle in his eye, Senghor responded, *"Excellence, je comprends."*

I offered to act as the senator's interpreter when he met with Senghor, but he bravely insisted on using his Cajun French. It was an unforgettable linguistic scene: a wide-ranging conversation, alternating between perhaps the most elegant French in the world and the Louisiana patois. On our way out, in the corridors of the presidential palace, Ellender said, "Phil, are you sure Senghor is all black?" "You saw him, Senator," I replied. "He must have some white blood," Ellender concluded. "He's too intelligent to be all black."

When I thought Senghor was off-base, I didn't hesitate to tell him. Once, in a long speech to his party congress, he picked up de Gaulle's line equating the Soviet Union with the United States. He talked about "les Deux Grands," the two superpowers, without really differentiating between them. He made the point that unlike the Soviet Union and the United States, France was no longer powerful enough to be "imperialist." He was overemphasizing his nonalignment while justifying his close ties to France. The speech was aimed primarily at the young radicals in his party who always attacked him for being too pro-French.

Equating the two superpowers was not only wrong, it was so out of character with what I'd heard him say before, both publicly and privately, that I decided to confront him about it. *"Monsieur le Président,"* I said, "I'm afraid I haven't represented my country very well if a man of your intelligence, your political understanding, and your knowledge of history can suggest that there's no difference between the Soviet Union and the United States. Obviously, I haven't been able to explain satisfactorily what the United States stands for, our traditions and our aspirations."

He was taken aback for a few moments, but quickly rallied and said, *"Excellence,* you have a point. The trouble is, I drafted a good deal of this speech before President Kennedy was inaugurated."

I didn't let him get away with that. "I'm talking," I said, "about something fundamental in American society. Among your favorite words are humanism and democracy, words that inspired our founding fathers, the remarkable group of men who drafted our Constitution. Thomas Jefferson," I added, "who had an influence on the early stages of the French Revolution, was one of the greatest figures in our history. No one has articulated more clearly than he the ideas that must be the basis of free and democratic societies. Have you read anything about Thomas Jefferson?" I asked. He replied that he hadn't and asked me to give him a biography of Jefferson. I then brought the conversation back to his speech. "Let me reread it," he said. "It hasn't been published for distribution yet and, before it is, I'll make a few changes." He kept his word. When the subject came up again, I felt he appreciated that liberalism, humanism, and democracy had a long history in America and did not emerge suddenly with John F. Kennedy.

During the Cuban missile crisis Senghor showed that he understood the difference between the superpowers. After President Kennedy decided to place a naval blockade around Cuba, our military realized that Soviet planes could fly atomic warheads to Havana if they were able to land and refuel in West Africa. Only two airports had the necessary facilities, Dakar in Senegal and

Conakry in Guinea. Kennedy sent messages to his ambassadors in these two countries instructing them to see Presidents Senghor and Sékou Touré and convey his request to deny Moscow the use of their airports.

In his book *Thirteen Days*, which tells his story of the Cuban missile crisis, Robert Kennedy writes: "In Dakar Philip M. Kaiser had a close personal relationship with President Léopold Senghor, who a short time before had had a very successful visit to Washington. He, too, quickly perceived the change and agreed not to permit Russian planes to land or refuel in Dakar." It was rather more complicated than Bobby suggested.

The cable with instructions from Washington wisely included the text of the speech the President was going to deliver that night, telling the American people and the rest of the world about the crisis in Cuba, and the action he was taking to deal with it. I had no trouble arranging an immediate meeting with Senghor. After underlining the seriousness of the crisis and President Kennedy's need for help, I presented him with the text of the speech. Senghor read it in English (there had been no time for a French translation) and said, "This is indeed very serious! I must help President Kennedy to the extent that I can . . . we're nonaligned and the Russians aren't using the airport now. It would violate our policy if we changed our practice."

Senghor was worried, however, about his prime minister, Mamadou Dia, who was much more to the left and had, in fact, just returned from a visit to Moscow. (Several weeks later, their disagreements came to a head with Dia's abortive attempt to overthrow Senghor.) Thinking out loud Senghor said, "You know I'm having some trouble with my prime minister." He paused before adding, "I'm having a cabinet meeting tomorrow morning. Can you write me a letter about President Kennedy's request and have it delivered to me personally at the palace before 8:00 A.M.?"

When he mentioned Mamadou Dia, I pointed out that I had had word that Sékou Touré was going to deny the Soviets the use of Conakry's airport. Bill Attwood, our ambassador to Guinea, had handled Touré skillfully, and Washington had done a good job in keeping both embassies informed. I added, "Of course, you realize, Mr. President, it would be incomprehensible to the American people and to President Kennedy in particular if Touré, the radical, closed down his airport and you didn't close down Dakar." "Oh!" he said. "You must include that in the letter, the fact that Touré is closing down Conakry."

I went back to the embassy, and with the help of my top colleagues (we all knew French) prepared the letter. The next morning I had my political officer, Steve Low, who in later years became our ambassador to Zambia and Nigeria, deliver it directly to Senghor before eight. Early in the afternoon Senghor informed me that Senegal would not let the Russians use the Dakar airport.

A few weeks later the ideological and personal differences between Senghor and Mamadou Dia came to a head. When Senghor's supporters in the National Assembly forced Mamadou Dia to resign, the prime minister responded by holing up in his offices at "Le Building," the government's principal administrative center, which in colonial days had served as the headquarters of French officials. After corralling the support of his gendarmerie (he served as minister of defense as well as prime minister), Dia moved to unseat Senghor. The president, however, was able to resist successfully because he had the backing of the large and more powerful Senegalese army as well as popular support. For several days there was great anxiety over the possibility of a bloody civil war.

At the critical moment, when the outcome was still in doubt, I felt that our embassy information on what was transpiring was inadequate. Before reporting to Washington I decided to call on my French colleague Lucien Paye, because the French had special intelligence assets in Senegal. In addition to the thirty-five thousand French civilians living in Dakar, there was a military garrison of some six thousand soldiers and about twelve hundred French "technical counselors" who were acting as advisers in every one of the government's ministries.

Paye was a distinguished French educator and public servant. He had served as rector at the University of Dakar, as de Gaulle's minister of education, and, after his diplomatic tour in Senegal, he became France's first ambassador to Communist China. He was an open, engaging individual and we had become close friends.

He received me warmly and showed me the cable he'd just sent to Paris, a collegial gesture that I very much appreciated. It was helpful, too, because it filled in gaps in our information. We were discussing the crisis when Paye's chief intelligence officer, a naval commander who had lost an arm in Vietnam, barged in, obviously to report something special to his ambassador. I rose to leave, but Paye insisted I stay. "No secrets between us," he said.

The commander then stated that Mamadou Dia had just been taken by Senghor's supporters on the fifth floor of "Le Building." This was dramatic stuff, but for the moment Paye and I played it cool and continued our conversation. A few minutes later the commander returned somewhat embarrassed to announce that he had been mistaken. Mamadou Dia had not been taken but was trapped between the fifth and seventh floors.

I left soon thereafter. As I walked back to the embassy I decided not to report that Dia was trapped. My doubts were justified. Dia was not taken between the fifth and seventh floors. He got up to the thirteenth, where control of the country's communications system enabled him to order the provincial gendarmerie to march on Dakar. The army stopped them, however, by blocking the three access roads to the capital. Dia was taken prisoner at 5:00 A.M. the next morning. French intelligence could also be wrong.

After my first year in Senegal, President Kennedy gave me another African assignment. He asked me to be his special ambassador to Rwanda, in central Africa, when it formally received its independence from Belgium. I agreed, though I was sorry it meant missing my first Fourth of July reception for the Senegalese. When I phoned the White House for more details about the mission I asked why the President had chosen me when there were five American ambassadors posted between the thousands of miles separating Dakar from Kigali, the capital of Rwanda.

The White House replied that some feared there would be the same kind of disturbance in Rwanda that had occurred in nearby Congo (now Zaire) when it became independent. There was a long history of bloody conflicts in Rwanda between the two main tribes, Tutsi and Huti. The President wanted someone he knew to represent him. I appreciated the compliment, but it didn't add to my sense of security. Typical of that Cold War period, soon after the White House announced that I was going as the President's special envoy to Rwanda, Paris, London, and Moscow announced that they, too, were sending their special representatives.

To reach Kigali in time I had to break away from my lunch in honor of Father Theodore Hesburgh, the president of Notre Dame University. I had first to fly north to Paris, then south to Athens, where I picked up a Belgian Sabena overnight flight to Bujumbura, the capital of Burundi, Rwanda's neighbor. It was a rough flight, one of the worst I've ever experienced. Upon arrival I was met by our local consul and the American air attaché from Leopoldville (today Kinshasa), whom the White House had asked to fly me to Kigali. The Air Force colonel told me that he would get me there safely, although there was no airport in Kigali, just a strip long enough for a DC-3 and a flag on a pole to indicate the direction of the wind. He had flown to Kigali the day before and was now confident he could safely negotiate the surrounding mountains.

I spent a vivid two days in the Rwandan capital. Because the local young American consul had no guest room in his modest quarters, he arranged to put me up in the best available facility, a room above a lively café run by a woman of somewhat doubtful reputation.

The President of Rwanda received me soon after my arrival. I conveyed President Kennedy's warm congratulatory message, and we then had a long discussion about the problems of the new nations of Africa. The Rwandan chief executive made the usual pitch for American economic aid for his newly independent country.

At the ceremony the next day, not surprisingly, I found myself seated between the foreign and finance ministers. All went off delightfully, and peacefully. At the dramatic moment when the president began to speak, immediately after the Belgian flag had been lowered and the Rwandan raised, an African baby, held in the lap of his beautiful mother seated behind us, began to cry loudly. When I turned around one of the ministers said to me, "There's no problem; the child is the son of the president."

The highlight of the celebration was the scintillating African dance of the Tutsi, strikingly handsome people all well over six feet tall who performed to a lively drum accompaniment.

The holiday spirit was sustained in the reception given by the president after the formal ceremony. I left soon after, before it was dark, the air attaché having emphasized that there were no facilities for a night takeoff. We made a special stop in Bujumbura where I was able to cable Washington a report of my two days in Kigali. I was happy to emphasize that there was no rioting, nor any sign of disorder. The festivities, I concluded, were very much like our Fourth of July celebrations.

From Bujumbura I flew to Leopoldville, where I picked up a Pan American flight that landed in Dakar at 2 A.M. July 5.

By the end of my tour in Senegal and Mauritania, U.S. interest in Africa began to lag. The glamour about the continent was wearing thin as we became increasingly aware of the depth of its problems. Furthermore, our government became heavily engaged elsewhere. Relations with the Soviet Union, Latin America, Western Europe, and the problems of Vietnam consumed more and more of the administration's time and energy. Senghor talked to me about it several times, as did Mokhtar Ould Daddah. "Why isn't more aid forthcoming? Why is Africa being neglected?"

In spite of the pressures from other parts of the world, Kennedy did not lose his interest in Africa. In October 1963, a few weeks before his assassination, he found time to receive the president of Mauritania and to be briefed about him before his arrival.

Mokhtar Ould Daddah was not as formidable as Senghor—he was younger, more reserved, less worldly—but still something of a persona in his own right. His poise and dignity reflected the fact that he was an aristocratic Moor. The son of a Maraboutic family, the religious elite of Mauritania, he was trained as a lawyer in France and was married to an attractive Frenchwoman who had been at law school with him. He had the intelligence, cunning, and patience required to preside over a barren country that was beset by economic and social tensions.* Its black population, inhabiting the northern shores of the Senegal River, was better trained and more prosperous than the Arab Moors who were in the majority. The blacks spoke French; the Moors, who spoke Arabic, resented the fact that French was the official language. A few years later, after I left Africa, Ould Daddah made Arabic the official language, which led to the outbreak of bloody riots.

*Ould Daddah was overthrown years later after unwisely joining his old enemy, Morocco, in the long and fruitless struggle with Algeria for control of Western Sahara, the former Spanish Morocco.

Since I didn't reside in the Mauritanian capital, I only saw the president about once a month. But distance had its advantages. Thanks to my chargé, William Eagleton,* who lived in the capital, Nouakchott, the agendas for my meetings were well prepared. I was invariably invited to luncheon or to dine with the President so that we conducted our business in a relaxed postprandial atmosphere. We developed a good personal relationship. On special occasions he provided a *méchoui*, when a whole sheep is roasted in sand. It was the centerpiece of the meal. After the second or third *méchoui*, Ould Daddah paid me the compliment of tearing off the most succulent parts of the animal and putting them on my plate. Luckily, I didn't receive the ultimate compliment, the eye, because I had told Eagleton to make sure Ould Daddah didn't offer it to me.

Being accredited to two governments tested one's diplomatic skill. Both presidents talked to me about the other. Although Senghor and Ould Daddah were basically friendly, some issues led to friction: Morocco, for example, didn't recognize Mauritania, while Senghor played up his excellent relations with Rabat. Ould Daddah sometimes resented the greater importance of Senegal, along with the fact that he was considered junior to Senghor. The continued dependence of Mauritania on the Dakar sea- and airports particularly irritated Ould Daddah. Several times he said to me, "We must liberate ourselves from Dakar." Needless to say, I never quoted one to the other. However, when I thought it appropriate, I tried tactfully to mitigate any difference.

Ould Daddah was also a great admirer of Kennedy, and as I accompanied him into the Oval Office, I could sense his awe for the President. Kennedy quickly put him at ease. The President began by congratulating Ould Daddah for voluntarily giving up direct French support for Mauritania's budget. Ould Daddah had taken this action to show that he was not just a "French stooge," a charge widely leveled against him. "This is wonderful," Kennedy said, "and so rare. So many of the new countries keep pressing us for budgetary support, and you voluntarily gave it up because you wanted to stand on your own two feet!"

---

*Eagleton later became U.S. ambassador to Syria.

Then followed a long *tour d'horizon* during which Ould Daddah impressed Kennedy by giving a reasonably objective analysis of the Algerian-Moroccan border war, even though it was clearly to his advantage to make Algeria look better. To Kenneth O'Donnell's annoyance (he was the President's appointment assistant), the conversation lasted an hour longer than scheduled. O'Donnell was waiting to bring in a delegation from Illinois and, as Ould Daddah and I left the Oval Office, O'Donnell muttered to me, "There are more votes in Illinois than in Mauritania!"

One subject not mentioned during the meeting between the two presidents was the problem with Mauritania involving Pan American Airways. Shortly before Ould Daddah's arrival, Pan Am had launched a third flight to Africa, whose route was New York, Lisbon, Rabat, and Conakry. The most direct route, Rabat to Conakry, was eight hundred miles over Mauritania. To show how tough he was, and that Mauritania was not just a "client state" of France, Ould Daddah refused to allow a plane that had touched down in imperialist, dictatorial Portugal, and then in Morocco, which had not recognized him, to use Mauritanian air space. This decision was costly to Pan American. In order to reach Conakry, planes had to fly westward across North Africa and down the coast to Guinea—several hundred miles more than the direct path over Mauritania. We had made representations to the Foreign Ministry about the matter, but without success. We decided to wait for Ould Daddah's visit to Washington to discuss it with him.

When the Pan Am problem came up at the presidential briefing it was apparent that Kennedy was loath to raise it with Ould Daddah. I suggested that instead we give him "the Arab treatment." On the way back to New York on the government plane, when we talked about his visit, I would say to Ould Daddah, "There was a matter President Kennedy wanted to bring up but because you were his guest, he didn't think it would be appropriate." The President was delighted with the idea and instructed me to proceed as proposed.

It worked, too. When Ould Daddah raved about his visit with Kennedy, I raised the Pan Am matter, explaining that because he was the President's guest, Kennedy had not done so. I repressed my smile when Ould Daddah acted surprised, saying that he was unaware of the restriction on overflying Mauritania. It is no secret that in Africa only chiefs of state make this kind of decision. When his foreign secretary, whom he called over from the other end of the plane, self-consciously confirmed the Pan Am restriction, Ould Daddah ordered, "I want the policy changed immediately."

Ould Daddah and his entourage returned to Africa the next day on a Pan Am flight that flew direct to Dakar. Within moments of their arrival in Nouackchott, the foreign minister called Bill Eagleton to inform him that the restrictions on Pan Am flights over Mauritania had been removed. Such was the impact Kennedy had on African chiefs of state.

The last time I saw President Kennedy was during Ould Daddah's visit. I remember the President's words. As we were leaving the Oval Office the two presidents walked together with an interpreter between them. Soapy Williams and I were about ten feet behind. Kennedy turned his head back toward me as he said, loudly enough, "Don't say these nice things about the ambassador to me. Tell them to the ambassador. He's the fellow who would particularly like to hear them."

7

The United Kingdom
in the 1960s:
American Minister

When he was secretary of state, Dean Rusk rarely meddled in personnel matters; yet fortunately he did in my case after I had finished my tour as ambassador in Africa in 1964. Rusk and I became friends when we were both members of Truman's Little Cabinet. He responded enthusiastically to the suggestion that I serve as minister, deputy chief of mission, in the London embassy. Having been a Rhodes Scholar—Rusk preceded me by four or five years—he appreciated the value of friendships Americans made with British students during their years at Oxford. He knew that several of my British contemporaries, with whom I had kept in touch over the years, were now key figures in the Labour and Conservative parties.

It took bureaucratic courage on Rusk's part to push my appointment to London. Although I had been a public servant for many years, I was not a Foreign Service officer, and this was the first time that the minister in London was not a member of the corps.

Happily, David Bruce, the ambassador in London, accepted Rusk's proposal that I serve as his deputy. Bruce was head of the Marshall Aid Agency (ECA) in France when we first met, and I saw him regularly after he became our ambassador to Paris, as I usually stopped in the French capital on my way to or from Geneva. We saw each other in Washington, too, when he served as undersecretary of state toward the end of the Truman administration.

My arrival in London, scheduled for August 1964, was delayed because my routine medical checkup revealed that I had picked up tuberculosis in Africa. I spent six weeks in Bethesda Naval Hospital, where I was treated royally, or rather, like an admiral. After a fortnight they allowed me to leave on weekends during which, with doctors' permission, I happily spent afternoons at Averell Harriman's pool in the garden of his Georgetown home. We now take for granted the miraculous drug discovered shortly after the Second World War, which can cure tuberculosis, a disease that at one time had been as deadly as cancer. In three weeks the doctors informed me that the drug was beginning to be effective, though for prophylactic reasons I had to take it for two years. Fortunately, I never felt any ill effects.

I arrived in London in October, a week after Labour had narrowly won the election, and was warmly received by Ambassador Bruce and my other colleagues in the embassy. I was cheered, too, by the welcome given me by old British friends, though in the first instance Ted Heath was a bit aloof. Apparently he was annoyed by the story that the embassy had predicted a Labour victory, a report that had appeared in the British press, and by an item in *Newsweek*'s Periscope that I had been sent to London because of my contacts with members of the Labour Party and British trade unionists. But these obstacles were soon overcome, and Heath and I saw each other regularly throughout my years in London.

On one occasion during those years a photo of Heath and me with a small group of friends, along with my wife, Hannah, and my youngest son, Charles, appeared on the front page of several newspapers in Great Britain. In late August 1967, Heath, then leader of the Conservative Party, had invited us all to a Sunday picnic at his father's home in Broadstairs, east of London on the sea. Since it was August, in the best British tradition, politics had effectively closed down. Heath had asked us to meet him at the town pub for a drink before adjourning to the garden of his father's house. There was so large a crowd in the pub that we were forced to stand in the street outside while Heath gathered up our drinks from the bar. As he was delivering them, the police came by and ordered us to squeeze onto the sidewalk, an ideal photo opportunity for the journalists covering the Tory opposition leader. My friendship with Heath was no secret, but this cozy photo still provoked amusing comment from my many friends in the Labour Party.

Among the ten guests of Heath that beautiful, sunny Sunday were Margaret Thatcher and her husband, Denis. At that time she was a political protégée of Heath's, which was one of the reasons he so resented her when she defeated him for the Conservative Party leadership in 1975, and was unable to adjust to the fact that she became prime minister.

My friendship with Heath was especially helpful during one potentially embarrassing situation. The relationship between President Johnson and Prime Minister Harold Wilson had its ups and downs. Wilson supported Johnson on Vietnam as far as he thought he could with many members of the Labour Party opposed to our military involvement in Southeast Asia, and very vocal about it. When we bombed Hanoi, Wilson felt compelled to criticize us, though he did so rather mildly. Johnson reacted with typical vehemence, sharply castigating the prime minister. As a consequence, relations between the two men, never too warm, deteriorated temporarily.

To reestablish a working rapport with his British colleague, Johnson invited Wilson to Washington. At midnight, after the dinner Johnson had given in honor of the prime minister, I received a phone call from Ted Heath. I was acting as chargé d'affaires in the embassy because Bruce was away. "This is the end," Heath said. "I want you to know that I'm going to blast your President tomorrow." "What are you talking about?" I asked. "Obviously you haven't heard the midnight news" was Heath's response. "At the President's dinner for Wilson tonight Johnson compared Wilson with Churchill and Churchill came out a poor second. This is too much." I urged Ted to hold his fire until we had a chance to see the text of what the President had said. I would call Washington immediately and ask them to cable me the President's speech. When I phoned Washington I couldn't reach Rusk but I found George Ball, the undersecretary, and reported my conversation with Heath. Ball said, "For God's sake, don't let him attack Johnson." "I'll do the best I can," I replied, "but first send me the text of the speech."

When the text arrived early the next morning I nervously dispatched a copy to Heath. Johnson had clearly been extravagant in his praise of Wilson. A few hours later Ted phoned me. "See what I mean," he said. "I'm going to blast your President." "Hold your horses," I replied. "Let me talk to you now as an old friend, *not* officially. Compared to Johnson, elephants suffer from amnesia. Johnson never forgets a criticism. The chances are that you will be prime minister while he is President, and if you criticize him, he will never forget or forgive you. Remember how he treated Alec Douglas-Home when Home was prime minister. On his way out of the Oval Office after seeing the President, Home met the press and criticized Johnson for chastising the British for sending buses to Cuba. The President never forgave Home, and never had contact with him again."

Heath heard me out. He was silent for several moments. Then he said, "I'll think about it." The next morning the Sunday press reported that high officials in the Conservative Party were unhappy about President Johnson's speech in Washington at his dinner for Wilson. But Heath made no direct personal attack.*

My contemporaries from Oxford days made up a fair share of the Labour cabinet. I had a casual acquaintance with Prime Minister Wilson, but among my friends dating back to the late thirties were Denis Healey, Dick Crossman, Roy Jenkins, Patrick Gordon Walker, and Lord Longford. Niall Macdermot, another Balliol classmate, was minister of state in the Housing Department. I had met Jim Callaghan when he visited Dakar in 1961 to represent the Labour Party at a conference sponsored by President Senghor, "The African Road to Socialism," and our friendship flourished after a weekend visit together to neighboring Gambia, which was still a British colony. I had easy access to all of them during my years in the embassy and they helped me develop close working relationships with their cabinet colleagues whom I had not known before, particularly Elwyn Jones, the attorney general, and the explosive George Brown, secretary of state for economic affairs in the first Wilson Cabinet, later foreign secretary. Several of them were of invaluable assistance in extricating us from some potentially embarrassing situations.

---

*Actually, Heath served as prime minister while Nixon was President, not Johnson.

On the Conservative side, old college contemporaries, now members of Parliament, included Hugh Fraser, Julian Amery, Tony Kershaw, and Maurice Macmillan, the son of the former prime minister, in addition to Ted Heath. I had seen them regularly during my frequent visits to London in the late 1940s and 1950s.

When I arrived in London, I was struck by the change in British-American relations over the preceding three decades. In spite of our common language, common traditions, and linked history, the ties between us were not particularly close in the 1930s. Exchanges occurred primarily among three communities of both countries: lawyers who shared the common-law tradition; bankers on Wall Street and in London's City; and stars of the New York and London stages and of Hollywood films. Thanks to the Rhodes Scholarships, there was also a growing community of interest in the academic world. By the 1930s about a thousand Rhodes Scholars had studied at Oxford, and a fair number had become professors at American universities.

There was, however, little contact between British and American politicians and our respective Foreign Services did very little collaborating before World War II. Nor was there any love between our two navies, while our armies had little to do with each other. Although FDR was highly regarded by many of the British, America would not have won a popularity contest in the old country while the United Kingdom would have done just as poorly in the United States. The familiar caricatures still persisted. Many English condescendingly found the United States strange, wild, and uncouth, while to many Americans the United Kingdom was a society dominated by a snobbish elitism. In addition, elements in American society were clearly hostile to Britain, particularly the Irish, who were becoming increasingly important politically.* There was resentment, too, over the British failure to repay debts from World War I.

In the years just before the outbreak of the Second World War relations between the two governments were not easy. While Britain, still a leading world power, was trying desperately to

---

*In the mid-1920s Wild Bill Thompson won an election as mayor of Chicago by running against King George V.

cope with the threat from Hitler's Germany, America was playing a peripheral role in international affairs. To underline our post–World War isolation we had passed new neutrality legislation. The British, and other Europeans, felt that our rejection of membership in the League of Nations after World War I and our subsequent reversion to isolationism had contributed to the European mess in the late 1930s. They resented, too, that this did not inhibit us from striking a moral pose and telling the British how to behave, particularly how to deal with Hitler, while making it clear that we did not intend to get directly involved.

The able corps of American newspaper correspondents stationed in London at this time contributed to some of the hard feelings between the United Kingdom and the United States. Ferdinand Kuhn of *The New York Times*, and his assistant, James Reston; Ed Murrow of CBS; Paul Ward of the *Baltimore Sun*; and William Stoneman of the *Chicago Daily News* all annoyed Whitehall by their continuous criticism of Neville Chamberlain's policies. Their reportage generated anti-British sentiment in the States. On the other hand, Margaret Halsey's book *With Malice Toward Some* stirred up considerable resentment in the United Kingdom. It was highly critical of British society and the government's foreign policy. A best-seller in America, it was also widely read in the United Kingdom. I was amazed when a respected Oxford figure seriously suggested that anti-British elements in America must have commissioned Halsey to write her book.

Not surprisingly, Chamberlain resented President Roosevelt's efforts to be helpful in light of America's official policy of neutrality. A secret message from FDR to Chamberlain contributed to Eden's decision to resign as foreign secretary in 1938, a major political event. The American President had recommended the convening of an international conference to deal with the mounting crisis posed by Hitler's aggressive expansionism. Chamberlain turned FDR down, without even bothering to consult his foreign secretary.

By the mid-1960s Anglo-American relations had changed dramatically. The "special relationship," a product of the wartime alliance and the subsequent Cold War, was still alive, though it had lost some of its steam.

It was altogether fitting that Winston Churchill was the author of the phrase "special relationship." He used it for the first time in 1946 in Fulton, Missouri,* in a speech more famous for his reference to the "Iron Curtain." Son of an American mother and a British father, Churchill proudly considered himself as much American as British; he felt he personally embodied the "special relationship." Long before the outbreak of hostilities, he thought the survival of Britain as a world power depended on a close friendship with the United States. The war, including Britain's magnificent repulse of Hitler's aerial onslaught, American entry into the struggle, and the extraordinary personal collaboration between Roosevelt and Churchill, the two "former naval persons," laid the foundation, emotional as well as practical, for the "special relationship" so close to Churchill's heart.

The relationship took on new substance in the years following the war, after FDR's death and Churchill's defeat in Britain's 1945 election. There had been differences between Churchill and Roosevelt on such issues as the future of the British Empire and the nature and extent of continued U.S. involvement in maintaining European security. Churchill had good reasons for fearing American reversion to a new isolationism. We forget that in the 1944 presidential campaign FDR felt compelled to deny Dewey's charge that he planned to keep our troops in Europe after the war—a charge that struck a responsive chord in the American electorate. However, the danger of the Soviet threat, which became clear to the West in the 1940s after Moscow lowered the "Iron Curtain," precluded the possibility of a U.S. withdrawal from Europe.

We looked for allies, and with France, Germany, and Italy still in postwar disarray, Great Britain became the logical, indeed the only possible, candidate. Once again practical considerations pro-

---

*Here is the relevant excerpt from that speech: "Neither the sure prevention of war nor the continuous rise of world organization will be gained without . . . the fraternal association of the English-speaking peoples. This means a special relationship between the British Commonwealth and Empire and the U.S. . . . Fraternal association requires not only the growing friendship and mutual understanding between our two vast but kindred systems of society but the continuance of the intimate relationship between our military advisers, leading to common study of potential dangers, similarity of weapons and manuals of instruction, and interchange of officers and cadets. . . ."

vided new substantive significance to our special relationship. Together we took the lead in creating the North Atlantic Treaty Organization, which so successfully institutionalized the Free World's defense against the challenge posed by the Soviet Union.

This new pragmatic basis for the special relationship persisted through the end of the 1950s—for as long as the United Kingdom remained Washington's most important NATO ally and still ranked as a major world power. The camaraderie U.S. and U.K. officials developed during the war came into play again. Many of the same individuals still held important positions, and both governments profited from these old friendships. Officials from both countries communicated frequently and easily. They cooperated in a manner unique in relations between two countries. This special mutual understanding also enabled the United Kingdom and the United States to handle differences without divisive fallout. Except for Eisenhower's sharp reaction to Eden's Suez invasion, the United States accepted with relative equanimity British diversion from U.S. policy on such issues as recognition of Red China, and the Jewish migration into Palestine.

By 1964, however, the United Kingdom no longer ranked as America's most powerful NATO ally. England had to adjust to a new reality; having lost her empire, she had become a middle-sized power seeking, in the words of Dean Acheson, "a new role" as Washington now directed attention to other allies, particularly Germany and France.

In spite of the disparity between British and American power, relations between our two peoples, and particularly our two governments, continued to be special in several important respects. In contrast to the situation thirty years earlier, Americans and Britons knew each other better and felt more comfortable with one another. Since the Second World War, when our servicemen were stationed in England, Americans and Britons had seen each other's countries in increasingly large numbers. Thanks to the revolution in air travel, tourism had expanded dramatically; there had also been a striking increase in student exchanges, and visits of businessmen, lawyers, and other professionals. The Fulbright and Marshall scholarships more than doubled the number of Rhodes recipients in the United Kingdom, and several American universities had arranged for their students to spend a junior year in London. In addition, a much larger number were doing graduate work in British universities while professorial exchanges were common. The 1960s also saw a considerable brain drain from British academia, with a fair number of professors permanently transferring to American universities. In fact, the universities and think tanks in both countries acted increasingly as a single community, with research, analysis, and discussion on social, economic, and political issues becoming transatlantic rather than national.

The growth in international trade influenced the relationship. Ties between Wall Street and the City, London's financial center, had become more extensive. Large New York and Washington law firms established offices in London to handle the foreign legal business of their major American clients. The membership roster of the American Chamber of Commerce in London included most blue-ribbon U.S. corporations and many other companies, reflecting the extent to which American industry had plants in the United Kingdom.

The 1960s saw a much greater interchange in the social and cultural worlds. London had become a "swinging" city. For young people who came of age then it was the undisputed cultural capital of the Western world. Everything from Carnaby Street fashions to the original James Bond movies with Sean Connery made anything English automatically "hip." British rock stars provided youth around the world with dozens of anthems, ranging from "Satisfaction" by the Rolling Stones to "Layla" by Derek and the Dominos.

The spectacular success of the Beatles made British popular culture dominant in the Western world. With their music, their movies, and their haircuts these four Liverpudlians seized what seemed to be absolute control of the hearts and minds of nearly every American under thirty. In the summer of 1967, with the release of their masterpiece, "Sgt. Pepper's Lonely Hearts Club Band," the Beatles imposed what one critic described as the greatest cultural unity the West had experienced "since the Congress of Vienna."

Americans flocked to London to enjoy its outstanding museums and renowned opera, ballet, and theater. London staged frequent productions of American hits and Broadway presented British successes. Hollywood movie producers were taking advantage of the superb corps of English actors and the fact that it was cheaper to produce films in England. Several American filmmakers settled in the British capital during this decade.

Douglas Fairbanks, Jr., was one of a group of American actors and writers who lived in London in the 1960s. Groucho Marx came for an extended stay and S. J. Perelman, the *New Yorker* satirist, who wrote several scripts for Marx Brothers films, moved to the British capital following the death of his wife. He intended to settle in England, but after a little over a year he returned to New York because, he said, "I can't write without regularly hearing New Yorkers speak in their native accents."

These American figures enhanced Anglo-American relations while enriching London's social life. I recall a dinner party that Mr. and Mrs. Douglas Fairbanks gave in honor of Mr. and Mrs. Charles Chaplin. Among the other guests was Chaplin's good friend Lord Mountbatten. When the men adjourned to the study, in accordance with the anachronistic British postprandial practice, Mountbatten turned to Chaplin and said, "Tell us about *A Countess from Hong Kong*, the movie you've just produced." Chaplin responded by acting out the roles of the main stars, Sophia Loren and Marlon Brando. It was vintage Chaplin, reminiscent of his great film performances. After several minutes he stopped short. "What am I doing?" he said. "If I continue, you fellows will never pay to see the movie." The film, incidentally, was a flop, probably because Chaplin himself played only a bit role.

None of this is to suggest that in the 1960s there was complete harmony between the people of both societies. The increase in exchanges and tourism helped dispel many old stereotypes, but could not overcome basic disagreements among certain elements in the two countries. Some British Conservatives, for example, had difficulty accepting the fact that the United States had replaced the United Kingdom as the leading world power. A few of them suggested yet again the old scenario—that now they would act as the wise, experienced "Greeks," counseling the raw, politically unsophisticated "Romans" how best to handle their new international role, an idea first articulated by Harold Macmillan when he served in North Africa as the top British adviser to General Eisenhower.

In the early 1960s, when Macmillan was prime minister, in

dealing with the young President Kennedy he tried to practice what he preached. I remember a dinner that Sir John Wheeler-Bennett, the distinguished diplomatic historian, gave in honor of his friend Harold Macmillan, at Garsington,* Wheeler-Bennett's historic Elizabethan home. Macmillan, whose mother was American, spoke avuncularly of his relationship with Kennedy, warmly describing his first meeting with him in Bermuda in 1962. He suggested that his personal appeal to the President influenced the latter's decision to allow Britain to replace Skybolt with the Polaris submarine. Macmillan made it clear that he enjoyed playing the role of the wise and experienced tutor to the young Chief Executive. The family connection between the two—Kennedy's sister Kathleen had been married to a close relative of Macmillan's wife—undoubtedly facilitated the special relationship between the prime minister and the President.

Ted Heath agreed with Macmillan's notion about Greeks and Romans, but was not so sympathetic toward the United States. Some thought that a factor in his passion for Europe was his belief that membership in the Common Market would make the United Kingdom less dependent on the United States.

For ideological reasons anti-American sentiment was strong among some British socialists, particularly left-wing members of the Labour Party who felt that the United States was the bulwark of world capitalism and obsessed with the Cold War. They vigorously, sometimes violently, opposed our involvement in Vietnam. Conversely, right-wing Americans were unhappy about the strong socialist strain in British society and what they considered an inadequate appreciation of the threat of Communism.

On the official level the relationship between the United States and the United Kingdom continued to be special, and no one appreciated its practical value more than those of us in the American embassy in London. Although no longer a world power, Britain was still the only Western country besides the United States that continued to have worldwide responsibilities. We shared interests in Europe, of course, in Africa, in the Middle East,

---

*The residence is described in great detail by Aldous Huxley in his novel *Chrome Yellow*. One of Garsington's previous owners was the famous hostess and mistress of Bertrand Russell, Lady Ottoline Morrell.

and, most important, east of Suez. Our interests also coincided in military strategy, disarmament, weapons technology, and particularly in nuclear weapons and intelligence. Moreover, the United Kingdom was a vital venue, "an invaluable aircraft carrier," for our military forces, particularly after de Gaulle withdrew French forces from NATO. Great Britain provided bases for the air squadrons that had to be moved from France and for our Polaris submarines.

Our embassy in London was structured and staffed to take advantage of the continuing convergence of Anglo-American interests. Experts on the British political scene, and on geographical areas around the world, were joined by officers who dealt with the wide range of new postwar responsibilities. There were sections on economics, labor, intelligence, information, culture, scientific, consular and legal affairs, and, of course, administration. The London embassy was a small-sized replica of the Washington bureaucracy, not just the arm of the State Department. Of the staff of more than seven hundred, only about seventy came from State.

More important than the structure of an embassy is the quality of its personnel. During the 1960s the London embassy was one of the most impressive in the U.S. Foreign Service. David Bruce, undoubtedly one of our outstanding ambassadors, set its tone and style. A student of American history and politics, he was also an expert on international affairs. He had been a member of both the Maryland and Virginia legislatures and author of a book, *America's First Sixteen Presidents*. During the war he served as the European director of the Office of Strategic Services, forerunner of the CIA, and was stationed in London. As assistant secretary of commerce under Averell Harriman in the late 1940s, he helped devise the Marshall Plan and subsequently became the head of the Marshall aid mission in France. Thereafter, he was ambassador to France, Germany, and then the United Kingdom, the only American ever appointed to all three posts. A close friend of Jean Monnet, he was an active supporter first of the Iron and Coal Community and then of the Common Market.

Unequaled in grace, wit, and charm, Bruce was an elegant host, a connoisseur of art and literature, and an outstanding gourmet.

His cable defending the quality of American compared to French wines is a vintage classic. He would have felt at home in Jefferson's Virginia. A personal paradigm of the special relationship, he was highly regarded in Washington, with whose bureaucratic idiosyncracies he was fully familiar, and deeply respected by all elements of British society. Keenly sensitive to the significance of political, economic, and defense developments in both countries, Bruce was a superb interlocutor between President and prime minister. Washington officials visiting London, particularly those at the highest level, sought his guidance in dealing with their British counterparts.

Bruce was equally skillful in handling the traditional functions of a chief of mission, as well as the new ambassadorial responsibilities in a world of instant communication, visiting presidents and roving foreign ministers. He took advantage of President Kennedy's letter of May 1961, which gave ambassadors ample authority to cover all the new operations of an embassy. Where possible he reduced superfluous personnel, though that was not always easy because his recommendations had to be carried out by different agencies in Washington. While State complied with his proposals, other departments were not so cooperative. He did succeed, however, in reducing the military attaché's office from seventy-two to twenty-three. Even the latter figure, he felt, was higher than necessary since London was the headquarters of the U.S. Navy in Europe, and England provided the bases for America's Third Air Force.

In the postwar world American ambassadors have become public figures who had to articulate the reasons for American policies and actions and to deal skillfully with an increasingly inquisitive media. Bruce performed this task with great style, and was held in high esteem by the British people and press, many of whom he and his beautiful wife, Evangeline, entertained in the ambassador's Regent's Park residence. He also found time for the large American community in England. Journalists, artists, actors, academics, and businessmen appreciated Bruce's continual efforts to advance their interests, and enjoyed his hospitality. They also took pride in the fact that he was so able and popular an ambassador.

An exceptional staff of officers, many of whom later became

outstanding ambassadors, served under Bruce. Ron Spiers, the political counselor, became ambassador to Pakistan and Turkey* while several members of the political section also became distinguished chiefs of mission: Monteagle Stearns served in the Ivory Coast and Greece, William Eagleton in Syria, and Hobart Spaulding in Singapore. Willis Armstrong, the embassy's economics minister, later served as assistant secretary of state for economic affairs while his deputy, Arthur Hartman, became the ambassador first to France and later the Soviet Union. Melissa Wells, our current ambassador to Zaire, was also a member of the economics section. Findlay Burns, the administrative counselor, was later our ambassador in Jordan and Ecuador. Burns and Peter Skoufis, his successor in London, were two of the ablest administration officers in the Foreign Service. Finally, Sheldon Krys, currently assistant secretary for security affairs, who was Ambassador Bruce's and my aide, was ambassador to Trinidad and Tobago.

The embassy's professional staff particularly appreciated the subtle ways in which Bruce would use his unique political knowledge and diplomatic experience, and his sensitivity to presidential and prime ministerial behavior, to advance U.S. interests. His cables to Washington were one of his major instruments. All cables leaving an embassy are signed by the ambassador, just as all cables leaving Washington bear the name of the secretary of state, but the ambassador's personal cables carried a rubric above the message that read "From the Ambassador to the Secretary of State," with the additional words "Please pass to the White House" whenever Bruce wanted the President to see it. And Presidents read David Bruce's cables. They were always drafted with a blend of wisdom, wit, and a clearly articulated objective—and they came sparingly.

Bruce understood that excessive reporting was counterproductive. Thousands of telegrams arrive daily in the Department of State and very few are seen by the secretary. I once asked Secretary Rusk how many cables he read a day, and he said usually between fifteen and twenty. When there was a crisis in a particular country he also would look at all the messages originating from that capi-

---

*He was also undersecretary for administration in the Reagan administration.

tal. Bruce saw to it that his messages were invariably among those few read, no mean bureaucratic achievement. In fact, Washington looked forward to receiving them.

I remember the impact on President Johnson of a cable Bruce sent while Alexei Kosygin was visiting London in 1967 during a Tet bombing truce in Vietnam. Harold Wilson had pressed the Soviet prime minister to urge Hanoi to enter into negotiations with Washington to settle the conflict in Vietnam. Wilson kept in close touch with the position of the United States, and Bruce drafted cables in his own handwriting well after midnight to keep the State Department and White House informed of the Wilson-Kosygin talks. In the early stages these conversations seemed to be producing results. The British had tapped Kosygin's phones in his Claridge's hotel suite and were encouraged by his remarks to Moscow suggesting that Hanoi should consider responding to the U.S. proposals. When the talks were aborted—they were not helped by a sudden hardening of our position—Washington informed the embassy that the United States would resume bombing of North Vietnam while Kosygin was still in London.

Bruce and I agreed that this was an unwise decision. We saw no reason why we couldn't wait until after Kosygin returned to Moscow, particularly since he had apparently tried to be helpful in his conversations with Wilson. We recalled, too, the bad impact on Kosygin when, months before, we had bombed Hanoi while he was visiting there. We decided to phone top officials in Washington urging them to hold off on the bombing until Kosygin had returned to Moscow. I talked to undersecretaries, Bruce to individuals at the secretarial level. When it became apparent we were getting nowhere, Bruce decided to send one of his personal cables directly to the President. When Johnson read it, he overruled his top advisers and ordered them to follow Bruce's recommendation to delay the resumption of bombing until Kosygin had returned home. In fact, the bombing was resumed about an hour after the Russian's plane touched ground in Moscow.

Not until several months later did I learn some of the details about how the cable was received. When it reached the State Department—of course, it was marked "IMMEDIATE"—it was brought to the President while he was meeting with his top advisers. Defense Secretary Robert McNamara apparently was the first to react, arguing in favor of resuming the bombing immediately. "What does Bruce know about Vietnam?" he asked. The President, who had a deep respect for Bruce, decided to accept his advice. Bruce was naturally delighted when he heard of the President's decision. He was also pleased when soon thereafter McNamara phoned to thank him for the cable, adding that it had proved very helpful.

Bruce dominated the embassy with an easy hand. He gave his officers great leeway in carrying out their responsibilities, providing support whenever they needed it. There was never any doubt, however, about his ambassadorial authority, which he always asserted whenever the embassy briefed a visiting congressional delegation. Bruce then put on an exceptional solo performance, leaving his senior colleagues gaping in silent admiration.

Serving as Bruce's minister was a delight. I administered the daily activities of the embassy, including signing off on the outflow of cables. In my almost five years as minister, only once did he question my approval of a particular cable. An event a week before Bruce left London summarized our relationship. We both used the same bathroom, located in the middle of a short corridor connecting the rear of our adjoining offices. On this occasion, for the first time during my tour as minister, we opened our doors at the same moment. "After you, Mr. Minister," said Bruce with mock formality. "After you, Mr. Ambassador," I replied and returned to my office. A few minutes later Bruce knocked at my door. "It's all yours, Phil," he said, "and I've just realized this is the first conflict we've had in five years."

Bruce encouraged me to cultivate my old and new friends in the political, intellectual, and journalistic worlds, thereby enhancing my status as minister and as chargé when he was absent from London. He also saw to it that I made practical use of these relationships in difficult and potentially embarrassing situations.

One of these centered on events immediately following the British capture of James Earl Ray, the assassin of Martin Luther King, Jr. On the day of Bobby Kennedy's funeral two officers of Scotland Yard seized Ray at Heathrow airport just before he could fly off to South Africa. Within forty-eight hours, without asking for British clearance, President Johnson sent Fred Vinson, Jr., assistant attorney general in charge of the Department of Justice's

Criminal Division, to inspect the cell in which Ray was incarcerated. "The President wanted assurances that the cell was secure," Vinson reported. This was Johnson in one of his less attractive modes: intensive and insensitive to the feelings of others, even foreign allies.

The request was so patently out of order that Bruce and I thought the British would be amused and indulge our President. We decided that I should phone my old friend, Jim Callaghan, then home secretary, and ask him to allow Vinson to look at Ray's cell. I mistakenly thought that I could handle the matter by joking about the President's unwarranted concern. I was wrong. Callaghan angrily responded, "What do you think we are, a banana republic?" After making it clear that he had no intention of satisfying Johnson's request, he hung up.

When I phoned Nicholas Katzenbach, the deputy secretary of state who had previously been attorney general, to tell him of our embarrassing situation, he replied, "The President is determined that Vinson see the cell." Then Katzenbach proposed a compromise: Vinson could "see" it from the end of the cell block's corridor and could subsequently tell the President that he had carried out his mission. This was an excellent idea, Bruce and I agreed, but how were we to open up the subject with Jim Callaghan?

Bruce bought my suggestion that I take it up with another friend, Elwyn Jones, the British attorney general, who in Wilson's later government became Lord Chancellor. Elwyn Jones was one of the noblest figures in British political life. The son of a poor Welsh laborer, he and his two brothers had won scholarships to Cambridge University. The father was so proud of their achievements that, to the delight of their small Welsh town, he always insisted on wheelbarrowing his sons' baggage to and from the rail station when they left for the university and returned for holidays. Elwyn Jones combined Welsh charm with ability, decency, and integrity. When I called on him to discuss our dilemma over Vinson's visit, he couldn't have been more responsive. "Surely this is one problem we ought to be able to resolve. As attorney general, I have a legitimate interest in it. I'll be glad to take it up with Jim." My delight in his response increased when he added, "And, of course, Phil, you wouldn't want me to mention to Jim that you came and discussed the matter with me."

Elwyn Jones's intervention with Callaghan did the trick. Vinson was permitted to see the cell from the end of the corridor, the President was satisfied, and Callaghan handled the extradition of Ray with discretion and dispatch. On the basis of several conversations between prison officials and Ray, Callaghan reported that he thought Ray may have had accomplices in plotting King's assassination.

This was but one example of the kind of cooperation between the embassy and British officials generated by the special relationship. We consulted frequently, frankly, and informally across the whole spectrum of political, defense, and economic issues, not just the usual bilateral ones. We took advantage of each other's expertise in our respective governments. Thus Washington would sometimes ask us to solicit the views of Murray Maclehose, the British government's leading Sinologist, on a particular situation in China.

We also filled in gaps in each other's information, even at the highest level. Whenever Wilson met with Johnson we could secure a copy of his memorandum to his cabinet on what had transpired long before we received any report from Washington. Sometimes Washington failed to provide us with any account, reflecting the fact, we thought, that 10 Downing Street was more efficient than the White House, as well as more sensitive to the obligations of the special relationship.

Social contacts strengthened our personal relations with British officials, making it easier to deal with them informally as well as in government offices. The ambassador, of course, entertained extensively. I did my share, lunching à deux at Wychwood House, the minister's residence, with government members and leaders of the opposition, and hosting with my wife larger parties for members of the House of Commons and top civil servants. At the suggestion of Ron Spiers we had separate luncheons for the Foreign Office officials in each of the world's geographic areas, and for officials in other departments, particularly Defense. Naturally, I took particular pleasure in entertaining politicians and officials who had been my contemporaries at Oxford.

The embassy's task was made easier by U.S. and U.K. agreement on a wide range of issues, though we did not always concur on specific policies and tactics. Particularly important was our agreement on nuclear weapons and intelligence. In the nuclear field the United States sold Britain Polaris missiles. It also furnished the United Kingdom with information on the design of certain nuclear warheads. For its part, the United Kingdom helped the United States by providing independent analyses of new weapon designs and the use of Christmas Island as a base for certain atmospheric tests.

The United Kingdom also granted the United States a base on Diego Garcia in the Indian Ocean in exchange for our waiver of research and development costs on Polaris. During the Persian Gulf war, American B-52's taking off from Diego Garcia bombed military targets in Kuwait and Iraq while the United Kingdom made airfields available in the home island where B-52's en route to the Persian Gulf refueled.

In the intelligence field our two countries gave each other more information than either gave to any of its other allies. We exchanged information on both overt and covert sources for the preparation of joint estimates. The weekly report of the Joint Intelligence Committee in London, read in the highest government circles, was the product of a combined effort with the chief of our CIA station responsible for the American contribution.

In addition to our cooperation on nuclear weapons and intelligence, Washington and London worked together during the crises in the Middle East and Rhodesia, and in maintaining the strength of the British army on the Rhine. We supported Britain's efforts to join the Common Market, believing that British membership would make the best use, politically and economically, of her new middle-sized status and create a stronger European "pillar" in the NATO alliance. We cooperated, too, on the international financial front. We felt that maintaining the parity of the pound protected the position of the dollar. We had difficulty, however, over Vietnam and Britain's steady withdrawal of forces from east of Suez.

We supported Wilson's efforts to stop Ian Smith, Rhodesia's prime minister, from a "unilateral declaration of independence," and subsequently in the sanctions that followed Rhodesia's breakaway. I was chargé when Smith was in London just before his declaration, and Washington instructed me to personally deliver a demarche urging him not to take the unilateral step. Smith was a tense, nervous man who tried to convey an impression of steadiness, determination, and toughness. He obviously was unhappy that the United States was putting pressure on him. "We're planning to do what you did in 1773," he said testily. I refrained from correcting his date: I didn't want him to think I was accepting his analogy. He was particularly nasty about Wilson. "He expects you to pull his chestnuts out of the fire," he said scornfully in that tight voice. During the next two years Smith showed he lacked the political foresight and personal courage to resolve the deadlock between Rhodesia and London even though he had two reasonable opportunities to do so. Twice Wilson met with him aboard a British naval ship and worked out deals not unfavorable to Rhodesia that Smith apparently accepted. However, when he returned to Salisbury, his capital, he couldn't resist the pressure from his hard-right racists, and reneged on his agreements with Wilson.

On the financial front we supported Wilson's determination to maintain the exchange value of the pound. In the 1964 election Labour had made a major issue of the Tory government's trade deficit that year of 400 million pounds. When Labour came to power, Wilson was absolutely determined to reduce the deficit without devaluing the pound. Some respectable economists and several of Wilson's ablest cabinet colleagues disagreed with what they saw as an "obsession" that could fatally undermine the Labour Party's *raison d'être*. For without devaluation, economic growth was stymied, and without growth the government would be unable to achieve its social and industrial aims. But Wilson was so adamant that for several years, until shortly before devaluation, he permitted his cabinet to discuss the subject only once, and regretted that he had done so.

Washington's nervousness about the British pound caused President Johnson to take insensitive advantage of the disparity of the power between our two countries. In April 1965, the weekend before the chancellor of the Exchequer was to present the government's annual budget to the House of Commons, the President sent Kermit Gordon, his budget director, to London to have a look at the budget, or at least find out enough about it to determine whether it would disturb international money markets.

This was a foolish act, an abuse of the special relationship. Preservation of the budget's secrecy until it was presented to the

House of Commons was a basic political principle. In 1948 Hugh Dalton had had to resign as chancellor of the Exchequer because a few minutes before he was to present his budget he met a friendly correspondent in the corridor of the House of Commons and revealed a minor detail about it.

It is not difficult, therefore, to imagine our concern. We were determined to keep Kermit Gordon's visit secret. Had it become public it might have raised a political storm.

Gordon, a Rhodes Scholar contemporary of mine at Oxford, had been one of Harold Wilson's students when the prime minister was an economics tutor in University College. That was why Johnson had chosen him for this delicate, unprecedented mission. It did, in fact, make it easier for Wilson to accept the visit.*

Because Bruce was out of town Gordon stayed with us at Wychwood House. At that time our eldest son, Bob, was living with us. He was taking a graduate degree at the London School of Economics and working as a part-time foreign correspondent for the *Washington Post*. Before Kermit arrived I told Bob he had to move out of the residence for the weekend, ask no questions, and refrain from letting the *Post* know I had asked him to do so. Bob proved then, as he has since in equally delicate situations, that he is a reliable son. He asked no questions and kept quiet.

Some American correspondents in London thought I was a major source for Bob. They were wrong. I leaned over backward to treat him no differently from his journalistic colleagues. His mother complained I didn't treat him as well. Only once did I favor him with a special piece of information. The morning after Patrick Gordon Walker resigned as foreign secretary, Bob phoned me in the embassy to say it was rumored on Fleet Street that Callaghan would succeed Gordon Walker. Bob added that he had noted I was scheduled to have lunch *à deux* with Callaghan at Wychwood House. Would I let him know if the rumor were true? He didn't want to go out on a limb.

Callaghan told me that Michael Stewart would be the new

*The prime minister was proud of his American students. Several times he had talked to me about Gordon; Dyke Brown, later a vice president of the Ford Foundation; Steve Bailey, who became one of America's leading educators; and Harlan Cleveland, who served as Kennedy's assistant secretary of state.

foreign secretary. Earlier that day, he added, Wilson had walked into 11 Downing Street, the chancellor's residence, and said, "Jim, if you ask me to appoint you foreign secretary I'll agree. So please don't ask me!"

I was prepared to be helpful to my son on this one occasion, but I wasn't going to let the *Post* scoop the embassy. Too often American foreign correspondents reported important events more quickly than embassy officers. Before passing on the information to Bob,* I sent it to Washington in an "immediate" cable.

Mirabile dictu, we managed to keep Gordon's visit out of the press. Wilson received him warmly. Of course he didn't show Gordon the budget, but he did assure him that Johnson had no cause for concern about money markets being disturbed by it.

The prime minister gave a small dinner for his old student during which we had an interesting discussion on the different ways in which our governments operated, particularly at the highest level. Wilson mocked our "amateurish" approach. Some of the individuals the President picked for his cabinet had no previous government experience, and in some cases they hadn't even met each other until the first cabinet session.

Wilson compared that with the British system. The prime minister was only "first among equals." All cabinet members were not only parliamentary colleagues; most of them had had previous ministerial experience. He proudly added that prime ministers almost always had been heads of several departments before reaching the top.†

There was merit to Wilson's argument, but it ignored the negative aspects of the British system. British politics are much more incestuous than American. Our legislators do serve in Congress for many years—with seniority still essential to their advancement to committee chairmanships. There are tensions bred by long

---

*Today Bob is the managing editor of the *Washington Post*, his professional home since he finished his studies in London in 1966. His latest book is *Why Gorbachev Happened: His Triumphs and Failures*.

†Not for the first time, Wilson was exaggerating. When he became prime minister he and Patrick Gordon Walker were the only two members of the new government with cabinet experience. Most of the others had been minor ministers in the Attlee cabinet, the previous Labour government.

familiarity among members. Senators and congressmen, however, do not make up future cabinets, though from time to time a President will choose a member. The fact that the success or failure of a British parliamentary career depends mainly on whether an MP becomes head of a department puts a premium on competition among members. This ever-present rivalry is further intensified by a system under which members of Parliament, not the British electorate, choose the prime minister when they select the leaders of their parliamentary parties.* When George Brown came to lunch in my residence a few days after Patrick Gordon Walker's defeat in a by-election meant he had to resign as foreign secretary, I greeted Brown by saying, "Isn't it too bad about Patrick." Brown responded, "Too bad! The shit got what he deserved. He voted against me for leadership of the party." Brown had run against Wilson in 1963.

When I was a student I heard Churchill state in the House of Commons, mocking the Chamberlain government, that yet another problem for the prime minister was the inclusion in his cabinet of "four ex-future prime ministers." Harold Wilson suffered from the fact that his cabinet included three or four would-be future prime ministers. And being a man who had even more than the usual amount of paranoia so characteristic of chiefs of state or government, he tended to imagine his colleagues were plotting against him even when his fears were not warranted.

On one occasion Eugene Rostow, the American undersecretary of state, accompanied Ron Spiers and me to a meeting in the cabinet room at 10 Downing Street with the prime minister and Jim Callaghan, then chancellor of the Exchequer. It was the end of a long day during which we had seen the relevant cabinet members to discuss the problem of German hard currency offset payments to cover the costs of the British army of the Rhine. The United States was anxious to maintain the British force at the current level, even though the Germans were not prepared to take care of the full foreign exchange expenditure. The British were threatening to withdraw unless they did so.

We had arrived at a proposed compromise that now needed

*The Labour Party has changed its selection procedure, but the vote of its MP's is still important.

cabinet approval. When Wilson and Callaghan agreed to accept our recommendation, the prime minister added that, of course, they were only two members of the cabinet and a majority would be required. Remembering that Wilson considered himself a Lincoln buff (I heard him boast several times that he had read all four volumes of Carl Sandburg's biography), I said, "We realize that, but with the PM's and the chancellor's support, it is certain the cabinet would approve," and then recalled the story of Lincoln at a cabinet meeting. All the members of his cabinet had voted "nay" on a particular issue. "The yeas have it," Lincoln said and moved on to the next subject.

"I remember that, of course," Wilson replied, "but I also recall Lincoln's response when one of his political managers warned him against putting all of his past opponents into his cabinet. 'Don't worry about that,' said Lincoln. 'They will neutralize themselves by chewing each other up!'"

"That's a Wilson story!" Callaghan interjected.

The Vietnam War created difficulties between our two countries, with the British people more critical of our policy than was the British government. One of Wilson's goals on assuming office was to maintain the special ties with Washington. He particularly wanted to establish a close personal relationship with President Johnson, continuing the easy rapport between Kennedy and Macmillan. Unfortunately, Wilson and Johnson were not temperamentally congenial. And their shaky rapport was hardly enhanced by Johnson's view that Wilson was not sufficiently helpful to us in Vietnam. The President deplored the failure of Britain to support us militarily even if the aid was essentially symbolic. "A platoon of bagpipes," Johnson said, would have been enough. He ignored Wilson's political difficulties—the fact that a majority of his cabinet, most of his party, and a large sector of the British populace opposed our involvement in Vietnam.

Nor was Johnson's dissatisfaction assuaged by Wilson's verbal tilt in our favor during the prime minister's efforts to act as a mediator between the United States and Hanoi. Immediately after Kosygin's visit to London in 1967,* Wilson made a public state-

*See page 221.

ment expressing his unhappiness over the failure of his mediation efforts—placing the blame on Hanoi, rather than the United States. That was not good enough for Washington. In a sharp cable I was instructed (as acting chargé) to call on the prime minister to express our displeasure over his comment that his mediation had almost succeeded. I thought it unfair. Fortunately, Wilson left on a three-day official visit to Germany that morning and his absence gave Washington a chance to cool down. I never delivered the message. Wilson persisted in his efforts to mediate even though some members of his cabinet, including Denis Healey and Dick Crossman, thought Wilson's leaning toward the United States ensured his failure. Crossman wrote, "We really can't play any part in the peacemaking process because we have not been able to denounce the Americans."

Britain's military withdrawal from east of Suez added to Johnson's disappointment with London. Heavily engaged in Vietnam, we were anxious to have a dependable ally maintain its military role in the Far East, even though she was not aiding us directly in Saigon. We feared that because of her economic difficulties Britain would precipitously remove her troops. Top American officials underlined our concern to Wilson before the withdrawal began, when the prime minister made his first visit to Washington in 1964.

Wilson favored maintaining the British presence east of Suez even as the pressures for withdrawal intensified with the continuing deterioration of Britain's economy beginning in the summer of 1966. In addition, the Common Market supporters in the Labour cabinet, particularly George Brown, insisted that withdrawal and the final liquidation of the empire were essential prerequisites to entering Europe.

In 1967 a day or two before George Brown was scheduled to make his first trip to Washington as foreign secretary, Michael Palliser, the prime minister's assistant for foreign affairs, asked me, as chargé, to drop in at 10 Downing Street to discuss a matter of importance to the prime minister. Palliser and I had first met in Dakar in 1961 when he was the Deputy Chief of Mission (DCM) in the British embassy. His ambassador, Adam Watson, had asked him to welcome me at the airport when I arrived to take up my post, a much-appreciated gesture. It didn't take long to realize that Palliser was what the British administrative elites call a "high flyer." Tall, handsome, and congenial, he was a superb "public" school–Oxford product. He combined a relaxed personal style with a thorough knowledge of international relations, a keen intellect, and an exceptional ability for easily and clearly articulating his ideas. I was delighted but not surprised that he had been appointed the prime minister's adviser on foreign affairs (10 Downing Street always seconded a Foreign Service officer for that task), and later when he became the permanent undersecretary of the Foreign Office, the highest official position in the ministry.

To say that I was surprised by what Palliser told me is to indulge in British understatement. The prime minister wanted to remind Washington of Brown's position on British withdrawal from east of Suez, and to suggest that both the President and the secretary of state try to educate Brown on the importance of maintaining a British presence in the Far East. I gulped, then asked Palliser for a pencil and a pad of paper and drafted what I thought would convey to Washington the kind of message the prime minister had in mind. Palliser took the draft into the PM's office and came back with a few editorial changes. I sent the cable as soon as I returned to the embassy. I don't recall whether the President and Dean Rusk worked on Brown. But he never changed his position.

Months later Palliser phoned and asked if he could drop in to see me at the embassy. This was unusual. Embassy officials went to 10 Downing Street rather than vice versa, but Palliser came to ask a special favor. When the prime minister was recently in Washington the President promised to make a statement about Vietnam that would help Wilson politically. Palliser added, diplomatically, that public comments by Johnson suggested he had forgotten about it. Could I get a message to the President reminding him of his recent conversation with the prime minister and be sure the message was passed on to the President? I agreed to send an appropriate cable, and then, in the presence of Palliser, phoned Walt Rostow, my Balliol classmate, and gave him the number of the cable I was about to draft to ensure that the President saw it soon after it arrived. Walt, who was Johnson's national security adviser, couldn't have been more cooperative. The President read the cable the next morning. He immediately called in the British ambassador to clear up any misunderstanding.

In contrast to the government, which tried to maintain a moderately favorable attitude toward U.S. policy on Vietnam, many British people opposed our policy, and sometimes expressed their views violently.

Students in universities around the country registered vocal protests. Despite David Bruce's personal popularity, he was booed off the rostrum when trying to defend our policy before a Cambridge University audience. Fortunately, a Scotland Yard agent, who, at my insistence, accompanied Bruce, skillfully hustled him out of the room before the audience became dangerously ugly. Similar sentiments in Oxford were reinforced by the anti-Vietnam views of a majority of the American Rhodes Scholars, who issued a public statement attacking U.S. government policy. Public demonstrations against our Vietnam policy were held in Grosvenor Square facing the embassy and sometimes turned violent. Rocks hurled at the embassy smashed its front windows. On one occasion the mob almost broke into the embassy, hoping to destroy it. Fortunately, police had been placed secretly in the lobby (counter to international law) and at the last moment turned back the surging mob. These demonstrations invariably resulted in injuries to police and participants, and in many arrests.

Other protests to the embassy were orderly. Multiparty parliamentary delegations usually presented letters condemning our policy, which we promised to transmit to Washington. The most publicized visit was from Bertrand Russell; the famous philosopher was then over ninety years old and a patriarchal figure venerated by his left-wing supporters. I was chargé when he called to present a petition from the Communist front organization over which he presided. I received him with as much dignity as I could muster, and assured him I would pass the petition on to the appropriate authorities in Washington. A large number of correspondents, awaiting him in the square, had been led by Russell's supporters to expect some fireworks. The reporters were let down when Russell told them that an American official called Kaiser had received him quietly and acted civilly. The press were as disappointed as Russell himself.

The effectiveness of the embassy's activities depended on detailed knowledge of the British political scene. We watched developments on a daily basis, evaluating the current mood of the government, its personalities, its plans and prospects, the public's attitude toward it, and the strength and strategy of the opposition. Labour came to power in October 1964, their first victory in thirteen years. At the Labour Party conference on the eve of the election, Harold Wilson had stirred the country, not just his Labour supporters, with his speech about "the white heat of the technological revolution." It suggested purpose and energy in contrast to the torpid, scandal-ridden latter years of the Tory administration. Wilson displayed confidence in his ability to deal with the country's economic difficulties, particularly its unfavorable balance of trade.

However, this hopeful sentiment was tempered by the narrowness of Labour's victory—a bare majority of three—and the uncertainty about Wilson's capacity to govern. He had become leader of his party after the untimely death of Hugh Gaitskell, a member of the party's moderate wing. The country was familiar with Gaitskell, and was comfortable with the idea that he would one day become prime minister. Although he was generally respected, his personal warmth was not fully appreciated by those outside of his circle of friends.

I had first met Gaitskell during one of my trips to London in the mid-1950s and saw him on several occasions thereafter, in New York, Albany, Vienna, and, of course, London. He had a lively and winning personality. In Vienna in 1957, after hosting a small dinner for six of us, including Anna Kethly, the Hungarian social democrat, a sentimental Gaitskell took us to the café he used to frequent in 1934, the year he spent in the Austrian capital as a Rockefeller Foundation fellow. At his insistence we all stayed, dancing and having a few drinks, until the closing at 6:00 A.M.

During the last week of April 1958 when I had stopped over in London on my way back from a visit to Israel, Gaitskell invited me for a drink in the opposition leader's office in the House of Commons. He insisted that I stay while he talked to Alf Robens, the shadow Labour minister, about how to handle in Parliament the busmen's strike scheduled for three days later. It was difficult to defend the stoppage because Frank Cousins, leader of the Transport Workers' Union, was objecting to a settlement that, in his view, provided too much of a wage increase to one sector of the industry. I witnessed a good example of how complicated was the relationship between the political Labour Party and the trade unions, its main financial supporters.*

When Gaitskell told me he was dining with his family in the House of Commons that evening to celebrate the birthday of his daughter Julia, I admitted that I, too, would be dining there—as the guest of my old Balliol classmate, the Tory chief whip, Ted Heath. Upon my arrival at the door of the dining room, the maître d' directed me to a particular chair at the table for two reserved by Heath. When Heath joined me a few seconds later he found on his plate a pamphlet entitled *Forward with Labour*, an official party document prepared for the next election. He scowled as he picked it up. I couldn't help turning my head toward Gaitskell's table; his face broke into a broad grin as he enjoyed his little joke.

Although Wilson's political orientation was somewhat suspect—he had been a supporter of the party's left wing led by Nye Bevan—opportunism had impelled him sufficiently toward the center to be elected the party's leader over George Brown and Jim Callaghan. Wilson was bright, articulate, a professional economist, and a highly effective performer in the House of Commons, far superior to Alec Douglas-Home, who had succeeded Macmillan as the Tory prime minister and whom Wilson had defeated in the 1964 election.

Working with a majority of only three suited Wilson's talents for political juggling. The narrow margin made it easier for him to manage the disagreements between the right and left wings of his party, as he happily and successfully focused on two or three short-term objectives. His first was to prove to the British people that after being out of power for thirteen years Labour could govern effectively. He did so by demonstrating that he had the necessary political sensitivity, personal energy, and flexibility. He often quoted Nye Bevan's remark, "A week is a long time in politics."

Substantively he dealt primarily with the pressure on sterling as he tried to fulfill Labour's promise to enhance the country's economic performance. His determination not to devalue the pound fitted nicely with his desire to strengthen Anglo-American

---

*Observers subsequently felt that this strike helped turn political sentiment against Labour in the 1959 election.

ties, and to develop close personal relations with President Johnson. Washington, which feared that because of his left-wing background Wilson would not be reliably supportive on international issues, was pleasantly surprised by his cooperative attitude on nuclear sharing, and his decision, at least for the time being, to maintain a British presence east of Suez. However, as already indicated, Johnson was disappointed over Wilson's refusal to send even symbolic military aid to Vietnam.*

Wilson was helped by the exceptional quality of his cabinet, of which the Oxford "mafia" was a powerful element. Eight members, including the prime minister, had earned first-class degrees, Oxford's highest academic honor: Michael Stewart, the foreign secretary; Denis Healey, minister of defense; Tony Crosland, minister of education; Roy Jenkins, minister of aviation; Dick Crossman, housing minister; Douglas Jay, president of the Board of Trade; and Lord Longford, leader of the House of Lords. Except for Michael Stewart, they had been at Oxford when I was, either as students or as faculty Fellows. All had been active in either student politics or, in the case of Crossman and Longford, Oxford city politics.

At least three of them—Healey, Crosland, and Jenkins—had an eye on 10 Downing Street. Healey, who in his student days had been a Communist, was perhaps the most intellectually agile, and certainly one of the most competent and charming men in the cabinet. Knowledgeable, dynamic, and decisive, he was to prove superbly successful as defense minister overseeing the radical reorganization of the department, and a continual cutback in his budget. He was more familiar with American society than any of his colleagues; but then he was more familiar with the four corners of the earth than was anyone else. Every now and then some of us in the embassy reminded him that we, too, knew something about our country.

Healey had good relations with most members of the American strategic community and was easily the intellectual equal of the U.S. secretary of defense, Robert McNamara, with whom he worked closely. He was justifiably proud of being the father of

*See page 230.

the NATO Nuclear Planning Group and took the lead in advocating the European defense caucus in NATO.

Healey was clearly a potential party leader, though he made no effort to develop a personal political following among the Labour members of the House of Commons. Our friendship of many years was based on frequent meetings and frank exchange of views. On one occasion I asked him why he thought he was not particularly popular with his parliamentary party colleagues. In his typically frank manner he replied that he had been too busy with other activities—journalism and travel—to massage egos, and what's more, many of Labour's back-benchers were not too bright or interesting. Healey still might have become prime minister and an outstanding one. He had the necessary intellect, energy, and drive, and a rich political background. He was, however, the victim of the costly left-wing domination of the Labour Party in the early 1980s. Subsequently, opinion polls indicated that, had Healey been the leader of the party instead of Michael Foote, Labour might have won the election against Margaret Thatcher.

Having lived through the McCarthy period, I couldn't help but be impressed by British political liberality. The fact that Healey had been a Communist as a student did not preclude his becoming minister of defense and chancellor of the Exchequer, and nearly prime minister. It is inconceivable that an American who had been a Communist as a student could have even aspired to reaching equivalent political positions.

Roy Jenkins, another Balliol man, differed from Healey in background and temperament. Considered a Labour "aristocrat" because of his father's background, Jenkins seemed to some of his colleagues to be more at home in a Mayfair drawing room than in a trade union rally, an impression reinforced by his deceptive languid style. Jenkins was bright, thoughtful, and articulate, a superb parliamentarian, sharp but never verbose in his exchanges with members of the opposition. Politics were not his only interest. He contributed regularly to periodicals and newspapers, and authored several books which won critical acclaim, including his prize-winning biography of H. H. Asquith, the former Liberal prime minister.

Jenkins moved from minister of aviation, his first post in Wilson's cabinet, to the Home Office, and finally, at a critical time in the late 1960s, to chancellor of the Exchequer. As home secretary he pushed successfully for the liberalization of laws on obscenity and homosexuality. As chancellor of the Exchequer he carried the hopes of the Labour Party that he could successfully overcome the country's economic difficulties before the next election.

He did not accept uncritically some of the Treasury's sacred cows. I remember his telling me that he thought the budget-making process was too restrictive. In his view, it was unrealistic for chancellors to be upset when the budgets they had devised in an "ivory tower" with just a handful of advisers were not enthusiastically welcomed by individuals and groups, who, though directly affected, had no idea of their contents until budget day.

Jenkins appreciated, of course, that the state of the economy affected political attitudes. He felt, however, that other less tangible factors like the style of government and its moral standing were also important. He was particularly unhappy about the Labour government's illiberal handling of immigration problems.

While he was chancellor, there was much talk of Jenkins as a future prime minister, a view reinforced by his selection as deputy leader of the party after George Brown stepped down and by the fact that, unlike Healey, Jenkins had developed a following among the Labour members of Parliament. Had Wilson lost the 1973 election, Jenkins might well have become leader of the party. But when Wilson suddenly retired as prime minister in 1976 and Jim Callaghan was elected to succeed him, Jenkins sensed his future now lay elsewhere. Later that year he left Parliament to become president of the European Commission. In the early 1980s he returned to British politics as one of the "gang of four" who organized a new Social Democratic Party. The party never fulfilled its bright hopes and, by splitting Labour, contributed to several Conservative electoral victories during the last decade. Meanwhile, Healey stayed in the Labour Party to fight for the moderate cause against the party's ascendent left wing.

Tony Crosland was the third influential member of the middle-aged group who was a possible heir to the premiership. In addition to being an outstanding Oxford graduate in philosophy, politics, and economics, he had been a president of the Oxford Union, the university's renowned debating society. After teaching economics, he entered full-time politics in 1950 as a protégé of Hugh Gaitskell. His book *The Future of Socialism* had a seminal influence among moderate elements of the Labour Party. As a Gaitskellite he was politically as well as personally close to Roy Jenkins— they had been friends since their student days—but an element of rivalry between them inevitably developed as they aspired to reach the top political post.

Crosland was one of the government's leading economists and an effective executive. Under Wilson he moved from minister of education to president of the Board of Trade, greatly enhancing the status of that ministry. His career was tragically cut short by his sudden death while serving as the foreign secretary in Jim Callaghan's government. Like several other British political figures, Crosland was married to an American, the attractive, highly intelligent, and literary Susan Barnes, whose biography of her late husband, *Tony Crosland*, became a best-seller.

But not all the leading members of the cabinet were Oxford graduates. George Brown and Jim Callaghan had never attended any institution of higher learning, one of the few things they had in common. Callaghan's confidence and competence did not suffer from a lack of a university education. He once told me that while he recognized Wilson's superior knowledge of economics, he felt when it came to political ability he was at least Wilson's equal. This was not the remark of a boastful man but one with healthy self-esteem. The Labour Party's "John Bull," Callaghan was able, relaxed, sensible, and moderate, qualities that subsequently made him a respected prime minister.

I recall Dick Crossman talking about Callaghan's political shrewdness and sagacity. In his view Callaghan's overall ability as a performer in the House of Commons, at a political rally, or at a Labour Party conference surpassed that of Wilson or Brown. Wilson was superb in the House but not exceptional on a political rostrum at a party conference, while Brown was at his best at a party rally.

Brown who, when sober, was bright, shrewd, and energetic, suffered from a deep sense of insecurity as a result of his working-class background and his lack of a university education. Remarkably, he was the Teflon figure, the least criticized in British politics. The public rarely criticized or blamed him for mistakes or unseemly behavior; instead, he evoked sympathetic and protective feelings. When obviously drunk during a television performance as was sometimes the case, rather than criticize him people would excuse him with such remarks as "Poor George, he was working so hard he had a drink too many."

Callaghan and Brown were perpetually at loggerheads when Callaghan was chancellor of the Exchequer and Brown was minister of economic affairs, a new ministry set up by Wilson. It prepared a National Economic Plan that incorporated many of the Labour Party's economic proposals, which had little relevance to the real world. Callaghan felt strongly that the Treasury was the only ministry necessary to handle the government's economic affairs. He scoffed at Wilson's idea that the two departments working at cross purposes would create tensions that the PM could then relieve for the greater public good. The scheme was typical of Wilson's inflated notion of prime ministerial power.

I saw a good deal of Brown when, to everybody's surprise, he became foreign secretary the summer of 1966 after the first crisis in Wilson's government following Labour's sweeping electoral victory of March 1966. It was agreeable to deal with Brown before noon. He had a good understanding of international issues; he was also particularly friendly to America. Several times he went along with Washington's proposals even though he didn't fully agree with them, as was the case on Middle East issues, where Brown was notoriously pro-Arab. "If that's what Washington wants," he would say, "then I'll support it."

Calling on Brown in the late afternoon or evening was not always a happy experience. If inebriated, not an infrequent occurrence, he could be aggressively unpleasant, with conversation deteriorating into a loud Brown monologue.

I saw him twice the afternoon and evening before his dramatic midnight resignation as foreign secretary. The second time, clearly under the influence of drink, he made so many wild statements that when we left his office in the House of Commons I assured his troubled aide I would not report the conversation to Washington. I always followed one of David Bruce's sensible working rules: don't report anything a top figure in your host country says that embarrasses him but has no substantive significance. Such cables

Governor Harriman signs bill providing pensions for retired teachers. PMK in rear amid women.

Harriman and PMK at latter's swearing-in as ambassador to Senegal and Mauritania.

PMK's youngest son Charles with Mokhtar Ould Daddah, president of Mauritania.

President Kennedy formally welcomes President Léopold Senghor of Senegal at Andrews Airfield. PMK stands at rear between them. *(Kennedy Library)*

The Kaisers welcome President Senghor to July Fourth reception at American ambassador's residence.

Hubert H. Humphrey with Morris Novick, media specialist who founded New York's WNYC, at left, and PMK, after Humphrey spoke at Liberal Party rally. *(Al Ben-Ness, Labor Press Photographer)*

Lyndon Johnson and PMK.

PMK's sons and their wives. Left to right, Hannah, Bob, David,
Cathy, Charles, and Joe.

Informal chat with Ambassador David Bruce.

PMK chatting with HRH the Queen Mother at reception at Ambassador Bruce's residence.

Secretary Cyrus Vance with PMK and Albert von Szent-Gyorgyi, Hungarian-American Nobel laureate, during visit to Budapest when the Crown was returned. *(Interfoto MTI Newspicture Service)*

Secretary Vance returns the Crown of St. Stephen to the Hungarians. *(Interfoto MTI Feature Service)*

The Reverend and Mrs. Billy Graham visit Budapest at the same time as Mr. and Mrs. Joseph Pechman. Joe was director of economic studies at Brookings Institution.

PMK, co-chair with Congressional Representative Yvonne Braithwaite Burke of foreign affairs section of Democratic Platform Committee, 1976. *(Ellsworth Davis, The Washington Post)*

Secretary of State Edmund Muskie meets the press during his visit to Vienna.

PMK arriving at presidential palace in Vienna to present his credential letters.
(Foto Haslinger)

PMK's farewell meeting with Chancellor Bruno Kreisky.

PMK in ambassador's office in Vienna with autographed photos of Presidents Kennedy and Truman in background.

are the wrong way to show Washington how well connected you are.

In neither conversation did Brown indicate that he planned to resign. He did so a few hours later when he learned that the prime minister had not consulted him before agreeing to close the gold market. Brown had offered his resignation more than once before in the belief it would not be accepted. He was stunned to discover the next day that this time Wilson had accepted it. From that moment on, Brown suffered a steady decline in political influence, ending with the loss of his parliamentary seat in the 1970 election.

There were other talented members in Wilson's cabinet: particularly Elwyn Jones and Barbara Castle. An additional group of able individuals—George Thomson, Harold Lever, Shirley Williams, David Owen, Fred Mulley, and Cledwyn Hughes—served in the second rank of Wilson's first government. Later all became full cabinet members. I counted them as friends.

Harold Lever combined wide-ranging knowledge with extraordinary intellectual energy. His mind reminds me of a perpetually erupting volcano; he never stops producing ideas for solving the world's economic problems. I particularly enjoyed our regular weekend walks in Hyde Park, during which our conversations were laced with Yiddish and Hebrew phrases. Wilson and Callaghan both wisely included Lever in their cabinets as minister without portfolio to advise on international financial issues.

During Labour's first halcyon eighteen months in office, Wilson's cabinet was effective and reasonably harmonious. Its high quality contributed to the stunning electoral victory in March 1966, which increased the government's majority to ninety-seven.

In that election the Conservatives were led by Ted Heath, who had defeated Reginald Maudling for the party leadership after Alec Douglas-Home had stepped down. Tory MP's voted for Heath because they thought he would be a tougher opponent for Wilson than the easygoing Maudling, but Heath was no match for Wilson in the House of Commons. In his campaign, Heath emphasized his support for British entry into the Common Market, and played down the United Kingdom's relationship with the United States. In fact, he suggested that Wilson was too close to Washington. He also criticized Wilson for the way he had handled the Rhodesian issue after Ian Smith had unilaterally declared independence, although initially he supported the prime minister. These were not winning issues.

Heath was able, a serious politician with a respectable record as a cabinet member, but he lacked the common touch and failed to generate enthusiastic voter support. Several of us who had known him since university days were struck by how his election as party leader apparently made him more introspective, in contrast to his rather easy sociability as a student and as a rising young politician.

I enjoyed following the election of 1966, the first one I had witnessed since the famous Oxford contest in 1938. It made me realize again how much better the British electoral process is than the American. Particularly impressive is the short, three-week campaign; the large turnout of voters; the equal access of all parties to television and radio, *without cost*; and the lively political rallies where candidates concentrate on issues and relish exchanges with hecklers.

The euphoria in the Labour camp following their victory was short-lived. Beginning with a seamen's strike four months after the election, the first by their union in many years, the government faced a series of setbacks that put continuing pressure on its sterling balances. Wilson responded to the seamen's stoppage by initiating drastic cuts in government expenditures and introducing a freeze on wages for six months in response to the trade unions' rejection of the government's wages and incomes policy. This was hardly what the Labour movement expected from a Labour government. Relations between the political party and the trade unions became increasingly frustrating.

Wilson's government never recovered from this first traumatic setback. Wilson had allowed a discussion of his taboo subject—devaluation—before announcing the unpopular deflationary measures. Several cabinet members, including Jenkins, Crosland, Brown, and Crossman, had argued that devaluation would have been preferable. Wilson regretted permitting the cabinet debate. He thought it was the beginning of a "plot" to remove him, an anxiety that persisted as his government seemed incapable of coping with a deteriorating economy.

By the fall of 1967, Wilson could no longer avoid devaluing the pound. The Arab boycott of oil exports after the 1967 war in the Middle East and the cutoff of Nigerian oil during the civil war between Lagos and Biafra added to the government's economic difficulties. Several Arab countries also threatened to withdraw their sterling balances from London. One amusingly did. I recall Callaghan telling me of how the government of Sudan "punished" the United Kingdom for being anti-Arab by withdrawing its sterling balances, about fifteen million pounds, from London and depositing them in Switzerland. As a result of this "punitive" action Sudan received three percent for its money in Zurich instead of seven percent in London; the Swiss redeposited the sterling in London, netting a four percent return, and there was no change in the British position.

The dock strikes in Liverpool and London, which followed the oil embargo, finally forced Wilson to devalue the pound on November 18, 1967. It was a serious blow to the prime minister. He foolishly compounded the negative impact of devaluation by his extraordinary remark on television that devaluation would not affect "the pound in your pocket." What he meant, apparently, was that your pound was okay so long as you didn't stray outside Britain. But the remark was perceived as dishonest, and the damage to Wilson's reputation could not be undone. Callaghan resigned as chancellor of the Exchequer and was succeeded by Roy Jenkins.

Ten days later de Gaulle vetoed Britain's application for entry into the Common Market. Wilson had applied in the hope that it would help ease the country's economic problems. He thought, unrealistically, that he could succeed in gaining admission where Macmillan had failed. It was an unexpected move because the Labour Party had never favored joining the Market. Dick Crossman, who had been a vigorous opponent of the EEC, was so defensive about the switch that he said to me aggressively: "If joining the Market is the price we have to pay for being less dependent on the U.S., I'm prepared to support it." He implied that several of his cabinet colleagues felt the same way.

I remember Wilson trying to soften his disappointment over the veto by telling me that he "took comfort from what he had read between the lines of a personal letter de Gaulle had sent after rejecting the application. The general's tone was not entirely negative." The prime minister had a propensity for self-delusion, a trait increasingly exasperating to his cabinet colleagues.

Other difficulties followed. There was bitter disagreement in the cabinet over lifting the arms embargo to South Africa and over a proposal to reform British trade unions developed by Barbara Castle, the minister for employment and productivity. This represented a courageous attempt to correct abusive trade union practices that not only adversely affected the economy but also made governing by a Labour government more difficult. Castle's recommendation, published in a document called *In Place of Strife*, provoked a storm of protest in every sector of the Labour movement, splitting both cabinet and party and arousing the hostility of the trade unions. Callaghan led the opposition to the proposal and after six months of bitter wrangling, Wilson felt compelled to withdraw it.

Under the pressures generated by these continuing failures and a steady increase in economic difficulties, what had seemed in its first eighteen months to be a happy, cooperative cabinet coterie, led by an effective prime minister, became a collection of frustrated cabinet members who did little to hide their rising dissatisfaction with the prime minister. Ministers complained privately about Wilson's inadequacy, about his lack of long-term plans, his tendency to avoid reality, and particularly his paranoia, which led him increasingly to believe that his colleagues were plotting his removal.

Cabinet members not only criticized the prime minister; relations among themselves also deteriorated. As one of them put it to me, "They have lived together for three years and most of the myths about each other have been washed away. Too much has gone wrong, and too many hopes dashed. . . . Cabinet members are all eyeing one another critically, particularly the PM."

A series of cabinet changes by Wilson failed to improve government morale. Wilson's colleagues deplored the fact that he had unrealistically set the American presidential system as his model. Several of them pointed out that, for practical as well as systemic reasons, it was an illusion to think that the presidential system could work in the United Kingdom. American Chief Executives have the personnel resources required to be presidential, including the Council of Economic Advisors, the Office of Budget and Management, the National Security Council staff, and a large number of presidential assistants who are expert on every governmental issue.

In Britain the cabinet departments assumed these responsibilities. For that reason, the PM had only a modest staff. As Callaghan and other ministers pointed out in informal conversations, Wilson's government suffered from his efforts to run "a one-man show," ignoring the responsibilities and competence of his "equal" cabinet colleagues. Two of his practices were particularly irritating: his failure to consult with members of his cabinet, and his effort to use the secretary of the cabinet, the top British civil servant, and the latter's small group of aides as the equivalent of a presidential staff. The responsibilities of the cabinet secretary covered all ministers. It was wrong for Wilson to use that key official as his own personal private secretary.

When I left the embassy in the late summer of 1969, the government was still struggling. Ironically, its focus was not on the Labour Party's social and economic programs but on improving the country's balance of payments. Clearly, Wilson had failed to fulfill his high hopes when he came to power five years earlier. He had been caught by the conflict between the ideological aspirations of his party, which had been incorporated into its election manifesto, and the imperatives of the real world.

In a democracy, politicians, particularly the challenging candidate, invariably make extravagant claims during election campaigns. The challenger tries to convince the voters that everything they find wrong in the country is the fault of the incumbents and he—the new man—will put it all right after he is elected. He alone has the answer to the country's problems. If he wins, how he adjusts to the realities, which often make a mockery of his campaign promises, will determine the success or failure of his administration.

American Presidents have an easier time than British prime ministers because American political parties are not so ideological as Britain's, particularly the Labour Party. American party platforms, drafted every four years at conventions nominating presidential candidates, are rarely taken seriously by either the candidates or the electorate. They can be ignored or repudiated with impunity. Kennedy did not suffer when he pursued a policy of détente with the Soviet Union after being a "cold warrior" as a candidate. Likewise, Nixon, as Chief Executive, bore little resemblance to the Nixon who, for years, led the anti-Moscow and anti-Peking forces in the United States. He was cheered, not criticized, for pursuing a policy of détente with the Soviet Union and establishing relations with China after a generation of nonrecognition.

Political leaders in the United Kingdom found it more difficult to move from the extravagance of campaign rhetoric to the tough reality of governing. Campaign manifestos were taken much more seriously, particularly in the Labour Party where they reflected anachronistic left-wing views that had little relevance to the problems Wilson's government had to face. The world had changed from the days when private industry and the free market were considered the roots of all social evil, and government nationalization and class-oriented politics the only possible road to social salvation. To continue to preach public ownership while trying to make a mixed economy work was a recipe for frustration and failure.

Wilson was basically a moderate. As an Oxford don he helped Sir William Beveridge develop the pragmatic welfare state established by Attlee's Labour government. But in order to win the support of the Labour Party's left wing, Wilson had to be a "closet" moderate. Once he was in power, and the extent of his "unsocialist" views began to become apparent, his more radical left-wing supporters felt let down. Meanwhile, because his election as leader had been based on left-wing support, the moderates suspected him even when he moved in their direction. Actually, Wilson devoted too much energy, too much of his resourcefulness in trying to maintain a balance between the two wings of his party. I recall his mentioning with pride how he would balance the appointment of a right-winger to his cabinet with the selection of a member from the left. His government might have been more successful had he concentrated on planning and pursuing appropriate public policies.

Wilson's loss of the election in 1970 left in its wake divisions within the party and between the party and the trade unions, overcome only temporarily after close Labour electoral victories in the mid-1970s. However, they would take their political toll with Thatcher's defeat of Callaghan in the 1979 election when damaging countrywide strikes were a crucial issue, and in the decade that followed. Buttressed by British success in the war over the Falklands, Margaret Thatcher had little difficulty in winning the 1983 election against a demoralized Labour Party controlled by its left wing, particularly after the defection of a splinter group of moderates who formed the Social Democratic Party.

The embassy naturally focused its attention on the British scene. Visitors, however, took up a great share of the embassy's time. They came in droves—relatives, friends, friends of relatives, relatives of friends, and, mostly, officials, including the secretary of state, Adlai Stevenson, the Vice President, and the President. I remember receiving a letter from Fanny Perlman, the widow of my Wisconsin economics professor, asking me to receive some old friends of hers. "You haven't the time to see them," said Harriet Curry, my loyal secretary who had served with me in Africa, and was to rejoin me in Budapest and Vienna. "I know," I replied, "but I must see them." Fanny was the wife of the teacher to whom I was most devoted—my mentor, intellectually and politically—whose class I had attended with Hannah. Two days later Fanny's friends, an elderly couple, entered my office. He was a retired teacher from Choate, the New England prep school, and told me with quiet pride that he had taught both Joe Kennedy, Jr., and his brother Jack. When I put the usual question to him, "When did you last see Fanny Perlman?" he replied, "A little over fifty years ago." Good manners prevented me from laughing as he added, "But we grew up together in Keene, New Hampshire, and we have been corresponding ever since."

Official visitors naturally took more time, and were not always so agreeable. Hundreds of officials descended upon us annually, a fair share of them expecting or demanding special treatment.

Of course, most attention was paid to a President visiting London, a Vice President, a secretary of state, and an Adlai Stevenson. Next in line were congressional delegations, who usually found time for sight-seeing, shopping, and amusing themselves in other ways. During my days in London two congressmen were particularly demanding: John Rooney from Brooklyn, New York, who chaired the House Appropriations Subcommittee which dealt with the State Department, and Wayne Hayes of Ohio, who chaired the Foreign Affairs Committee which handled the substantive legislation affecting the department. Shamelessly exploiting their powerful positions, they expected the embassies to turn themselves inside out to satisfy their purely personal and often unreasonable requests. They added to their unpopularity by invariably indicating they had no love for the Foreign Service and the State Department.

Fortunately, Rooney and Hayes behaved a little better in London because they were awed by the stature and reputation of Ambassador Bruce. He never went to the airport to meet them (in fact, Bruce only did that for the President, Vice President, secretary of state, and chairmen of the Senate Foreign Relations and House Foreign Affairs committees), and hardly ever entertained them individually. On one occasion I received a desperate phone call from our embassy in Paris. Congressman Wayne Hayes had just visited the French capital for several days and, reacting hostilely to something one of the embassy's officers had said or done, had heaped unrelenting abuse on the Foreign Service. "Please have Ambassador Bruce butter him up by inviting him to the residence for a drink," the embassy officer said. When I urged Bruce to do so, for the sake of the Foreign Service, he said, "I'll do it. But you know, Phil, Hayes is a real shit." This was the only time in five years I heard Bruce, the quintessential gentleman, use that kind of language.

Secretary Rusk was a pleasant and easy visitor. He usually spent a day or two in London after a NATO foreign ministers' meeting, and devoted most of his time to seeing top British officials to exchange views on current international issues. His stay in London usually ended with a small informal dinner hosted by Ambassador Bruce with, of course, the foreign secretary as the special British guest. One couldn't help but observe how frank and relaxed were the relationships between the two top officials, the same atmosphere that characterized contacts between embassy and British officials.

Rusk himself had a warm sentimental feeling toward the British dating from his happy years as a Rhodes Scholar in the early 1930s. On one occasion, because Bruce was suffering from a very bad cold, I met Rusk at the London airport. In anticipation of questions from Rusk, I had briefed myself on every international issue I could think of. But on the ride back to the ambassador's residence, the first question Rusk put to me was: "When did you last visit Oxford?" Happily I could tell him that I had dined at All Souls College the Saturday before. After reminiscing about his happy days at Oxford, he talked about his modest southern background. He noted that on several occasions President Johnson and he had argued about who had been born in a smaller log cabin. When I suggested that the easy solution for that argument was to send someone to measure the size of both, Rusk replied that they had long since been torn down.

Rusk's attachment to Britain was put to the test by what he felt was London's inadequate response to the war in Vietnam. When I was in Washington for consultation he always received me as an old friend. Invariably he criticized the British for not fulfilling what he contended was their obligation under SEATO, adding, in the years before the disastrous Tet offensive, that he was sure we would win the war. On one occasion he emphasized that we were dropping more ammunition on North Vietnam than we had on Germany during the Second World War. I usually replied by pointing out that Prime Minister Wilson's moral support was the best he could do in light of the hostile attitude of the many Labour members of Parliament, and the party's rank and file.

In spite of his keen disappointment over Vietnam, Rusk remained deeply attached to the British. I saw him in Washington in the late fall of 1967, just after the British government devalued the pound. The United States was unhappy about this because our Treasury Department thought a stable pound protected the value and international status of our dollar. At the same time we realized that Wilson had resisted devaluation as long as possible. Rusk proudly told me he had drafted the warm personal message President Johnson had cabled to Wilson after the announcement of the devaluation, in which the President emphasized his understanding of Wilson's action and pledged U.S. financial support to the British during their difficult period of adjustment.

On another occasion Rusk felt that the British were not acting as responsively as they should. In 1965, the day after the outbreak of hostilities between India and Pakistan, Rusk phoned me from Washington and asked me (I was acting as chargé) to get the prime minister to immediately make a public statement similar to the one just issued by President Johnson and U Thant, the secretary general of the United Nations. It was about 6:45 P.M. in Washington and five hours later in London.* I told Rusk that I knew Wilson was planning to make such a statement in the House of Commons the following day, and that it would be difficult, if not impossible, to get the British government to act now, at midnight.

"Well, do what you can tonight," said Rusk. I phoned Murray Maclehose, the principal private secretary to George Brown, the foreign secretary. Maclehose was a dour Scotsman with whom, however, I had good personal relations going back to our acquaintanceship at Balliol. "You can't be serious," he said, "about getting the prime minister to issue a statement before tomorrow." Fortunately, Rusk also had asked me to get some information immediately about one or two other matters, and Maclehose volunteered to see whether he could satisfy me on that score. He phoned back with the answers a few minutes later. Then I called Rusk and eased his disappointment slightly by providing satisfactory replies to the other questions he had raised. But he was still clearly unhappy about the failure to secure an immediate prime ministerial statement.

Ironically, a few minutes after I hung up—it was now well past midnight—I received a call from Secretary of the Treasury Henry Fowler, who was on an official visit to Rome. Fowler and I were old friends—he had been my immediate boss in the Foreign Economics Administration—and I had introduced him to Jim Callaghan. They soon became close Anglo-American colleagues. "Where the hell is your friend, Jim Callaghan?" Fowler irately asked. "Early this afternoon he phoned me here in Rome and asked me urgently to do him a special favor. It was a reasonable request. I took care of it before the end of the day, and I've been unable to reach him all evening to inform him that I was able to do so. Will you tell your friend to phone me at our ambassador's residence before I leave at eight tomorrow morning?" I promised I would and added, "When you get back to Washington, would you please tell Dean Rusk about the trouble you had reaching the

---

*Not infrequently we received late-night calls because Washington forgot the time difference.

chancellor of the Exchequer throughout the evening even though Callaghan had requested a special favor and wanted an answer urgently?" I would explain, I added, why I wanted him to do that when I next saw him. I called Callaghan at 11 Downing Street shortly after 7:00 A.M. and he gratefully promised to contact Fowler.

In 1967 Vice President Humphrey made an official visit to London. It took Johnson three years to allow Hubert Humphrey to take this trip. Johnson had planned to attend Churchill's funeral in 1965, immediately after his inauguration, but an emergency operation compelled him to stay home. The logical surrogate was the Vice President, but that was too much for the Johnson ego. Instead he sent Chief Justice Earl Warren, using as his rationale the fact that under Washington protocol the Chief Justice outranked the Vice President.

When Humphrey finally came to London in 1967, he received a warm welcome. He was the most popular American politician among members of the Labour Party and was generally liked by the British public. A speech he delivered to members of Parliament was the highlight of his visit. Just before he gave it, we had listened to the prime minister answer questions in the House of Commons during the often dramatic weekly confrontation between him and members of Parliament. On our way to the Commons committee room where Humphrey was to speak—a walk of just a minute or two—he turned to me and asked, "What should I talk about?" I was surprised that Humphrey had no prepared text, but then I remembered that Hubert Horatio Jr. was probably the most impressive extemporaneous speaker in American politics. "Why not tell your audience about the Johnson administration's remarkable domestic achievements," I replied. "Most of the British are unaware of them and members of Parliament associate Johnson only with Vietnam."

Humphrey liked the idea, and captivated his audience with an outstanding performance, substantive, clear, witty, and not too long. He did equally well replying to questions—until the very last one. The chairman, Lord Gardiner, the Lord Chancellor, who presided over the House of Lords, the analogue of Humphrey's position in the Senate, had taken what he announced would be the last question. After the Vice President had answered it, but before Gardiner had formally concluded the meeting, Humphrey noted that there were still hands raised. Typically, he couldn't resist. He volunteered to continue. The next question—it turned out to be the last—came from a left-wing member of the Labour Party. It was a hostile question about our Vietnam policy. Unfortunately Humphrey compared the situation in Vietnam to Munich—an analogy that the British, particularly members of the Labour Party, had long since deplored. The Vice President's response produced some loud booing. Though the meeting ended on that unhappy note, it did not overshadow the generally applauded Humphrey performance.

The prime minister's lunch in Humphrey's honor, the final event before his departure, was billed as a "business" session. However, because all the formal agenda had been covered, the lunch turned out to be an informal and relaxed occasion. We were a group of six: three British, the prime minister, Foreign Secretary Stewart, and Defense Secretary Healey; and three Americans, the Vice President, Ambassador Bruce, and me. The fact that we were all old acquaintances added to the informality of the occasion. After some general conversation, the discussion focused on corruption in politics, in both the United Kingdom and the United States. Forgetting for the moment that Wilson represented a Liverpool constituency, I quoted Denis Brogan's remark some years back to a British student who expressed concern about municipal corruption in America. "If you want to see what municipal corruption is really like," Brogan had responded, "let me take you to Liverpool or Glasgow some weekend." To my great relief, the prime minister stated that he agreed with Brogan.

There then followed an exchange of anecdotes between Wilson and Humphrey about corruption in their respective cities, Liverpool and Minneapolis. Two stories stood out. Humphrey said that the day after he was inaugurated mayor of Minneapolis, he phoned J. Edgar Hoover to ask him to provide a list of untainted officers in the city's notoriously corrupt police force. Humphrey wanted to be sure he picked an honest chief of police. A few days later Hoover replied, "There's only one clean officer in the Minneapolis police department."

Wilson responded with the story of how, in 1943, in the midst of a major government effort to use all economic resources for military production, a Liverpudlian not only managed to receive permission to build a pub but also secured the supplies to construct it that same year.

When I saw Humphrey off at the airport, he made a request that saddened me. It revealed the extent to which his ebullient self-confidence had been deflated by Johnson. When I told the Vice President that he had been very impressive during his visit, he thanked me, and then added, "Will you ask David Bruce to write a letter to the President praising my performance?" When I passed on this request to the ambassador, he told me he had already done so.

We were delighted when Adlai Stevenson came to London in July 1965. Like so many of my generation—but unfortunately not enough American voters—I greatly admired Stevenson. I had campaigned for him in 1952 and saw him several times in the years that followed. He brought to the political arena an unmatched intelligence laced with charm and wit, and an understanding of domestic and international problems facing our country. He raised the level of political dialogue, inspiring many Americans to take an interest in our elections for the first time in their lives. His campaign in 1952 was one of the most honest and courageous in our history. He focused on issues, not sound bites. Particularly impressive were the frank speeches to groups like the Veterans of Foreign Wars and the American trade unions. He did not try to curry favor by catering to their prejudices; on the contrary, when he thought their views were counter to the broad public interest, he took them to task—frankly, clearly, and elegantly.

I heard Eisenhower and Stevenson speak before the AFL Executive Council on successive days in October 1952. Eisenhower made the usual campaign speech, catering to what he and his advisers thought the labor audience wanted to hear. He even tried to suggest that the Republican Party had a tradition of being pro-labor. Stevenson did exactly the opposite. After making it clear that he appreciated the positive role labor played in American life, he catalogued what he thought were the faults of the labor movement, and urged his audience to take steps to correct them. The labor "skates" couldn't resist his honesty, his frankness, and his wit. They voted to support him, the first time the AFL had endorsed a presidential candidate since 1924.

Stevenson was clearly unhappy at the UN. He might have been appointed secretary of state had he come out for Kennedy before the Democratic convention in 1960. Instead, he reluctantly accepted the ambassadorship to the UN, one of the most frustrating jobs in the government. In the spring of 1965 a review of Viscount Montgomery's memoirs in a London newspaper quoted the field marshal as saying that when he saw General Douglas MacArthur in New York in September 1956, the general was so bitter about Eisenhower that he was supporting Stevenson in the forthcoming presidential election. I thought it inconceivable that MacArthur favored Stevenson and, at the suggestion of my youngest son, Charles, enclosed the review in a note to Stevenson, suggesting that he'd be amused to learn who one of his supporters was in 1956. Back came a reply in which, to my amazement, Stevenson wrote, "Some day I'll tell you what we had to do to prevent MacArthur from publicly announcing that he was backing me against Eisenhower!" Stevenson concluded his letter with a sad comment: "I hope, my friend, you are enjoying London more than I am New York."

Stevenson was in good spirits when he arrived in London to consult with British officials on UN business. He was accompanied by Ambassador Marietta Tree, one of his deputies in his UN mission in New York. Soon after Stevenson was settled in the embassy's office reserved for VIP visitors, he asked me to review his draft reply to a letter from Paul Goodman, making any editorial changes that I thought appropriate. Goodman, who had become a well-known writer and social critic and had developed a considerable following among antiwar youth, particularly college students, urged Stevenson to resign as permanent U.S. representative to the UN in protest against American policy in Vietnam. Coincidentally, Goodman and I had been in the same summer camp forty years earlier.*

In his draft reply Stevenson wrote that the U.S. military effort in South Vietnam was necessary to check Chinese Communist expansion because of its threat to all of Southeast Asia. He ex-

*See page 12.

pressed the hope "that relatively small-scale resistance now may establish the fact that changes in Asia are not to be precipitated by outside force. This was the point in the Korean war. This is the point in Vietnam. . . . ." A more stable Asia will result from "a just and honorable peace which leaves the future of the people of South Vietnam to be decided by them and not by force from North Vietnam. . . . ." I made a few editorial suggestions in Stevenson's draft and sent it along to him.

Since Bruce was out of London for a day during Stevenson's visit, I thought it appropriate to put Stevenson in the ambassador's office. Forgetting that Stevenson was occupying his suite, I failed to lock the door when I used the facility between our two offices. As I was buttoning up Stevenson barged in. Before I could feel embarrassed he grinningly said, "My God, Phil, I thought you had risen above that sort of thing!" This was July 13, 1965, the day before our son Bob was marrying the lovely Hannah Jopling. That evening, at the prenuptial reception the Bruces generously gave in honor of the young couple, I had a relaxed chat with Stevenson. We talked briefly about the letter he had received from Goodman. He planned to send his reply the next day.

The wedding the following morning went off happily and smoothly. At four o'clock, after most of the guests had left the wedding reception, I decided to go to the embassy to read the daily take of cables. Soon after my arrival Irv Fuller, an aide to both the ambassador and me, came in to report that Governor Stevenson wanted to see me. When I immediately phoned the governor, his secretary said he had been looking for me, but had just left for the day with Ambassador Tree. A few minutes later Fuller dashed back into my office. "I've just heard," he said, "that Governor Stevenson collapsed in front of the Grosvenor House Hotel." Bill Brubeck, an embassy colleague, and I ran to the hotel, which was fifty yards from the embassy. As we arrived, Stevenson was being carried into an ambulance. Marietta Tree was standing beside the door waiting to follow. Her beautiful face was lined with anxiety, but as always she was poised and in command of the situation.

I jumped into the ambulance with Marietta. We watched prayerfully as ambulance medics worked desperately over the governor, one holding an oxygen mask over his face, the other pumping his chest. They were guided by a cardiologist who happened along within seconds after Stevenson collapsed.

When we reached St. George's Hospital on Hyde Park Corner, only a few minutes away, a doctor and several orderlies were waiting to move the governor into the emergency room. Marietta and I were led into the waiting room. About ten minutes later the doctor in charge came in to tell us that Governor Stevenson was dead. Marietta broke down, and I found myself weeping, too.

Then she pulled herself together and asked me to phone the governor's son Adlai Jr., giving me the number. I did so after I called the ambassador at his residence. He said he would go straight to the embassy and we should join him there. At the steps of the embassy Marietta and I ran into Eric Sevareid and Kay Graham. (She was staying with the Bruces.) Kay, Marietta, and I went to the ambassador's office. We were received by the deeply saddened Bruces who, as always, were poised, dignified, and kind. The ambassador wrote out a statement for the press, and the rest of us made a few international calls: Marietta to her daughter, Kay Graham to her mother, and I to Adlai Jr. and Newt Minow, who was with him, to fix the details about moving the body. Then we left the embassy.

It was a day I can never forget, with emotions swinging from the joy of our first son's happy wedding to the awful sadness of the death of one of America's outstanding men.

Nothing engages an embassy more than a presidential visit, and London was the first stop of Nixon's initial trip abroad shortly after his inauguration in the spring of 1969. David Bruce and I were still serving as ambassador and minister. Advance men came weeks before the President was scheduled to arrive. The first one, who had no experience with embassies, was relatively unintrusive, though he couldn't conceal his suspicion of the embassy so characteristic of all the President's men. Unfortunately, newly elected Presidents, particularly those replacing incumbents from the opposition party, have made it a habit not to trust the State Department, especially its Foreign Service. They refuse to believe that the first rule of a responsible civil servant is to be loyal to political authority. This distrust was particularly true of Nixon and his top aides. They insisted on checking out themselves every detail relating to the President's visit even though embassy personnel had considerable expertise on events of this nature.

We took this treatment in stride. Nixon's minions also had no compunctions about ignoring the legitimate sensitivities of the host country. And British government officials were not so amenable. The President's agents behaved like advance men during a presidential campaign, giving orders to the local party officials of a city that their candidate was about to visit. John Ehrlichman, the last advance man to appear, was able, tough, and certainly demanding as he reviewed the scenario for the stay in London, including the prearranged event in Westminster Abbey where an American tourist was to "spontaneously" greet the President during his visit.

The climax of the preparations was a last-minute Ehrlichman conference call from Washington to the administrative officers in the embassies of the three countries the President was planning to visit, during which he ruthlessly changed plans made several weeks before, and for different reasons shamelessly castigated each one of the three embassies. He insisted, for example, that we in London tell the prime minister whom he should invite to the dinner he was giving in honor of the President, and whom he should disinvite.

Bruce reacted strongly to this behavior. He asked Ron Spiers, our political counselor, and me to join him in drafting a cable to the White House responding to some of Ehrlichman's unreasonable demands.* He minced no words. I particularly remember what he said about the prime minister's dinner. "As for telling the prime minister whom he should invite to dinner, the suggestion is too ridiculous for any further comment." The White House caved in on all the changes Bruce requested.

There was a last-minute crisis in the preparation for the visit because of an argument over helicopters. The President's plane was scheduled to land at Heathrow airport late in the afternoon, and the prime minister had decided to entertain the President that first night at Chequers, his official country residence. Instead of

---

*This was the only time Bruce asked for collaborators in drafting a cable.

an hour-and-a-quarter car ride to Chequers, Wilson wanted to fly the President there by helicopter, which would take no more than ten or fifteen minutes. The White House agreed with this plan, and informed the British that it would bring over the presidential helicopter. The British took that as an insult. They manufactured their own helicopters, they said, which in their view were at least as good if not better than the American product. As the hosts, they insisted on using their machine. For twenty-four hours the British refused to give in to the Americans. Finally, a potentially damaging brouhaha was resolved: we pointed out that only the President's helicopter included the special equipment that enabled him to respond to a sudden nuclear crisis.

After all that, cloudy weather precluded the use of any helicopter. Instead the President and Prime Minister were driven together to Chequers. After dinner the President rode back to London with Bruce.

Late the following morning when I walked into Bruce's office, he said to me, smiling, "I'm a great ambassador, Phil, I'm a great ambassador." When I asked him what he was talking about, he told me about his ride back to town with the President, during which Nixon asked him for his frank opinion of Harold Wilson. "As you know," added Bruce, "I like Wilson and I made it clear to the President why I have a high regard for him. I also mentioned one or two of the criticisms leveled against him and concluded by saying, 'Some people, Mr. President, think he's tricky.' " As we both laughed, Bruce repeated, "I'm a great ambassador."

Nixon's visit seemed to abound with "incidents." The President stayed in the Royal Suite at Claridge's rather than at the ambassador's residence in Regent's Park. On their own initiative the British informed Bruce and me that "of course" the telephone tapping equipment in the suite would not be used during the President's visit.

Then there was the matter of the President's informal meeting with a small group of private citizens. He and Kissinger thought that by excluding the ambassador and me from this session, the President would get a franker view of how the British felt about America. There were several things wrong with this idea. Nobody knew more about the British scene than Bruce. Secondly, private citizens were more likely to be more relaxed in the company of a

President if their old and universally respected friend David Bruce also was present.

And then there was the question of which twelve or fifteen British citizens to choose. Here we had trouble with Henry Kissinger, who thought he knew more about British personalities than those of us who had lived and worked in the country for many years. We finally resolved our disagreements by arranging an extra private meeting for just the publishers and editors of all the British newspapers. I introduced them to Kissinger, who acted as the nominal host until the President "dropped in" about ten minutes later, and led a lively discussion. Needless to say, the other "private" meeting, which the press publicized, made quite a few uninvited Englishmen very unhappy.

Those British and Americans participating in the official meetings held during the visit could observe that the President paid much more attention to Kissinger, his national security adviser, than to William Rogers, his secretary of state. Time and again Nixon solicited Kissinger's advice while ignoring Rogers. At one point Nixon sloughed the secretary of state off to discuss the Middle East with Foreign Office officials while Kissinger remained with the President and the prime minister.

The main substantive meeting took place the last day of the visit in the cabinet room at 10 Downing Street. On the British side Wilson had his top cabinet members present, while Kissinger, Rogers, Ambassador Bruce, and I accompanied the President. It was an impressive session. Wilson himself and his cabinet colleagues—Stewart, Jenkins, Healey, Crosland, Crossman, and Benn—sparkled intellectually as they described the work and problems of their respective departments.

The President's response approached the level of the British performance. He spoke easily, clearly, and to the issues that had been raised. He flattered the British by asking them how best to handle de Gaulle during his imminent visit to Paris.

It was in the cabinet room that *en passant* Nixon somewhat self-consciously mentioned to me the difficulty we had about the arrangements for his London visit. He suggested it was due to a misunderstanding rather than any criticism of what the embassy had proposed. And, during another moment with me, he recalled the lunch we had in the Hôtel Crillon in Paris in 1952 when he was on his way home from a World Health Organization conference and I en route to the annual ILO meeting, and the chance encounter immediately thereafter with Victor Reuther, Walter's brother and the international representative of the CIO. I was surprised that Nixon remembered.

Ambassador Bruce left his London post shortly after Nixon's visit and I stayed on as chargé d'affaires until the arrival of Walter Annenberg. I served for several months thereafter. When the White House announced Annenberg's nomination shortly before the President's scheduled arrival in London, Bruce had offered to depart. But Nixon asked Bruce, whom he greatly respected, to remain for the visit.

Whatever Nixon's motives may have been in choosing Annenberg to replace Bruce—some thought it was his way of showing his hostility to the "Eastern establishment"—the President's choice underlined his lack of regard for professionalism at the ambassadorial level. Bruce had the ability, the knowledge of foreign affairs, the diplomatic experience, and the social style that made him one of the outstanding ambassadors in American history. Annenberg's main qualification was a talent for making money and, more important, a willingness to spend it. Three Presidents enjoyed his lavish hospitality, and appreciated his substantial campaign contributions. While out of office and practicing law in New York, Nixon also profited from handling Annenberg's considerable legal business generated by his large publishing and communications enterprises.

In selecting Walter Annenberg, Nixon was continuing a practice of most previous Presidents: awarding individuals for their campaign contributions or other personal services, or because they were old friends. Though more than a few of these ambassadors were embarrassingly inadequate, picking noncareer ambassadors is not necessarily a bad practice. Some of our outstanding diplomats have been noncareer: Bruce, Averell Harriman, Ellsworth Bunker, Kenneth Galbraith, Edwin Reischauer, Daniel Patrick Moynihan, and Bill Attwood. They had exceptional backgrounds and special qualifications for the posts to which they were assigned. President John Kennedy in particular appreciated the importance of choosing qualified noncareer individuals. A *Christian Science Monitor* foreign correspondent viewed John Kennedy's noncareer appointments as "noncareer professionals." Kennedy knew how to use ambassadors, career and noncareer. He made it clear to the host countries that they were his personal representatives, and he looked to his ambassadors' advice on how to deal with key bilateral issues.

There should, however, be a limit on the number of noncareer appointments. A good majority of the posts should be left for men and women who are Foreign Service officers. Without the prospect of reaching the top they will lack the normal career motivation for exceptional performance. Moreover, in the course of many years of service, career officers amass the variety and depth of experience that can prove invaluable in dealing with difficult, unanticipated issues.

When still a U.S. senator, the eminent Charles Mathias introduced a bill limiting the number of noncareer ambassadors to twenty-five percent of the total. The bill never became law because it was argued that it would curtail presidential flexibility. However, Mathias's proposal underlined an important point: the health of our Foreign Service depends on keeping a majority of ambassadorial posts available for qualified career officers.

The selection of Walter Annenberg was illuminating. Despite his diplomatic inexperience and his lack of knowledge of British history and politics, he often rejected the advice of his embassy officers. When the media criticized or laughed at him for some of his missteps, his paranoia led him to believe that embassy staff were responsible for these stories, because he knew we had many friends in the press.

Annenberg overcame some of his early difficulties by sparing no expense in entertaining the British after he had "refurbished"* the residence. He also contributed to British charities. Although he had little impact on substantive issues between the United Kingdom and the United States, he did become a social success, particularly among the titled members of British society who relish diplomatic partying but have little influence on the country's politics. The social side of ambassadorial life can be useful as well as enjoyable. Dining and wining government officials, members

---

*He revived the use of the word when at his presentation of credentials he told the queen that the residence was in need of "refurbishment."

of Parliament, members of the press, academics, artists, actors, British and American industrialists, trade union leaders, and local Americans can provide an easy setting for serious exchanges, depending on whether the host has the appropriate substantive background. Bruce was richly endowed with the right background and skillful in using it. Annenberg was not.

Selecting ambassadors with the caliber of a Bruce underlines the fact that an ambassador can and should make an invaluable contribution to the management of our foreign affairs. Choosing an Annenberg, on the other hand, encourages those who argue that with modern communications and frequent travel of top officials, the role of the ambassador has become obsolete. Henry Kissinger and Zbigniew Brzezinski are strong supporters of the latter view. Kissinger has stated, "Ambassadors don't count anymore," while Brzezinski feels that "for the most part serious business is not conducted by an ambassador." Are these two gentlemen omniscient? Their attitude recalls the story of the French colonel in World War I who was transferred from the staff of one general to that of another. The latter asked the colonel's first chief, "What sort of an individual are you sending me?" "A very interesting type," came the reply. "He knows everything, but that's all he knows."

In spite of the arrogance of some top officials in Washington, properly equipped ambassadors are perhaps more necessary than ever for the effective conduct of American foreign policy. Even Kissinger could not be in two places at the same time. Ambassadors who know the politics, history, culture, and economics of the country to which they are assigned, who are in regular contact with its top officials and have earned their respect, and who know the mood of the country at any particular time are an essential antidote to the misunderstandings easily generated by instant communication and the quick visits of top officials. As Ellsworth Bunker, one of our most distinguished noncareer ambassadors, observed, "Instant communication does not produce instant understanding, let alone instant agreement." On-the-spot ambassadorial competence is more important than ever to minimize confusion and disagreements between home base and the host country, assuming Washington and roving emissaries have the wisdom and humility to use the knowledge of a truly qualified chief of mission.

Moreover, faster communication provides new opportunities for ambassadorial effectiveness. If he is knowledgeable, articulate, and respected by Washington, an ambassador can use quick communication to ensure his input on vital policy decisions. David Bruce, Ellsworth Bunker, and Averell Harriman were among those ambassadors whose views were not only listened to by Washington, but solicited as well.

When I came to London in 1964 it was no secret that I had been an admirer of the United Kingdom since my days as a student at Oxford. For those three years I had the good fortune to be a participant in British life, while observing it from the perspective of my own country. I came to appreciate more fully England's unique civility as well as its rich cultural traditions—its decency, its sense of fairness, and its love of diversity. Nor could I ever forget the warmth with which our Oxford friends joined Hannah and me in the celebration of our marriage. I learned then, and during my many visits to England in the years that followed, that the British, shy at first, had no equal in cultivating the art of genuine friendship.

After my five years as minister I happily appreciated that in spite of a costly war, the loss of empire, and the difficult, sometimes painful transition from a world power to a middle-sized state, Britain remained a liberal democracy, with a continuing emphasis on the values of a humane society.

On the governmental level I found that belittling the special relationship was not justified—that the pronouncement of its demise, so frequent since the late 1950s, was premature. The relationship had obviously changed from the postwar period, when our joint status as world powers was its chief characteristic. However, for practical as well as sentimental reasons, Anglo-American ties continued to be special. There has been a tendency, particularly among academics and journalists, to deprecate the value of a common language, common traditions, linked history, and a broadly shared outlook. But the fact remains that they have made our diplomatic and defense as well as our social and business relations much easier to conduct.

Recent history underlines the continuing, unique nature of U.S.-U.K. collaboration. The relationship between Margaret Thatcher and Ronald Reagan was as close as any between Anglo-American chiefs of government since the end of the war. Thatcher probably had more influence on the President than any member of Congress. And Reagan's active support of the British during the Falkland war reflected his commitment to the Anglo-American alliance. U.K.-U.S. collaboration reached new heights during the conflict with Iraq. No Western country matched British popular, diplomatic, and military support of Washington throughout the Persian Gulf crisis.

8

Carter's Ambassador to Communist-Controlled Hungary

After leaving the American embassy in 1969 I lived in London until my departure for Hungary eight years later. During that period while in private business there—I worked as chairman and managing director of the British branch of Encyclopaedia Brittanica—I was active in Democrats Abroad, an affiliate of the National Democratic Party in Washington, which made me its delegate to the National Democratic convention in Miami in 1972. In 1976 I represented Democrats Abroad on the Democratic Party's Platform Committee. I was named co-chair of the subcommittee on foreign relations after Pat Moynihan's supporters objected to the selection of Bella Abzug, who was opposing Pat for the Democratic nomination for senator from New York.

In the course of several committee meetings in Washington and New York we produced a document that reflected the positions taken by Jimmy Carter in the primaries, particularly his desire to pardon young men who had left the country to avoid serving in the Vietnam War. We had few illusions about the significance of most of the platform beyond the presidential campaign.

When I saw Cy Vance, whom I first knew during the Johnson administration and whom Carter had just picked to be secretary of state, we talked about my taking up another diplomatic post, possibly Yugoslavia. After President Carter and Secretary Vance established a committee to advise them on ambassadorial appointments, I learned that I was short-listed for Belgrade. Old friends familiar with my past performance in government including Dean Rusk, Averell Harriman, and Steve Schlossberg, who was the United Auto Workers representative in Washington, sat on the committee.

In April I was surprised but not disappointed when Warren Christopher, deputy secretary of state, phoned to tell me the President had chosen me for Hungary instead of Yugoslavia. Later I learned that Henry Kissinger had asked Cy Vance a special favor— to appoint his assistant, Lawrence Eagleburger, to Belgrade, which Vance was happy to grant. Democrats always have been more cooperative on such personnel matters than Republicans. Four years later the new Republican administration turned down Vance's request to appoint his executive secretary, Peter Tarnoff, an outstanding Foreign Service officer, to an appropriate diplomatic post. Today Tarnoff is president of the Council on Foreign Relations.

Once again second choice proved to be more interesting and more challenging than my first preference. In 1977 Washington's interest in Yugoslavia focused on the potential impact of Tito's death on the country's stability. The Yugoslav leader was in his late eighties. The old fear about possible Soviet intervention persisted.

The situation in Hungary was more promising, with real possibilities for creative American diplomacy. By 1977 Hungary had become the most liberal country in Soviet-dominated Eastern Europe, a remarkable achievement on the part of János Kádár who, as first secretary of the Hungarian Communist Party,* was the leader of the country. During the Hungarian revolution in 1956, which was ruthlessly repressed by Moscow, Kádár had behaved perfidiously. He was a member of Imre Nagy's government, which was attempting to liberate Hungary from Soviet domination. However, six days after telling Yuri Andropov, then the Soviet ambassador to Hungary, "If necessary I will fight your tanks with my bare hands," Kádár shamelessly emerged as Moscow's stooge. Later, as the new head of the Hungarian regime, he directed a draconian policy of repression, disbanding free institu-

---

*It was called the Hungarian Socialist Workers Party.

tions that had emerged during the revolution and imprisoning or executing supporters of the uprising. When Nagy, the Hungarian reform leader whom the Soviets had deposed, and his top colleagues had received asylum in the Yugoslav embassy, Kádár did nothing to prevent Soviet military intelligence from kidnapping and exiling them to Romania. Nor did he try to deter the Russians from subsequently executing Nagy.

As a result of his repressive policies in 1957 and 1958, Kádár was despised by practically all Hungarians. Yet by the summer of 1977, when I arrived in Budapest, it was generally agreed that he would be overwhelmingly elected president in a free democratic contest. Several Hungarian Americans who had fled the country in 1956 and visited their old homeland in the late 1970s told me that they couldn't help but be impressed by Kádár's widespread popularity.

This extraordinary reversal was due to the policies initiated by Kádár after he had ruthlessly consolidated his authority. Painfully aware of why the Hungarian people had revolted against the repressive Stalinist regime, Kádár moved to improve economic conditions for the masses and ease political, religious, and intellectual restraints. On the economic front he launched a policy of economic reform (NEM) whose major goal was the establishment of a market economy and a genuine price system. The central role of government economic agencies was somewhat reduced, competition encouraged, and some private enterprises, particularly in the service industries, permitted. For the first time a Soviet-dominated country was challenging Soviet gospel that a completely controlled economy was the sole road to economic and social salvation.

Under the reform program managers were freer to determine prices and wages and to decide how to use profits. I saw the new economic program working at Raba, Hungary's leading engineering company, where axles are produced for General Motors. Horvath, the company's manager, was appropriately dubbed "the Red Baron." He ran the vast enterprise with its thousands of employees with an authority that American and British CEO's might have envied. During one of my visits to company headquarters in Gyor, about one hundred miles from Budapest on the road to Vienna, Horvath proudly showed me his modern equipment bought from the United States, Germany, and other Western countries. He complained about the government's attempts, particularly its trade unions, to interfere with his management when it came to wage differentials for more skilled workers, and to reducing the number of employees. He made it clear that he usually got his own way. He also told me that he traveled abroad freely whenever business required it, and that he played the major role in determining how to invest company profits.

The modernization of Hungarian agriculture was NEM's biggest success. Cooperatives, covering three-quarters of the country's fertile land, were efficiently and democratically run. In secret elections members chose the top officers, who were free to buy machinery and fertilizers from the West, to set the prices of their produce, and to market it abroad or at home. Members of the cooperatives also farmed their individual family plots, which, in the 1970s, produced almost fifty percent of the country's hogs and chickens. Peasants prospered as never before, and agricultural products became major exports to the West as well as the East. It is not surprising that Gorbachev was impressed by the country's agriculture when he visited Hungary in the early 1980s.

Industrial workers, however, particularly the less skilled, profited little from the economic reforms. They resented the increase in wage differentials and the prosperity of the peasants. I remember my meeting with Gaspar, the leader of the government's trade unions and, incidentally, the president of the Communist World Federation of Trade Unions.* At the instigation of the Hungarian Foreign Office, which was aware that I had been assistant secretary of labor, I was the only Western ambassador Gaspar received. He expressed his concern over the failure of the industrial workers to do as well as the peasants under the new economic program. He was one of the more conservative party leaders who, in 1972, with encouragement from Moscow, forced Kádár to temporarily slow down the process of reform.

---

*Amusingly, Gaspar praised George Meany as a great trade union leader. At that time the United States, at the instigation of Meany, had withdrawn from the International Labor Organization, and Gaspar asked me to urge Meany to change his position. The organization, particularly trade union representatives, needed his knowledge and influence.

Though there had been few systemic political changes by the late 1970s, the social and intellectual atmosphere had eased noticeably. Kádár wisely dealt with the postrevolutionary trauma of his people by pursuing a policy of tolerance and reconciliation. "Those who are not against us are with us" became his key motto. Persuasion rather than force became his way of engaging public support for government policies. Practically, this meant that organized religions could pursue their traditional activities in the few churches still open, although they were benignly regulated by the secretary of state for religious affairs. Academics and writers, allowed more intellectual leeway, displayed less fear about expressing their views in private conversation. The government even allowed a weekly, uncensored TV program on political and social issues. However, criticism deemed provocative to the Soviet Union or any of Hungary's bloc neighbors was prohibited, and "self-censorship," as it was called, inhibited self-expression.

The attitude about incarceration for political reasons was more relaxed. We found credible the claim that the number of political prisoners had been drastically reduced. Foreign travel became easier. Kádár boasted that almost all of the million Hungarians who visited the West in 1976 were happy to return home.

I remember a story Kádár told in reply to an American congressman's question about Hungarian emigration to Israel. After stating that there were hardly any restrictions against such travel, Kádár smilingly added the apocryphal tale about Mr. Schwartz, an elderly Hungarian, who had decided to join his younger relatives in Israel. After living there for several years, the tug of his old country impelled him to return to Budapest. However, at the renewed insistence of his relatives, he tried living in Israel again, only to come back once more to Hungary. After his second return one of his friends asked, "Schwartz, you've had the unusual experience of having lived in two countries. Tell me, which of the two do you really prefer?" "Frankly," replied Schwartz, "I like it best in between."

The U.S. government observed with increasing approval the developments in Hungary. Improved church-state relations, an openness to Western information, a forthcoming travel and emigration policy, a relatively tolerant attitude toward dissidents, and an innovative, decentralized economic system made Hungary unique among members of the Warsaw Pact countries, even though it continued to support Moscow loyally on international issues. We also liked the skillful way Kádár secured Moscow's acquiescence to his reforms. From time to time he wisely indicated to the Russians that his policies were the best guarantee against a recurrence of 1956. More than any other Eastern European leader he had the knack of knowing when he could expand the limits of Soviet toleration. Moreover, improving relations with the West, particularly the United States, became a major Kádár objective, since the success of his economic reforms depended on a substantial increase in trade with the non-Communist world, and the West's willingness to make large capital loans to facilitate the restructuring of the Hungarian economy.

I arrived in Washington in May 1977 for several weeks of briefing before my departure for Budapest. I soon realized that the prospects for an active and creative ambassadorial tour seemed promising. U.S.-Hungarian relations, badly strained during the decade following the repression of the revolution, had taken a favorable turn. We had signed a cultural and scientific exchange agreement. Hungary had settled all outstanding property claims, and had paid off its debt arrears to the U.S. government, including its post–World War I debt, the only country in addition to Finland to have done so. However, two major issues remained unresolved—our return of their Crown of St. Stephen and the negotiation of a new trade agreement, which would grant the Hungarians most-favored-nation treatment (MFN).

The highest priority for the Hungarians was the return of their Crown. A gift of Pope Sylvester II to Hungary's first king, the Crown symbolizes the establishment of the Hungarian state and a thousand years of continuous history. "Where the country is, there must be the Crown" expressed a nationwide sentiment. The United States had kept the Crown at Fort Knox for thirty-two years—since the end of the war, when our soldiers in Germany had received it from Hungarian guards for safekeeping while the Soviet and German troops were battling in Budapest. It was clear that it would take skill and persistence within the bureaucracy and Congress, as well as presidential political courage, to effect the return of this venerated symbol of Hungarian national identity and legitimacy to a country still under Communist control.

The State Department felt that the time had come to respond favorably to the Hungarian government's urgent request for the Crown's return. This was the view of Arthur Hartman, still serving as assistant secretary of state for Europe but about to leave to be ambassador to France. It also became the view of Matthew Nimetz, a very able young lawyer and partner of Secretary Vance, whom Carter had appointed counselor of the State Department. It was at Nimetz's instigation that the European Bureau at State prepared a draft memorandum from Vance to Carter strongly recommending that the President agree to giving the Crown back to the Hungarian people. Nimetz, working with Peter Tarnoff, Vance's executive secretary, received Vance's enthusiastic approval.

About ten days after Vance had sent the memorandum on to the President, Zbigniew Brzezinski, Carter's national security adviser, replied that the President had decided to delay a decision until we had determined our overall Eastern European strategy. In the meantime the President wanted the secretary to ask Hungarian officials to make a proposal on how the Crown would be received and then displayed if it were returned. The President stressed, however, that we should make no commitment and that we should keep our inquiry confidential. Subsequent actions by Brzezinski confirmed our suspicions that he was against the return of the Crown.

A few days later I had another chance to discuss the subject with Secretary Vance. Strongly in favor of returning the Crown, he stated that he would take it up again orally with the President at the earliest opportunity. After I left the secretary's office I told Peter Tarnoff about our conversation. Early the following week Tarnoff informed me that the Crown issue would be discussed at a presidential breakfast meeting the following Friday, which would be attended by the Vice President as well as the secretary. At this point I decided to contact Senator Hubert Humphrey—our friendship went back to the late 1940s—and ask him to talk to his protégé, Vice President Walter Mondale, about the issue.

I knew how Humphrey felt about the Crown. Several weeks earlier, when I had called on him while making the rounds of members of the Senate Foreign Relations Committee, Humphrey had raised the issue of the Crown before I even mentioned it, stating that it was "a disgrace" that it had not yet been returned. "What," he asked, "can I do to help?" This was typical Humphrey. He knew more about more subjects than any senatorial colleague. He answered his own question by suggesting that at my confirmation hearing he would ask me directly where I stood on the issue. He realized, of course, that as long as the President had not yet taken a position I would have to be noncommittal in my response. At that point he would make a strong statement urging return of the Crown. He asked me to draft such a statement for him. I did so with the help of Tom Gerth, the department's Hungarian desk officer, and sent it up to the senator several days before my hearing. Unfortunately an unanticipated urgent matter prevented Humphrey from appearing. However, he sent Secretary Vance a strong letter urging return of the Crown using text I had suggested. This was the background for my request to Humphrey that he brief Mondale before the Friday breakfast.

I was in New York that day speaking before a meeting of bankers and industrialists with interests in Hungary arranged by the Businessmen's Council on International Understanding. When I phoned Humphrey's office that afternoon I was told that the senator had not only talked to Mondale, he had raised the matter with the President as well and had received positive responses from both. Upon my return to Washington Tarnoff informed me that the President had agreed in principle to Secretary Vance's proposal that the Crown be returned and had asked him to draw up a realistic scenario for doing so.

My wife and I then left town to spend a week at our son Bob's new country cottage in the Pennsylvania mountains before departing for Budapest. Two days later I received word that Secretary Vance wanted to see me urgently. When I met with him he asked me to have an appropriate scenario drafted. It should include, he emphasized, the following conditions to be met by the Hungarians: various segments of the Hungarian public, including the Roman Catholic cardinal, would participate in the ceremonies welcoming the return; the ceremony would emphasize the national religious and cultural nature of the Crown and its regalia, and underline the fact that the American people were returning it to its legitimate owners, the Hungarian people, not the government. We also wanted assurances that the Crown would be displayed publicly in a historic location, and finally we would request the Hungarian government to state officially and publicly that Hungarians all over the world would be welcome to visit Hungary and view the Crown.

The scenario for the President would also include a strategy for dealing with the Hungarian-American community, for whom the Crown was a highly emotional issue. A large number, particularly those who had emigrated to the United States after the 1956 revolution, opposed the return because, in their view, it would legitimate the Kádár government. There were those, however, who appreciated that giving back the Crown would reinforce the deeply felt nationalism of the Hungarian people, which was much stronger than any Communist sentiment, and would help weaken the artificial ties between Hungary and the Soviet Union. President Carter would be facing the kind of domestic political problems familiar to American Chief Executives when they deal with issues affecting countries like Ireland, Poland, and Israel. Carter knew that there were large numbers of Hungarian-American voters in key states like Ohio and Illinois. In the close 1976 election he had carried Ohio by a majority of just over eleven thousand. I soon became aware of the domestic aspects of the Crown's return. When my appointment was announced, several members of Congress, particularly Mary Rose Oakar from Cleveland, tried to exact a commitment from me to oppose giving back the Crown.

I asked Herb Wilgis, whom I had chosen as my deputy chief of mission, to draft a scenario based on my conversation with the secretary. Wilgis, an able Foreign Service officer, had served in Budapest as a political counselor several years before. Tom Gerth, Matt Nimetz, and I reviewed Wilgis's draft before I sent it up to the secretary. When I left for Hungary shortly thereafter, the President had not yet made the final decision to return the Crown. The potential domestic political fallout was still troubling him.

Before leaving Washington, however, I had taken one last important step, securing the support of Senator Henry "Scoop" Jackson for the return of St. Stephen's Crown. I had first met Jackson when he was a young congressman from Washington State and I was in the Labor Department. When I flew to Europe in November 1948 to attend my first ILO governing body meeting, Jackson was a fellow passenger. I had arranged for his selection as the government delegate to an ILO meeting on the maritime industry, a subject of special interest to him.

Jackson and I became good friends. In 1952 I supported his successful campaign for the U.S. Senate against the Republican incumbent, Harry Cain, who at that time was an arch McCarthyite. I helped raise campaign contributions, particularly among labor groups, and spoke on Jackson's behalf in Everett, his hometown, during my speaking tour for Stevenson. Eisenhower carried the state of Washington by a large majority, but Jackson did just as well in defeating Cain.

Jackson's friendship never faltered. He was always available when I turned to him for advice and help. I appreciated, too, his easy, relaxed manner. When you were with him he made you feel you were the most important person on his schedule. On domestic issues his liberalism was impeccable. Internationally he was a hardliner, but he was a good listener even when you didn't fully agree with him.

By the late 1970s Jackson had become one of the Senate's prime movers with special influence on our Soviet policy. The Jackson-Vanik amendment to our 1974 trade law was one of the senator's landmarks. Under its key provision no country could be granted most-favored-nation (MFN) status unless its citizens were allowed to emigrate; this provision was aimed at the Soviet Union's severe restrictions of Jews and Armenians who wanted to leave the country.

Although this time there was no likelihood of the Soviet Union complying with Jackson-Vanik, the senator hoped that one of the bloc countries would do so. I convinced Jackson that the Hungarians were anxious to receive MFN status and he accepted my view that the favorable Hungarian attitude toward the United States generated by the return of the Crown would encourage Hungary to consider securing MFN status under the Jackson-Vanik provisions. We would secure both objectives through practical rather than official "linkage." Jackson told me that I could inform the State Department and White House that he supported the return of the Crown. He stuck by his word, even when domestic opposition to giving it back became highly vocal.

I recall how surprised the Hungarian ambassador to Washington was when he saw Jackson, the hard-liner, at my swearing-in. He assumed, I later learned, that the senator would oppose return of the Crown. Other friends like Averell Harriman and Ben Cohen, the mythical New Deal figure, were also present. In the course of my brief remarks at the ceremony I said that I was delighted to see so many old friends, some of whom had been distinguished members of every Democratic administration in this century except President Wilson's and, I added, "had Averell Harriman not waited until 1928 to become a Democrat, he undoubtedly would have been a star in the Wilson government." A few moments later Warren Christopher, deputy secretary of state, who was filling in for Vance, gracefully introduced Ben Cohen who, he pointed out, had served with distinction as counselor of the department under Secretary James F. Byrnes. He asked the shy Cohen to say a few words. In his mild, squeaky voice Cohen acknowledged the introduction and added, "And what's more, I *was* a member of the Wilson administration!"

When I presented my credentials to the Hungarian president of the Presidential Council, soon after my arrival in Budapest, he expressed his government's satisfaction with the improved atmosphere between Washington and Budapest, and then passionately emphasized that the return of the Crown of St. Stephen and a trade agreement granting MFN status were the essential next steps toward the normalization of U.S.-Hungarian relations. The best I could do in response was to say that we fully appreciated his position and hoped that in due course we could satisfactorily deal with both issues.

In my cable to Washington about my conversation with the president I reiterated my belief that U.S. objectives in Hungary and other Eastern European countries would be well served by our return of the Crown. I awaited instructions for the next move.

In the meantime my wife and I enjoyed settling into Budapest. We took an immediate liking to the Hungarian people, and our regard for them increased during our three-year residence. We were aware of the contributions of Hungarian immigrants to our scientific and cultural life. The work of four Hungarian scientists, all, incidentally, of Jewish origin, had been vital to the making of the nuclear bomb: John von Neumann, Leo Szilard, Edward Teller, and Eugene Wigner. I had heard the story, apocryphal, no doubt, of how Albert Einstein, after receiving the famous reply from President Roosevelt to go ahead with the production of the bomb, had turned to this group of Hungarians at a meeting he had called of leading physicists and said, "Now you gentlemen can work out the details in Hungarian."

We were amused, too, when George Lehel, a Hungarian symphony conductor whom we met soon after our arrival in Budapest, told us that he had received a letter from an American friend, a musicologist, in which the latter jokingly wrote, "I've just been reading a book on American conductors who are not of Hungarian origin—it's a very thin volume." Eminent Hungarian maestros included George Szell of the Cleveland Orchestra; Eugene Ormandy of the Philadelphia Orchestra; Sir Georg Solti of Chicago, and his predecessor, Fritz Reiner; and Antal Dorati, of Washington and Detroit. Hungarians are even more proud of their composers: Franz Liszt, Béla Bartók, Zoltán Kodály, and Ernst von Dohnányi, whose grandson Christoph is now the musical director of the Cleveland Orchestra.

We enjoyed the current musical scene—its extended opera season, its symphony orchestras, and the trio of very young piano virtuosi who were gaining international reputations: András Schiff, Zoltán Kocsis, and Dézso Ránki. Schiff, whom some critics have come to compare with Alfred Brendel, the brilliant Austrian pianist, often visited our residence. In recent years it has been a special pleasure to see Schiff perform in the United States several times.

Thirty years of Communist rule did not diminish the Hungarians' regard for their literary figures. No contemporary Hungarian was more revered than Gyula Illyés, an outstanding poet who also wrote *The People of the Puszta*, a classic portrayal of the life of the poor farmers in the western plains. We cherished our friendship with Illyés, which we fully enjoyed without benefit of interpreters. We communicated in French.

Particularly impressive was the continuing effort of Hungarians to expand their political and intellectual elbow room in a society still controlled by a Communist dictatorship, even though it was the most "liberal" in Eastern Europe. The Communist political infrastructure was still in place, with party domination over all institutions, a powerful and pervasive secret police, a controlled press, and a powerless parliament. Free assembly was prohibited and phones were tapped. Moreover, eighty thousand Soviet troops occupied Hungary. Western ambassadors, particularly the American, were closely watched; our servants reported on us regularly, on our personal habits, our movements, and our guests.

I recall an amusing incident when I visited the ham canning plant about one hundred miles from Budapest, which in the late 1970s produced the largest Hungarian export to the United States. János Bartha, the Foreign Office official in charge of the Western European and American Bureau, insisted that I see it. I was struck by the plant's efficiency, inspired no doubt by the regular inspection of officials from the U.S. Department of Agriculture. I sat down to lunch in the dining room assuming that ham would be served. To my amazement, three different kinds of meat appeared: veal, chicken, and beef, but no ham. Our servants had obviously told Hungarian officials that I never ate ham or pork.

Other aspects of the surveillance were not so amusing. Officials, journalists, even academics who were invited to our residence had to seek permission to enjoy the hospitality of the American ambassador, or, as the bolder of them put it, "We 'informed' our superiors or editors that we were dining with you." Even private individuals were sometimes skittish about accepting our invitation. A few refused to come, still remembering the Stalinist days when visiting the American embassy could hurt politically and professionally. I recall one top official, who ran the country's agricultural experimental institute, refusing to accept our invitation because he felt it demeaning to ask for official permission to do so.

A sad example involved Nyers, the able economist who had been the architect of NEM and had served as the secretary of the Communist Party in charge of economics until 1972 when, due to right-wing reaction against the reforms and Moscow's concern about them, he had been forced to resign. By 1977 he had been reduced to doing research in a government economic agency. Nyers was a close friend of Lord Kaldor, born and reared in Hungary, who had become a distinguished professor of economics at Cambridge University and an adviser to British Labour Party politicians. Hannah and I knew Kaldor well from our days in England. He stayed with us during his annual visits to Budapest to see his relatives. One morning in the fall of 1977 he announced to us that he was having lunch that day with Nyers (to whom, incidentally, he had acted as an unofficial adviser). We suggested that he invite Nyers to the dinner we were giving in Kaldor's honor a few nights later. After returning to the residence, Kaldor told us that Nyers would have been delighted to come but there wasn't enough time for him to secure permission.

A year later, after the Crown had been returned, Kaldor was again staying with us. This time when he invited Nyers to dinner in our residence, Nyers accepted, although again he didn't think he had enough time to secure permission. It was no longer so necessary, he said, a sign of the easing of the social and political environment and the changing attitude toward the United States. Incidentally, in the 1980s, Nyers became a powerful figure once more. He played a leading role in the reform of the Communist Party and was instrumental in bringing about the downfall of Kádár.

My wife and I never stopped inviting as many Hungarians as time would permit, and increasing numbers accepted. Some were dissidents or near-dissidents. Among the latter were people like the talented writer Arpad Goncz, who had been freed from jail after seven years of a commuted sentence to life imprisonment due to his participation in the revolution of 1956. During his incarceration he learned English and became the Hungarian translator of modern American novelists like William Faulkner, Ernest Hemingway, and E. L. Doctorow. Today he is the popular, highly respected president of democratic Hungary. It has been a special delight for my wife and me to see him in recent years in Washington; in Charlottesville, Virginia, where he was the guest of honor at the bicentennial celebration of our Constitution; and, of course, in Budapest.

Almost all the private people we met—journalists, intellectuals, musicians, and artists—were anti-Communist and anti-Soviet. While appreciating Kádár's reforms and admiring the skill with which he handled Moscow, they had no illusions about the system under which he continued to govern. When I asked Hungarians whether they felt freer under Kádár or less repressed, they invariably answered "Less repressed." They were adept, however, at taking advantage of Kádár's relative tolerance. The country continued to produce internationally respected historians like Georgi

Ranki and Ivan Berend, and outstanding economists like Janos Kornai, who divided his academic year between Harvard, where he had tenure, and the university in Budapest. Kornai's *The Economics of Shortage* is considered the definitive book on the subject. In fact, economists were probably the freest individuals in the country, reflecting the government's need to deal uninhibitedly with the problems posed by Kádár's economic reforms. Hungarian economists had regular and increasingly frank exchanges with their American colleagues after the launching in 1973 of the U.S.-Hungarian economic roundtable.

During this period Hungarians also managed to produce films that increasingly breached the restraints of censorship. A fair number of their productions were highly regarded in the West, and *Mephisto* won the Hollywood Oscar for the best foreign film of 1981.

Also evident was the increase in the religious activity of the Hungarian people. Catholic and Jewish clergy both were encouraged by the number of young people, now disillusioned with Communism, who attended their services. When the American prelates John Cardinal Krol of Philadelphia and Archbishop Joseph Bernardin of Chicago visited Hungary in September 1977, they led a special Mass to commemorate the Pope's eightieth birthday. The cathedral was packed and, surprisingly, Kádár's wife was one of the people present; this I learned from my chauffeur, Steve Bihari, who had seen Mrs. Kádár enter the cathedral and had visited with her chauffeur while both waited for the end of the service.

Hungary is predominantly Catholic and its primate, Cardinal Lekai, played an important role in the return of the Crown. He also had a delightful sense of humor. The day after Karol Wojtyła was elected Pope, he smilingly said to me, "I think a Pole was chosen because only God can help the Polish economy." Lekai's role was not an easy one. Some of his priests thought that he was not tough enough with the regime. There were still onerous restraints on the Church, particularly with regard to Catholic schools. Lekai, on the other hand, felt he was attuned to the realities he confronted and adept at taking advantage of whatever new openings were provided by state authorities.

Religious participation also increased in the Jewish community, which had been decimated by the Holocaust. Over half a million Hungarian Jews had been rounded up by the governing fascist Arrow Cross between October 1944 and the spring of 1945, just before the end of the war, and consigned to their deaths in Auschwitz. Thousands more would have suffered the same fate had it not been for the heroic efforts of the Swedish diplomat Raoul Wallenberg. The 100,000 Jews living in Hungary in the late 1970s were still the largest surviving Jewish community in Eastern Europe outside of the Soviet Union. After attending Day of Atonement services in the large Budapest synagogue, I disagreed with Erne Salgo, the chief rabbi of the country, over the number of people present. I said about two thousand; he claimed at least thirty-five hundred.

The Jewish community was particularly proud of the fact that Budapest was the home of the last rabbinical seminary in Eastern Europe. So was Kádár. On several occasions I heard him boast of the seminary in Budapest because it was training rabbis for the Soviet Union. The seminary, incidentally, was run by an outstanding Hebraic scholar, Rabbi Scheiber, who handled his delicate role with a firmness and finesse that any diplomat might envy. He told me that one of his students had ties to the KGB.

Hungarian Protestants hosted the most dramatic religious event of the fall of 1977, a visit by the evangelist Billy Graham, his first to an Eastern European country. In addition to his highly successful public appearances Graham diplomatically handled his personal meetings with church and government leaders.

The highlight of Graham's visit was his sermon at a service held outdoors about seventy-five miles from Budapest in a large field nestled between tree-lined hills. Thousands were present, including men, women, and children from neighboring countries. Like hundreds of thousands around the world who have heard Graham, they responded warmly to his sermon, which lost none of its impact in its sentence-by-sentence translation. The interpreter, a Hungarian medical doctor and Baptist minister who had settled in Atlanta, Georgia, almost enhanced the sermon's effect by successfully imitating Graham's preaching style, particularly his unique cadences.

Graham's visit to Hungary came at the time President Carter was deciding what to do about the return of the Crown. The warmth with which Graham was received and the goodwill he generated in Hungary undoubtedly made an impact back home. It also underlined the desire of the Hungarians for closer ties with the United States. Not surprisingly, the Hungarians emphasized to Graham how essential was the return of the Crown for better relations between our two countries. Graham's report on his visit after his return home may well have influenced President Carter's subsequent decision.

Shortly before Graham arrived in Budapest I received a cable from Washington instructing me to make the first approach to the Hungarian government about the return of the Crown. The President had reviewed the scenario that Secretary of State Vance had presented to him and had decided to delay a decision so that it could be considered in the context of an overall review of our Eastern European strategy. In the meantime, without making any commitment, I was instructed to ascertain how the Hungarian government would receive the Crown and its regalia, and whether they would be displayed publicly should they be returned. We wanted to know, too, whether Hungarians living abroad would be able to see it without restrictions. The cable concluded that I was "probably being placed in a difficult position because we were making no commitment about the return." Nevertheless, Washington expressed the hope that I would be able to elicit specific Hungarian ideas for the scenario, and report back by the end of August.

I didn't mind being "placed in a difficult position," but I was disappointed. I thought the issue had been settled before I left Washington.

When I informed János Nagy, the deputy foreign minister who dealt with U.S.-Hungarian relations, of the substance of my instructions, he made no effort to conceal his unhappiness over the fact that we still hadn't decided to return the Crown. He told me that he would bring my message to the highest authorities immediately, and give me their answer as soon as he received it. His response, which came two days later, hedged its replies to our questions. I bluntly told him that unless its substance was changed, it would have a negative effect on Washington, perhaps delaying indefinitely a decision to return the Crown. When he asked what I thought would be the right answer, I took paper and pencil and drafted the cable I would have liked to send to Washington. After reading it, Nagy asked me to delay my reply until I had heard from him again.

Two days later, August 26, he informed me that I could send the cable I had drafted in his office. Specifically, if the United States decided to return the Crown, the Hungarian government would receive it with the dignity and honor appropriate to this "unique national and cultural treasure, valued by all segments of society." In addition, the government would be happy to work out the actual details of the transfer after our decision had been taken and we had indicated how we intended to return the Crown. The Hungarian government would place the Crown in an appropriate building in Budapest. And, he concluded, it has always been the intention of the government to place no restrictions on foreigners or Hungarians living abroad wishing to see it.

I cabled the State Department these unequivocally positive answers to our questions. Ten days later Billy Graham told me that during a meeting with Deputy Prime Minister Gyorgy Aczel, an intimate of Kádár, Aczel had made it clear that if the United States decided to return the Crown, the Hungarians would receive it in whatever way fit the requirements of the President.

I was delighted when the President decided in late September to return the Crown. Secretary Vance then planned to inform Fryjes Puja, the Hungarian foreign minister, of the decision when he saw him on October 1, during the usual round of the secretary's meetings with foreign ministers attending the UN General Assembly.

Washington agreed to my request that I be present at this turning point in Hungarian-American relations. I arrived in New York the evening before and phoned George Vest, assistant secretary of state for Europe, immediately after checking into my hotel. Vest told me that apparently there was still some hesitation at the White House about what Vance should say to the Hungarian foreign minister, and suggested I call him the next morning for the final word before the meeting between Vance and the foreign minister.

When I did so, Vest told me that under an arrangement Secretary Vance had worked out with President Carter at the beginning of the administration, Vance wrote nightly a short memorandum, seen only by the President, in which Vance laid out immediately important issues for the President's information and consideration and, when necessary, for approval. The President sent back his written comments, if any, scribbled in the margin of the memorandum the next morning.

With Vance in New York, Warren Christopher, the acting secretary, prepared the memorandum on September 30. In it he informed the President that the next day the secretary was planning to tell the Hungarian foreign minister that the U.S. government had decided to return the Crown of St. Stephen. In the reply of the following morning, the President gave his approval.

George Vest, one of our ablest Foreign Service officers, immediately phoned Vance to tell him of the President's action. When Brzezinski called the secretary thereafter to suggest that he delay conveying approval to the foreign minister, Vance crisply informed Brzezinski that the President had given him the green light.

The secretary handled the meeting with Puja in his characteristic straightforward and dignified manner. He stated that we wanted to continue to strengthen relationships between our two countries. We realized that an important next step would be the return of the Crown of St. Stephen, a step we now wished to take. "The question," Vance added, "is when and how. We believe that we should try to finalize this act at an early date. We will be giving the necessary instructions to Ambassador Kaiser so that we will be able to move forward." In reply Puja said that he was delighted with the secretary's message. "Undoubtedly," he concluded, "the return of this sacred relic of the Hungarian nation will greatly influence the feelings of the people toward the United States." It was then agreed that the decision to return the Crown should be kept secret until we arrived at a mutually acceptable time to announce it.

Cyrus Vance was an excellent choice for secretary of state. He had wide experience in international affairs, had served as undersecretary of defense in the Johnson administration, and, with Averell Harriman, in the negotiations with the North Vietnamese in 1968, which, unfortunately, were cynically sabotaged by Nixon's people before the presidential election that year. As secretary of state, Vance negotiated the Salt II Agreement with the Soviet Union. Though the accord was vehemently attacked by right-wing Republicans and never ratified by the Senate, President Reagan complied with its provisions.

Vance's outstanding characteristic is his integrity. It was always apparent in the calm and judicious way he handled tough issues. Vance found it difficult to believe that the people he dealt with were not equally honorable and reliable. His gentle manner belied his political courage. When he thought using military force to free our hostages in Iran was wrong, he resigned as secretary of state. Though the resignation was not announced until the day after this aborted effort, Vance had submitted it to the President a few days before the mission, making it clear that even if the mission succeeded, he would not change his mind.

Serving as an ambassador when Vance was secretary of state was a happy experience. Always thoughtful, considerate, and fair, he welcomed ideas and suggestions and found time to discuss them. We were all particularly pleased that the President asked him to lead the U.S. delegation accompanying the return of the Crown to Hungary. He had played a major role in making it happen, and was highly respected by the Hungarians. I remember his comment on the ride from the airport to the residence the day he arrived in Budapest. "I'm delighted to be here," he said. "Nothing gives me more pleasure than being involved in an act that is morally right."

Three weeks after the Vance meeting with Puja a cable from Washington instructed me to meet with the foreign minister to work out details of the transfer, emphasizing the following essential points: (1) various segments of the Hungarian public, including the Roman Catholic primate, should participate in the return ceremonies; (2) the Crown would be displayed publicly and appropriately in a historic location, one not associated with the Communist Party; (3) the ceremony would emphasize the national religious and cultural nature of the Crown and the fact that the American people were returning to the Hungarian people a national treasure that rightly belongs to Hungarians. We anticipated a public statement from the government that Hungarians from all over the world were welcome to visit Hungary and view the Crown.

After Puja told me that the Hungarian government agreed with our proposals, the embassy and the Foreign Office negotiated the practical details for implementing them. As expected, there were several technical hitches and, except for one, all were resolved smoothly. We had insisted on an exchange of letters between the foreign minister and me setting out the agreements (we avoided using the word "conditions") covering the Crown's homecoming. When the foreign minister argued that this sort of thing was never done by their regime, I replied that never had the Crown been returned before. We "compromised." At the appropriate time, the full text of my letter was published in the party and government newspapers with an authentic summary of the foreign secretary's reply.

Washington now proceeded to take the final steps before a public announcement of the President's decision to return the Crown. Congressional members were consulted and plans made to inform representatives of the Hungarian-American community. Unfortunately, before the completion of these moves, due to some government leaks, *The New York Times* broke the story in a page-one article on November 3, 1977, the anniversary of the very day on which the Soviet Union had crushed the Hungarian revolution in 1956.

Opponents of the return, particularly elements of the Hungarian-American community who had emigrated to the United States after 1956, reacted passionately. They focused their complaints on Congress and the White House and, as a last resort, the federal courts. A predominantly hostile crowd attended hearings on the issue before the House Foreign Affairs Committee. Not surprisingly, the noisy expression of their sentiments during the hearings, as well as a demonstration outside the Capitol, received most of the media's attention. Almost ignored was the fact that two key Hungarians supported the return because of their conviction that this unique symbol of a thousand years of Hungarian history would strengthen the country's appreciation of its national identity. The first was Ferenc Nagy, the last Hungarian prime minister democratically chosen, who, forced to leave the country in 1948, resided in northern Virginia. The second was General Béla Király, the commander of the revolutionary forces during the revolt in 1956, who had become a professor of international relations at Brooklyn College in New York City. These two distinguished Hungarians could hardly be accused of being soft on Communism or oblivious of Kádár's past history.

President Carter received a delegation opposing the Crown's return. While appreciating their feelings about the return of the holy Crown of St. Stephen to a nation under Communist control, Carter made it clear that his decision was based on the evidence that Hungary's record on human rights, while hardly perfect by U.S. standards, was superior to that of any other Soviet bloc country. His act reflected the President's "differentiation" policy in Eastern Europe—a policy that recognized that, although Moscow-controlled, each one of these nations cherished a unique history despite decades of Communist rule. American interests were best served when we responded to those differences.

Carter emphasized this point in his remarks to the Hungarians. He also told them that the United States had always recognized that the Crown belonged to the Hungarian people. And it was only right that it be returned to its home before a whole generation of Hungarians came of age without being aware of its existence and its symbolism.

The public reaction of the Hungarian-Americans to the premature newspaper disclosure of the decision to return the Crown temporarily affected Washington's plans. The date that had been set for the Crown's arrival in Budapest was put aside while the administration coped with some of the wildest charges of those who opposed the return. Washington asked me, for example, to inquire whether it was true that not long after receiving the Crown the Hungarians would allow the Soviets to move it to Moscow. When I questioned the government about this foolish rumor, they helped me cover my embarrassment by being amused rather than annoyed by the question. Of course, they had no such intention.

More seriously, Washington wanted me to solicit the views of Cardinal János Lekai about the attitude of the Catholic Church, since American opponents contended that the Church was against its return. Accompanied by Herb Wilgis, who spoke excellent Hungarian, I called on Cardinal Lekai, with whom I had developed a friendly rapport.

Lekai left no doubt of his full-hearted support of President Carter's decision to return the Crown. He spoke with deep feeling, calling it the most important act affecting Hungarian-American relations. "A historic, as well as religious, symbol," he added, "the Crown stands for Hungarian freedom and independence."

Lekai stated that he would be pleased to make a public statement or write an article in the Catholic press about his support of the return of the Crown. "Tell Washington," he concluded, "I support the return of the Crown, the Catholic Church supports it, and the Hungarians as well."

After the United States and Hungary agreed on a new date for the Crown's return, Washington made a highly sensitive request: I was to tell the Hungarian government that President Carter would be politically embarrassed if Kádár were present at the ceremony celebrating the Crown's homecoming. Would the head of the Hungarian state be willing to absent himself from Budapest on that day? The response was impressive: Kádár understood the sensitivity of the situation and would not be present.

It was a remarkable gesture, one that reflected Kádár's mature political persona. The only head of an Eastern European country who discouraged the development of a personality cult, Kádár was rarely praised in the press, or on radio or TV. His picture hardly ever appeared in the newspapers, and I never saw his photo in any office of a top government official.

I had my first meeting with Kádár a month before the Crown was returned. We talked for almost two hours in his office at Communist Party headquarters, covering a wide range of topics that included the President's decision to return the Crown, and its impact on our bilateral relations and Hungary's domestic and international policies, particularly economic reform.

Although Kádár had been jailed by Mátyás Rákosi, his Stalinist predecessor, and it was widely believed he had been severely tortured, Kádár showed few signs of it. After greeting me at the entrance to his office, he led me to a chair facing him across a conference table. The only other person present was the interpreter. Ambassadors can be somewhat awed during a first meeting with the chief of state, or government, or, in a Communist country, the head of the party, but Kádár didn't seem to take himself too seriously. He quickly put me at ease by quietly asking how my wife and I were adjusting to life in Budapest. He warmly welcomed me as the new U.S. ambassador to Hungary, adding a comment about the importance of the role of ambassador because it was through his eyes that his home country saw Hungary's society. It was essential, he emphasized, that ambassadors be as objective as possible and report fully and frankly to their home capitals. He put a premium on a realistic approach to international and domestic affairs.

After a member of Kádár's staff produced two Scotch-and-sodas (not my usual drink at 10:00 A.M., but obviously his), Kádár expressed his gratitude for a friendly oral message I gave him from President Carter, and then proceeded to use it as his lead for an exposition of Hungarian policies that lasted for over an hour, including the time for interpretation. He spoke easily, intelligently, and with animation.

He said that although Hungary was a member of one alliance and the United States the leader of another, that should not inhibit the development of meaningful relations between our two countries. He wanted to make it clear that Hungary was an independent country with its own domestic and international policies, although of course it was loyal to its alliance. Hungary had its own traditions, history, and culture, and its own national interests. These factors, plus the "size of our country, our location on the map, and the nature of our economy, were the main criteria" of the policies pursued by Hungary.

Kádár spoke at considerable length about changes in the Hungarian economy, stressing that it was the most important aspect of Hungarian life. He urged me to appreciate the political significance of his economic reforms. Continuing economic progress, he explained, depended on expanding foreign trade, particularly with the West. Compared to West Germany, Austria, and Italy, American trade was just a trickle, and our failure to grant MFN status to Hungary was inhibiting its growth.

He then talked about U.S.-Hungarian relations. He recounted our joint history since World War I, ending with the story of the Crown. He wanted me to convey to the President his deep appreciation of the decision to return this historic Hungarian symbol, particularly in light of the domestic political obstacles the President had to overcome. He also asked me to report that he agreed with the President's view that the Crown was being returned to the Hungarian people by the American people.

He concluded by recalling in great detail his meeting with Governor Harriman in 1963, when the governor was in Moscow to sign the Test Ban Treaty. Khrushchev introduced Kádár to

Harriman in the Sports Stadium, where they were watching a track meet between the United States and the U.S.S.R. Kádár spoke warmly of the governor, stating that no man understood East-West relations better than Harriman. He knew of our friendship and asked me to convey his greetings to Harriman.

In responding to Kádár's main points, I emphasized that President Carter and Secretary Vance had always recognized that the Crown was Hungarian property. The President's decision was morally right as well as politically courageous and, of course, it removed a major obstacle to our improving relations. It reflected his broader approach to East-West relations, his commitment to cooperation, not confrontation, as evidenced by his determination to reach a SALT agreement and to prevent nuclear proliferation. Because of his technical training no chief of state had a better appreciation of the significance of the nuclear threat. When I suggested to Kádár that he read the President's recent speech in Charleston, South Carolina, to understand Carter's views on world affairs, Kádár said he was familiar with it.

Realizing that ambassadors should always try to take practical advantage of private meetings with chiefs of government, particularly in a state ruled by one man, I then raised several specific issues on our bilateral plate. I told Kádár that the Executive Branch of our government favored granting MFN status to Hungary, but we had to meet the requirements of the 1974 Trade Act. We felt this could be done without adversely affecting the self-esteem of either country. As Kádár undoubtedly was aware, we had made our first proposal for meeting the political requirements of the act and were waiting for the Hungarian government's response. Once we solved the political aspects we would proceed to negotiate a trade agreement incorporating MFN.

The next practical issue was the need to increase contacts between Hungary and America. We were pleased with the new cooperation between members of the embassy and officials of the Foreign Ministry and other government departments. We now wanted to develop similar relationships with party officials. When Senators George McGovern and Joseph Biden had visited Budapest, they found their meetings with several top party leaders very helpful. To break new ground we had invited the director of the party's international department to visit the States. We hoped he would be allowed to accept. It was not necessary to tell Kádár we knew that in a Communist-controlled country top party people were more important than government officials. We also wanted to increase Hungarian and American contacts between private individuals and organizations, particularly in the fields of education, science, technology, and culture. Kádár reacted positively to these suggestions, stating in his direct laconic way, "Exchanges are reality."

Kádár concluded the meeting by emphasizing that with the return of the Crown he foresaw increased cooperation between our two countries. We could, in his view, accomplish a great deal on a realistic basis and, he added, we didn't have to announce our achievements in "bright neon lights." Two days later Kádár gave permission to party officials to accept invitations to visit the United States. Thereafter a regular flow of such visitors enhanced the rapport between our two governments.

The meeting with Kádár reflected the fact that we were entering a new, more open phase in the relationship between our two countries. This became even more evident after the return of the Crown on January 6, 1978, in the magnificent gilded Central Hall of the Parliament Building constructed in the late nineteenth century, the heyday of the Austro-Hungarian Empire. The accompanying ceremonies went off flawlessly before an audience of the two countries' delegations, American embassy and local personnel, some two hundred representatives of the Hungarian people, and the international and Hungarian press. The colorful and dignified ceremonies were covered in their entirety on radio and TV.

The American delegation, which brought the Crown on a U.S. government plane, was made up of private individuals like my old friend Monsignor George Higgins, America's "labor priest"; Rabbi David Shneyer, who had spent his youth in Budapest, as a refugee from Nazi Vienna; and government officials, including Senator Adlai Stevenson III and Congressmen Lee Hamilton, Fortney Stark, and Ted Weiss. Everyone, including the Hungarians, was delighted that the chairman of the delegation was Secretary Vance. We were pleased, too, that he was accompanied by Gay, his attractive, charming, and highly intelligent wife.

We happily noted that, like the U.S. delegation, the Hungarian delegation represented the people of the country. A sprinkling of high government officials, members of Parliament, and the mayor of Budapest were joined by two hundred invited Hungarian guests, including members of trade unions, the Council of Hungarian Women, youth organizations, outstanding factory and agricultural workers, and personalities from the academic, scientific, and art worlds. A Jewish religious leader later remarked that it was the first time ever in Hungary that leaders of all faiths had come together in a ceremony associated with the Crown, and that they rarely met on any other occasions.

Highlights of the ceremonies were speeches by Secretary Vance and Antal Apro, president of the Hungarian Parliament. Vance stressed the link between the event and improved relations between the United States and Hungary, adding that it also reflected our joint commitment to the final Helsinki Act signed in 1975 by all European countries, the United States, and Canada. The secretary referred particularly to Chapter III of the act, which committed the signatories to the protection of the full range of human rights, and called for regular consultation among countries to implement this provision.*

Apro replied in the same spirit, stating that he was honored to receive the Crown and regalia in the name of the Hungarian people and expressing appreciation to President Carter and the American people. He also affirmed that the return of the Crown corresponded to the spirit of the final Helsinki Act and concluded, "We are ready to further develop our relations, the conditions of which are considerably improved by the spirit of this day."

In the later private session between Secretary Vance and Prime Minister Lázár, the discussion focused on MFN status and the application of the human rights provisions under the final Helsinki Act. In reply to press questions before leaving Budapest, Secretary Vance referred to the discussions with the Hungarians on both subjects. He was, of course, in full agreement on the implementation of the final Helsinki Act, adding that he had asked me to carry forward the negotiations for granting MFN status to Hungary.

There was a touch of international irony in the emergence of

---

*Vance's remarks were elegantly translated by Czanad Toth, a young Hungarian who had escaped from Hungary in 1956 and had become a State Department official.

the final Helsinki Act as a major instrument for regular communication on human rights between the United States and Eastern European countries. When the act was approved in 1975 by the CSCE (Conference on Security and Cooperation in Europe), right-wing elements in Western countries, particularly the United States, criticized the signatories for accepting the post–World War II territorial changes in Europe. Conservatives derived little comfort from the fact that the Soviet Union and the Communist-controlled Eastern European countries had all approved the human rights provisions in Chapter III of the Helsinki Act. They scoffed at the thought that these countries would possibly comply. Yet in bilateral discussions and in international conferences under the aegis of the CSCE established by the Helsinki Act, human rights continued to be a front-burner issue; and, thanks to the dramatic developments in the late 1980s, the Soviet Union has not only accepted the reunification of Germany—a dramatic territorial change considered inconceivable by Moscow in 1975—but also its membership in NATO. Moreover, today there are those who believe that a permanently structured CSCE could be the institution best suited to regulate peacefully disagreements in the post–Cold War, all-inclusive Europe.

A provision on free emigration in Chapter III of the Helsinki accord provided the key to granting MFN status to the Hungarians. Some relatively minor changes in language, agreed upon in Budapest, enabled Washington to rule that Hungary was in compliance with the Jackson-Vanik provision of the 1974 Trade Act. Thereafter I chaired the American team that in meetings in Washington and Budapest negotiated a new trade agreement with the Hungarians that granted mutual MFN status.

Thanks to Washington's initiative in settling the Crown and trade issues, relations between our two countries improved steadily during the remainder of my three-year tour in Budapest. We achieved substantial progress in economic and commercial cooperation, in cultural exchanges, and in high-level political dialogue on a variety of issues.

After MFN status was established, trade deals between our two countries increased, including joint ventures that brought U.S. technology and more sales to Hungary. Major American companies opened offices in Budapest. We signed agreements on double taxation and on export-import bank loans and extended Commodity Credit Corporation credits. We settled major patent infringement disputes and established a joint economic committee to meet annually to discuss economic developments in both of our countries.

After agreeing on a new cultural and scientific program, our cultural exchanges were at the highest level ever. Our professors were lecturing in Hungarian universities and other institutions. For the first time we were able to mount a major cultural exhibit in Budapest. Hungarian tourism to the United States, including whole families, was up and American travel to Hungary had expanded substantially. Also encouraging was the dialogue we developed under the final Helsinki Act tent that contributed to our success in reunifying American families with their Hungarian relatives, some of whom had been waiting to join their families since the late 1940s.

High-level political dialogue was helped by visits of congressional delegations, one headed by Speaker Tip O'Neill, another by Senator Abraham Ribicoff, and a third by Congressman John Brademas. Kádár broke personal precedent by receiving these groups and spending several hours with them, and his frankness on all issues made a strong impression. He quickly won over Speaker O'Neill by observing that because they were both sixty-five years old ("He sure has done his homework," O'Neill whispered to me) they had a more mature perspective on political and social issues. I remember Congressman (now Speaker of the House) Tom Foley, after hearing Kádár's reply to the congressman's question about the NEM, saying to me, "That's one of the best explanations of a market economy that I've heard in a long time." I also recall the comment of Oklahoma's Senator Henry Bellmon after the senators' two-hour meeting with Kádár: "That was one of the most impressive political performances I've ever witnessed."

No American was received more warmly and with greater respect by Kádár than Averell Harriman, who, with his beautiful wife,* Pamela, honored us with a four-day visit. During a conver-

*Marie Harriman died in 1970.

sation that lasted almost three hours, Harriman and Kádár frankly exchanged views on a whole range of international issues, particularly those affecting East-West relations. Kádár listened intently when Harriman suggested that during Kádár's forthcoming meeting with Brezhnev he clear up some of the latter's confusions about Washington's attitudes on Soviet-American disagreements. Harriman, then eighty-seven years old, enjoyed every minute of the meeting, handling Kádár with a master's touch.

Between an official lunch, a reception, and dinner I drafted a long, detailed memorandum of the conversation, which I gave to Harriman for his approval before changing for dinner. While I was showering I heard Harriman loudly ask Hannah, "Where's Phil?" She replied, "Having a shower." A few seconds later my bathroom door opened and, with the water cascading over my head, I heard Harriman ask, "Phil, did I really say that to Kádár in the last paragraph on page three?" This was vintage Harriman behavior on matters that really interested him.

The media gave unusually wide coverage to Harriman's visit, including a one-hour interview on television, all of it exceptionally favorable. He was one American, they emphasized, who clearly understood East-West relations. It seemed, too, as if all of Budapest sought to be invited to our reception in honor of the Harrimans.

Hungary also continued to expand its contacts and trade with Western Europe. Kádár visited Paris in 1979, received German chancellor Helmut Schmidt and Greek prime minister Konstantinos Karamanlis that same year, and scheduled visits to Belgium and the United Kingdom. He had already traveled to West Germany, and his annual meetings with Chancellor Bruno Kreisky of Austria were dubbed "the K and K alliance."

Nothing in the favorable developments between Hungary and the West, however, suggested any change in Hungary's attitude toward Moscow. We at the embassy were continually reminded that we still lived in a Warsaw Pact country, and no improvement in our bilateral relations was to bring into question Hungary's loyalty to the Soviet Union. Bridging gaps between a democratic and a Communist society, even in a more enlightened Hungary, was not an easy task. Though we had contacts with Hungarian journalists and TV and radio commentators, we realized that we were still operating in a media environment that was neither free nor entirely friendly.

On international issues the media continued to be as pro-Soviet as ever, though, thanks to our embassy's periodic protests, somewhat less critical of America. While our relations improved, we had regular access only to top-echelon Hungarians in the ministries of foreign affairs, foreign trade, economics, culture, and the national bank. Moreover, though embassy officers saw more of Hungarian editors, intellectuals, artists, religious leaders, trade unionists, and industrialists, we realized that some of them still thought twice about contacts with Americans.

Because Budapest was sensitive about its ability to handle the Soviet Union while expanding its relations with the West, I was particularly curious about the reaction of top officials when Leonid Brezhnev visited Budapest in May 1979. In fact, Washington asked for my impressions of the Russian leader's physical condition. He was thought to be in poor health, and he and President Carter were scheduled to meet in Vienna ten days later to sign the Salt II Agreement.

All members of the diplomatic corps were present at Brezhnev's arrival and departure at the Budapest airport. We noted that as he stepped down from his plane, the Russian leader, aggressively rejecting any help, seemed determined to demonstrate that he was very much in control of his physical movements. He walked deliberately. When he shook hands with the Hungarian brass and then with each member of the diplomatic corps, it was with a quick, identical handshake, as if the handshake button on an automaton had been pressed. He greeted no one verbally. The lack of spontaneity and the carefully calculated quality in every gesture looked surreal.

The behavior of the Hungarian leadership naturally caught our attention. Hungarians are always excellent hosts, and in this situation they naturally outdid themselves. They couldn't conceal, however, the anxiety that permeated the airport. It was not only Brezhnev's physical security that preoccupied them; they were concerned, too, about what Brezhnev and his entourage, which included Andrei Gromyko and Konstantin Chernenko, would have to say about Hungary's economic policies. Hungarian officials did not conceal their relief when, in a speech on Budapest radio the night before his departure, Brezhnev expressed his full support of Kádár's policies. We learned later that the speech had been recorded in Moscow before the Soviet leader came to Hungary.

This sense of relief dominated the scene at the airport when Brezhnev departed, with smiles rather than strain on the faces of the Hungarian leaders. Kádár was noticeably bouncy and talkative, and with a big grin on his face gestured to several of us Western ambassadors while Brezhnev was talking to the Cuban ambassador. Even Brezhnev was more relaxed, unself-consciously now walking with a slight limp. He even spoke to some of the ambassadors as he bid them farewell. When he tried but couldn't quite manage to say anything to me after shaking hands, Gromyko covered his leader's embarrassment by filling the void with "Good-bye, Mr. Ambassador." Outside the airport I ran into several Hungarian officials talking to Vladimir Pavlov, the Soviet ambassador, and couldn't resist remarking how relaxed they looked. At this they all laughed, including the usually dour Russian. Brezhnev's blessing of Kádár's policies indicated that even as Kádár pursued his economic reforms and expanded his contacts with the West, his relations with Moscow continued to be in good order.

My wife and I left Budapest in 1980, but thanks to my membership on the board of the Soros Hungarian Foundation, annual visits enabled us to continue to follow developments in the country. Born in Hungary, George Soros came to America after taking his degree at the London School of Economics in the late 1940s. A genius at making money, he had an extraordinary talent for spending a fair share of it to advance the objectives of his practical idealism, particularly the development of free societies in Eastern Europe.

After creating his Open Society Foundation in New York, which financed the visits to the states of near-dissidents and dissidents, in 1983 Soros established the Hungarian Foundation with main offices in Budapest and a backstop administrative unit in New York. The foundation was launched after an agreement with the Hungarian Academy of Science, not the government. Soros successfully insisted on the foundation's independence, a remarkable achievement considering that the country was still Communist-controlled. On several occasions when the government made a pass at interfering with its operations, Soros threatened to close down the foundation.

The original goal of the foundation was to contribute to the transformation of Hungary into an open society. The fact that it was allowed to function in the early 1980s reflected the increasing tolerance in the country. Through the financing of literary and social science scholarships, of grants to Hungarian experts to attend international conferences, of postgraduate studies by Hungarian students at Oxford and other universities, and the provision of photocopy machines to schools and libraries, as well as thousands of books, the foundation handsomely advanced its objectives in Hungary, so much so that Soros proceeded to establish similar foundations in Poland, the Soviet Union, Czechoslovakia, Romania, and Bulgaria, and more recently in the Baltic States, Ukraine, and Albania.

Nineteen eighty turned out to be the apex of Kádár's success and popularity. As a result of his economic reforms, particularly his emphasis on consumerism, for almost a decade Hungarians had enjoyed a steady increase in their standard of living and more political and social tolerance. The populace believed that this trend would continue. It did politically, but not economically.

A new stage of economic reforms, including a further increase in prices, higher taxes, and more rational use of labor, which led to unemployment, generated serious social and economic problems. Their satisfactory resolution would have required a systemic change to a genuine market economy, a change Kádár was neither psychologically nor politically prepared to make. Instead he held on to the fundamentals of the socialist economy, even while pushing for some reforms within it. Industry and agriculture were still state-owned. Most new investments in the country were also still government-controlled and competition among Hungarian enterprises remained minimal. Kádár hesitated to reduce subsidies, fearing a political backlash. Substantial foreign loans, which made Hungary the largest per-capita debtor of any Eastern European country, were used mainly to sustain consumption rather than for industrial modernization, their avowed purpose.

By the mid-1980s a stagnant economy, unable to meet rising expectations, was creating widespread dissatisfaction with dramatic political repercussions. Stimulated by the liberalizing effect of Gorbachev's perestroika in May 1988, reformers in the Communist Party's Central Committee, many of whom had been influenced by the freer spirit generated by Kádár in the 1970s, forced him to resign as the party's general secretary and ousted eight of his old-guard colleagues from the thirteen-member politburo. The average age of the new politburo was fifty-two, remarkably young by Eastern European standards.

The key figures in this peaceful coup were Nyers, the leading reformer under NEM, and Imre Pozsgay, whom I had first met when he was minister of culture in the 1970s. He now publicly set democratic socialism as the goal of a new Hungary. When I saw him the year before he hadn't hesitated to articulate his liberal, democratic views, emphasizing the need for doing away with party control of the government as a major step toward establishing a multiparty democracy.

Under Pozsgay's leadership the Hungarian Socialist Workers Party became the only Communist party in Eastern Europe to develop a genuine, democratically oriented reform movement. He played an important part in the preparation of the party document that rejected the official view that the 1956 revolt was counterrevolutionary and Soviet intervention justified. The party's reformers then participated in ceremonies attended by hundreds of thousands of Hungarians to mark the reburial of Imre Nagy and other leaders of the 1956 revolution. This remarkable reversal broke the remaining influence of the older party types who had reluctantly rolled with the wave of reform, particularly Karoly Grosz, an apparatchik who had succeeded Kádár as general secretary.

A series of important steps toward democracy followed. In January 1989 Parliament legalized free assembly and association. A month later the Hungarian Socialist Workers Party, on its own initiative, approved the creation of independent political parties, recognizing that competition with other parties "entails the possibility of losing power." In no other Eastern European country did the Communist Party voluntarily give up its monopoly role and then organize a multiparty commission to develop procedures for holding free elections.

In September the government, still controlled by the party, made a historic decision that contributed to the democratic revolutions that subsequently swept through several Eastern European countries. It allowed thousands of vacationing East German tourists to leave Hungary for West Germany. Although this act was a technical violation of its treaty with East Germany, the Hungarian government argued that it had the right to apply to citizens of another state the provision in the Helsinki Accords concerning the free movement of people. The Hungarians' courage contributed to the fall of the Communist regime in East Germany, which in turn inspired the "people's revolt" in Czechoslovakia.

A month later, in October, an extraordinary congress of the Hungarian Socialist Workers Party came out in favor of "democratic socialism" and reorganized itself as the Hungarian Socialist Party. Other parties now sprang up and began campaigning for the first free election in over forty-five years, scheduled for March 1990.

I was a member of the international delegation, chaired by former vice president Walter Mondale, that observed the election. Representing sixteen countries, we broke up into teams that visited three hundred polling booths from their opening at 6:00 A.M. to their closing twelve hours later. One of the American members jokingly remarked that the practices he observed were more open than those of Chicago in the old days.

We concluded that the new electoral law had provided an effective means for the Hungarian people's participation in a genuinely free parliamentary election. Like the other members of the delegation, I was deeply moved by what I had seen. During my three years in Hungary, when we were trying to improve Hungarian-American relations and help the Hungarian people expand their political and social elbow room, I didn't dream that a decade later I would witness an event that signaled the end of forty years of dictatorship.

My sentiments paled in comparison with those expressed by an elderly white-haired man whom I met in one of the polling stations. He told me that he was a veteran of the 1956 revolution and spoke of the courage and sacrifice of the people during that struggle for freedom. He had been imprisoned and his brother executed. With tears in his eyes he concluded, "I never believed I would live to see a free election in Hungary."

9

Austria's Postwar Democracy: Ambassador to Vienna

When it was announced that I was leaving Hungary to become our ambassador to Austria, Cardinal Lekai said, "This is a historic event, the first time in a thousand years that Budapest is sending the Kaiser to Vienna rather than vice versa." It was a charming reminder of the old imperial relationship, and delighted citizens in both countries.

The Austro-Hungarian Empire had collapsed in 1918, and the histories of separated Austria and Hungary in the subsequent two decades were marked by revolution, reaction, dictatorship, and alliance with Nazi Germany. After the Second World War Hungary was forcibly included in the new Soviet empire while Austria, with the help of the Western countries, particularly the United States, successfully avoided Moscow's clutches and emerged as a democracy. In spite of decades of social upheaval and differing political paths, Budapest and Vienna never lost completely their special relationship. It was sustained by historic sentiment, geographic contiguity, and connections between families and friends.* Following the Hungarian revolution in 1956, when Vi-

---

*A large number of Hungarians continued to live in Vienna after the breakup of the empire. I remember the reply of the wife of the Hungarian ambassador to Austria when the Hungarian foreign minister asked how she could possibly manage in Vienna without knowing German. "Easily," she replied. "I use my English in the diplomatic world, and my Hungarian is indispensable when I do my shopping."

301

enna courageously accepted 200,000 Hungarian refugees, the two old imperial partners developed increasingly close ties. By the 1970s Austria was Hungary's main bridge to the West. Given their common history and Austria's declared policy of neutrality between the blocs, Moscow found it difficult to object to this seemingly inevitable development.

I saw evidence of the strengthening of Austro-Hungarian relations during my years in Budapest. Austria became a major source of foreign loans to Hungary and an important trading partner. Much of the new construction in Hungary, particularly the hotels, was built and financed by Austrians. By 1980 when I left Budapest, visas were no longer required for travel between the two countries, increasing an already large flow of visitors who crossed both borders. Austrian women patronized the cheaper hairdressers in Hungary, and Austrian car owners filled their tanks there with less expensive gas.

There were contacts between various groups, particularly the Austrian and Hungarian trade unions, even though the Hungarian labor movement was government-controlled. Encouraging these developments were Kádár and Bruno Kreisky, the Austrian chancellor, who met regularly in Budapest and Vienna. The "K and K" relationship pleased Hungarians and Austrians, and students of the empire's history observed that Austria and Hungary had never had better relations.

Much as I enjoyed my tour in Budapest, I appreciated being posted again to a democratic country with untapped telephones and a free (though largely irresponsible) press. It was also agreeable to have easy access to opposition leaders, as well as government officials; to writers, artists, and academics; and to industrialists and labor leaders.

Ever since serving in Truman's Labor Department I had enjoyed good relations with the powerful Austrian trade unions. Anton Benya, their leader and also president of Parliament, remembered that soon after the war we had launched the highly successful exchange program for Austrian and German trade unionists who had survived Nazi repression and imprisonment. When I called on him, I delivered a warm personal message from his old friend Lane Kirkland, president of the AFL-CIO. American labor's contribution to the postwar revival of the Austrian trade unions had helped create a strong fraternal relationship.

Vienna's cultural life, the beauty of the city itself, the famous "Vienna woods," and the country beyond all helped make our stay particularly agreeable. The Vienna Philharmonic is considered the best orchestra in the world by many musicians, though, inexcusably, it is the only major orchestra still excluding women. Happily, ambassadors had free access to the diplomatic box of the Musikverein, where the orchestra and other musical ensembles and artists performed. The equally famous Vienna State Opera—the Philharmonic is its accompanying orchestra—rivals Covent Garden in London, Milan's La Scala, and the Met in New York, while the Volksoper is renowned for its production of such light-opera gems as *Die Fledermaus* and *The Merry Widow*.

Vienna was also a favorite of art lovers. The Kunsthistorisches Museum houses a collection of masterpieces including several Rembrandt self-portraits, a stunning Brueghel room, and countless paintings of other great artists. In addition the gallery in the Belvedere Palace featured some of the best-known Klimt and Schiele paintings and several Kokoschkas, while the Albertina could boast of one of the world's best collections of drawings.

Ambassadors do not spend all their time in the capital. I enjoyed visiting all corners of Austria. While Vienna dominated the country it did not overshadow the glorious mountains and lakes that make Austria a mecca for thousands of tourists.

I was happy returning to an Austria that differed radically from the one I had first visited in 1937 when I was a student at Oxford and spent the full five weeks at the famous Salzburg Festival. The scene then was grim. You could feel the country's malaise. Unemployment stood at over twenty percent of the work force. A fascist regime had ruled the country for three years and Hitler's increasing threat to take over the country culminated in the Anschluss the following year. Nazi sentiment was particularly strong in Salzburg, but I didn't allow it to spoil the joy of hearing operas and concerts directed by the great Arturo Toscanini and Bruno Walter. I shall never forget Walter's virtuoso performance at a dress rehearsal of *The Marriage of Figaro*. In addition to conducting, he played the harpsichord and, without interrupting the performance, intermittently turned around to quickly discuss a particular scene or aria with Lothar Wallerstein, director of production.

When I made my ambassadorial call on the governor of Salzburg Province, he told me of an experience he had immediately after Hitler took over Austria. The Nazis arrested his father, the editor of a liberal Catholic newspaper, and himself, although he was only twelve years old at the time. Shortly after they released him a few days later, he went for a haircut in the shop that had taken care of three generations of his family. This time, however, the barber, refusing to accept him, said, "I won't cut the hair of a little anti-Nazi pig."

There had been many remarkable changes in Europe since 1945, but perhaps none more dramatic than those in Austria. By 1980 the fascist country that had become part of Nazi Germany had been transformed into a prosperous, independent democracy. Learning the appropriate lessons from their costly hostility in the interwar period, the two leading political parties, the Socialists and the People's Party (formerly the Christian-Social Party), first collaborated to frustrate Moscow's attempt to take over the country. They have never stopped working together to achieve and maintain a vigorous democratic society. This continuing political cooperation has been buttressed by a social partnership that is largely responsible for Austria's economic prosperity. The country's strongly organized economic interest groups—labor, business, and agriculture—established a Party Commission for Prices and Wages to facilitate their cooperation in dealing with the problems arising from inflation. The commission had evolved into the country's main instrument for resolving economic conflicts peacefully. The fact that since 1955 Austria has had virtually no strikes attests to its remarkable success. Austria's per-capita income is higher than the average per capita of the European Community.

Austrian recovery was helped, too, by massive Western economic aid under the Marshall Plan. I was impressed by the number of older Austrians who, recalling the bitter years immediately after the war, expressed their gratitude for American aid.

A leading architect of Austria's postwar success was Bruno Kreisky who, by 1980, was serving his tenth year as chancellor. His personal story was remarkable. Born Jewish, he had become head of government in a country that had a long history of anti-

Semitism, culminating in the atrocities during the Nazi Anschluss. No one in the late 1930s would have dreamed that an individual of Jewish origin,* and a socialist to boot, would become a highly regarded chancellor three decades later.

Kreisky, the child of a wealthy and politically liberal Jewish family, was born in Vienna in January 1911.† The young Kreisky witnessed the misery resulting from the postwar transformation of Vienna from the capital of a multiethnic empire of fifty million to that of a small impoverished country of a little over six million people. In later years Kreisky spoke of the impression made on him by the large number of Vienna's homeless and hungry, and of his parents' help to them.

When he was fifteen Kreisky decided to join the workers' wing of the Socialist Youth Organization and work his way up the ranks. When the Social Democratic Party was outlawed following the civil war in 1934, Kreisky engaged in covert activity against the fascist regimes of Engelbert Dollfuss and Kurt von Schuschnigg. Early in 1935 the young socialist was arrested and sentenced to a one-year prison term for "high treason." Subsequently, after being expelled from the University of Vienna's law school, he spent two years as a factory worker and as an underground political organizer.

Kreisky was imprisoned again immediately after the Anschluss. By the sheerest luck he succeeded in getting out of the Nazi prison a day before he was scheduled to be sent off to a concentration camp. When incarcerated by the Schuschnigg fascist government a few years before, Kreisky had a Nazi cellmate who became a police officer soon after the Anschluss. When he saw Kreisky's name on a deportation list he helped arrange his escape.

I remember Kreisky's response to a comment by an elderly Viennese lady at a small private dinner party. "I suppose," she said, "you were treated better in jail by Dollfuss's people than by the Nazis." Coolly, Kreisky replied, "I would have preferred avoiding both."

---

*That was the phrase Kreisky used. He considered himself an agnostic.

†Wolfgang Petritsch, director of Austria's Information Service in New York, provided much of the information on Kreisky's earlier years.

Following his escape, Kreisky made his way to Sweden, which became his home for the next eleven years. In Stockholm he worked as a journalist and participated in the activities of the Social Democratic Party, experiences which influenced his subsequent political orientation and tactics. Most important, Kreisky met Willy Brandt, a fellow socialist who had escaped to Sweden from Nazi Germany. The two became friends—and close collaborators twenty years later when they were elected chancellors of their respective countries. They worked together on international issues, particularly after Brandt was chosen chairman of the Socialist International and Kreisky vice chairman in charge of foreign policy.

After the end of the war Kreisky joined the foreign service of the newly established Austrian Republic and helped organize relief for war-impoverished Austria from neutral Sweden. In 1953 he became adviser to the federal president Theodore Koerner, who appointed him state secretary for foreign affairs, the beginning of a remarkable political career that spanned three decades. In that position Kreisky played a key role in the negotiation of the State Treaty of 1955, under which Moscow agreed to withdraw its military forces in return for an Austrian promise of permanent neutrality. The Austrians made it clear, however, that they were militarily, not ideologically, neutral.

Elected a socialist member of Parliament in 1956, Kreisky served as foreign minister from 1959 to 1966 in a Conservative-led "grand coalition government." An election in 1966 gave the People's Party a majority; for the first time in the postwar period the new government, led by Josef Klaus, was not a coalition. Despite widespread fear, the absence of a coalition did not adversely affect the country's stability, which was soundly based on its social and industrial consensus, and a realization on the part of both parties that cooperation was essential even when only one of them was governing the country.

In 1970 Kreisky took over as chancellor when his party, the Socialists, won an electoral plurality, and once again the two main parties failed to agree on a coalition. In October of the following year Kreisky called for another election and won a majority for his party, which he maintained for the next thirteen years, dominating Austrian political life.

I asked several Austrians—politicians, diplomats, journalists, and intellectuals—to account for this remarkable achievement by a socialist of Jewish origin. Heinz Fischer, a leading socialist parliamentarian and Kreisky's close political colleague, told me that during the 1960s, when Kreisky was moving upward politically, he himself doubted that he could overcome the Jewish obstacle. He underestimated the favorable impact of his abilities and personality on the Austrian people.

As foreign minister, Kreisky's knowledge and diplomatic savoir faire came to the fore. He proved to be equally skillful as a political leader. Beginning in 1966, when he succeeded Bruno Pitterman as chairman, Kreisky reshaped the Socialist Party. Under his leadership it became more liberal and pragmatic, more like the Swedish Socialist Party—no longer a "working-class" party emphasizing the "class struggle." To win the support of farmers and the new middle class, particularly salaried employees between the ages of twenty-five and thirty-five, the product of Austria's new industrial growth, Kreisky focused on such practical issues as full employment and steady economic growth without inflation. To change the party's orientation Kreisky traveled to every part of the country and gained the active support of local Socialist Party members and officials. Kreisky also cultivated the business community—he often referred to "my father, the businessman"—and was mainly responsible for several substantial foreign investments in the country, including a large General Motors plant.

Always elegantly tailored, Kreisky was blessed with charm as well as boundless energy. Skillful in dealing with the press, almost all of which editorially opposed his party, he was pleased to be dubbed the "journalistic chancellor." He was always available to correspondents who didn't hesitate to phone him at home.

In fact, Kreisky made a fetish of being accessible to all the people. His home telephone number was listed in the Viennese directory, and he drove his own car around town. I was struck by the spontaneous, warm reaction to his informal presence in a Viennese restaurant or in a country inn miles from the capital. He was clearly the most popular political figure in postwar Austria.

His Jewish background actually became an asset. His election as chancellor provided psychological absolution to those Austrians

who felt guilty about anti-Semitism and their association with
Nazism. Kreisky helped by defending former Nazis, appointing,
in fact, several to his cabinet. He stated that individuals were
influenced by sweeping events that left them with little choice. In
later years, during the tensions aroused by revelations about Kurt
Waldheim's wartime record, Kreisky remarked, "Things were
different then. People were faced with a catastrophe. It looked like
the Nazis and their successors would rule forever, so people—
even Waldheim—accommodated."

An Austrian friend suggested another interesting reason to explain how Kreisky overcame the Jewish obstacle. Many Austrian
families apparently had what was called a "house Jew"—the family doctor, lawyer, or other person of special importance—about
whom they would never allow anyone to express any prejudices.
Kreisky succeeded in becoming the national "house Jew."

Kreisky's position on the Middle East added to his popularity
in Austria. He was anti-Zionist, though he helped support a
brother who lived in Israel. Believing that at least one Western
political leader should be in a position to act as a credible channel
between the Israelis and the Palestinians, he was prepared to play
that role himself. He established good personal relations with
Yasir Arafat, chairman of the Palestine Liberation Organization
(PLO), and through his position as vice chairman for foreign
affairs of the Socialist International, he had regular contact with
leaders of Israel's Socialist Party, including Shimon Peres.

Kreisky hoped that eventually the Israelis would conclude that
security and prosperity could only be achieved through peace with
their Arab neighbors. At the same time, he maintained, the PLO
would give up its terrorist ways only if it were accepted as a
participant in any Israeli-Arab negotiations. He also thought that
the Palestinians must be accorded the right to live in their own
state. Kreisky felt his was a balanced position, but it did not
evoke the desired response from Israel or from Washington. As a
consequence his frustration often got the better of him, and he
became increasingly critical of Jerusalem while tilting more and
more toward Arafat and other Arab leaders. The Free World
reacted sharply when Kreisky welcomed Muammar Qaddafi in
Vienna with an embrace. Inevitably this made him particularly
suspect to most Israelis and many Jews in other parts of the

world—a situation he seemed to relish. Vienna enjoyed a popular joke about the success of the Austrian government's public diplomacy. "The Foreign Office is so able," wags said, "it has succeeded in convincing the world that Beethoven was an Austrian, Hitler a German, and Kreisky an Arab."

During an informal conversation several months after my arrival in Vienna, Kreisky expressed his annoyance over something Israeli prime minister Begin and his Likud Party had just done. "You know," Kreisky said, "Jews acting as a group are not always so smart." "That may be true of any group of people," I replied, "but wouldn't you agree that three Jews—Marx, Einstein, and your fellow Viennese, Freud—were major architects of the modern world?" "Yes," he said, and to my surprise added, "and what about Disraeli?" Kreisky, the socialist, referred to the fact that Disraeli, the conservative, "was the father of 'Tory democracy.'" He was also, I suspect, associating himself with the first politician of Jewish origin to become prime minister of a Western country.

I remember my first call on Kreisky in the baroque palace on the Ballhausplatz, the site of the Austrian government. The chancellor's historic office, once occupied by Prince Metternich, the famous nineteenth-century Austrian leader, was enormous. Kreisky's desk was at the far end of the room. As he walked briskly toward the front of the office where his guests were seated, Kreisky greeted me cordially, adding, "I've received letters about you from several mutual friends—Jim Callaghan, Denis Healey, Harold Lever, and Kitty Carlisle. How do you know Kitty Carlisle?" I told him of my early friendship with her husband, Moss Hart. He expressed admiration for her and then spoke warmly about the others, particularly Jim Callaghan, the former British prime minister. My association with his longtime social democratic colleagues—and Kitty Carlisle Hart—obviously pleased Kreisky, and doubtless contributed to what became a friendly and frank relationship. He also liked the idea that during my government service I had dealt with trade unionists, Third World as well as European socialists, and an Eastern European Communist regime.

Substance as well as sociability marked this initial meeting. In fact, we discussed two issues that came up regularly during my tour in Vienna—the Middle East and Afghanistan. I had already

told Kreisky's foreign minister, Willibald Pahr, about our dissatisfaction over Austria's recent recognition of the PLO. As instructed
by Washington I now emphasized that it would be unfortunate if
the Arab states, responding to PLO pressure, initiated a debate
at the UN on Palestinian rights, an unhelpful maneuver when
President Carter had invited Menachem Begin and Anwar Sadat
to come to Washington.

Kreisky replied that, a few days before, he had told Arafat that
it would be inopportune to make any provocative moves at this
time. And then he dramatically picked up the phone and asked his
secretary to call someone (unfortunately I couldn't catch the
name). When he hung up, the chancellor explained that he was
trying to reach his main contact with Arafat to tell the PLO leader
again to lie low; but that individual was on his way to Paris. Had
he reached him, Kreisky would undoubtedly have talked to him
in my presence. I learned later that this was the way the chancellor
loved to operate.

Kreisky then proceeded with his well-known line about the
Palestinians and the PLO. In response to my query, he said that a
public statement by Arafat that he recognized the right of Israel
to exist would be counterproductive. It would almost certainly be
scoffed at by Israeli leaders and consequently Arafat's stature as a
"moderate" would be seriously damaged. Kreisky was confident
that the PLO would recognize Israel when Israel recognized the
Palestinians' rights. When the chancellor stated that he was pessi-
mistic about any progress in the negotiations for West Bank autonomy so long as Begin was in office, I stressed again President
Carter's commitment to the Camp David agreement and his determination to have it fully implemented.

Kreisky talked, too, about the Soviet invasion of Afghanistan,
noting that the Politburo had decided to move militarily after the
generals had assured them that it would take only days to finish
the job. His source was a minister in one of the Warsaw Pact
countries. (This, too, I realized later, was typical Kreisky. He
always had his "reliable" special informers in key parts of the
world.) Moscow, he added, was surprised not only by the setback
in Afghanistan, but also by the international reaction to its invasion. To demonstrate his knowledge of the Soviet scene, Kreisky
added that in his view Brezhnev was no longer the dominant

figure in Moscow. Mikhail Suslov and Gromyko, he said, were the real powers in the leadership.

The chancellor then talked about the prospects for Soviet withdrawal from Afghanistan. He showed me a letter he had recently received from Indira Gandhi, the prime minister of India, in which she stated that she had stressed to Gromyko how essential it was for the Soviets to withdraw from Afghanistan before any stability in the region could be established.

However, Kreisky didn't think that India could significantly influence the situation, nor, in his view, could pressure from the United States and Western European countries. Kreisky suggested that a nonaligned country could mediate the issue and, to my great surprise, he concluded that Cuba, as the current chairman of the Non-Aligned Movement, and because it was anxious to appear less of a Soviet puppet, was the one to play that role. I made it clear that this suggestion was way off base. When he persisted about Cuba at a subsequent meeting, I bluntly told him that Washington considered his proposal utterly unacceptable.

At the end of this initial meeting the chancellor said his door would always be open and he hoped there would be a regular exchange of ideas between us. He concluded by emphasizing how much he and the Austrian people appreciated the fundamental role the United States was playing in sustaining freedom throughout the world.

This first meeting set the pattern for our relationship. On the personal level it was easy, friendly, and uninhibited in discussions of substantive issues. On several occasions Kreisky came to the residence or asked me to drive out to the airport with him when that was the most convenient way for him to discuss urgent matters.

The subjects Kreisky raised during my initial call reflected the fact that, in addition to maintaining good U.S.-Austrian relations, his passion was the world scene. Because of his consuming interest in foreign affairs, during my year in Vienna I saw more of him than of any other top official, and found dealing with him always interesting and sometimes challenging.

Kreisky was determined to play a major role on the world stage, and felt he had special assets for doing so. Firmly established as chancellor of his country—in 1979 he had won his third successive election with his biggest majority—he also had had long experience in foreign affairs. He often cited Austria's strategic location in the center of Europe, and the fact that its past imperial history provided the basis for Vienna's special ties with Eastern European countries. Austria's neutrality, in Kreisky's view, enabled him to act as a channel between Washington and Moscow. And, last but definitely not least, his position as vice chairman of the Socialist International in charge of foreign policy inevitably involved him in international issues.

Not surprisingly, maintaining détente between East and West was a major objective of Kreisky's foreign policy. In fact, he considered himself "an architect of détente." In his view Austria's survival was inexorably tied to the détente process; a threat to détente was a threat to Austria's neutrality and independence.

To strengthen détente Kreisky saw to it that Vienna developed cultural, economic, and political relations with the bloc countries, particularly those that were formerly part of the old Austrian empire, and he often boasted of the special personal ties he had with key Eastern European political leaders. He also felt he had good rapport with Moscow. He didn't conceal his pleasure over the fact that Vienna was the first capital visited by Nikolai Tikhonov, the newly appointed Soviet prime minister. Substantial trade with the East was financed by large Austrian credits. Per capita, Austria held the largest proportion of Eastern European debt.

Although Kreisky always emphasized Austria's total commitment to Western ideals and frequently mentioned the crucial U.S. role in the preservation of European freedom, his seemingly excessive support of détente was not always appreciated by Washington. He felt, for example, that he could not support the boycott of the Olympic Games in Moscow after the Soviet invasion of Afghanistan. Although Kreisky condemned Iran's taking of the American diplomats as hostages, he believed that Austria's neutrality prevented it from supporting sanctions against the Ayatollah Khomeini's government.

A major string to Kreisky's international bow was his association with the Socialist International. It provided a special rostrum for his worldwide interests. Organized by European socialists before World War I, the Socialist International had had a turbulent history from 1914, when it failed to prevent the outbreak of war, to 1918, and in the period leading up to the second global conflict, during which it opposed both the fascists and the Communists. By 1980 the International's membership included socialists and social democrats in various parts of the world. Europeans, however, continued to dominate the organization because social democratic parties controlled governments or were the leading opposition parties in Germany, France, England, Scandinavia, Spain, Portugal, Belgium, and Holland. As Kreisky remarked to me on several occasions, the American commanders of NATO appreciated that the success of U.S. policy in Europe depended on cooperation with the Continent's social democratic parties.

Social democratic old-timers like Kreisky took pride in the history of the Socialist International. Its members had fought for freedom and democracy against the repression of fascism and the onslaughts of the Communists. Social democratic governments also had demonstrated that democracy and a welfare state were not incompatible. The International resented and vigorously opposed Soviet Communism, because it had defiled the democratic ideals of authentic social democracy. In the postwar period the development of democracy in the Third World and especially in Latin America had become one of its major objectives. The Socialist International, and particularly Kreisky, pushed for more substantial economic aid by the northern industrial countries to the undeveloped southern areas.

As vice chairman of the International in charge of foreign policy, Kreisky had earned the respect of such colleagues as Willy Brandt, the chairman of the International; Helmut Schmidt, who had succeded Brandt as chancellor of West Germany; Olaf Palme, the prime minister of Sweden; and Felipe Gonzalez, the able young socialist who was soon to become prime minister of Spain. These men combined political compatibility with warm personal friendships which Kreisky used to enhance his international influence. He adopted the International's positions on foreign issues because invariably he had inspired or supported their adoption. It enabled the Austrian chancellor to assume a role far exceeding Austria's intrinsic weight in foreign affairs.

Kreisky did not hesitate to push the International's views, even if they irritated Washington. When I raised our objections, Kreisky would sometimes say, "Friends have a right to criticize." He tried continuously to reconcile his desire for cordial U.S.-Austrian relations with positions taken by the Socialist International, particularly on the Middle East, Latin America, and the Third World.

Some of our disagreements reflected the ambivalence of the Socialist International about the United States. Social democrats, and Kreisky in particular, recognized and appreciated America's role as the world's most powerful champion of democracy and bulwark against Soviet Communism. In addition to being committed to democracy, however, social democrats considered themselves the true heirs of the "leftist" tradition. They vigorously opposed Communism, condemning it for debasing socialist ideals, but they had mixed feelings about capitalist America, and what they thought was our excessive concern about the military threat from Russia. They were particularly critical of U.S. support of military dictatorships in Latin America.

I discussed this with Kreisky on more than one occasion, pointing out that sometimes the Social Democrats operated on a double standard. They had, for example, attacked the United States for its policies in Vietnam, encouraging mass demonstrations against us, but there was no evidence in Western Europe of any mass demonstrations against the utterly immoral Soviet invasion of Afghanistan.

During the spring of 1980 the Socialist International tried hard to be helpful about our diplomats taken hostage in Iran. They authorized a mission to Teheran under Kreisky's leadership. The group, which included Olaf Palme and Felipe Gonzalez, visited Iran from May 22 to 26. In advance of the mission, Harold Saunders, the assistant secretary of state for Near Eastern affairs, came to Vienna to brief Kreisky on how we were trying to resolve the problem and what we hoped the mission might accomplish. He emphasized that we would not countenance any attempt by the Iranians to put the hostages on trial.

Kreisky couldn't have been more cooperative. The day after his return he gave me a full account of his mission. His report was vintage Kreisky, with comments about the main individuals he saw: Ayatollah Muhamed Beheshti, the mullah leader who had close ties to Khomeini; Sadiq Ghotzbadeh, the foreign minister; and Prime Minister Abu'l Hasan Bani Sadr. Beheshti, "a combination of Robespierre and Stalin," was "intelligent, dangerous, and fascinating," and aware of his own power. Other mullahs disliked him. He told Kreisky that the hostages would be released but he warned against undue haste. To release them before the people were ready for it would be a serious mistake.

Kreisky found Bani Sadr to be the opposite of Beheshti. He didn't believe the prime minister could manage a revolution; "he would be more plausible as a mild Harvard University professor." Kreisky thought that Ghotzbadeh was an able, not very likable person, given to double talk. He took one line in the presence of Bani Sadr, and an opposite, more enlightened position on the hostages when driving alone in the car with Kreisky. These government officials were more optimistic than Beheshti about the release of the hostages. Bani Sadr actually suggested that Kreisky might want to indicate in any subsequent press conferences that the hostages would be released "soon." Kreisky preferred "sooner or later."

Kreisky was impressed by the depth of anti-American feeling. Most Iranians did not believe that the Shah's illness was genuine. They thought this was simply a cover for a U.S. scheme to return the Shah or his son to power. Bani Sadr told Kreisky that a secret poll showed more than fifty percent of the population to be against any renewed U.S. influence in Iran, but only two percent favored a trial of the hostages.

The chancellor discussed the possibility of following up the mission's visit to Teheran when the Socialist International met in Oslo ten days later. Ghotzbadeh had asked to attend the International's meeting as an "observer" to report on the hostage question, adding that there would be no discussion in Parliament about the hostages before his proposed trip to Oslo. On Kreisky's recommendation the International informed Ghotzbadeh that he could appear the day after it had completed its formal agenda.

Here again Kreisky was most cooperative. In response to my request to see him prior to his departure for Oslo, Kreisky called at the residence at ten o'clock the night before he left. I passed on to him a message from Washington. We would appreciate it if once again Kreisky would tell Ghotzbadeh that we were deeply concerned over the continuing Iranian threat to put the hostages on trial. Kreisky recalled that he had discussed this with both Ghotzbadeh and Bani Sadr during his recent visit to Teheran, and they had stated that there was no question of *all* the hostages being tried, though there was some suggestion that a few of them might be. The Iranians told the delegation about incriminating documents that had been picked up after the aborted U.S. rescue attempt. Kreisky would be more than willing to bring up the matter again with Ghotzbadeh in Oslo.

Receiving me the day after he got back from the Oslo meeting, Kreisky said Ghotzbadeh had told him that, "as things look now," there would be no trial of the hostages, and that he hoped to convince a majority in Parliament that the time had come to release them. When he had succeeded, he would try to secure Khomeini's support for their release. Kreisky added that the hostage issue was the main subject of his colleagues' conversations with the Iranian foreign minister. They all unequivocally stated that the Iranians had to release them. Unfortunately these and subsequent efforts by Kreisky did not convince the Iranians to free the hostages, but our diplomats were not put on trial. Bani Sadr escaped to France and Ghotzbadeh was executed long before the release of the hostages.

Not all of my time in Austria was devoted to dealing with international issues and to supervising the activities of the embassy. With tourism a major Austrian industry—and Vienna and Salzburg renowned musical centers—it was not surprising that in this post, too, we entertained a large number of visiting Americans. Two of the most interesting and enjoyable were Leonard Bernstein and Zubin Mehta. The Viennese artistic and intellectual community loved these maestros, whose concerts always produced full houses in the Musikverein. As one Austrian put it, "When they are here Lenny is King of Vienna and Zubin the Crown Prince." Key to this special status was their genius as musicians, and the dramatic persona of Bernstein and the charming, though less histrionic, Mehta, who had studied music in Vienna. While the Vienna Philharmonic admired the ability of both, Bernstein was their favorite.

Bernstein's presence in Vienna also generated a special excitement among politicians, many of whom were his friends. With his passion for politics, he followed Austrian developments as closely as American. I remember a small dinner we gave in Bernstein's honor after a special performance of his *Mass* in German by the Vienna Opera Company, its first nonoperatic production. The other guests were Chancellor Kreisky and two couples who were close friends of both the chancellor and Bernstein. At that time the most dramatic domestic issue in Austrian politics was the break between Kreisky and his onetime protégé Hannes Androsch, who had been his minister of finance and deputy chancellor. Androsch was destined to be Kreisky's successor until the split in what some observers had called a "father-son" relationship. The dramatic growth of business in Androsch's family accounting firm while he was finance minister had caused his removal from office. I knew how strongly Kreisky felt about it because on several occasions after we had finished our diplomatic agenda, he would express his unhappiness over his need to replace Androsch as minister of finance.

The moment after the guests at this dinner party were seated, Bernstein said to Kreisky, "Bruno, I had dinner with Hannes two nights ago and heard his side of the story. Now I would like to hear what you have to say." The other guests were taken aback by Bernstein's directness, but Kreisky took it in stride. He responded quietly, "What would you like to know?" Bernstein then relentlessly cross-examined the chancellor, plying him with one question after another, to each of which Kreisky calmly replied, except for a slight rise in his voice midway when he said, "Lenny, you're like a fox terrier tonight." But even with that comment, Kreisky did not suggest that his old, dear friend Lenny was out of bounds. The exchange concluded with Bernstein stating authoritatively, "Your account pretty much coincides with Hannes's"

In spite of this exchange—no Austrian would have dared cross-examine the chancellor in this way—their friendship was not affected. A warm, cordial atmosphere permeated the remainder of the evening as we talked about political and cultural subjects. The next day Bernstein conducted a concert of the Vienna Philharmonic and the chancellor was very much present. He vigorously applauded Bernstein's conducting of a Mozart symphony and Bernstein's own "Kaddish" Symphony.

We had our share of official visitors to Vienna, too. Secretary of State Edmund Muskie came in the spring of 1980 to join the Austrian celebration of the twenty-fifth anniversary of the state treaty that had ended the wartime Allies' military occupation of the country. It was a gala event to which the government had invited the current foreign ministers of the U.S., U.K., France, and the Soviet Union as well as the still-surviving foreign ministers who were original signatories of the treaty.

I had met Muskie before. In fact, I was an active supporter of his presidential campaign in 1972 and I am still sorry that he was not nominated. He had been an outstanding senator and an effective campaigner as Hubert Humphrey's running mate in 1968. Watching Muskie during his meetings with Kreisky and the foreign ministers made me appreciate his exceptional qualities. It was a delight to observe how warmly they responded to his easy manner, his intelligence, his wit, and his political savoir faire.

Harold Macmillan, one of the former foreign ministers present, was particularly impressed with the secretary of state. Two years later at a Balliol alumni dinner, recalling his visit to Vienna, Macmillan highly praised Muskie. "He should have been elected president," Macmillan said to me. "I understand that he lost his chance because he shed a tear when, during a political speech, a heckler in the audience accused his wife of drinking too much.* That was too bad," Macmillan added. "If, while I was campaigning, some scalawag had shouted 'Macmillan, we know about your wife. She's a drunkard,' I would have simply replied, 'Yes, but you should have known her mother.'"

One issue was impossible to avoid while living in Vienna: Austria's involvement with Nazism. In May 1980 I was invited to attend a ceremony to be held at Mauthausen, the concentration camp in Austria. Its survivors were commemorating the thirty-fifth anniversary of the camp's liberation by Combat Command B of the U.S. Army's 11th Armored Division commanded by Colonel Richard R. Seibel. Now retired as a brigadier general, Seibel was scheduled to be present at the ceremony. I naturally agreed to attend and accepted Kreisky's invitation to accompany him in his car. The camp, located near Linz, was a two-hour drive from Vienna through some of Austria's loveliest country. During the drive Kreisky expressed his concern about the hostages in Iran and the Soviet invasion of Afghanistan, both of which he

---

*Macmillan was wrong about what actually happened to Muskie.

condemned. He once again stressed his friendship toward the United States, especially for our role in World War II and his gratitude for the assistance we gave Austria after the war. He also praised us for the security we provide to the free nations of the world. As we reached Mauthausen I remember Kreisky's remarking, "Unbelievable, isn't it, that such a terrible concentration camp was located in such a beautiful setting." It was the only remark he made about Austria's Nazi past.

I knew of Mauthausen's existence but did not realize until my visit that day that it was one of the vilest of the concentration camps. The U.S. War Crimes Commission stated that the atrocities committed there were the worst they had investigated. As a result of the Nuremberg Trials more Nazi personnel from Mauthausen were executed than from any other concentration camp. In addition to Jews, the camp included partisans from Greece, Italy, Yugoslavia, Poland, France, and the Soviet Union, as well as Englishmen, Americans, and French. A handful of survivors from almost all of these groups was present at the memorial service.

It was a soul-searing day. I saw the death block, gas chamber, crematorium, and execution corner. I also saw the quarry works where inmates suffered indescribable cruelties. I heard about some from a remarkable British survivor named Sheppard who was chairman of the International Committee of Mauthausen Survivors. During the formal ceremonies he spoke eloquently on behalf of his fellow inmates. A British intelligence officer, Sheppard had been parachuted into Europe on a special assignment. After fulfilling his mission he worked his way to the French border in the Pyrenees, where he was picked up by the Nazis before he could reach Spain.

Sheppard was soft-spoken, calm, and dignified. I sat between him and Kreisky during the ceremony. Quietly, he began to tell me about the cruelties he and the other inmates had experienced in the camp. After a few minutes he stopped and said, "There is no need, Mr. Ambassador, to trouble you with any further details. Let me just add that I was in Mauthausen for two years. Fortunately, I was transferred to Dachau where I spent a third year in a concentration camp. That saved my life," he softly concluded. "I don't think I could have survived a third year in Mauthausen."

On the way back to Vienna Kreisky invited his Communist cellmate when he was jailed by the Dollfuss government to join us. This individual—I can't recall his name—was a survivor of Mauthausen. He had long since turned against the Communists and joined the Socialist Party. In fact he had been largely instrumental in frustrating the Communist effort to make Mauthausen only a symbol of the Nazi oppression of Communists. I was struck by the easy comradeship of the former political prisoners in spite of the vast chasm in rank between them. We stopped off for lunch in a country inn where the chancellor, an unexpected visitor, was received warmly but not fawningly. The other guests were obviously pleased to be joined by so distinguished a figure, but didn't fuss about him while we were lunching. They applauded him as we left.

The visit to Mauthausen as the guest of an Austrian chancellor of Jewish origin was deeply moving. I was aware, of course, of the Holocaust and personally involved—several of my relatives were victims—but I had never seen a concentration camp, its instruments of torture, or a group of survivors. It focused my attention on the way Austrians were dealing with their Nazi experience now that the country had emerged as a prosperous democracy after the destruction of the war and the terrible aftermath.

After several months in Vienna I was familiar with many Austrians who were nostalgic about the past, particularly the glorious days of the old empire. They found it difficult, however, to face up to the country's behavior during the years leading up to the Anschluss, and the time they were part of Hitler's "Greater Germany." Many Austrians felt they had been absolved by the Allies' 1943 declaration that "Austria was Hitler's first victim." They were helped, too, by the State Treaty signed in 1955, which not only established Austria's neutrality in exchange for the withdrawal of Soviet troops but also dropped all reference to joint German-Austrian responsibility for wartime aggression.

Austria's record as part of Nazi Germany was scarring. Not all Austrians succumbed to Nazism. Many Catholics, socialists, and liberals were imprisoned for their resistance to the Anschluss. There was a courageous though relatively small resistance movement whose dramatic story is told in Fritz Molden's *The Fires in the Night*. He was the Austrian underground's liaison with Allen

Dulles, chief of U.S. wartime intelligence in Europe. His visits to Bern, Switzerland, where Dulles was stationed, were not devoted entirely to business. Dulles's daughter became Molden's first wife.

The fact is, however, that thousands of Austrians wildly cheered Hitler on his triumphant entry into Vienna. Some socialist and conservative leaders, including the cardinal of Vienna, actually welcomed the Nazi absorption of Austria as an act of liberation. By 1945 over 500,000 Austrians were members of the Nazi Party, a higher proportion of the population than in Germany itself. About one-quarter of all convicted Nazi war criminals were Austrian. Although Austrians made up about ten percent of the population of Greater Germany, Simon Wiesenthal, the indefatigable Nazi hunter, told me that they provided more than fifty percent of the administrative personnel of all the concentration camps. Several Austrians were key figures in the Nazi extermination program, including the notorious Adolf Eichmann and his key aide Alois Bruner, SS General Ernst Kaltenbrunner, and Odilo Globocik.

Of the 200,000 Jews who lived in Austria before the war, 70,000 died in concentration camps, and most of the others fled before 1941. In 1981 the total Jewish population in Austria was approximately 6,000. Small wonder that the Austrian capital is the only large European city whose postwar population is smaller than it was in the late 1930s. There was a special irony, too, in the destruction of the Viennese Jewish community. Much of the intellectual and cultural fame and glory of the imperial capital was due to the contributions of such Austrian Jews as Wittgenstein, Schnitzler, Berg, Freud, Schoenberg, and Mahler.

Inevitably I found myself discussing the "Greater Germany" period with Austrian friends and, as one would expect, their attitudes were mixed. Some were deeply embarrassed by the subject and reluctant to talk about it. Others, including Hugo Portisch, the country's leading journalist and an outstanding producer of TV historical documentaries, faced up to the truth about Austria's Nazi involvement. One of Kreisky's able young assistants spoke frankly about his mother being an active member of the Nazi Party. He "understood" her decision to join, but definitely did not condone it. He urged me to mention Austria's recent past in my public speeches.

Others were more circumspect or defensive. They blamed the rise of Austria's fascism and Nazism on the failure of Western diplomacy during the period between the two wars, particularly France's unwillingness to allow an economic Anschluss with Germany in the early thirties. There were those who emphasized the country's dreadful economic conditions, especially the massive unemployment, as justification for people's support of the Nazi takeover. They admired Hitler's success in putting people to work, ignoring the ominous fact that it was largely due to his massive rearmament program. Many felt, however, that it was best to accept the Allies' 1943 statement that Austria was Nazi Germany's first victim, to forget about the ugly aspects of the past, and to enjoy the continuing prosperity of the new, democratic Austria.

Several private individuals suggested that the Austrian government should face up to the truth, and follow the example of West Germany's Konrad Adenauer by adequately compensating the victims of Nazi atrocities. Only then could the country purge itself of its tortured past. They regretted that no Austrian political leader had spoken out publicly and frankly about the extent of Austria's involvement with the Nazis.

It took Kurt Waldheim's presidential candidacy in 1986, five years after I left the embassy, and his subsequent election, to dramatically and painfully reopen the issue of Austrian behavior during the Nazi Anschluss. There was no proof that Waldheim was directly involved in the deportation of Jews, as charged by the Austrian weekly *Profil* and the World Jewish Congress. The fact remains, nevertheless, that in his autobiography, *The Eye of the Storm*, Waldheim avoided mentioning his service in the Balkans as a lieutenant in the intelligence unit of a division led by the notorious Nazi commander General Lohr.

In his campaign for the Austrian presidency, Waldheim reacted aggressively to the charges leveled against him. He charged that unfriendly outsiders were unfairly, if not maliciously, meddling in Austrian affairs. In addition, by emphasizing that in serving on the Eastern Front, "I did what hundreds of thousands of Austrians did—I did my duty," Waldheim identified the whole country with his behavior, including his effort to repress his activities during the war.

Waldheim's tactics, observers agreed, stirred up anti-Semitism. During my visit to Vienna after the election a Social Democratic leader told me that a careful analysis of the presidential election results revealed a significant defection of typical socialist voters in areas where, historically, anti-Semitism had been prevalent. Waldheim won the election, but it was a Pyrrhic victory for him personally and an embarrassment to the country. His presidency was crippled. If he had visited the United States he would have had to face charges regarding his wartime activities, and other countries of the Free World also made it clear that he was unwelcome, all terrible blows in light of the fact that representing his country abroad was a major function of the Austrian president.

The election had its positive impact. In its aftermath, Austrians realized it was no longer realistic to ignore their Nazi past; in fact, in order to rid itself of any stigma, the country had to honestly face up to its ugly aspects. It wasn't until July 1991 that Chancellor Franz Vranitzky, a Social Democrat and the country's most popular political figure, stated in Parliament that many Austrians had backed the Nazi regime and participated in its crimes. This was shortly after Waldheim announced he would not run for reelection, and Joerg Halder, the leader of the right-wing Freedom Party, was ousted from his post as a provincial governor for praising Nazi Germany's labor policies. During a debate in Parliament on the crisis in Yugoslavia Vranitzky said that the Austrian government had little moral credibility on current issues so long as it failed to deal honestly with its own past. "We acknowledge all of our history," he said, "and the deeds of all parts of our people, the good as well as the evil. As we lay claim to the good, so must we apologize to the survivors and the descendants of the dead for the evil. . . .

"Many Austrians took part in the repressive measures and persecution of the Third Reich, and some of them in prominent positions. Even today we cannot brush aside a moral responsibility for the deeds of our citizens." Vranitzky then went on to say, "Austrian politicans have always put off making this confession. I would like to do this explicitly, also in the name of the Austrian government as a measure of the relationship we today have to our history." And Vranitzky added that "the federal government would assume new responsibilities for reparation payments for victims and survivors of the Holocaust and help those not included before, or not sufficiently included, or whose moral or materials claims were until now not covered."

Vranitzky's courageous speech should help the Austrians put to rest the Nazi aspects of the past, and with a clearer conscience enable them to enjoy the fruits of their remarkable achievements since the end of the war.

After Reagan's election in 1980, Kreisky expressed public concern about possible changes in U.S. foreign policy, especially toward Latin America. Meeting in Madrid soon after Reagan's victory, the Socialist International passed a resolution stating that overall U.S. foreign policy should be judged by what the United States was perceived to be doing in Latin America. They were critical of Reagan's plan to support authoritarian regimes. I met with Kreisky shortly thereafter to tell him Washington felt the Madrid resolution had gone much too far. It was unfair to attack President Reagan before he had even assumed office, and to judge overall U.S. policy on the basis of what it did in one part of the world.

Always anxious to reconcile the objectives of the Socialist International with U.S. policies, Kreisky was rather defensive in his reply and indicated that he also thought the resolution had gone too far. However, he was concerned about the impact on social democrats in Western Europe of "wrong" U.S. policies in Latin America. In his view Catholic as well as socialist youth were more interested in Latin American developments than in Europe itself. When leading Latin American Catholic figures—politically active bishops, for example—came to Vienna to lecture, the largest halls were overcrowded. This was not the case with European speakers.

Attempting to smooth things over, Kreisky expressed his pleasure over President-elect Reagan's meeting with the Mexican President. He hoped President López Portillo would convince Reagan to attend the North-South Summit scheduled for June 1981, a project originated by Kreisky to stimulate the northern industrial countries to become more involved in the improvement of conditions in the less-developed world. He was encouraged by the emphasis that President Reagan was placing on good relations with Mexico and was sure Portillo had stressed the importance of pursuing moderate policies in Latin America.

Kreisky emphasized again the importance of cooperation between the social democrats and the new Reagan administration. He was urging his social democratic colleagues to demonstrate their readiness to support administration policies aimed at strengthening the free world. Socialists and social democrats, he pointed out, played key political roles in Germany, Scandinavia, Spain, Portugal, Belgium, Holland, and England, and no American foreign policies would be successful without their cooperation. Interestingly, he added that they knew from Haig's performance as NATO commander that the new secretary of state recognized that fact.

In one of my last official meetings with Kreisky after Reagan had been inaugurated, I had a long discussion with the chancellor on international issues and expressed the hope that we would not allow differences on one or two issues to adversely affect our longstanding friendship. Latin America continued to preoccupy him. Shortly after Reagan's inauguration, Secretary Haig decided to send several personal representatives to European capitals to explain U.S. policy in Latin America, particularly our actions in El Salvador. When Kreisky told me that he had no intention of receiving such a representative, I replied that he was making a mistake. His refusal would hardly help him to develop a workable, personal relationship with the new secretary of state and the President. Kreisky changed his mind. Because Haig's representative was the son of Luigi Einaudi, the former president of Italy and Kreisky's old political friend, it made it easier for him to receive the American.

My tour in Vienna came to an abrupt end. When Reagan was elected President I realized, of course, that as a Democrat and technically a noncareer officer, there was little likelihood that I would stay on. I was aware of the unfortunate history of rough treatment of incumbent ambassadors when an opposition party came to power. Democrats, as well as Republicans, were sometimes guilty of crude behavior in their removal of political ambassadors regardless of their performance in office. Such treatment has not been one of our government's most intelligent or elegant practices, and should be discontinued.

The Reagan administration, however, behaved more rudely than any predecessor. It ordered all noncareer ambassadors to leave in two weeks, an act of obvious hostility that shocked the host government. It made a mockery of diplomatic behavior, and left far too little time to bid farewell to Austrian officials, friends, and members of the diplomatic corps.

I reacted to my instructions to leave in a fortnight by cabling Washington that I had invited the chancellor to an informal dinner at the residence three weeks later, the day after he returned from a state visit to Egypt, and, if I were not granted an extension, I would entertain Kreisky in a private hotel suite. The State Department quickly responded that I could stay long enough to officially entertain the chancellor. Kreisky was in particularly good form that evening, witty and charming and generous in his comments about me.

My wife and I hastily packed and bade farewell to top government officials and as many friends and colleagues as time would allow. Before leaving Vienna, however, with the help of my administrative officer and my DCM, I did manage to send a farewell cable to Washington that created a stir back home, at least among the State Department's administrative officers. Using the perspective of a nonmember of the Foreign Service who had had considerable experience on the inside, I discussed at considerable length Washington's failure to provide the State Department with the resources necessary to perform its role as the first line of national defense. State Department officials have informed me that my cable is as relevant today as it was a decade ago.

It is unfortunate that we continue to treat the Foreign Service as a stepchild of our government. American commitments overseas have expanded greatly since World War II, with only a negligible increase in the Foreign Service corps overseeing these responsibilities. The Department of State has the smallest budget of any cabinet department. In an era in which we have been devoting nearly three hundred billion dollars a year to defense, we spend less than one percent of that to keep the peace through diplomacy.

The time has come, too, for the American people to forget some of their stereotyped notions about the Foreign Service and its activities abroad. The false perception of the glamorous diplomat from the "Eastern establishment" is still too widely held. Foreign Service employees are recruited from all walks of life to represent all Americans. From my experience over four decades I can attest to the ability and dedication of these men and women. In the several embassies in which I have served I was struck by their loyalty and competence, and their commitment to the best interests of our government and the welfare of the American people. Among others the names of ambassadors Ron Spiers, Melissa Wells, Stephen Low, Arthur Hartman, William Eagleton, Sheldon Krys, and Robert Pelletreau come to mind. In Vienna, my DCM, Sol Polansky, who later became ambassador to Bulgaria, was an outstanding example of the exceptional quality of many of our Foreign Service officers.

We should not forget that in the past thirty years, a period that included the Vietnam War and the Persian Gulf conflict, more ambassadors have been killed than generals and admirals, and more Foreign Service employees have lost their lives than agents of the FBI.

Reflections at the
End of the Century

I was born in 1913, four months after Woodrow Wilson was inaugurated as President. As I look back at these last eight decades, I am struck by the extent to which the world in which I lived and worked was shaped by Wilson's Presidency. His legacy of ideas, policies, and style greatly influenced succeeding Presidents. He was the first President to confront the great foreign and domestic challenges of the twentieth century: the role of the United States as a world power and the role of the government in dealing with the social and economic problems of an industrial society. American Chief Executives have had to cope with the same basic issues and have acted largely within the framework set by Wilson's successes and failures.*

Insisting that active government was required in an industrial society, Wilson used the power of the Presidency to press Congress to enact a wider range of economic and social legislation than the country had ever seen before. The Federal Reserve Act, the Clayton Antitrust Act, the establishment of the Federal Trade Commission, workmen's compensation, the Child Labor Law, and an eight-hour day on interstate railways were among the reform measures passed during his administration.

*I've dealt in some detail with this subject in my essay "Woodrow Wilson" in The History Makers, edited by Lord Longford and Sir John Wheeler-Bennett (London: Sidgwick and Jackson, 1973), pages 38–52.

Wilson's approach set the stage for the performance of subsequent presidents, particularly his Democratic successors. When FDR assumed office in 1933 he faced a desperate economic and social crisis that was the product of the Harding/Coolidge era of "normalcy," whose chief characteristic was laissez-faire government. FDR's temperament and personality, his appreciation of the institutional legacy of the Wilson administration in which he had served as assistant secretary of the navy, and his commitment to the Wilsonian conception of the Presidency helped him meet the demand of the American public for immediate remedial action and long-term reform.

Through personal contact with members of Congress, effective use of patronage, executive formulation of bills, and direct appeal to the public against special interests, all Wilsonian techniques, Roosevelt not only dealt with desperate immediate needs, he also pushed through a program that greatly increased government involvement in the economic life of our nation. When he assumed office, the state of the nation was such that had he so desired FDR could easily have broken radically with American principles and traditions. He could, for example, have nationalized the banks and met little or no resistance. I remember Secretary of Labor Frances Perkins telling me about business executives coming to Washington in the early days of the New Deal to ask the President to take over their companies. FDR turned down these requests; instead, he helped establish a welfare state within the framework of a regulated capitalism, and he did so without limiting our individual freedoms.

I was a student at the University of Wisconsin during the dramatic early years of the Roosevelt administration, and I can never forget the violent attacks leveled against him. He was accused of being a dictator, a fascist, and a Communist. Time and again it was predicted that his policies would undermine our society and that they were bound to lead to disaster. These reactions to Roosevelt were extreme expressions of the passive government views of those who were in power during the twelve years between the end of Wilson's administration and the beginning of FDR's.

Of course, none of the dire predictions of conservatives ever materialized. In fact, most of the reforms of Wilson, Roosevelt,

Truman, Johnson, and Kennedy have become essential parts of the warp and woof of American social and economic life. Mentioning some of the outstanding reforms that we take for granted today underlines that fact: Social Security, unemployment insurance, labor law reform, veterans' benefits, housing and education reforms, minimum wages, Head Start, Medicare and Medicaid, insurance of bank deposits, civil rights laws, voting rights reform, freedom of information laws, and environment protection. Almost all of these Democratic initiatives were opposed by the Republicans.* But they constitute the "safety net" of economic security that has helped sustain our capitalist system.

Opponents of the pragmatic and progressive Democratic tradition argue that it is outmoded, too costly, and irrelevant to today's needs. They prefer the laissez-faire, deregulated, more passive government. For twelve years now we have experienced administrations based on this doctrine. The results are reminiscent of the Coolidge era of the 1920s. The rich have become richer, while the middle class and the poor have lost economic ground. Despite their patriotic rhetoric, two successive Republican administrations have presided over American economic decline, domestically and globally. Almost every measure of social and economic health has declined on the conservative watch. While federal deficits have soared to historic levels, the quality of our education has declined and the cost of our health care has spiraled out of control. Our homeless have increased, race relations have deteriorated, and we are best with crushing crime and drug problems. The real estate market has collapsed and our banking system is tottering while foreign competition has eroded key sectors of our once-dominant economy. Industry after industry has given way to Asian and European competition. We have lost substantial parts of our steel, textile, machine tool, shipbuilding, and electronics industries in less than one generation, and our automobile industry is on the ropes.

For the first time since the Great Depression, the percentage of middle-class Americans declined—by about a tenth—during these past twelve years. The American dream became more elusive for

---

*Reagan's claim during the 1984 presidential campaign that his record was in the tradition of FDR, Truman, and Kennedy was a flagrant distortion of the truth.

millions of our citizens, while the wealthy elite was rewarded in Washington with bigger tax breaks and lax regulation.

My experiences during the journeys recounted in this memoir convince me that passive government will not provide the solutions to this wide range of problems. What the country needs is a fresh application of the progressive legacy initiated by Wilson, a willingness to use government imaginatively and creatively. And, unless we solve our domestic problems, there's a danger that we may lose the opportunity to play a leading role in the post-Communist world.

In international affairs, too, Wilson broke new activist ground. In the spring of 1917, when he asked Congress for a declaration of war, he emphasized that "America was fighting for democracy, the rights and liberties of small nations and for a universal dominion of rights by such a concert of free nations as shall bring peace and safety to all nations and make the world at last free."

In his famous Fourteen Points, made public in January 1914, Wilson articulated the principles of his new world society. He called for open diplomacy; freedom of the seas; frontiers based on national self-determination; freedom of the subject people of the Austrian, German, and Russian empires; and the establishment of a world organization of nations dedicated to lasting peace.

Wilson had become the spokesman of progressive liberalism at home and was now projecting this view on the world scene, relating his own vision of the postwar world to that of the nonrevolutionary liberal, democratic forces of Europe. The spread of parliamentary democracy and reformist capitalism would help preserve the peace. America, he felt, had a mission to lead the world toward an orderly international society of the future. The League of Nations was for him a key element in the fulfillment of that mission. This was the first time an American President had called for the establishment of a "new world order." It was a dramatic break from our historic isolationism.

Unfortunately, Wilson failed. Hampered by illness as well as political weakness—the Republicans, dominated by isolationists, gained control of the Congress in 1918—Wilson was unable to overcome the resistance of the conservatively led Allies to major elements of his Fourteen Points. He made many compromises to gain acceptance of the establishment of the League of Nations, which, he argued, would justify the sacrifices of the war. Tired and sick, harassed by a Republican Senate led by Henry Cabot Lodge of Massachusetts,* Wilson unfortunately eschewed the political flexibility that had proved so productive in the early years of his Presidency. When he insisted that the Senate accept the text of the League covenant without significant changes, the Senate refused to approve the treaty. Our failure to join the League of Nations may well have contributed to the developments that led up to the Second World War.

In the presidential election of 1920, the Republican candidate, Warren G. Harding, called for "a return to normalcy" and won by a landslide. The voters had rejected the foreign and domestic policies of Wilson's active Presidency. During the following decade there was a return to passive administrations in Washington, where President Coolidge expressed the prevailing sentiment when he said, "The business of government is business."

When FDR became President after the financial crash of 1929, the Wilson experience became his guide, internationally as well as domestically. As the Democratic candidate for Vice President in 1920, FDR supported the League of Nations. He did not, however, ignore the isolationism still prevalent in the 1930s. For practical balance of power as well as ideological reasons, FDR's sympathies lay with the Allies, but until the fall of France in 1940, he moved cautiously in foreign affairs. As Robert Sherwood observed in his book *Roosevelt and Hopkins*, "FDR was haunted by Wilson's ghost." He took steps to avoid his former chief's mistakes. Even before Pearl Harbor he appointed two distinguished Republicans to his cabinet as secretaries of war and navy. He arranged for Republican congressional leaders to be involved in the peacemaking process in its earliest stages, and was able to commit the United States to membership in the United Nations before the end of hostilities, a major step in postwar America's new foreign policy.

In the Atlantic Charter FDR reverted to Wilsonian idealism in an effort to arouse support for the war. On the other hand, his belief until just before his death in the possibility of coexistence

---

*A member of the group was Senator George Maclean of Connecticut, my wife's grand-uncle. She was born in the senator's house in Simsbury, Connecticut.

with Stalinism and his attempts to prepare the American people for a less-than-perfect peace settlement reflected his determination to avoid the pitfalls of Wilson's excessive idealism. His death foreclosed the possibility of his trying to put his mixture of idealism and realism into practice.

Within two years after Roosevelt's death, Harry S Truman had produced an activist foreign policy that was reminiscent of Wilson's moral fervor and idealism. By 1947, it was clear that Western Europe was economially prostrate and that the Soviet Union represented a major threat to Western democracies. Determined to contain Soviet Communism, and deciding that the situation called for an American commitment on a worldwide scale, Truman used Moscow's threat to break through the barriers of isolationism where Wilson had failed. Through his Greek-Turkish policy, through Marshall aid and membership in NATO, Truman allied the United States to Western Europe, made it possible for her to revive economically and politically and resist Stalin's aggressive pressure. Significantly, it was a Labour government in Britain that took the lead in organizing the European side of the new Euro-American alliance. As I can attest from my own involvement, the success of Truman's policies was largely due to the close collaboration between his administration and the anti-Communist left in Western Europe.

Ironically, the moral atmosphere against Communism that Truman helped inspire created a climate in which extremist critics of his policy could make political capital out of any Communist success. It was this atmosphere that helped spawn McCarthyism, and enabled the Republican political opponents to unjustly charge that Democrats were "soft on Communism," a charge that influenced the direction of American politics.

Those of us who helped Truman implement his creative policies, which were so instrumental in changing the course of world history, will never forget his political skill and courage. The Cold War could not have been won without the political-military infrastructure established by Truman with the aid of Dean Acheson, George Marshall, and Senator Arthur Vandenberg. Bipartisanship was an essential element of Truman's success. Truman recommended postwar aid to Western Europe when his popularity was near its lowest level and only nineteen percent of the American people supported foreign aid. Nevertheless, he got his key international legislation through a Republican-controlled Congress, and then won the 1948 election by campaigning against the "do-nothing, good-for-nothing" Eightieth Congress.

Mutatis mutandis, Truman's successors, Republicans as well as Democrats, have tried to manage foreign affairs along his version of the Wilsonian tradition. A sense of moral obligation to defend freedom anywhere in the world and a continuing open-ended political, economic, and military commitment to that objective have been the basic ingredients of that policy. Eisenhower, the first military commander of NATO, strongly supported his predecessors' foreign policies. Kennedy reflected their spirit when he stated in his inaugural address in 1961, "We shall pay any price, bear any burden, meet any hardship, support any friend, oppose any foe to assure the survival and the success of liberty." He practiced what he had preached during the Cuban missile crisis. In Africa I was at the receiving end of the skill with which he handled that dangerous confrontation.

After that crisis Kennedy realized that an accommodation in nuclear arms with the Soviet Union would serve our mutual interests. Due to his initiative, implemented by Averell Harriman's skill as a negotiator, the United States and the Soviet Union signed the Test Ban Treaty of 1963. Negotiating arms agreements with the Soviet Union became a major element in the foreign policy of all subsequent Presidents with the most impressive results during Gorbachev's perestroika.

Johnson's Presidency, innovative and successful domestically, was undermined by Vietnam. The combination of an open-ended American commitment to combat Communism during the Cold War and Johnson's hypersensitivity to the unjustified charge of "Democratic softness on Communism" led to his decision to launch a full-scale military effort in Vietnam.

In spite of Nixon's campaign claim that he had a "secret plan" to end the conflict, he admitted later that this was just a campaign ploy. Nixon continued the war for five more years; it ended in humiliating defeat after the tragic increase in the number of our casualties. At the same time Nixon, who claims that Wilson was one of his heroes—Wilson's portrait was one of two former Chief Executives that hung in Nixon's White House—pursued an aggressive Wilsonian foreign policy, opening up relations with Communist China and negotiating the first SALT agreement with the Soviet Union.

The trauma of Vietnam shook American faith in international commitments and raised the specter of a regression into isolationism. To Carter's credit, in spite of his rough passage politically, he continued to involve the United States in international affairs. His accomplishments were impressive—in Panama, in the Middle East with the Camp David Israeli-Egyptian agreement, and, as I know from my own direct experience, in Eastern Europe, particularly Hungary. His emphasis on human rights was in the best Wilsonian tradition. Thanks to Carter, human rights has become an essential element in our foreign policy.

In spite of his tepid attitude toward abuses of human rights, particularly in military dictatorships, Reagan followed the Wilsonian international path with special success during his second term when, anxious to restore his popularity after the Irangate scandal, he took advantage of the Soviet openings inspired by Gorbachev's perestroika. This resulted in significant arms-reduction agreements and a change from the historic confrontational American-Soviet relationship.

Bush, a fervent internationalist, has had the good fortune of being President when Communism collapsed. Thanks to the foreign programs launched by Truman after World War II and sustained by his successors, the West has won the Cold War. Bush impressively arranged the international coalition that was so successful in the Persian Gulf conflict, and enhanced the prestige of the United Nations, though thus far he has failed to achieve one of his main objectives, the removal of Saddam Hussein. He is also making the first serious effort since Camp David to bring peace to the Middle East.

Bush boasts that we are "the undisputed leaders of the world." Unfortunately, we are not playing that role in Eastern Europe. During this century two world wars started in that part of the world because of ethnic and national conflicts, the kind that Yugoslavia has been experiencing. The best insurance against the revival of these dangerous tensions is the development of economically viable democracies in the countries liberated from Communism and the newly established commonwealth nations.

These countries are attempting to create such societies. They are trying to accomplish in a few short years what Western democracies took decades to achieve. To succeed they need Western help. The new commonwealth countries require short-term humanitarian aid to meet the shortages of food and medical supplies. Without it they face the danger of riots, strikes, and civil war. There is an American tradition to helping the Russians. The Hoover Commission fed millions in the early 1920s when Lenin was ruling the Soviet Union. Russians still remember the food we provided under Lend-Lease during World War II. The aid recently offered by our government has fallen short of the amounts provided on those occasions.

Beyond humanitarian aid for the new commonwealth nations, there is urgent need for long-term assistance to them as well as to the old Central and Eastern European countries to prevent an early loss of faith in democracy and a reversion to authoritarian government. New democratic leaders in Eastern Europe like Lech Walesa and Boris Yeltsin are warning us of this danger to international stability.

Closing down military production facilities and inefficient government enterprises, removing subsidies from food and housing, essential steps in moving toward a free-market economy, will cause enormous social and economic dislocations, including large-scale unemployment and runaway inflation. Aid is required to help provide a safety net for the social casualties resulting from these changes. It is also required to enable these countries to rebuild their infrastructure, to deal with disastrous environmental conditions, and to establish stable, convertible currencies.

So far U.S. aid has been modest, noticeably so in comparison with German assistance. I've heard leaders of Central European countries say that they do not want to be too dependent on Germany. They want the American influence that comes with American aid, and we need that influence to maintain our international leadership. The United States has spent over three trillion dollars to win the Cold War. We should be willing to spend a much smaller amount—about thirty billion over the next three years—in cooperation with Western Europe to consolidate our victory.

Stung by one of our worst economic recessions since the end of World War II, the American people are turning against foreign aid and insisting that more resources be devoted to domestic economic and social needs. Moreover, without the threat of Communism Americans are less likely to appreciate the importance of foreign aid. Political leadership and courage are required, the kind provided by President Truman in the late 1940s, to convince a skeptical American public that even in these difficult times adequate aid to Central and Eastern Europe is essential to our long-term security, and the establishment of a "new world order" first envisaged by Woodrow Wilson almost eighty years ago.

Index

339